'A comprehensive guide full of insightful information for those who want to enhance their current stock of knowledge on international best practices for accounting, governance and accountability in emerging economies ... a must-read primer for higher degrees by research students, practitioners and consultants.'

Professor Zahirul Hoque, La Trobe Business School,
La Trobe University, Australia

'This handbook is a welcome and timely addition to the limited literature on accounting in emerging economies – timely in particular because there is a need to shift the focus away from the much-examined developed capital market economies, towards settings and jurisdictions of which less is known and published in the English language. It is a welcome reminder that accounting practice, regulation and the accounting profession are not homogenous, but subject to local as well as global socio-economic and political influences. In essence, this book provides a wealth of resources for the classroom as well as for researchers.'

Professor Lisa Evans, University of Stirling, UK

'It is a privilege to endorse Part IV of this book, especially Chapter 21 offers an authoritative and up-to-date overview of research in accounting in emerging economies from the leading researchers in the world, including its main originator, Professor Trevor Hopper.'

Professor Collins Ntim, Professor of Accounting and Deputy Head of Southampton
Business School, University of Southampton, UK

THE ROUTLEDGE COMPANION TO ACCOUNTING IN EMERGING ECONOMIES

As researchers reveal the increasing complexities of accounting practices in emerging economies, there is a growing need for an overview of the topic. *The Routledge Companion to Accounting in Emerging Economies* is a prestige work offering an introduction to current scholarship in the field, with indications of future directions for enhancing the contribution to knowledge.

With regional coverage of key emerging economies such as Brazil, Russia, India and China, the team of contributors analyse issues in accounting in detail, while shedding light on the role of the accounting profession in providing accountability and governance across the developing world. Each chapter is headed up by an internationally recognised author who is a leading expert in designing and implementing research approaches to the topic. Within the team of authors, some are experienced senior contributors while others are developing new avenues of exploration on the basis of high-quality doctoral study. This range of author experience has been deliberately chosen to allow the reader to envisage working in such a team while growing in confidence.

This unique reference offers a comprehensive guide to advanced students, academics, practitioners and policy makers on the current state of, and potential developments in, accounting in developing economies globally. This work will be of particular interest to students and researchers looking to identify topics in emerging economies, academics and practitioners seeking convenient access to an unfamiliar area, and established researchers seeking a single repository on the current state of knowledge, current debates and relevant literature.

Pauline Weetman is Professor Emerita in Accounting at the University of Edinburgh and holds the Distinguished Academic Award 2005 of the British Accounting and Finance Association. She is a co-author of *International Corporate Reporting: A Comparative Approach*.

Ioannis Tsalavoutas is Professor of Accounting and Finance at the University of Glasgow and holds a PhD in Accounting from the University of Edinburgh. His research on financial accounting and reporting has featured in leading journals such as *Accounting and Business Research*.

ROUTLEDGE COMPANIONS IN BUSINESS, MANAGEMENT AND ACCOUNTING

Routledge Companions in Business, Management and Accounting are prestige reference works providing an overview of a whole subject area or sub-discipline. These books survey the state of the discipline including emerging and cutting-edge areas. Providing a comprehensive, up to date, definitive work of reference, Routledge Companions can be cited as an authoritative source on the subject.

A key aspect of these Routledge Companions is their international scope and relevance. Edited by an array of highly regarded scholars, these volumes also benefit from teams of contributors which reflect an international range of perspectives.

Individually, Routledge Companions in Business, Management and Accounting provide an impactful one-stop-shop resource for each theme covered. Collectively, they represent a comprehensive learning and research resource for researchers, postgraduate students and practitioners.

Published titles in this series include:

The Routledge Companion to Critical Marketing
Edited by Mark Tadajewski, Matthew Higgins, Janice Denegri Knott and Rohit Varman

The Routledge Companion to the History of Retailing
Edited by Jon Stobart and Vicki Howard

The Routledge Companion to Innovation Management
Edited by Jin Chen, Alexander Brem, Eric Viardot and Poh Kam Wong

The Routledge Companion to the Makers of Global Business
Edited by Teresa da Silva Lopes, Christina Lubinski and Heidi J.S. Tworek

The Routledge Companion to Accounting in Emerging Economies
Edited by Pauline Weetman and Ioannis Tsalavoutas

For more information about this series, please visit: www.routledge.com/Routledge-Companions-in-Business-Management-and-Accounting/book-series/RCBMA

THE ROUTLEDGE COMPANION TO ACCOUNTING IN EMERGING ECONOMIES

Edited by Pauline Weetman and Ioannis Tsalavoutas

Routledge
Taylor & Francis Group

LONDON AND NEW YORK

First published 2020 by Routledge

2 Park Square, Milton Park, Abingdon, Oxon, OX14 4RN
605 Third Avenue, New York, NY 10017

Routledge is an imprint of the Taylor & Francis Group, an informa business

First issued in paperback 2020

British Library Cataloguing-in-Publication Data
A catalogue record for this book is available from the British Library

Library of Congress Cataloging-in-Publication Data
Names: Weetman, Pauline, editor. | Tsalavoutas, Ioannis.
Title: The Routledge companion to accounting in emerging economies/edited by Pauline Weetman and Ioannis Tsalavoutas.
Description: 1 Edition. | New York: Routledge, 2020. | Series: Routledge companions in business, management and accounting | Includes index.
Subjects: LCSH: Accounting–Developing countries. | Accounting–Standards–Developing countries. | Finance, Public–Developing countries–Accounting.
Classification: LCC HF5616.5 .R68 2020 | DDC 657.02/18–dc23
LC record available at https://lccn.loc.gov/2019015148

ISBN: 978-0-8153-5620-2 (hbk)
ISBN: 978-0-367-78381-5 (pbk)

Typeset in Bembo
by Wearset Ltd, Boldon, Tyne and Wear

CONTENTS

ILLUSTRATIONS

Figures

Tables

CONTRIBUTORS

Tarek Abdelfattah is a Senior Lecturer in Accounting and Financial Management at the University of Portsmouth. Previously he worked at Hamdan Bin Mohammad Smart University, UAE, The British University in Egypt and Mansoura University, Egypt. Dr Abdelfattah obtained his PhD at Durham University. His research interests cover corporate governance, financial reporting, earnings quality, risk management, audit quality and Islamic banking and finance. He has published papers in leading journals and textbooks. He is an expert in training and consultancy in the field of accounting and auditing and is a member of the advisory committee of some international companies.

Mazni Abdullah is a Senior Lecturer in the Faculty of Business and Accountancy, University of Malaya. Prior to joining academia, she worked as an accountant in Malaysia. She obtained her PhD from the University of Stirling. She is a member of the Malaysian Institute of Accountants, the Malaysian Institute of Certified Public Accountants and the Malaysian Institute of Management. Her research areas include financial reporting, taxation, Islamic finance and corporate governance. She has published her articles in academic journals and has also authored two books: *Financial Accounting and Reporting 2* and *Veerinder on Malaysian Tax Theory and Practice*, third edition.

Gloria Agyemang is a Professor of Accounting and Head of the School of Management at Royal Holloway University of London. Gloria's diverse research interests include performance management; NGO accountability, management control in public sector organisations; funding issues in public sector organisations; management of educational institutions; race, culture and diversity issues; accounting and sustainability issues in less developed and emerging economies. Gloria's publications appear in leading accounting journals including *Accounting, Auditing and Accountability Journal*, *Critical Perspectives on Accounting* and *Accounting Forum*. She is on the editorial board of several accounting journals.

Kamran Ahmed is Professor of Accounting at La Trobe University. His research interests are in corporate disclosure, corporate accounting policy choice, earnings management, international accounting harmonisation, accounting and reporting practices in South Asia, and microfinance reporting. He has published in several scholarly journals including *Abacus, Accounting and Business*

Research, Accounting and Finance, British Accounting Review, Corporate Governance: An International Review, Journal of Accounting and Public Policy and *Journal of Business Finance and Accounting.* He is currently Associate Editor of *International Journal of Accounting, Auditing and Performance Evaluation* and is an editorial board member of several journals including *International Journal of Accounting.*

Saiful Alam is an Assistant Professor of Accounting at the University of Dhaka, Bangladesh. Previously, he worked at the University of Hull and obtained his PhD at University of Glasgow. His research interests cover management accounting, accountability and control in post-modern organisations of less developed countries. He has presented papers at AFEE, BAFA-SAG, CPA, ScotDoc and other conferences. Funding for his research has included grants from Commonwealth Scholarship Commission, Adam Smith Business School, University of Glasgow, and Bureau of Business Research, University of Dhaka.

Cătălin N. Albu is Professor of Accounting at the Bucharest University of Economic Studies, Romania. His current research and teaching areas are IFRS enforcement and auditing in transitional economies. He is 2011 Senior Fulbright Grantee at the University of Dayton, US, KPMG Professor and Visiting Professor at ESSEC Business School, Paris. His research has been published in (among others), *Critical Perspectives on Accounting, Australian Accounting Review, Journal of International Financial Management & Accounting, Journal of Accounting in Emerging Economies* and *Accounting in Europe.* He is an editorial board member of *Accounting Forum* and *Journal of International Accounting, Auditing and Taxation.*

Nadia Albu is Professor of Accounting with the Bucharest University of Economic Studies, Romania. Her research currently focuses on the role of national states and changes to accounting systems in emerging markets. She is 2014 Senior Fulbright Grantee at the University of Dayton, US, and Deloitte IAAER Scholar between 2013 and 2017. She has published papers in (among others) *Critical Perspectives on Accounting, Australian Accounting Review, Journal of International Financial Management & Accounting* and *Accounting in Europe.* She serves on the editorial board of *Accounting in Europe* and is the editor of the *Journal of Accounting and Management Information Systems.*

Muhammad Jahangir Ali is currently an Associate Professor of Accounting in the Department of Accounting and Data Analytics, La Trobe University. He was a visiting scholar at Otago University, the University of Kebangsaan, Independent University, Rajshahi University and Asian University. His research interests focus on corporate governance, earnings management, harmonisation of accounting and reporting practices, international accounting, accounting policy choice and audit quality. He has published papers in leading journals including *Accounting and Business Research, British Accounting Review, Journal of Accounting and Public Policy, Journal of Accounting Literature, Pacific-Basin Finance Journal* and the *International Journal of Accounting.*

Habiba Al-Shaer is a Lecturer in Accounting at Newcastle University, UK. She obtained a PhD degree at Durham University, UK. Her research interests cover corporate social responsibility, corporate governance and financial reporting. She has published work in journals including *Journal of Business Ethics, Business Strategy and the Environment* and *Journal of Contemporary Accounting and Economics.*

Junaid Ashraf is an Associate Professor of Accounting and Control at the Lahore University of Management Sciences, Pakistan. He obtained his PhD at the University of Essex, UK. His research interests cover management control changes in public sector organisations and corruption. He has published papers in prominent accounting journals and has provided extensive consultancy/executive training to government organisations in Pakistan in his field of research.

Kathryn Bewley is an Associate Professor of Accounting at the Ted Rogers School of Management at Ryerson University, Toronto, Canada. Prior to joining Ryerson she was on faculty at York University. She obtained her PhD at the University of Waterloo. Before joining academe she pursued a professional career in auditing. Her research interests have involved examining environmental performance reporting, regulation of financial reporting via accounting and auditing standard setting, and other compelling emerging issues in accounting and auditing standards development. She has published her research in several academic and professional journals.

Pran K. Boolaky is a Senior Lecturer in Griffith Business School, Griffith University, and is an FCA member of the ICAEW with 20 years' experience in professional practice including four years as a partner at Grant Thornton. He worked in a number of sub-Saharan African countries on projects funded by international agencies, including the implementation of IFRSs in different sectors. He obtained his PhD from the University of Reading. In 2009, he joined Griffith University. He researches on reporting and auditing quality and has published papers on international auditing standards and their application in leading academic journals.

Sudipta Bose is a Senior Lecturer in Accounting at the University of Newcastle, Australia. He was awarded his PhD in Accounting from the School of Accounting, UNSW Sydney. He is a Chartered Accountant and a Certified Management Accountant. His research interests include capital markets, cost of equity capital, carbon emissions and assurance, sustainability reporting and assurance, and corporate governance. He has published scholarly articles in the *British Accounting Review*, *Journal of Contemporary Accounting and Economics*, *Asia Pacific Journal of Management* and the *Journal of Banking and Finance Law and Practice*.

Guillermo Braunbeck is a Lecturer at the University of São Paulo, where he obtained his PhD degree. He is also a board member of the Brazilian Accounting Standard Setter (CPC) and of several audit committees in Brazilian public companies. Dr Braunbeck has worked for the International Accounting Standards Board in London as a project manager in the IFRS Education Initiative. He has been part of several initiatives to promote high-quality reporting, including initiatives of the World Bank and the United Nations. His research interests cover IFRS adoption, impacts and Framework-based teaching of IFRS.

Maria Clara Bugarim is a full Professor of The University of Fortaleza. She has PhD degrees in Engineering and Management of Knowledge from UFSC and in Accounting from the University of Aveiro/Minho, Portugal. She is currently Controller-General of Alagoas and President of the Brazilian Academy of Accounting Sciences. She is vice president of Institutional Relations of the Inter-American Accounting Association and technical advisor to IFAC. Holding several national certificates and medals, she is the first woman to receive the highest and most important commendation of Brazilian Accounting Science, the Medal of Accounting Merit João Lyra, awarded at the twentieth Brazilian Congress of Accounting.

Russell Craig is Professor of Accounting at Durham University and an adjunct professor at the University of Canterbury, NZ, and Victoria University, Australia. A central concern of much of his research is to expose the folly of unquestioning acceptance of measures contained in published accounting reports and in narrative accounts by CEOs. Professor Craig has published in major journals such as *Accounting, Organizations and Society*, *Human Relations* and *Research Policy*. His two major scholarly books are *CEO-Speak: The Language of Corporate Leadership* (with Joel Amernic) and *John Croaker: Convict Embezzler* (with John Booker).

Sonja Gallhofer is Professor of Accounting Governance and Accountability at the Adam Smith Business School, University of Glasgow. Her research is interdisciplinary and critically analyses accounting, corporate governance and corporate social responsibility practices. A major focus of her research to date has been the exploration of the possibilities for more enabling and emancipatory accounting, corporate governance and corporate social responsibility practices through theoretical, historical and contemporary social analyses. She has published in leading international journals and is a co-author of *Accounting and Emancipation: Some Critical Interventions* in the series of Routledge Studies in Accounting.

Natalia V. Generalova is an Associate Professor of Statistics in the accounting and audit department at Saint Petersburg State University. She obtained her PhD in Economics in 2004. Her research focuses on financial accounting and reporting, including goodwill and consolidation. She is the author of more than 80 works in Russia, including papers on the presentation of financial statements, the application and adoption of IFRS in Russia, goodwill, consolidation, evolution of consolidated reporting in Russia, and impairment of assets.

Peter Ghattas is an Assistant Professor at MacEwan University, Canada. After obtaining an MSc from the University of Central Florida, Peter became a Certified Public Accountant and obtained his PhD from the University of Southampton in 2017 for a study of auditing professionalisation, standards and oversight in Egypt. Prior to joining MacEwan University, he worked at the University of Nottingham, China, the University of Southampton, the University of Winchester (UK) and Nile University (Egypt). His research focuses on audit practices; professionalisation, international standards on auditing, and public oversight, particularly in the context of developing countries.

Iurii N. Guzov holds a PhD in economics. He is an Associate Professor in St Petersburg State University, and First Deputy Dean of the faculty of Economics. He is a member of the board of the self-regulating Association of Auditors of Russia, SODRUJESTVO. He is the author of more than 100 publications on the theory and history of accounting and auditing. He took part in developing financial and auditing legislation in Russia.

Jim Haslam is Professor of Accounting, Governance and Society and head of the division of Accounting and Financial Management at the University of Sheffield. His previous main institutions have been Aston, Bangor, LSE, Essex, Waikato, Heriot-Watt, Dundee, Durham and Newcastle. His research focuses on the critical and social analysis of accounting and related practices. He has published papers in several leading journals and is a co-author of *Accounting and Emancipation: Some Critical Interventions* in the series of Routledge Studies in Accounting. He is on several leading editorial boards.

Trevor Hopper is Emeritus Professor of Management Accounting at Sussex University, and a visiting professor at Victoria University of Wellington, Essex University and Stockholm School of Economics. Previously he was a cost accountant in industry, a lecturer at Wolverhampton and

Sheffield Universities and professor at Manchester Business School. He has co-edited eight books, including *A Handbook of Accounting in Developing Countries*, and his accounting- and development-related papers include intensive case studies in Bangladesh, Benin, Ghana, Malawi, Nigeria, Pakistan, Sri Lanka and Indonesia; and several reviews of research on accounting and development.

Guoqiang Hu is an Associate Professor in the Accounting School at the Tianjin University of Finance and Economics in China. He obtained his PhD at Tianjin University of Finance and Economics. His research interests cover corporate governance, and financial and accounting issues in the Chinese capital market. He has published papers in such journals as *The European Journal of Finance*, *Accounting Research* (in Chinese) and *Auditing Research* (in Chinese). He has led research projects sponsored by the National Natural Science Foundation of China, the Philosophy and the Social Science Foundation of the Education Ministry.

Bopta Chan Huot is attached to the Ministry of Economy and Finance in Phnom Penh, Cambodia. Prior to joining the ministry she obtained her PhD at La Trobe University, Melbourne, Victoria, Australia. Her research interests cover the accounting profession and accounting education. She has published papers in leading journals including *Accounting, Auditing and Accountability Journal*. She has been involved with several committees in the Ministry of Economy and Finance in Cambodia.

Khaled Hussainey is a Professor of Accounting and Financial Management at the University of Portsmouth. His research focuses on market-based accounting research, narrative reporting and corporate governance. He has published papers in leading journals and his work has received international recognition through the award of prizes for articles in the *British Accounting Review* (2007) and the *Journal of Risk Finance* (2012). Funding for his research has included grants from the ESRC, the British Academy, Qatar National Research Fund and Abu Dhabi University, UAE.

Kelum Jayasinghe is a Professor of Accounting and the Director of the Centre for Environment and Society, University of Essex. He has published on management accounting, NPM, corporate governance, microfinance and ethno-accounting. Geographically, his publications draw from varied research sites located in Asia, Africa and Europe. Methodologically, his research is in qualitative traditions drawing from sociology, anthropology, development economics and philosophy. He has published in leading journals such as *Accounting, Auditing and Accountability Journal*, *Critical Perspectives on Accounting*, *Qualitative Research in Accounting and Management*, *Accounting Forum* and *International Journal of Entrepreneurial Behaviour and Research*.

Rania Kamla is a Professor of Accounting at Heriot-Watt University, School of Social Sciences (previous institutions include University of Aberdeen and University of Dundee). Her research focuses on critical analysis of accounting and culture, particularly in relation to the Muslim and Arab world. In her previous publications she explored the impact of globalisation, imperialism and colonialism on the accounting profession and professionals in Arab and Muslim contexts. Rania serves on the editorial boards of several leading journals and has published work in leading international journals including in relation to the experiences of Muslim women in the accounting profession.

Svetlana N. Karelskaia is an Associate Professor of Statistics in the accounting and audit department at Saint Petersburg State University. She obtained her PhD in 2008. Her research focuses on IFRS, accounting and statistics history. She has published more than 80 works in Russia, and a chapter on accounting for Vodka in Russia (with co-authors Viatcheslav Sokolov and Ekaterina Zuga) in *Accounting for Alcohol: An Accounting History of Brewing, Distilling and Viniculture* (Routledge, 2019). She was an investigator in the fundamental scientific research *Harmonization of the Accounting and Statistics Methodology in order to Increase the Reliability of Economic Data* from 2011–2013 at Saint Petersburg State University.

Sarada Rajeswari Krishnan is a Lecturer in Accounting at the University of Sussex, having obtained her PhD from Alliance Manchester Business School. Her research interests cover various issues surrounding the diffusion of international accounting standards, accounting policy decisions of nation states, transnational policy networks and processes in accounting regulation. She is currently working towards publishing in leading journals and has recently published a paper on the influence of transnational economic alliances on the IFRS convergence decision in India from an institutional perspective, in *Accounting Forum*.

Philippe Lassou is an Assistant Professor of Accounting at the University of Guelph. Previously, he worked at the University of Southampton and obtained his PhD from the University of Birmingham. His research interests cover the interplay between accounting, governance and development, and accounting issues in emerging economies. He has published papers in leading journals including *Critical Perspectives on Accounting, Financial Accountability & Management* and *Journal of Accounting in Emerging Economies*. Funding for his research has included grants from the African Development Bank, and the Social Sciences and Humanities Research Council of Canada.

Hui Lin is an Assistant Professor of Accounting at Minjiang University in China. She obtained her PhD from Xiamen University in China. Her research interests cover corporate governance and accounting issues on China's capital market. She has published papers in leading journals. She is also a certified public accountant in China.

Isabel Lourenço is an Associate Professor of Accounting at the ISCTE-IUL (Lisbon University Institute) and Visiting Professor at the University of São Paulo. She obtained her PhD at ISCTE-IUL. Her research interests cover international accounting, consolidation and sustainability issues. She has published papers in leading journals, namely *European Accounting Review, Accounting in Europe* and the *Journal of Business Ethics*. She is on the editorial board of the main scientific accounting journal in Brazil, *Accounting & Finance Review*. She has actively collaborated with professional associations and standards setters. She now has a position at the Portuguese Accounting Standards Board.

Oliver Marnet is Associate Professor of Accounting at Southampton Business School. His research focuses on corporate governance and external audit. He has published papers in leading journals and is the co-author of 'Audit within the Corporate Governance Paradigm: A Cornerstone Built on Shifting Sand?' published in *British Journal of Management*. He has been invited to give comments by the European Commission and PIRC, and the ICSA Review of the Higgs Guidance. Funding for his research has included grants from the Leadership Foundation for Higher Education and the ICAEW.

Mohammad Zakaria Masud is a PhD candidate at the La Trobe University, having studied for his Master's degree in Bangladesh at the University of Dhaka. He is a fellow member of the

Institute of Cost and Management Accountants of Bangladesh. His doctoral study investigates the sophistication of management accounting practices in association with firm characteristics to develop a performance optimisation model. He has published in academic and professional journals and co-authored a book on Bangladesh income tax. He was the principal investigator for research projects funded by the International Finance Corporation and the University Grants Commission of Bangladesh.

Melita Mehjabeen is an Associate Professor of Accounting and Finance at the Institute of Business Administration, University of Dhaka, Bangladesh. Melita obtained her PhD from the Alliance Manchester Business School, University of Manchester, under the Commonwealth Scholarship in the UK. Her research interests cover CSR reporting, politics, corporate governance and accountability, primarily in emerging economies.

Marizah Minhat is a professionally qualified accountant and a Lecturer in Finance at Edinburgh Napier University. She is a member of Chartered Accountants Australia and New Zealand, Malaysian Institute of Accountants, Institute of Chartered Accountants in England and Wales, and Association of Chartered Certified Accountants. She holds a PhD and an MSc in Banking and Finance from the University of Stirling and a Master of Laws (Financial Law and Regulation) from the London School of Economics. She has published widely on Islamic finance and corporate governance, covering executive remuneration, risk-taking incentives and financial reporting.

Olayinka Moses is a lecturer at Victoria Business School, Victoria University of Wellington, New Zealand, where he teaches Management Accounting and Accounting Information Systems in the School of Accounting and Commercial Law. His recently completed PhD from Victoria University of Wellington investigates the effectiveness of the Extractive Industries Transparency Initiative (EITI) in mitigating corruption in poor but resource-rich countries, and the economic value of extractive companies' non-tax payment information disclosed under the EITI implementation regime. His research interest is in the area of financial reporting and financial management with a particular focus on developing economies.

Sirinuch Nimtrakoon is an Assistant Professor in the School of Accountancy at the University of the Thai Chamber of Commerce, Bangkok, Thailand. She received her MRes and PhD from the University of Hull. Her research interests and journal publications are in management accounting practices and corporate reporting of intellectual capital. She has worked as the university liaison with the Federation of Accounting Professions, the Thai professional accounting body.

Brendan O'Dwyer is Professor of Accounting at the University of Amsterdam Business School (ABS) and the Alliance Manchester Business School. He was previously Head of the Accounting division and Associate Dean of Research at ABS. Brendan researches in the fields of non-financial reporting, corporate and NGO accountability, sustainability reporting and assurance, and the regulation of professions. He sits on the editorial boards of numerous leading international academic journals and has published several award-winning and highly cited papers in these journals. Brendan is also a member of the Strategic Sustainability Committee of the Institute of Chartered Accountants in England and Wales.

Charles Antwi Owusu is a Lecturer in Accounting at Brunel University, London. Prior to joining this university, he worked at the University of Cape Coast, Ghana, and obtained his

PhD at Royal Holloway, University of London. His research interests cover accounting, accountability and performance management in NGOs. He has published papers in leading journals. He has presented papers at British Accounting and Finance Association Conferences and Management Accounting Summer Schools in the UK, and in other countries in Europe.

Songlan (Stella) Peng is an Associate Professor of Accounting at the Faculty of Liberal Arts and Professional Studies at York University, Toronto, Canada. Her research focuses on financial reporting and auditing issues, critical perspectives on the standard-setting process, and the economic consequences of accounting and auditing standards. She is also interested in corporate social responsibilities research. She has published papers in leading journals such as *Journal of Accounting Research* and *Accounting, Auditing and Accountability Journal*. Her research has been supported by funding from CPA Canada and the Canadian Academic Accounting Association.

Nguyen Cong Phuong is an Associate Professor of Accounting at the School of Economics, the University of Danang. He obtained his PhD at Paris Dauphine. His research interests cover accounting regulation, transition in relation to IFRS, corporate governance and earning quality. He has published papers in leading journals such as *European Accounting Review* and *Journal of Accounting & Organizational Change*. He is a contributor to books entitled *IFRS in a Global World* and *Routledge Handbook of Accounting in Asia*.

Sharmin Shabnam Rahman is an Assistant Professor at BRAC University, Bangladesh. She obtained her PhD from the University of Manchester, UK. Her PhD study, on the accountability of global fashion-industry supply chains, looked into the post-Rana Plaza regulatory initiatives in the ready-made garments sector of Bangladesh. Her research interests cover accounting for human rights, auditing and accountability, emerging market and inclusive supply chains and corporate governance.

Seuwandhi B. Ranasinghe is a Senior Lecturer in the Department of Management and Organization Studies, Faculty of Management and Finance, University of Colombo. She obtained her PhD from the University of Glasgow through a scholarship awarded by the Adam Smith Business School. Her research interests cover postcolonial and feminist perspectives of organisations in developing countries.

Lúcia Lima Rodrigues is Professor of Accounting at the University of Minho. She is Vice President of the Portuguese Standards Setter, representing Portugal at the Accounting Regulatory Committee and European Financial Reporting Advisory Group (EFRAG), and is on the EFRAG Academic Panel. Her research focuses mainly on financial and non-financial reporting, and accounting history. She has published papers in leading international journals. She is recognised internationally through editorial membership of journals and international accounting academic associations. Funding for her research has included grants from the Portuguese Chartered Accountants Association, the Portuguese Foundation for Science and Technology, and the European Union.

Javed Siddiqui is a Senior Lecturer in Accounting at the University of Manchester, UK. His research focuses on areas such as human rights accountability, the politicisation of corporate social responsibility, and the relationship between the state and the accountancy profession, especially in the context of developing countries. His research has been funded by the Institute of Chartered Accountants of Scotland and by the Commonwealth Scholarship Commission,

UK. He works as a consultant for a number of international development agencies, as well as national level professional accountancy bodies, such as the Institute of Chartered Accountants of Bangladesh.

Abdus Sobhan is a Senior Lecturer in Accounting and Financial Management at the University of Northumbria, Newcastle. Previously, he obtained his PhD at the University of Edinburgh and Master of Accounting at the University of Melbourne, Australia. His research interests cover institutions, corporate governance and accounting reforms in developing countries. He has published a paper in *Corporate Governance: An International Review*. He has been awarded research grants by the Committee of Department of Accounting and Finance (CDAF) of the UK and by the Association of Commonwealth Universities.

Viatcheslav I. Sokolov is a Professor of Economics at Saint Petersburg State University, doctor of economics and a Partner of PricewaterhouseCoopers, responsible for accounting consultancy. He is the author of more than 150 publications on the theory and history of accounting.

Teerooven Soobaroyen is Professor of Accounting at the University of Essex. He is currently Head of the Accounting Group at Essex Business School and Vice President of the African Accounting and Finance Association and of the British Accounting and Finance Association. His research focuses on accounting, accountability and governance, with an emphasis on emerging and developing economies. He has published papers in leading journals, such as *Accounting, Auditing and Accountability Journal*, *Accounting Business Research* and *Critical Perspectives on Accounting*. Funding for his research has included grants from the Worldwide University Network and the Chartered Institute of Management Accountants.

Mike Tayles is an Emeritus Professor of Accounting and Finance at The University of Hull Business School, having previously been Director of the Centre for International Accounting and Finance Research at the University. His research interests include management accounting practices, particularly cost systems and developments in strategic management accounting, including accounting for intellectual capital. Funding for this research has included grants from the UK professional accountancy bodies, CIMA and ACCA, who have subsequently published his reports. Prior to entering academia Mike worked in the manufacturing industry as a Chartered Management Accountant in such roles as Financial Controller and Divisional Management Accountant.

Ioannis Tsalavoutas is Professor of Accounting and Finance at the University of Glasgow. Previously, he worked at the University of Stirling and obtained his PhD at the University of Edinburgh. His research interests cover financial accounting and reporting. In particular, he is interested in investigating companies' reporting practices under International Financial Reporting Standards across different jurisdictions, along with any economic consequences that may arise from divergence in practice. He has published papers in leading journals and has given oral evidence inter alia to members of the International Accounting Standards Board.

Shahzad Uddin is a Professor of Accounting and the Director of Essex Accounting Centre. He is a qualified cost and management accountant. He is the co-editor of *Journal of Accounting in Emerging Economies* and the founding chair of British Accounting Association special interest group, Accounting and Finance in Emerging Economies. Shahzad began his academic career in the UK in 1998 at Queen's University of Belfast upon finishing his MSc and PhD from the

University of Manchester. His research is in qualitative traditions and he has published widely on management accounting, accounting and development, public management, corporate governance and CSR, all in leading journals.

Sarath Ukwatte is a Lecturer in Accounting in the School of Accounting at the RMIT University, Melbourne, Australia, where he also previously studied for his PhD. His doctoral study investigates the professionalisation of accounting in developing countries. He has published in some accounting journals and has presented papers on international issues at the annual meetings of the American Accounting Association and the European Accounting Association, and in conferences associated with Asian Pacific accounting.

Jeffrey Unerman is Professor of Sustainability Accounting at Lancaster University. He has published several articles on sustainability accounting (including NGO accounting and accountability) in leading academic journals. He was recipient of the British Accounting and Finance Association's 2016 Distinguished Academic Award and in 2018 was awarded a Fellowship of the Academy of Social Sciences. Among external roles, Jeffrey is a co-opted member of the ICAEW Council and vice-chair of the ICAEW Research Advisory Board. He is also a member of the Expert Panel of the Prince of Wales' Accounting for Sustainability Project.

Shraddha Verma is Senior Lecturer in Accounting at the Open University. Prior to joining this university, she worked at the University of York and Birkbeck College and obtained her PhD at the University of Warwick. Her research interests cover the professionalisation of accounting and accounting disclosure and risk. She has published papers in leading journals including *Critical Perspectives in Accounting*, *Business History* and *British Accounting Review*.

Pauline Weetman is Professor Emerita in Accounting at the University of Edinburgh. The work of her doctoral students, in researching a range of accounting issues in emerging economies, has added to her enthusiasm for supporting research topics that make new contributions in drawing on the unique features of this area of study. She is a co-author of *International Corporate Reporting: A Comparative Approach*, which uses a framework of institutional and cultural factors to describe and evaluate approaches to accounting. She has been the editor of *Accounting and Business Research* and received the Distinguished Academic Award of the British Accounting Association in 2005.

Danture Wickramasinghe is the Chair in Management Accounting at the Adam Smith Business School in the University of Glasgow. His research interests lie in accounting and management control issues in public sector reforms in developing countries; NGO accountability and development; global supply chains and production networks; the interface between management accounting and corporate governance and enterprise risk management; microfinance, social controls and accounting; and participative development, governance and accounting. He adopts qualitative methodologies with structural and post-structural/postmodernist theoretical perspectives. He currently serves on editorial boards of several leading international journals.

Jason Zezhong Xiao is a Professor of Accounting and director of the Centre for China Business Research at Cardiff University. His research focuses on accounting and corporate governance, with published papers in *Accounting Horizons*, *Accounting, Organizations and Society*, *British Journal of Management*, *Journal of Accounting and Public Policy* and *Journal of Corporate Finance*. He has served as a joint founding editor of *China Journal of Accounting Studies*, as an associate editor for *Abacus* and *China Journal of Accounting Research*, and on editorial boards of such journals as *Auditing Research* (Chinese), *British Accounting Review* and *Journal of International Accounting Research*.

Prem W. Senarath Yapa is an Associate Professor of Accounting at the RMIT University. His research focuses on the accounting profession, education and public sector accounting in developing countries. He has received best paper awards in leading journals for work on the professionalisation of accounting in developing countries. Funding for his research has included grants from CPA Australia, the Accounting and Finance Association of Australia and New Zealand, The Association of Southeast Asian Institutions of Higher Learning, the Asia-Pacific Economic Cooperation Human Resource Development in Industrial Technology Network, the Centre for Sustainable Regional Communities, and the Public Sector Governance and Accountability Research Centre.

ACKNOWLEDGEMENTS

We are immensely grateful to the researchers who have contributed chapters to this volume. They all have very demanding research careers and we appreciate the time they have taken to share their experiences with us and with the readers of this volume. All the chapters bring out their passion for their research and their deep understanding of the research issues they and colleagues in the field have investigated. Our aim is to encourage those who are starting out on the road to researching accounting in emerging economies, and also to give a focus for those who may already have begun the exploration but are seeking the theories and methodologies or methods that will take their work to a higher level.

We would also like to give special thanks to all the staff at Routledge who have assisted with the editorial and production stages of the book, particularly to Terry Clague for proposing the topic.

1
INTRODUCTION

Ioannis Tsalavoutas and Pauline Weetman

'Accounting is the process of identifying, measuring and communicating financial information about an entity to permit informed judgements and decisions by users of the information' (American Accounting Association, 1966, cited in Weetman, 2016: 6). As such, accounting is multi-dimensional. Its principles and regulations are shaped and developed by human behaviour and the characteristics of the context in which it is practised. Accounting is also influenced by defining the expected or known users of accounting information, and the intended use. Moreover, accounting communication, to be effective, requires robust accountability and governance.

Countries around the world are usually classified into dichotomous groups such as developed contrasted with less developed, or advanced economies contrasted with emerging economies. The most commonly used reference for such a classification is the International Monetary Fund's (IMF) *World Economic Outlook*. The IMF explains (2018: 130) that it divides the world into two major groups: one described as 'advanced economies' and the other described collectively as 'emerging markets and developing economies'. It explains that the classification is not based on strict criteria and has evolved over time. It first of all identifies 39 advanced economies, using such key indicators as their relative size (GDP valued at purchasing power parity, total exports of goods and services, and population). The remainder (155 countries in total) are classed as 'emerging markets and developing economies'.[1] The countries covered in this book are constituents of this latter group and we use the shorter phrase 'emerging economies' for this group of countries.

The majority of the countries regarded as emerging economies, taken individually, are relatively small in terms of the global economy and have one or more characteristics of weak institutional environments, non-existent or underdeveloped capital markets, and a lack of suitably valid and reliable data for research purposes. Those factors have hitherto limited the scope for researchers to provide sufficient valid evidence to support high-quality research, and consequently academic research on accounting in these countries has only recently begun quickening its pace. We are now seeing initiatives to recognise the field of study, such as the *Journal of Accounting in Emerging Economies* and the Accounting and Finance in Emerging Economies Special Interest Group of the British Accounting and Finance Association. However, it remains the case that many high-quality academic papers are spread across a range of journals, which may prevent quick and easy access for those seeking to enter this field of study or to locate the relevant body of work on a specific topic.

To provide access to the range of research output and future potential of accounting in emerging economies, this book provides readers with chapters written by an international selection of authors who are experts in the relevant subject. These chapters shed light on the current state of, and potential developments in, accounting across a diverse range of emerging economies. Each chapter draws on the unique nature of one country or a group of countries, showing the scope for further development of study within that country, but at the same time demonstrates the potential for extending the research topic to other countries which may have similar, or different, characteristics. The volume assists academics and students seeking convenient access to an unfamiliar area as well as established researchers seeking a single repository on the current state of knowledge, current debates and relevant literature. In this way, we aspire to stimulate further research and debates in this area.

The chapters encompass four themes. Part I concentrates on the state of adoption of and/or convergence to International Financial Reporting Standards (IFRS) in a variety of emerging economies. Part II examines issues around the formal establishment of the accounting profession as well as education and training of accountants in emerging economies. Part III focuses on the fundamental aspects of audit, governance and accountability. A particular feature of the chapters covering these three themes is that they draw on relevant academic literature as well as local regulations. Shedding light on the specific socio-economic contexts of these countries allows for a better understanding of how accounting regulations develop, how accountants are trained, how accounting is practised, and how the issues of audit, accountability and governance complement accounting in emerging economies. Part IV is primarily addressed to scholars who want to embark on conducting research on emerging economies. Authoritative colleagues with a wealth of research experience in those settings share these experiences and personal reflections in an attempt to inform future researchers on the potential challenges as well as opportunities for conducting research in these countries.

Overall, this volume complements other recent Routledge Companions in Business Management and Accounting[2] such as those edited by Hoque *et al.* (2017), Livne and Markarian (2018), van Mourik and Walton (2013) and Zhou (2018). It also complements the *Handbook of Accounting and Development* edited by Hopper *et al.* (2012). In offering a combination of covering technical issues and offering reflections on the potential avenues for future research in emerging economies, we envisage that this volume will be of interest to academics but also a wider audience such as practitioners, investors and regulators.

IFRS in emerging economies

According to the IFRS Foundation, as of 2018, 144 jurisdictions around the world required IFRS for all or most companies.[3] This wide implementation of IFRS around the world really began in the mid-2000s when the European Union imposed on listed companies in its member states the requirement to apply IFRS in the preparation of consolidated accounts. Aiming at greater accounting comparability and harmonisation, other countries around the world, such as South Africa and Australia, moved in the same direction at the same time.

Although it appears as a natural step for governments around the world to follow a similar approach and either adopt IFRS or converge national accounting standards with IFRS, it has been argued that such a decision in emerging economies in particular has been mainly driven by pressures from various institutional bodies with significant power (e.g. the World Bank, the IMF, the Organisation for Economic Co-operation and Development (OECD), the World Trade Organisation (WTO) and the Asian Development Bank (ADB), as discussed in Perera, 2012). Moving to IFRS would involve significant costs in these countries given the substantial differences between local accounting standards and IFRS, along with the unfamiliarity of auditors and accountants with IFRS.

Reflecting this background, Chapters 2–6 draw on the relevant regulations and academic literature and inform readers about the processes around the adoption of IFRS in key emerging economies: Brazil, India, Russia, China and Malaysia. Although they are emerging economies, these countries play an important role in the world's economic growth. China effectively reached convergence in 2007, while Brazil, India, Russia and Malaysia have more recently aligned with IFRS in varying ways, as described and analysed in the respective chapters. This analysis is complemented by Chapter 7, which explores accounting issues in Vietnam, and Chapter 8, which provides an overview of the corporate reporting environments and adoption of IFRS in the countries of the South Asian Association for Regional Cooperation (SAARC) (i.e. Afghanistan, Bangladesh, Bhutan, India, Maldives, Nepal, Pakistan and Sri Lanka). Chapter 9 reflects on the extent to which professional investors in China appreciate financial reporting information differently, following the move to IFRS. The key messages from each chapter are summarised in the following paragraphs.

Empirical evidence, according to Lourenço and Braunbeck (Chapter 2), suggests that the positive effects of IFRS adoption in Brazil are confined to entities with better governance and those with incentives to opt out of the weak institutional and poor governance environment. The evidence also indicates that Brazilian firms show a lower level of accounting quality than Continental European and Anglo-Saxon firms. Despite applying IFRS as a set of high quality accounting standards, country-specific characteristics still affect the implementation of IFRS.

After many delays the phased implementation of IFRS in India was scheduled to apply to accounting periods from 1 April 2019 onwards. Verma and Krishnan (Chapter 3) discuss how delays have been attributed to a lack of preparedness, taxation and legislative issues raised by industry, unworkable deadlines and ambiguity. Delays have occurred despite the efforts of the professional body, ICAI, which has worked towards convergence with IASs/IFRSs, and has played a significant role in influencing IASs/IFRSs through ongoing negotiations with the International Accounting Standards Board (IASB).

The development of accounting in Russia is at the government's initiative and under its control. Use of IFRS took effect under law from 2011. A significant and growing body of work published in Russian is identified by Sokolov *et al.* (Chapter 4). One challenge is the potential for conflict between IFRS and the Russian accounting and legal tradition. Another challenge is translating IFRS into Russian. The authors point out that the Russian language does not have a strict word order, and the words have no clear hierarchy, which contrasts with the structure of IFRS in English. Initial research is largely descriptive but is identifying new topics such as applying standards in the state sector.

In the development stages, fair value accounting was a notable impediment to the full adoption of IFRS in China and hence received special attention from both standard setters and accounting academics. Peng and Bewley (Chapter 5) offer a critical perspective on the institutional, political and social environments that may act as drivers of China's IFRS adoption and the implementation of fair value accounting, along with contrasting aspects that may impede convergence or challenge its fundamental appropriateness.

Despite Malaysia's experience of slow progress to IFRS convergence, respondents to research surveys have supported IFRS adoption and perceive that the new standards help to improve comparability and transparency in reporting. Abdullah and Minhat (Chapter 6) focus on three areas that are unique in the context of Malaysia: the application of MFRS 141 *Agriculture*; the IC Interpretation 15 *Agreements for the Construction of Real Estate*; and the question of accounting for Islamic financial instruments that has not been given adequate attention but matters significantly to Malaysia as a pioneer country in Islamic finance.

In response to significant changes in the accounting environment in Vietnam, reform was carried out in 1995 that established an accounting system moving towards a private capitalist accounting model. Phuong (Chapter 7) observes that the co-existence of IFRS-type accounting standards and a Uniform Accounting System in Vietnam reflects the specific circumstances of a 'socialist market-oriented economy' where the State-Party plays a supreme and pervasive role in leading and controlling society. While changes are made in legal and policy documents in Vietnamese accounting, it takes longer to change the social values and beliefs needed for effective implementation of new regulations based on the IASB's standards.

SAARC was established in 1985 by Bangladesh, Bhutan, India, Maldives, Nepal, Pakistan and Sri Lanka, to be joined later by Afghanistan. The South Asian Federation of Accountants, a forum of professional accountancy bodies in the SAARC region, works towards positioning, maintaining and developing the accountancy profession in the region. It is expected that financial reporting practices will be improved after adoption of the whole set of IFRS standards by 2021 in the region. Ali *et al.* (Chapter 8) provide detailed insight into developments, which are of particular value in respect of those smaller countries, where institutional developments are relatively rarely researched.

Although China is one of the largest recipients of inward investment and one of the largest outward investors, it is challenging for researchers to collect evidence about investors' information needs and the decision usefulness of reporting in this emerging economy. Hu *et al.* (Chapter 9) report results from a survey of professional investors in China. The authors find that accounting information, particularly where it is forward looking, is most important for an investment decision or an investment recommendation. Buy-side analysts favour accounting information while sell-side analysts view non-accounting information as more important. An overwhelming majority consider accounting information to have both confirmative and predictive value.

The accounting profession in emerging economies

Various countries which gained independence, some in the postcolonial era and others following the dissolution of the Soviet Union, have faced important dilemmas and challenges in relation to the formation of the accounting profession and future training and certification of accounting professionals. Even though many countries opted for adopting Western models of the profession or curricula from universities based on Western and developed countries, it has been documented in the literature that the original formation and further development of 'the audit profession in an emerging economy may exhibit significant organisational differences from the dominant Anglo-American model' (Dedoulis and Caramanis, 2007: 393). In such economies, the profession may serve state policy objectives instead. Additionally, the significant differences between the local accounting standards and those from foreign countries meant that foreign curriculars needed significant adaptations to embed the local accounting culture.

For example, the accounting profession in the post-socialist Central and Eastern European countries has experienced a significant transition from a totalitarian regime to a market economy. Albu and Albu (Chapter 10) draw mainly on Romania as a representative country case study and conclude that accountants' competencies may be influenced by the state–profession boundaries and efforts for professionalisation, the role and image of accountants in society, and changes in the economic, technological, social and organisational context. Research into accounting competencies should be informed by the local institutional challenges, not merely replicating studies performed in developed contexts.

Syria, prior to the outbreak of extreme violence in 2011, was seeking increased economic liberalisation and aspiring to gain a larger stake in the global economy after a long period of isolation and animosity with the West. Kamla *et al.* (Chapter 11) elaborate, with critical insight, on how, before the violent events of more recent times, Syrian accountants were mobilising debates and shaping their professional identity vis-à-vis the new role they envisaged for the accountancy profession in this era of globalisation.

By applying an historical institutional analysis reflecting the social, economic and political contexts in Brazil, Rodrigues *et al.* (Chapter 12) show that new accounting practices have often been introduced because of prevailing government ideologies (especially of corporatism) and policies that have sought to modernise society and expand commercial activity. Due to the more complex requirements of IFRS, from 2004 the Brazilian accounting profession has required a university degree as a pre-requisite for entry to the accounting profession. Two current challenges are the improvement of the quality of higher education institutions offering accounting education and the expansion and improvement of the limited development of academic research in accounting.

In the 1970s the Khmer Rouge regime, led by Pol Pot, destroyed most of the professionals in all disciplines in Cambodia, including accountants, as well as the social and physical infrastructure in the country. Subsequently, the economy was rebuilt with the help of the Vietnamese, Western countries and donor agencies such as the World Bank and the ADB. Yapa *et al.* (Chapter 13) discuss how the accounting profession was rebuilt but point out that there have been comments that the Kampuchea Institute of Certified Public Accountants and Auditors remains relatively weak. Accounting and financial policies are mainly handled by the Cambodian government. Public sector accounting is highly influential on economic performance in Cambodia.

Audit, governance and accountability

It is well established that 'different cultural and institutional backgrounds play an important role in the way accounting is practised and how accounting information is perceived' (Tsalavoutas, 2009: 2; with reference to a wide range of prior work). Similarly, such differences influence the way the concepts and purposes of audit, governance and accountability are perceived and put into practice across different countries. In emerging economies in particular, shareholders' protection from a legal perspective is weaker compared to that found in developed economies (Michas, 2011). Moreover, standards and regulations regarding audit and corporate governance are usually imposed on emerging economies by external institutional pressures. However, the way they are shaped and/or enacted is influenced by local norms (Hopper *et al.*, 2012: 5). Further, it has been found that although emerging economies may 'adopt the Anglo-American shareholder model of corporate governance … such adoption may be prompted by exposure to legitimacy threats rather than efficiency reasons' (Siddiqui, 2010: 253). Boolaky *et al.* (Chapter 14) comment that International Standards of Auditing (ISAs) in an emerging economy function as a technical artefact of regulation and as a social practice of ways of working in an audit firm.

Accountability is a broad topic that brings a focus on issues affecting progress towards a better society, particularly in emerging economies. We have invited researchers to reflect on their observations in two vital areas – the work of non-governmental organisations (NGOs) and the establishment of human rights. Both chapters provide a theoretical framework for analysis as well as carefully documented insight into the cases considered.

Boolaky *et al.* (Chapter 14) observe that, from a perspective of policy making and jurisdiction, there seems to be some consensus on the benefits of ISAs for developing countries, building confidence and paralleling the adoption of IFRS. However, issues of relevance, enforcement and fit to the local (professional) circumstances emerge at the regulatory and firm levels. The chapter questions implications of ISAs from a social, economic and political perspective, with regard to the status of accounting and audit practices in a national context.

Egypt has implemented, over the past two decades, a number of initiatives and corporate governance reform activities aiming to increase the awareness of corporate governance and encourage the application of its best practices. However, as indicated by Abdelfattah and Hussainey (Chapter 15), research indicates that challenges remain. The method of appointment of non-executives and independent members and the tenure of non-executive directors are potential factors that may threaten board independence in Egypt. Other challenges lie in the culture of high power distance and uncertainty avoidance, the strength of family relationships in firms and the costs of establishing good governance. The authors call for action by regulators, educators and the accounting profession.

The economic growth of Bangladesh is phenomenal but most of the formal institutions (e.g. family concentrated ownership and control of companies, an inefficient and ineffective judicial system, and rampant corruption) co-exist with informal institutions (such as high power distance and a secretive culture). Sobhan and Bose (Chapter 16) observe how these local institutional settings are distinct from those prevailing in Anglo-American countries and conflict with recently imported corporate governance guidelines based on an Anglo-American model.

Studies undertaken in Ghana provide examples of the issues that NGOs working in emerging economies have to manage, and the roles of accounting and accountability in enhancing the effectiveness and efficiency of this management. In framing the reporting practices between NGOs' funders and their beneficiaries, Agyemang *et al.* (Chapter 17) distinguish 'hierarchical accountability' and 'holistic accountability'. Development and refining of theories in the area of NGO accounting and accountability is an additional direction and important element of future NGO accounting and accountability studies that can make an impact both on the academic literature and on policy and practice around NGO accounting and accountability.

The role of the State in accountability for human rights is examined by Siddiqui *et al.* (Chapter 18) in the context of violations in the Bangladeshi garment industry relating to the Rana Plaza collapse of 2013. They draw on a 'responsibilisation' framework, to demonstrate how brands may assume a political role, taking complete responsibility by co-authoring and implementing regulations, to significantly allay concerns regarding labour governance in supply chains in developing countries. The efficacy of auditing and assurance practices are often questioned in emerging economies, where the State lacks resources and political will to safeguard the working conditions and the rights of workers breached by businesses.

Researchers' experiences and reflections

One key objective of this book is to stimulate further research on accounting in emerging economies. In line with this objective, many of the chapters identify gaps in the relevant literature and indicate avenues for future research, either for single country case studies which could examine specific topics relevant to these countries or for cross-country studies which would deal with one particular theme applicable to many countries. However, before the researcher embarks on a project s/he needs to make key decisions about research design that will determine the feasibility and later contribution of the intended study. These include the methodological approach for the research questions examined, the availability of or access to the relevant data, and the theories that may be suitable for these settings. Such decisions need particular consideration before starting a study on an emerging economy. This is because many of these issues can be decided with relative ease for studies on countries with developed economies but may not be appropriate or feasible for an emerging economy. With this in mind, authors were invited to contribute chapters which provide guidance and advice to new scholars in the area, based on their experiences and reflections from conducting research in these countries.

Applying an ethnographic methodology allows the researcher to show how people's everyday lives are manifested in management accounting and control practices. Alam *et al.* (Chapter 19) reflect on two cases. One studied Bangladesh's microfinance practices where illiterate women produce 'oral accounts' as part of alleviating rural poverty, while the other studied the management control practices of a Sri Lankan tea plantation where tea-plucking women exploited the opportunities of neoliberalism to reconstruct the prevailing system of management controls. Validation is achieved by the interaction of theory with the story. A story may act as an illustration of theory, or a theory may illuminate the story.

In an in-depth review, Nimtrakoon and Tayles (Chapter 20) show that management accounting in Thailand has grown in scale, scope and profile, although with a focus on manufacturing. A significant proportion of GDP is now generated by the service sector and there is potential for research to generate further insights here. More research would be welcome related to small or micro businesses, which are an engine for growth, and to the distinctive use of management accounting practices in indigenous businesses. They note that while there are examples of very good research papers, in some cases the arguments, constructs and interpretations tend to be a little unclear and this needs attention in developing higher quality papers.

The final chapter recounts the experiences of a team of highly experienced successful researchers who have published, reviewed and edited works on accounting in emerging economies. Ashraf *et al.* (Chapter 21) reflect on the growth of research and publications in this field, and recognise the significant potential for scholars with expertise regarding emerging economies to make further substantial contributions. While acknowledging the major hurdles faced, they advise that what is unique or common must be systematically teased out and the results tied to related work in both developed and emerging economies.

Cross-cutting themes

Qualities that make for successful and meaningful research into accounting in emerging economies are indicated by Ashraf *et al.* (Chapter 21). We take here three of their themes to illustrate how they create common threads that may be traced across the diversity of subjects in the chapters. Our three themes are: the choice of country for the project; the choice of research method and data sources; and the approach to conceptualising the research.

Choice of country for the project

Ashraf *et al.* (Chapter 21) comment that 'authors often presume that their selected country has unique features, intriguing to others. However, these are often common to other emerging (or even developed) countries.' Researchers find themselves challenged to identify the incremental contribution from what appears to be a replicative of the same problem. Ashraf *et al.* (Chapter 21) point to potential points to create incremental value: 'However, a weak institutional environment, unstable democratic traditions, low literacy rates and many other factors in emerging economies can create conditions where some issues, e.g. corruption and good governance, become more pronounced.'

We discuss in this section examples of how the choice of country for a particular study is matched to unique aspects of the context of that country, and how the researchers focus on the context in their research design.

In the chapters on setting accounting and auditing standards (Chapters 1 to 9 and 14), it is relatively clear in each case how the authors identify the country-specific factors that have slowed down the pace of change, or have led to convergence rather than direct adoption of standards. Culture, political power and institutional structures all play their part in different ways and with different impact in each case. The insight gained from the interpretation of the progress towards convergence or full adoption of IFRS is heavily dependent on the ways in which the authors demonstrate their understanding of the country, with first-hand knowledge and experience. These chapters also demonstrate the careful attention given to technical details such as dates of adoption of standards, or the titles of legislation. Ali *et al.* (Chapter 8) on the introduction of IFRS in eight countries of SE Asia show the value of establishing a thorough knowledge of the framework of standard setting in a country as a basis for commencing research projects.

In Part II, our four studies of the development of the accounting profession indicate ways in which experienced researchers have identified unique contexts that provide a basis for a new contribution.

Albu and Albu (Chapter 10) point to the significance of creating a profession while experiencing a transition from a totalitarian regime to a market economy. Some might say 'upheaval' in relation to that political transition.

Our current image of Syria is one of appalling destruction in the terrible and tragic events impacting it in recent times, but Kamla *et al.* (Chapter 11) draw on research studies from a period before that upheaval to comment on a moment in Syria's history as it shifted from a formally more socialistic to a more neoliberalistic socio-economic positioning.

An historical institutional analysis reflecting the social, economic and political contexts in Brazil is offered by Rodrigues *et al.* (Chapter 12) to show that new accounting practices have often been introduced because of prevailing government ideologies (especially of corporatism) and policies that have sought to modernise society and expand commercial activity.

Yapa *et al.* (Chapter 13) argue that the field of accounting cannot simply be understood in terms of professional associations and professionalisation projects but rather the space of political and economic influences experienced by nations. Cambodia has experienced brutal and life-changing political upheaval from which its economy is relatively recently emerging, and provides a unique setting for research where the accounting-related issues become more pronounced.

Although we have placed Chapter 3 in Part I, on moving towards IFRS, the development of the profession also features in the discussion by Verma and Krishnan (Chapter 3) of the effects of moving from colonial rule to independence, where they observe that, although professionalisation in India commenced pre-independence, it was not until post-independence that an indigenous accounting institute was established.

Our chapters on corporate governance and accountability provide further examples of the contribution being enhanced by the context. Regulators in emerging economies have sought to give assurance about the quality of corporate governance by instigating laws or codes that are recognisable to developed economies, but local factors may impede the reality of implementation.

Potential factors that may threaten board independence in Egypt are the focus of Abdelfattah and Hussainey (Chapter 15). They indicate the challenges arising from the method of appointment of non-executives and independent members and the tenure of non-executive directors. Other challenges lie in the culture of high power distance and uncertainty avoidance, the strength of family relationships in firms and the costs of establishing good governance.

Sobhan and Bose (Chapter 16) point to a context where in Bangladesh most of the formal institutions (e.g. family concentrated ownership and control of companies, inefficient and ineffective judicial system, rampant corruption) are said to co-exist with its informal institutions (e.g. high power distance and secretive culture). They point to the need for researchers to look beyond agency or institutional theory to acknowledge the role of institutional dynamics and individuals' social and human capitals simultaneously while conceptualising the causal relationships between corporate governance and firm outcomes.

Ghana is the subject country in which Agyemang *et al.* (Chapter 17) examine accounting and accountability mechanisms in NGOs, because NGO accountability issues remain important for the development of emerging countries such as Ghana. They point out that well-designed accounting and accountability mechanisms are crucial in improving the effectiveness and efficiency with which this finite aid is deployed by and through NGOs, thus improving the life experiences of those living in extreme poverty.

Turning again to Ashraf *et al.* (Chapter 21), the chapters we cite here all meet their stipulation:

> What is unique or common must be systematically teased out and the results tied to related work in both developed and emerging economies. In brief, the reader will only be intrigued if the study adds new theoretical and/or empirical contributions.

Choice of research method and data sources

Ashraf *et al.* (Chapter 21) open their observations on research methods with the opinion:

> Questionnaire surveys, large-scale archival data analysis, cross-sectional econometric analysis in pursuit of 'objective' measurement can provide a truncated view of reality. Surveys can be unreliable, given many subjects in emerging economies are unused to doing them and suspicious of their eventual usage.

This view is echoed by Nimtrakoon and Tayles (Chapter 20) in their review of research into management accounting in Thailand. They observe that much of the research they review is positivistic, based on quantitative analysis. They comment that only more recently has some extensive qualitative and longitudinal research emerged. In noting that cross-sectional surveys are the most popular method used, even where it would appear the researcher has visited a site and administered a questionnaire to which qualitative insight could be added, they recommend that the use of more interviews and qualitative research insight would be welcome to create more context and to explore with greater depth, aspects which are not easily achievable in survey work.

Management accounting research is also the focus of Alam *et al.* (Chapter 19) but with a very different research method, describing the use of ethnographic research into management accounting and controls. They explain how they address the validity issue through the process of iteration between the contextualisation of a text and textualisation of a context. They use forms of involvement that include interviews, conversations, observations and documentary reviews, and provide an explanation by way of two case studies.

Attention to detail in using secondary sources of evidence is very well illustrated by Siddiqui *et al.* (Chapter 18). They illustrate and discuss a 'State of denial' by careful reference to secondary sources in the public domain, ranging from statements by politicians, through reports in newspapers and other media, to policies of organisations set up by multinational companies, and academic research papers.

Kamla *et al.* (Chapter 11) comment on how an appreciation of the local perspective reflects the commitment of Gallhofer *et al.* (2011) to appreciate and learn from the other by going 'beyond listening' towards 'engaging' thus promoting 'co-operation and better ways'. They indicate the use of interview research methods but it is clear from the reported research that the interviews are primarily a rich source of narrative – it is very much a case of letting the interviewee speak.

Some chapters, particularly those on the movement towards IFRS, indicate a very thorough descriptive, analytical and critical approach to desk-based analysis of archival material, particularly in relation to setting accounting standards. It is a very important part of providing a valid base for analysis, although it may in some cases be the first stage of creating a research question that permits deeper conceptualisation.

Conceptualising the research

In their discussion of the importance of the theoretical framework applied in research studies, Ashraf *et al.* (Chapter 21) say:

> We need to know more about the actual indigenous economy, how it can be conceptualised, the influence of social, cultural, religious and political factors, and the nature and role of accounting therein. Accounting research emphasising sociological rather than economic theories helps inform these interesting accounting issues, which need further exploration.

Some of our chapters are deliberately descriptive, setting the scene in a relatively underresearched area, to provide a basis for further research that builds on a solid base. Other chapters demonstrate how researchers have identified theoretical frameworks that relate to the focus of their inquiry.

In discussing the introduction of fair value accounting in China through IFRS, Peng and Bewley (Chapter 5) discuss how a social movement analytical framework can be used for research analysing future developments in IFRS-based standard-setting initiatives in non-Western societies. They indicate that extending the research findings from China to the challenges of international standardisation more broadly can lead to new insight in countries that struggle to maintain their own unique identity in the face of dominant international powers.

Albu and Albu (Chapter 10) consider the social image of the accounting profession and the ways in which the role and image of accountants in society influence the interaction of professionals with other social actors.

The tensions between a desire for movement towards globalisation and an attitude of caution against Western influences are brought out by Kamla *et al.* (Chapter 11). They point to this evidence as contributing to mobilising new emphases in the theory and methodology of interpretation (hermeneutics). They indicate how critical insights into the context can seek to deepen appreciation but also problematise and challenge the local views.

Agyemang *et al.* (Chapter 17) discuss how theories of upward, downward, hierarchical and holistic NGO accountability, developed over a decade ago, have been very helpful in structuring interpretive analyses that highlight key elements from complex data about NGO accounting and accountability practices. They comment that, as this field matures, there is a need for more-refined theories to be developed that both help derive more context-specific insights and are adapted to evolving (and improving) NGO accountability practices.

The discourse of denial forms the theoretical framework for the chapter by Siddiqui *et al.* (Chapter 18). They point out that although the term 'denial' is relatively uncommon in accounting and management literature, it is frequently used in the field of psychiatry, psychology and personality. They show that the stages in the discourse of denial explain their observations in the case based on a tragedy in the ready-made garment industry of Bangladesh.

The creation of a variant of control society (through social ties, mutual relations and everyday interaction is the theoretical framework used by Alam *et al.* (Chapter 19) to frame two ethnographic studies, one of microfinance practices in Bangladesh and the other of management control practices in a Sri Lankan tea plantation.

A significant word of advice, which should be kept to the forefront by researchers, is taken from Ashraf *et al.* (Chapter 21): 'The underlying theory must be strong, explicit and connected to the research questions and the empirical analysis, especially in qualitative work.'

Final word

Our authors include experienced senior academics, colleagues whose careers are advancing fast and those who are at early stages. In some of the teams there are researchers who have been doctoral students and are now writing as co-authors with former supervisors. The academic research community creates families and this volume brings out those families, both in the teams who have written each chapter and in the citations, where we see many themes crossing over.

We hope that future researchers will find this volume a starting point for productive and rewarding work and that they will regard themselves as part of this family of researchers into accounting in emerging economies. There is scope for such research to have a real and meaningful impact in those economies if disseminated to policy makers. We also encourage researchers to make their work accessible to policy makers, practitioners, regulators and opinion formers.

Notes

1 The IMF also explains further how it identifies a country or an economy for statistical purposes (IMF, 2018: 130–131). Detailed tables are provided in the Statistical Appendix to the 2018 full report, which may be downloaded from: www.imf.org/en/Publications/WEO/Issues/2018/09/24/world-economic-outlook-october-2018.
2 The full list can be accessed here: www.routledge.com/Routledge-Companions-in-Business-Management-and-Accounting/book-series/RCBMA.
3 www.ifrs.org/-/media/feature/around-the-world/adoption/use-of-ifrs-around-the-world-overview-sept-2018.pdf?la=en.

References

Dedoulis, E. and Caramanis, C. (2007). Imperialism of influence and the state–profession relationship: The formation of the Greek auditing profession in the post-WWII era. *Critical Perspectives on Accounting*, 18(4), 393–412.
Gallhofer, S., Haslam, J. and Kamla, R. (2011). The accountancy profession and the ambiguities of globalisation in a post-colonial, Middle Eastern and Islamic context: Perceptions of accountants in Syria. *Critical Perspectives on Accounting*, 22(4), 376–395.
Hopper, T., Tsamenyi, M., Uddin, S. and Wickramasinghe, D. (Eds.) (2012). *Handbook of Accounting and Development*. Edward Elgar Publishing.
Hoque, Z., Parker, L. D., Covaleski, M. A. and Haynes, K. (Eds.) (2017). *The Routledge Companion to Qualitative Accounting Research Methods*. Routledge.
IMF (2018). *World Economic Outlook*. International Monetary Fund, Washington, DC.
Livne, G. and Markarian, G. (Eds.) (2018). *The Routledge Companion to Fair Value in Accounting*. Routledge.
Michas, P. N. (2011). The importance of audit profession development in emerging market countries. *The Accounting Review*, 86(5), 1731–1764.

Perera, H. (2012). Adoption of international financial reporting standards in developing countries, in Hopper, T., Tsamenyi, M., Uddin, S. and Wickramasinghe, D. (Eds.), *Handbook of Accounting and Development*. Edward Elgar Publishing.

Siddiqui, J. (2010). Development of corporate governance regulations: The case of an emerging economy. *Journal of Business Ethics*, 91(2), 253–274.

Tsalavoutas. I. (2009). *The Adoption of IFRS by Greek Listed Companies: Financial Statement Effects, Level of Compliance and Value Relevance*. Doctoral thesis, University of Edinburgh, UK.

van Mourik, C. and Walton, P. (Eds.) (2013). *The Routledge Companion to Accounting, Reporting and Regulation*. Routledge.

Weetman, P. (2019). *Financial and Management Accounting: An Introduction*, 8th edition. Pearson Education.

Zhou, H. (Ed.) (2018). *The Routledge Companion to Accounting in China*. Routledge.

PART I

IFRS in emerging economies

2

IFRS ADOPTION IN BRAZIL

Isabel Lourenço and Guillermo Braunbeck

Introduction

This chapter identifies and discusses the process of adoption of the International Financial Reporting Standards (IFRS) in Brazil, which was initiated in the late 1990s and required a change in national corporate law and engagement of members of the Congress. We then discuss the main changes in the previous generally accepted accounting principles (GAAP) regarding IFRS adoption in Brazil, which happened in three different phases (limited convergence, transition period and full adoption). We continue by characterising the broad set of empirical studies that analyse the effect of IFRS adoption in Brazil on accounting quality, on the capital markets and on audit fees. We observe that accounting practices of Brazilian companies can remain significantly different from those of non-Latin-American companies even when they are all applying the same accounting standards, the IFRS, depending on different incentives for Brazilian firms. We conclude with recommendations for future research.

The process of IFRS adoption in Brazil

According to the World Bank *Report on the Observance of Standards and Codes (ROSC) – Accounting and Auditing* (World Bank, 2013), Brazil's robust growth performance has led to a widespread improvement in economic and social indicators over the first decade of the millennium. Brazil is not only one of the largest countries in terms of area and population, but has also become one of the largest economies in the world. In 2016, Brazil ranked in ninth position in the world ranking of countries for gross domestic product (GDP), accounting for US$1.8 billion of GDP. Among the emerging economies, Brazil is behind only China and India, which have much larger populations. In the Americas, Brazil is the second largest economy (behind the United States).

Silva and Nardi (2017) characterise Brazil as a code-law country with a relatively low level of investor protection, with a relatively weak institutional environment and with corporate governance practices that are not entirely able to ensure the rights of shareholders. This is a disincentive in terms of attraction of foreign resources.

However, Brazil is an emerging market in which firms have substantial growth opportunities that cannot be funded internally (Lopes *et al.*, 2016), creating incentives to provide transparent information to foreign investors. Brazil is the third largest capital market in the Americas, after those of the United States and Canada, and the most important in Latin America, as shown in Table 2.1.

Before the 1960s the market for capital in Brazil was limited and investors focused mainly on tangible assets (i.e. real estate). In the 1960s, several initiatives were undertaken to promote the development of the financial markets. The Banking Reform Act (Law 4.595/64), together with the first Capital Markets Act (Law N. 4.728), established a framework for the regulation of the capital markets (Comissão de Valores Mobiliários, 2018).

However, it was only in the 1970s that these reforms were complemented by two other significant laws. A securities and exchange commission (the Comissão de Valores Mobiliários – CVM) was created in 1976 to monitor the stock market and protect investors, among other duties. In that same year, the Brazilian Corporate Law (Law 6.404/76) was passed and still governs corporations in Brazil. The law is applicable to corporations (Sociedades Anonimas), whether listed or not (Comissão de Valores Mobiliários, 2018).

The accounting requirements in the original version of the Corporate Law, issued in 1976, were inspired by US GAAP and this law is considered as a landmark in modernisation compared to the preceding accounting framework (Salotti and Carvalho, 2015: 3). The Corporate Law covers several accounting topics, including the type of financial statements to be prepared, presentation of financial reports, the content of the footnotes, valuation methods for assets and liabilities and consolidation of financial statements.

Although the law issued in 1976 represented a substantial step in the development of Brazilian capital markets, it turned out to be a restriction on the evolution of the accounting model a few decades down the road (Salotti and Carvalho, 2015: 81). Given the lengthy and rather complex legislative process in Brazil, the fact that important financial reporting requirements were (and continue to be) set in law made it difficult to incorporate new concepts that were demanded by the development of transactions that are increasingly complex (World Bank, 2005: 5). Over the years, the very same law that represented the modernisation of accounting in Brazil became a significant restriction to evolution towards the international standards (Martins *et al.*, 2013: 14). Especially in the second half of the 1990s, when Brazil was eventually able to

Table 2.1 Characteristics of capital markets in the Americas as of 2018

Stock exchange	Country	Market capitalisation (US$ millions)	Number of listed companies	
			Domestic	Foreign
Bermuda Stock Exchange	Bermuda	2,874.8	13	42
B3 SA Brasil Bolsa Balcao	Brazil	954,711.1	335	8
Bolsa de Comercio de Buenos Aires	Argentina	108,739.9	96	6
Bolsa de Comercio de Santiago	Chile	294,675.8	212	81
Bolsa de Valores de Colombia	Colombia	121,477.1	67	2
Bolsa de Valores de Lima	Peru	99,218.6	218	15
Bolsa Mexicana de Valores	Mexico	417,021.6	141	7
NYSE	United States	22,081,367.0	1,791	495
Nasdaq – US	United States	10,039,335.6	2,545	404
TMX Group	Canada	2,367,131.6	3,278	50

Source: Data extracted from World Federation of Exchanges (2018).

reverse the hyperinflation scenario and open the way to a new cycle of investments and development, the limitations of the Brazilian GAAP (BR GAAP) as set in the law became clearer.

The need for change mobilised a task force of accounting experts that included members of various Brazilian regulatory agencies, auditors and academics, among others. Its work started in 1996 (UNCTAD, 2006: 5) aiming to draft a bill to amend the law to converge BR GAAP to international best practices. The bill (PL 3741) was eventually authored by CVM in consultation with a wide range of stakeholders, and discussions in Congress started in 2000 (World Bank, 2005: 12).

The PL 3741 bill officially started its legislative process in November 2000, when the President of Brazil, Mr Fernando Henrique Cardoso, sent the Congress a bill proposing amendments to the law. The transmittal letter signed by the Minister of Finance, Mr Pedro Sampaio Malan, presented the main motivations for proposing the bill, which were increasing the quality of accounting information, enhancing the quality of resource allocation decisions and promoting the economic development of the country. To achieve these goals, it was stated that the law should be adapted to allow the implementation of principles, norms and standards in accounting and auditing that were internationally recognised (Brasil, 2000).

The bill proposed several changes in the law, ranging from technical matters such as replacing the statement of changes in financial position (i.e. changes in working capital) with the statement of cash flows, to administrative and institutional matters, such as determining that accounting and auditing standards could be set by technical (and independent) bodies, following due process and subject to the endorsement of the regulators (CVM and others) (Brasil, 2000).

According to Brazilian legislative due process, the bill had to be analysed by three different Congressional committees (Brasil, 2000). Member of Congress Emerson Kapaz was the rapporteur of the first committee (Brasil, 2000b). He was recognised for his knowledge about industry, innovation and entrepreneurship. As a businessperson himself, Mr Kapaz had been the rapporteur of another bill, sanctioned in October 2001, which made changes in corporate governance aspects of the law.

Mr Kapaz supported the idea that to increase the flow of investments in Brazil, including foreign investments, and to foster the economic development of the country, the law had to be modernised and minority interests had to be protected. His views on the PL 3741 bill were supportive of harmonising accounting practices in Brazil with those accepted in the main capital markets around the world and with the conceptual framework from the International Accounting Standards Committee (IASC, the predecessor of the International Accounting Standards Board (IASB)) (Brasil, 2000b). This rapprochement with the international accounting standards reflects the significant changes promoted by the IASC/IASB and the growing interest in the International Financial Reporting Standards (IFRS), particularly considering the decision made by the European Union in 2002 to require IFRS-consolidated financial statements from its public companies from 2005 onwards.

However, in 2003, Brazil gained a new president (Lula, Labour Party) and all seats in the lower chamber of Congress were renewed. In the new political environment, the bill lost traction for a few years. The legislative process continued with the bill being analysed by the other committees, which reported in favour of the bill. The last committee approved the bill on 6 December 2007, which was eventually sanctioned by President Lula on 28 December 2007. The changes introduced in the law set the way to a process of accelerated convergence of BR GAAP with IFRS. Full adoption of IFRS standards was reached for financial reporting years ending on 31 December 2010 and thereafter, whereas 2008 and 2009 were transitional years in which IFRS were progressively adopted on a standard by standard basis.

In summary, the process of adopting IFRS in Brazil had three phases:

1   Limited convergence (prior to December 2007): before the Corporate Law was amended, some of the accounting requirements applicable to public companies were adjusted by CVM (Securities Commission) in order to reduce differences with international standards. However, because of the restrictions imposed by the law, convergence was limited. For instance, before December 2007 financial instruments could not be measured at fair value. Therefore, CVM required public companies to disclose the fair value of financial instruments in the notes of the financial statements.

2   Transition period (from January 2008 until December 2010): after the Corporate Law reform was passed, IFRS were progressively incorporated into BR GAAP (IFRS Foundation, 2017). Financial statements prepared for the years 2008 and 2009 were not fully compliant with IFRS because during this period IFRS were issued by the were issued by the Brazilian Accounting Pronouncements Committee (CPC), as the national standard setter, and endorsed by the regulators and endorsed by the regulators on a standard by standard basis and the complete set of standards was not finished until 2010. During this period, a Memorandum of Understanding (IASB/CFC/CPC, 2010) was signed by the IASB, CFC (Conselho Federal de Contabilidade) and CPC documenting the goal of eliminating these differences between BR GAAP and IFRS by the end of 2010.

3   Full adoption (from 31 December 2010 onwards): on and after 31 December 2010, BR GAAP incorporated all IFRS and consolidated financial statements of public companies are compliant with IFRS as issued by the IASB (IFRS Foundation, 2017).

In the period before the law was amended and IFRS adoption became possible, an important landmark was reached in 2005 with the formal creation of the Brazilian Accounting Pronouncements Committee (CPC) by the CFC Resolution 1055/55. CPC is the standard-setting body engaged in the study, development and issuance of accounting standards, interpretations and guidance for Brazilian companies. Its rules are enforced by the securities commission for public entities and by the Conselho Federal de Contabilidade, the national body of the accounting profession for non-public entities. Some other agencies enforce these accounting pronouncements in specific industries, such as electrical energy and health insurance. The creation of CPC was key to bringing together the main forces necessary to move towards the adoption of IFRS, which nominated its voting members, representing academia, analysts, preparers, the stock exchange, the auditors and the accounting profession (Salotti and Carvalho, 2015). Regulators join CPC's due process. Standards and interpretations go through a thorough due process involving drafting, discussion in working groups, and mandatory public hearings before final approval and issuance (Comitê de Pronunciamentos Contábeis, 2018). The CPC standards and interpretations are the translation, word for word, of current versions of IFRS, except for some minor adjustments in comparison with the official translations of the IFRS *Red Book* to Brazilian Portuguese (e.g. CPC standards do not set an effective date for mandatory application, which is set by the regulators).

The IFRS that were progressively incorporated into BR GAAP in 2008 and 2009, and the IFRS fully adopted in 2010, are those as issued by the IASB, but some options were eliminated, for example, the revaluation of property, plant and equipment under IAS 16 *Property, Plant and Equipment*, and the revaluation of intangible assets under IAS 38 *Intangible Assets* (Salotti and Carvalho, 2015). Nonetheless, the resulting financial statements can still be in full compliance with IFRS as issued by the IASB (IFRS Foundation, 2017).

CPC standards, which are equivalent to the IFRS, are mandatory for the consolidated (and individual) financial statements of companies whose debt or equity securities are traded in a public market (i.e. entities subject to the regulation of CVM) and for financial institutions (those subject to the regulation of the Brazilian Central Bank). Large non-listed companies must also prepare consolidated and separate financial statements in accordance with CPC (and, therefore, with IFRS). Small and medium entities must apply CPC for SMEs, which is the translation of IFRS for SMEs (small to medium-sized entities). Micro entities must comply with CFC pronouncement ITG 1000, which is a simplification of IFRS for SMEs but has no direct equivalence to this standard issued by the IASB (IFRS Foundation, 2017).

Therefore, Brazil is a case of complete adoption of IFRS, required not only for consolidated financial statements, but also for the individual/separate financial statements for both listed and non-listed entities (with limited exceptions). Jurisdictions often opt for the approach of consolidated-only adoption, probably to reduce potential impacts and conflicts regarding taxation and dividends. Brazil changed the Company Law and altered the income tax legislation in such a way that a safe path was built to bridge the old BR GAAP standards and IFRS (Carvalho and Salotti, 2013). Before the Corporate Law reform enacted in 2007 and the beginning of the period of transition to full IFRS adoption, financial reporting in Brazil was heavily influenced by tax legislation (Silva and Nardi, 2017). The new Corporate Law itself determined that the changes in accounting policies should be tax neutral. In order to ensure tax neutrality, a transitional tax regime was implemented in 2009 until 2014, which basically determined that accounting numbers for taxation purposes should be obtained using the GAAP in place before the changes brought by the Corporate Law reform of 2007. The transitional tax regime was eventually replaced in 2014 by a permanent tax regime, which has been mostly guided by the same idea of tax neutrality of IFRS (Silva *et al.*, 2014); i.e. in general terms, the changes brought by IFRS in determining pre-tax net income continue to be neutral to the computation of taxable income. Brazil is one of the five G20 jurisdictions that has adopted the IFRS for SMEs standard (IFRS Foundation, 2018).

Wider changes arising from the adoption of IFRS in Brazil

The main areas of divergence of BR GAAP from IFRS before the PL 3741 bill was sanctioned on 28 December 2007, i.e. before the transition period started and IFRS were eventually adopted on 31 December 2010, were as follows:

1   All leases were accounted for as operational leases (World Bank, 2005; UNCTAD, 2006);
2   A variety of costs could be deferred (i.e. capitalised) over several years, including pre-operating and start-up costs (World Bank, 2005);
3   In general terms, BR GAAP tended to follow the historical cost model for the valuation of elements in the financial statements (World Bank, 2005);
4   Presenting the statement of cash flows was voluntary, but entities had to present the statement of changes in financial position, which presents the changes in working capital in three categories (operating, investing and financing) (World Bank, 2005; UNCTAD, 2006);
5   Benefits received by entities from government were recognised directly in retained earnings (World Bank, 2005; UNCTAD, 2006);
6   BR GAAP required the presentation of certain items in the statement of income as non-operating (World Bank, 2005);
7   BR GAAP tended to be less precise than IFRS, leaving more room for interpretation (World Bank, 2005);
8   BR GAAP were less detailed than their equivalent IFRS regarding disclosure requirements (World Bank, 2005).

IFRS adoption represented a true revolution in Brazil's approach to accounting education. The departure from the country's local 'code law' philosophy and 'tax-inspired' accounting in favour of a 'principles-based' approach continues to be a major educational challenge for faculties and students (Carvalho and Salotti, 2013).

Initiatives in accounting education to tackle these challenges include changing the approach in accounting courses to active learning strategies, having the fundamental concepts of IFRS as a starting point in the learning process, and emphasising concepts of corporate finance, economy, market forces, informational asymmetry, and conflict of interests, fair value, and objectivity versus relevance, among others (Carvalho and Salotti, 2013).

The process of convergence towards full adoption of IFRS in 2010 has resulted in a need for professional development in exercising choices, judgements and estimates, due to the degree of subjectivity contained in these standards. Marked improvement was necessary in teaching materials (textbooks, cases, etc.) but mainly in teaching philosophy and attitude. Classes in Brazil tended to be rather technical, focusing on double-entry procedures and not on conceptual questions. Students were expected to be able to account for transactions and there was almost no judgement or decision making involved (Lopes, 2011). In order to change this environment, case studies like the 'Open Safari', developed by the IASB Education Initiative (Wells and Tarca, 2014) as part of the so-called Framework-Based Teaching – FBT (Wells, 2011) started to be applied by Brazilian professors, who found that the skills most improved by using FBT were linked to the ability to consider more than one solution for real problems, to interpreting scenarios, to consolidating various aspects of the discipline and the course, to associating these with practice, and developing critical thinking and an individual responsibility for one's own learning (Costa *et al.*, 2018).

IFRS adoption in Brazil is also associated with a significant change in the accounting profession. Because of the more complex requirements of the international accounting standards, the CFC, which is responsible for enforcing legal requirements of the accounting profession, moved to require a bachelor degree in accounting as a pre-requisite for entry to the accounting profession (Rodrigues *et al.*, 2019).

Brazil has also been learning about how to engage in the standard-setting process since IFRS adoption. An example is the creation of the GLASS (Group of Latin American Accounting Standard Setters) in 2011, in which Brazil played a leading role. GLASS is one of the three members for the Americas, together with the Canadian Accounting Standards Board and the Financial Accounting Standards Board, of the Accounting Standards Advisory Forum (ASAF). The objective of ASAF is to provide an advisory forum in which members can constructively contribute to achieving the IASB's goal of developing globally accepted, high quality accounting standards.

Brazil has seats in other consultative bodies of the IASB (IFRS Advisory Council, Capital Markets Advisory Committee, Global Preparers Forum, Emerging Economies Group, SME Implementation Group and the World Standard Setters conferences), including, since 2009, one seat at the IASB for The Americas being occupied by a former senior official of the Brazilian Central Bank. Furthermore, there has always been one Brazilian trustee at the IFRS Foundation (and its predecessor body, the IASC Foundation) since 2000. Brazil has also been represented on the IFRS Interpretation Committee since 2014.

Investigating the effects of IFRS adoption in Brazil

The mandatory adoption of IFRS in Brazil had a significant effect on the financial statements of listed companies. Pires and Decourt (2015) analysed the Notes to the 2010 financial statements of 83 Brazilian public companies in order to measure the impact of full IFRS adoption on the net income, shareholders' equity and total assets of Brazilian public companies. The results show that IFRS adoption generated a significant increase in the net income of companies (mean value: 21 per cent), which, as an immediate consequence, increased the number of mandatory dividends to be distributed. IFRS adoption also generated an increase in shareholders' equity (mean value: 11 per cent) and in total assets (mean value: 7 per cent). Although on average there are increases in these three accounting measures, the results also show that most companies recorded a growth in net income, shareholders' equity and total assets.

The effects of IFRS adoption in Brazil have also been examined by several other studies, taking different perspectives, such as the effect on accounting quality, on the capital markets and on audit fees. Most of these studies provide empirical evidence of a positive effect of IFRS adoption on the accounting quality of Brazilian listed firms, as discussed in the following paragraphs.

Vieira *et al.* (2011) examined the impact of IFRS partial adoption (in 2008) on accounting quality using a sample of Brazilian public companies and data for the period 2005–2008. They provide empirical evidence of a positive impact of the IFRS partial adoption on earnings smoothing and on the value relevance of financial information.

Eng *et al.* (2018) also found an improvement in the value relevance of earnings after the mandatory adoption of IFRS in 2010. However, they did not find an improvement in the information content of earnings. A possible explanation identified for these partial results is related to the two-step transition from Brazilian GAAP to mandatory IFRS. It is possible that in the pre-IFRS period (i.e. during 2008 and 2009), some companies had already started making changes to their financial reporting practices to be in line with the IFRS reporting framework.

Pelucio-Grecco *et al.* (2014) examined the impact of IFRS adoption on earnings management, measured by the level of discretionary accruals, of Brazilian non-financial public companies, and documented a reduction of earnings management after full IFRS adoption in 2010.

Lourenço *et al.* (2015) examined the impact of IFRS adoption on earnings management practices to avoid losses for a sample of Brazilian public companies for the period 2004–2011, and found that mandatory adoption of IFRS by Brazilian companies was associated with a decrease in earnings management, especially during the period of full adoption of IFRS (post-2010).

Silva and Nardi (2017) also examined the impact of full IFRS adoption on earnings quality based on data from 2000 to 2011, and found an increase in earnings quality for all dimensions they analysed (earnings management, conservatism, value relevance and timeliness). Rodrígues García *et al.* (2017) found that changes from local accounting regulations to the IFRS increased the value relevance of accounting information in Brazil and in other Latin American countries.

Lopes *et al.* (2016) used a panel of Brazilian public companies from 1998 to 2014 to examine the impact of IFRS adoption on two indicators of accounting quality (value relevance and conservatism). Their findings show a positive association between accounting quality and IFRS adoption, with a larger effect in the case of companies with poorer corporate governance practices (measured based on a Corporate Governance Index developed by the authors).

However, Lourenço and Branco (2015) provide opposite findings regarding the role of corporate governance on the effect of IFRS adoption. They provide empirical evidence that IFRS adoption had a positive effect on the value relevance of accounting information, but only in the case of companies that signal better corporate governance practices (by belonging to the New Market or the Level 2 Market, a segment including only the listed firms that comply with a set of requirements that are associated with better corporate governance practices). This last finding is consistent with the literature based on other countries that provides evidence on the positive effect of IFRS adoption on the accounting quality of firms with better corporate governance mechanisms (e.g. Zéghal *et al.*, 2011). It seems that the economic consequences of adopting IFRS can be differentiated according to the characteristics of the companies that adopt these standards.

Black and Nakao (2017) provide additional evidence on the role of firm incentives on the effect of IFRS in accounting quality. They examined the effect of IFRS adoption in three classes of Brazilian public companies (firms listed in the US, firms not listed in the US classified as serious compliers, and firms not listed in the US classified as label compliers). The empirical findings show that only in the case of firms listed in the US and firms not listed in the US classified as serious compliers did an increase in accounting quality occur following IFRS adoption, which is not the case for the firms not listed in the US classified as label compliers. This finding is also consistent with the literature based on broader international samples (e.g. Daske *et al.*, 2008, 2013).

Silva and Nardi (2017) argue that rather than serving the information needs of corporate stakeholders, financial reporting practices are more likely to be motivated by opportunistic aims. This aside, many Brazilian companies seek foreign financing in the North American market through American Depositary Receipts, which means that they have to incorporate good quality corporate governance rules and provide more transparent information to the market.

Overall, the accounting literature suggests that in Brazil, a country characterised by weak investor protection and legal and enforcement regimes, the mandatory IFRS adoption is likely to impact positively on accounting quality. However, IFRS adoption cannot be seen as the only guide to accounting information quality. The companies with economic incentives given by the stock market are more likely to achieve increased quality after IFRS adoption. Therefore, a global set of accounting standards may not guarantee that the accounting numbers would converge to the same level of quality.

We now discuss studies providing empirical evidence of a positive effect of the IFRS adoption on the Brazilian capital markets. Silva and Nardi (2017) examined the impact of full IFRS adoption on the cost of capital, based on data from 2000 to 2011, and found a significant decrease in the cost of capital after IFRS adoption by the Brazilian public companies. Figlioli *et al.* (2017) analysed the effect of IFRS adoption on the synchronicity of the shares of listed Brazilian companies using data from 2005 to 2015. The term synchronicity refers to the extent to which company-specific information and market information is reflected in stock prices. The more that share prices reflect company-specific information rather than market information, the greater the informational content will be in terms of representing the economic value of a particular company. The results obtained by this study show a reduction in the synchronicity levels in the period of full IFRS adoption (from 2010 onwards).

These findings regarding the effect of IFRS on the cost of capital and on the synchronicity of shares are also consistent with the literature based on broader international samples (e.g. Armstrong *et al.*, 2010; Kim and Shi, 2012).

Although there is empirical evidence on the benefits of IFRS, the adoption of these international standards may also be associated with increased costs. Murro *et al.* (2015) investigate the effect of the mandatory IFRS adoption on the audit fees paid by Brazilian companies to their auditors. Based on data from 2009 to 2012, the findings show that the mandatory adoption of IFRS represented a significant increase of 20.71 per cent in the auditing fees. This finding is also in accordance with the literature on the effect of IFRS adoption on audit fees developed, based on audit fee data from European countries (Kim *et al.*, 2012).

Accounting practices in Brazil in the IFRS era

There is a stream of international literature on IFRS adoption suggesting that significant differences in accounting practices remain even in the IFRS era (e.g. Kvaal and Nobes, 2010; Nobes, 2006, 2008, 2011, 2013). Reasons explaining the existence of national versions of IFRS practice include the existence of gaps, overt and covert options, vague criteria and interpretations, and measurement estimations (Nobes, 2006). Another reason pertains to the incentive for companies to provide transparent information (Daske *et al.*, 2013). Therefore, it is expected that there may be some differences found in the accounting practices of Brazilian companies when compared to those of companies from other countries. Some studies provide evidence on this issue.

Rathke *et al.* (2016) analysed an indicator of accounting quality (discretionary accruals) in the main Latin American countries applying IFRS (Brazil and Chile), when compared to the main Anglo-Saxon countries with IFRS tradition (United Kingdom and Australia), and with the main Continental European economies (France and Germany). The results reveal that Brazilian and Chilean firms have a higher level of earnings management than Continental European and Anglo-Saxon firms. Thus, even with a single set of high quality accounting standards (IFRS) and reporting incentives, countries' specific characteristics still play an important role in the way IFRS is implemented.

Santos *et al.* (2014) evaluated the level of compliance with IFRS disclosure requirements of Brazilian non-financial public companies in the first year of mandatory IFRS adoption in Brazil (2010). Their findings provide empirical evidence of low levels of disclosure compliance, which range from an average of 16.04 per cent (strict criterion and dichotomous approach) to 33.72 per cent (tolerant criterion and partial compliance unweighted approach). This study emphasises the importance of increasing institutional support conditions for enhanced enforcement mechanisms, enabling Brazilian firms to better attain the full economic benefits of IFRS adoption.

Lourenço *et al.* (2018) developed a classification of national versions of IFRS practices based on 27 countries in which IFRS adoption is a widespread practice, as well as the US. The results suggest a classification distinguishing three groups of countries based on the similarity of their accounting practices: (1) Australia and New Zealand; (2) US-influenced countries; and (3) South Africa, Oman and European countries. The group classified as US-influenced countries includes Brazil, Chile and Peru, among others.

Lourenço *et al.* (2018) identify economic proximity to the US as an important factor influencing the accounting practices of the US-influenced countries. Regarding the case of Brazil, they highlight the importance of economic trade with the US and the significant number of large Brazilian firms cross-listing their shares in the US. The data regarding Brazil show, for example, that all the Brazilian firms present their income statement by function, instead of by nature, and their statement of cash flows using the indirect method. These choices are in accordance with the practices found in US firms.

However, the literature that compares the accounting practices of Brazilian firms with those of firms from other Latin American countries provides different findings, by showing greater similarity between the companies in this group of countries (e.g. Rathke and Santana, 2015; Sarquis and Luccas, 2015).

Rathke and Santana (2015) compare the level of earnings management in the first three Latin American IFRS adopters: Brazil, Chile and Peru. Their results show that firms from each country evidence different levels of earnings management before IFRS adoption, and that those differences no longer remain after the adoption of IFRS. Hence, the results indicate that IFRS has enhanced information comparability and has made financial information more homogeneous in Latin America.

Sarquis and Luccas (2015) developed a classification of the accounting systems of five Latin American countries that have adopted IFRS (Argentina, Brazil, Chile, Mexico and Peru). They provide empirical evidence that accounting practices in Latin American countries are harmonised in the IFRS era, considering that the five countries analysed have similar characteristics in terms of accounting systems. These authors identify the efforts of The Latin America Group of Issuers of Financial Reporting Standards (Grupo LatinoAmericano de Emisores de Normas de Información Financiera) as a possible explanation for the harmonisation of accounting practices in Latin America. This group, together with IASB, seeks to promote the adoption and convergence of international accounting standards in Latin American countries, consequently helping to improve the quality of financial accounting statements from these countries. All five countries analysed are members of this group and, thus, the harmonisation of accounting practices of these countries may occur because of the harmonisation efforts promoted by this group. Also identified is the role that the economic and political blocs that exist in Latin America (Mercosul bloc and Andean Community) may have on the harmonisation of accounting practices in these countries.

However, in spite of the harmonisation of accounting practices among the Latin American countries, there are still some significant differences in accounting practices and in the quality of accounting information among Brazilian firms, especially when compared to countries with more developed economies.

Future directions

The accounting literature suggests that in Brazil, a country characterised by weak investor protection and legal and enforcement regimes, the mandatory adoption of IFRS is likely to lead to an increase in accounting quality and to a decrease in the cost of capital.

However, in spite of the favourable effects of IFRS adoption in Brazil, empirical evidence suggests that those positive effects are confined to entities with better governance and those with incentives to opt out of the weak institutional and poor governance environment, as is the case of cross-listed entities.

The literature also shows that Brazilian firms have a lower level of accounting quality than Continental European and Anglo-Saxon firms. Thus, even with a single set of high quality accounting standards (IFRS) and reporting incentives, countries' specific characteristics still play an important role in the way IFRS is implemented in each country.

In this regard, among potential directions for future accounting research concerning Brazil, it would be useful to analyse more deeply, through case studies, the country- and firm-specific characteristics that contributed most to improving the quality of accounting information following IFRS adoption in Brazil. However, this type of analysis implies that there is a relationship of proximity with the Brazilian companies in order to make possible the accomplishment of said case studies.

It would be also useful to identify the role of national culture and CEO personality traits in successfully adopting IFRS in less developed countries compared to countries with higher levels of investor protection. This research could bring a significant contribution to the literature on the influence of culture and individual characteristics of executives on corporate financial reporting.

References

Armstrong, C. S., Barth, M. E., Jagolinzer, A. D. and Riedl, E. J. (2010). Market reaction to the adoption of IFRS in Europe. *The Accounting Review*, 85(1), 31–61.

Black, R. and Nakao, S. (2017). Heterogeneity in earnings quality between different classes of companies after IFRS adoption: Evidence from Brazil. *Revista Contabilidade & Finanças*, 28(73), 113–131.

Brasil (2000). Projeto de Lei no 3.741. Diário da Câmara de Deputados (Congress Gazette), Year LV (189): 56002–56025.

Carvalho, L. N. and Salotti, B. M. (2013). Adoption of IFRS in Brazil and the consequences to accounting education. *Issues in Accounting Education*, 28(2), 235–242.

Comissão de Valores Mobiliários (2018). History of the capital market. www.investidor.gov.br/menu/ Investidor_Estrangeiro/o_mercado_de_valores_brasileiros/Historia_Mercado_Capitais.html (accessed 4 September 2018).

Comitê de Pronunciamentos Contábeis (2018). Regimento Interno. www.cpc.org.br/CPC/CPC/ Regimento-Interno (accessed 4 September 2018).

Conselho Federal de Contabilidade (2005). Resolução CFC No 1.055/55. www1.cfc.org.br/sisweb/sre/ docs/RES_1055.doc (accessed 4 September 2018).

Costa, P. de S., Gomes, G. de S., Braunbeck, G. O. and Santana, M. E. G. (2018). A safari in Brazil: Evidence regarding the framework-based approach to teaching. *Revista Contabilidade & Finanças*, 29(76), 129–147.

Daske, H., Hail, L., Leuz, C. and Verdi, R. (2008). Mandatory IFRS reporting around the world: Early evidence on the economic consequences. *Journal of Accounting Research*, 46(5), 1085–1142.

Daske, H., Hail, L., Leuz, C. and Verdi, R. (2013). Adopting a label: Heterogeneity in the economic consequences around IAS/IFRS adoptions. *Journal of Accounting Research*, 51(3), 495–547.

Eng, L., Lin, J. and Figueiredo, J. (2018). International Financial Reporting Standards adoption and information quality: Evidence from Brazil. *Journal of International Financial Management and Accounting*, forthcoming.

Figlioli, B., Lemes, S. and Lima, F. (2017). IFRS, synchronicity, and financial crisis: The dynamics of accounting information for the Brazilian capital markets. *Review of Accounting and Finance*, 28(75), 326–243.

IASB/CFC/CPC (2010). Memorandum of Understanding among the International Accounting Standards Board – IASB, the Brazilian Federal Council of Accounting – CFC and the Brazilian Accounting Pronouncements Committee – CPC. www.ifrs.org/-/media/feature/around-the-world/mous/mou-brazil.pdf?la=en&hash=8A0DE96C0EA825EBAF2267ECF88087C898B62210 (accessed 4 September 2018).

IFRS Foundation (2017). IFRS application around the world – jurisdictional profile: Brazil. www.ifrs.org/-/ media/feature/around-the-world /jurisdiction-profiles/brazil-ifrs-profile.pdf (accessed 4 September 2018).

IFRS Foundation (2018). Analysis of the G20 IFRS profiles (updated 12 January 2018). www.ifrs.org/ use-around-the-world/use-of-ifrs-standards-by-jurisdiction/#analysis (accessed 4 September 2018).

Kim, J. B. and Shi, H. (2012). IFRS reporting, firm-specific information flows, and institutional environment: International evidence. *Review of Accounting Studies*, 17(3), 474–517.

Kim, J., Liu, X. and Zeng, L. (2012). The impact of mandatory IFRS adoption on audit fees: Theory and evidence. *The Accounting Review*, 87(6), 2061–2094.

Kvaal, E. and Nobes, C. W. (2010). International differences in IFRS policy choice. *Accounting and Business Research*, 40(2), 173–187.

Lopes, A. B. (2011). Teaching IFRS in Brazil: News from the front. *Accounting Education: An International Journal*, 20(4), 339–347.

Lopes, A. B., Walker, M. and Silva, R. L. M. (2016). The determinants of firm-specific corporate governance arrangements, IFRS adoption, and the informativeness of accounting reports: Evidence from Brazil. *Journal of International Accounting Research*, 15(2), 101–124.

Lourenço, I. and Branco, M. C. (2015). Corporate governance and the effect of IFRS Adoption: The Brazilian Case. *Revista Universo Contábil*, 11(1), 157–172.

Lourenço, I., Branco, M. C. and Curto, J. D. (2015). Do IFRS matter in emerging countries? An exploratory analysis of Brazilian firms, in Lourenço, I. and Major, M. (Eds.), *Standardization of Financial Reporting and Accounting in Latin American Countries*. IGI Global, 103–125.

Lourenço, I., Sarquis, R., Branco, M. and Magro, N. (2018). International differences in accounting practices under IFRS and the influence of the USA. *Australian Accounting Review*, 28(4), 468–481.

Martins, E., Gelbcke, E. R., Santos, A. and Iudícibus, S. (2013). *Manual de Contabilidade Societária*, 2ª edição. Ed Atlas.

Murro, E. V. B., Munhoz, T. R., Teixeira, G. B. and Lourenço, I. (2015). The impact of the mandatory adoption of IFRS in the fees of auditing in companies of BM&F Bovespa, in Lourenço, I. and Major, M. J. (Eds.), *Standardization of Financial Reporting and Accounting in Latin American Countries*. Hershey: IGI Global.

Nobes, C. W. (2006). The survival of international differences under IFRS: Towards a research agenda. *Accounting and Business Research*, 36(3), 233–245.

Nobes, C. W. (2008). Accounting classification in the IFRS era. *Australian Accounting Review*, 18(3), 191–198.

Nobes, C. W. (2011). IFRS practices and the persistence of accounting system classification. *Abacus*, 47(3), 267–283.

Nobes, C. W. (2013). The continued survival of international differences under IFRS. *Accounting and Business Research*, 43(2), 83–111.

Pelucio-Grecco, M. C., Geron, C. M. S., Grecco, G. B. and Lima, J. P. C. (2014). The effect of IFRS on earnings management in Brazilian non-financial public companies. *Emerging Markets Review*, 21, 42–66.

Pires, C. O. and Decourt, R. F. (2015). The impacts of the final phase of transition to IFRS in Brazil. *Review of Business and Management*, 17(54), 736–750.

Rathke, A. A. T. and Santana, V. F. (2015). Has IFRS improved comparability regarding earnings management in Latin America? in Lourenço, I. and Major, M. (Eds.), *Standardization of Financial Reporting and Accounting in Latin American Countries*, IGI Global, 56–78.

Rathke, A. A. T., Santana, V. F., Lourenço, I. M. E. C. and Dalmácio F. Z. (2016). International Financial Reporting Standards and earnings management in Latin America. *Revista de Administração Contemporânea*, 20(3), 368–388.

Rodrigues, L., Bugarim, M. and Craig, R. (2019). The Brazilian accounting profession and accounting education: An historical perspective, in Weetman, P. and Tsalavoutas, I. (Eds.), *Routledge Companion to Accounting in Emerging Economies*. Routledge.

Rodrígues García, M. P., Cortez Alejandro, K. A., Méndez Sáenz, A. B. and Garza Sánchez H. H. (2017). Does an IFRS adoption increase value relevance and earnings timeliness in Latin America? *Emerging Markets Review*, 30(C), 155–168.

Salotti, B. and Carvalho, L. N. (2015). Convergence of accounting standards towards IFRS in Brazil, in Lourenço, I. and Major, M. (Eds.), *Standardization of Financial Reporting and Accounting in Latin American Countries*, IGI Global, 79–102.

Santos, E. S., Ponte, V. M. R. and Mapurunga, P. V. R. (2014). Mandatory IFRS adoption in Brazil (2010): Index of compliance with disclosure requirements and some explanatory factors of firms reporting. *Review of Accounting and Finance*, 25(65), 161–176.

Sarquis, R. W. and Luccas, R. G. (2015). Accounting systems' classification in Latin America: Is there harmonization in the IFRS era? in Lourenço, I. and Major, M. (Eds.), *Standardization of Financial Reporting and Accounting in Latin American Countries*, IGI Global, 32–55.

Silva, R. L. M. and Nardi, P. C. C. (2017). Full adoption of IFRSs in Brazil: Earnings quality and the cost of equity capital. *Research in International Business and Finance*, 42, 1057–1073.

Silva, C. L. P. M, Santos, M. A. C., Koga, G. H. and Barbosa, R. A. C. (2014). Taxation and IFRS in Brazil: Changes in the law of IRPJ, CSLL, PIS/PASEP and COFINS introduced by Law No 12.973/2014. *Revista de Estudos Tributários e Aduaneiros*, Brasília-DF, 1(1), 393–422.

UNCTAD (2006). Review of practical implementation issues of international reporting standards: Case study of Brazil. Intergovernmental Working Group of Experts on International Standards of Accounting and Reporting, Twenty-third session, Geneva, 10–12 October 2006.

Vieira, R. B., Martins, V. A., Machado, A. and Domingues, J. C. A. (2011). Impacts of partial adoption of IFRS in Brazil: Effects on financial information quality of publicly traded companies. *British Journal of Economics, Finance and Management Sciences*, 1(2), 93–112.

Wells, M. J. C. (2011). Framework-based approach to teaching principles-based accounting standards. *Accounting Education: An International Journal*, 20(4), 303–316.

Wells, M. J. C. and Tarca, A. (2014). Stage 3 – Non-financial assets: The open safari case study. IFRS Foundation. http://archive.ifrs.org/Use-around-the-world/Education/Documents/Framework-based %20teaching%20materials/2014%20Stage%203%20Open%20Safari%20case%20study%20final.pdf (accessed 11 September 2018).

World Bank (2005). Brazil: Report on the Observance of Standards and Codes (ROSC) – accounting and auditing (English). World Bank. http://documents.worldbank.org/curated/en/484861468237862800/ Brazil-Report-on-the-Observance-of-Standards-and-Codes-ROSC-accounting-and-auditing (accessed 11 September 2018).

World Bank (2013). Brazil: Report on the Observance of Standards and Codes – accounting and auditing. World Bank. https://openknowledge.worldbank.org/handle/10986/16681 (accessed 11 September 2018). License: CC BY 3.0 IGO.

World Federation of Exchanges (2018). The WFE annual statistics guide (volume 3). https://focus.world-exchanges.org/statistics/articles/wfe-annual- statistics-guide-volume-3 (accessed 17 September 2018).

Zéghal, D., Chtourou, S. and Sellami, M. Y. (2011). An analysis of the effect of mandatory adoption of IAS/IFRS on earnings management. *Journal of International Accounting, Auditing and Taxation*, 20, 61–72.

3

IFRS IN INDIA IN THE CONTEXT OF DEVELOPING THE PROFESSION

Shraddha Verma and Sarada Rajeswari Krishnan

Introduction

This chapter reviews the literature on accounting developments in India from independence in 1947, focusing on socio-economic and political influences on the process of accounting change. In particular, we focus on the key elements of the accounting system that was implemented post-independence and the process leading towards the adoption of International Financial Reporting Standards (IFRS) from 2006. We start with a brief overview of the socio-economic and political context of India, followed by an outline of legal and professional accounting regulation in India post-independence. We then review the IFRS adoption process within India and conclude with potential avenues for future research.

Socio-economic and political context of India

India, at independence from the British in 1947, inherited an economy which was very underdeveloped with low per capita income, poor economic growth, many living under the poverty line and little industrialisation. What little Indian industry there was produced low technology, low productivity, low wages and labour intensive goods, and was concentrated in only a few selected areas such as textiles. There was little production of capital goods, a lack of infrastructure industries and a lack of modern banking and insurance (Spear, 1978; Kumar, 1982; Rothermund, 1993; Tomlinson, 1993).

Thus, a priority for the Indian government at independence was economic development. Led by Prime Minister Nehru, the government of India (GOI), dominated by the Indian National Congress (also called the Congress Party), introduced a mixed economy system, in which there was a role for both private and public enterprise and in which socialist ideals were operated within a secular democracy.

The key elements of this economic system included central planning of the economy, setting up a large public sector, a nationalised banking system and control and licensing of private enterprise. State control of foreign investment was seen as important to prevent foreign capital and interests from dominating the interests of India. Protection of indigenous industry through the use of import substituting policies, import restrictions, high tariffs and production for the domestic market rather than for exports was also seen as important. These were implemented, by and large, through the use of statutory legislation and by setting up government bodies and agencies to oversee policy initiatives. However, these policies did not lead to economic success, but instead to low economic and industrial growth, economic inefficiency, lack of modernisation in the corporate sector and lack of private and foreign investment (Kumar, 1982; Rothermund, 1993; Tomlinson, 1993; Joshi and Little, 1994, 1996).

Despite some attempts at liberalising the economy in the 1980s, India reached a position of economic crisis in the early 1990s, and faced persistent and growing fiscal deficits which were financed by public borrowing and borrowing from the Reserve Bank of India (RBI). This led to high debt and high inflation in the economy. India also showed a large deficit on its current account and its balance of payments, very low foreign exchange reserves and high foreign debt. There were problems in the public sector with poor management, overmanning and lack of new technology (Kulke and Rothermund, 1990; Rothermund, 1993; Joshi and Little, 1994, 1996; Wolpert, 1997).

In response to this crisis, the Finance Minister, Dr Man Mohan Singh, in 1991 initiated major changes to stabilise the economy and start a long-term programme of liberalisation and deregulation of the economy, moving away from control to competition. Tight fiscal control to reduce fiscal deficits was introduced and the rupee was devalued by 19 per cent, supported by standby credit from the International Monetary Fund (IMF). Import controls were reduced on raw materials and components and exporters were allowed to maintain foreign currency accounts for the first time. Industrial licensing was reformed, restrictions on large companies to expand capacity were reduced and areas reserved for the public sector were decreased. In addition, controls over foreign trade were reduced, tariffs and subsidies were reduced, foreign direct investment was encouraged and the tax system reformed (Kulke and Rothermund, 1990; Rothermund, 1993; Joshi and Little, 1994, 1996; Wolpert, 1997). Later reforms continued the liberalisation of the Indian economy and contributed to India being among the fastest-growing economies of the world with projected 7.3 per cent real growth of GDP in 2009 (IMF 2019). It is within this socio-economic context that accounting in India developed post-independence.

Accounting in India post-independence

There were two main planks to accounting regulation post-independence in India: legal regulation of accounting and regulation by the accounting profession. In terms of legal regulation, accounting regulations were incorporated within the Indian Companies Act and to date this remains a key form of accounting regulation. In addition, an indigenous accounting profession was instituted in 1949 with the establishment of the Institute of Chartered Accountants of India (ICAI), which became increasingly involved in accounting regulation over time.

Legal regulation

During the colonial period, the British introduced Indian Companies Acts to regulate the corporate sector within India. These were mainly based on British Companies Acts, but did contain some provisions which related to the Indian context.[1]

At independence in 1947, the GOI chose to retain the use of a Companies Act to regulate joint stock companies and this has remained an important means of legal regulation in India to date. The Companies Act 1956[2] was the first major companies act to be promulgated post-independence and incorporated key accounting regulations for joint stock companies.

Some of the provisions were in line with British law but some were specific to the Indian context and were drafted in line with the socio-economic context of India and India's social and economic objectives. For example, the accounting provisions included a requirement for books of accounts to be kept, specifying the books of accounts needed and a requirement for accounts to show a true and fair view. The formats for the balance sheet were specified, extending previous requirements and a detailed list of items to be disclosed in the profit and loss account was given. Provisions relating to the appointment, independence, powers, duties and qualifications of auditors, extending previous requirements and powers for central government to direct special audits, for example for fraud, and the rights of auditors in special audits were also included. A requirement for a cost audit for companies in specified industries was added in 1965 (Companies Act 1956).[3]

Overviews of the provisions of the Companies Act 1956 and its development have been provided, as part of wider studies, in books by Das Gupta (1977) and Chakravorty (1994). A more in-depth study of the promulgation of the Companies Act 1956 has been undertaken by Verma and Gray (2009). They study the promulgation of the Companies Act 1956 and explore interactions between key stakeholders in relation to the accounting regulations incorporated into the Act. The impact of imperialism in a post-imperial context is indicated with choices made by the GOI to use the Companies Acts as one of the means to regulate the corporate sector being very much in line with the British model, which they had inherited at independence, continuing post-independence.

Responding to calls for more research on the role of the state within accounting (Wilmott, 1986; Chua and Poullaos, 1993), Verma and Gray (2009) show the importance of the State in accounting regulation within India with the GOI choosing to incorporate key accounting regulations into the Companies Act, very much in line with the socio-political context of India in which strong State involvement was seen in all areas of social and economic life post-independence. Key reasons for incorporating accounting regulations within the Companies Act included a perceived need to improve information available to shareholders so that they could become more involved in running their companies as well as giving information to other users such as the government to monitor the running of companies. In addition, the government wanted to ensure fairness in the rewards earned by labour, capital and management in companies and considered that this might be made more transparent with better accounting provisions. Finally, the government needed information for economic planning purposes and it was felt that company reports may be able to provide such information and might also encourage companies to contribute more fully to national economic aims. Thus, the importance of the socio-economic political context and the role of the government are highlighted within the study.

Major changes to accounting regulation within the Companies Act took place in 1974 and 1988. For example, the Companies Act 1974 introduced provisions requiring the disclosure of higher paid employees and whether they were relatives of the directors of the company.[4] The Companies Act 1988 introduced regulations relating to depreciation and requirements for the disclosure of energy, technology absorption, research and development and foreign exchange earnings and outgoings.[5] Following a major revision in 2013, previous legislation was replaced by the Companies Act 2013 and introduced many new provisions, for example requiring the presentation of consolidated financial statements by any company with a subsidiary or a joint venture. The interaction between the Companies Act 2013 and IFRS is discussed later in the chapter. In addition to legal regulation, professionalisation of accounting and professional regulation of accounting also developed post-independence and this is discussed in the next section.

Accounting professionalisation in India post-independence

Professionalisation of accounting within the period of Empire and in postcolonial states has been an important strand of research within the field of accounting history, exploring professionalisation in both settler and non-settler states.

Common themes of studies in settler colonies such as the US, Australia and South Africa include tracing the impact of British accountants emigrating to these colonies, the establishment of local professional accounting institutes and the interactions between these and the professional institutes in the United Kingdom, closure activities of professional accounting bodies and the interactions of the state and the profession (Johnson and Caygill, 1971; Johnson, 1973; Parker, 1989; Carnegie and Parker, 1999; Carnegie and Edwards, 2001; Chua and Poullaos, 2002; Poullaos, 2010, 2016; Richardson, 2010).

This directly contrasts with the trajectory of accounting in non-settler colonies of the British Empire. Professionalisation of accounting was usually seen after independence in the latter half of the twentieth century, very much supported by the newly formed State with accounting professionalisation linked to wider social, economic and political agendas and the continuing influence of British accounting bodies and qualifications (Annisette, 2000; Uche, 2002; Sian, 2006, 2011; Bakre, 2010; Susela, 2010; Yapa, 2010).

Accounting professionalisation in India has taken a trajectory that falls in between that seen in settler states and that of non-settler states. Professionalisation in India commenced pre-independence but it was not until post-independence that an indigenous accounting institute, the ICAI, was established.

One major study on the professionalisation of accounting in India, undertaken by Kapadia (1972), covers a range of accounting developments from ancient times to 1972. This also includes a review of the establishment of the Indian Accountancy Board (IAB) pre-independence, the establishment of the ICAI under statute in 1949 and interactions between the ICAI and a rival accounting body, the Institute of Cost and Works Accountants (ICWAI), which was established under statute in 1959.

Extending this work, Verma and Gray (2006) and Verma (2010), using the concepts of closure and profession–state relations (Chua and Poullaos, 1993, 1998) together with the role of imperialism, have explored the establishment of the ICAI under statute in 1949. The studies note that the ideal of an autonomous and independent accounting profession had been inherited from the colonial period and the groundwork for an independent profession, based on the UK model, had been put in place with the creation of the IAB in 1932. The Board had been set up to advise the British government in India on issues relating to accounting and auditing, including the registration of Indian auditors and continued in existence until 1949.

The intention of the Indian members of the IAB was to develop an indigenous accounting profession headed by an independent institute but such a profession had not emerged at independence. At independence, the Indian members of the IAB wished to establish an accounting profession based on the UK model. However, in discussions with the GOI, a very different model emerged – one in which the ICAI was established under statutory charter with state representation on the Council of the ICAI. This was more in line with the socio-economic context of India at this time with strong GOI involvement seen in all areas of social and economic development.

Once again some of the main reasons that persuaded the GOI to support the development of an accounting profession was the perception held by the GOI that accounting was an important tool to help them achieve their socio-economic goals.[6] In particular, among the key aims of the government at independence was rapid economic growth together with social development, leading to a fairer distribution of wealth among the population. The perception held at this time was that accounting could help facilitate these aims by allowing for the provision of comparable information across the corporate sector, which would facilitate decision making. It was also thought that the provision of information within the accounting system might help encourage the private sector to act in ways congruent with the government's aims, rather than just for private gain, and that a stronger audit framework would help to monitor the actions of directors and perhaps curb abuses within the corporate sector.[7]

The direct involvement of the State was important in the establishment of the ICAI, which was established under statute in direct contrast to the more private-sector approach of the development of British accounting institutes and accounting institutes in settler states. In common with research on the Companies Act 1956, the continuing influence of the British model within accounting developments in India is indicated post-independence. The ICAI was, as far as was possible, modelled on its British chartered counterpart despite the statutory basis for the Institute and strong State involvement within the ICAI. The studies of Verma and Gray (2006) and Verma (2010) also explore interactions between the ICAI and the Institute of Chartered Accountants of England and Wales (ICAEW) with the ICAEW objecting, albeit unsuccessfully, to the adoption of the chartered designation by the Indian institute.

Once established in 1949, the ICAI put in place its organisational structure and dealt with issues such as examinations, disciplinary procedures and reciprocity. Part of their role included issuing recommendations and guidelines on accounting and auditing practices, which were issued until 1977, when the ICAI set up a system to promulgate accounting standards. This was a key development in the history of the ICAI and is discussed next.

Standard setting in India

The ICAI promulgated recommendations and guidelines in relation to accounting which were not mandatory under the auspices of its Research Committee, which was established in 1952, but it was not until 1977 that the ICAI promulgated Indian accounting standards, which was, at least in part, a response to international developments and joining the International Accounting Standards Committee (IASC) by the ICAI as an associate member in 1974. This placed some obligation on the ICAI to ensure that published financial statements complied with international accounting standards. The ICAI chose to incorporate international accounting provisions into national standards if deemed appropriate, rather than fully adopting international accounting standards. The Council of the ICAI constituted an Accounting Standards Board ('ASB (Ind)') to promulgate Indian accounting standards in April 1977 following a due process system similar to that used by the accounting profession in the UK and the IASC (Chander, 1992; Chakravorty, 1994).

Currently, Indian accounting standards are prepared under the supervision of the ASB (Ind). The standards are then recommended to the National Advisory Committee on Accounting Standards (NACAS) which reviews the standards and recommends accounting standards to the Ministry of Corporate Affairs (MCA), who notify the adoption of the standards by the corporate sector. The process towards International Accounting Standards (IAS) and IFRS convergence was initiated in 2006 and this is discussed next.

Move towards IFRS convergence in India

The decision-making process for IAS/IFRS convergence marked a key milestone in the development of the accounting profession in India. Convergence with international accounting standards is an important policy decision made by any nation state. Extant literature on convergence clearly indicates the importance of studying the relevant economic, legal and political context of the country within which convergence decision-making processes are embedded and within which the convergence process is actually enacted (Mir and Rahman, 2005; Tyrrall *et al.*, 2007; Cieslewicz, 2014; Krishnan, 2016; Krishnan *et al.*, 2017). Various legal, economic and conceptual factors have influenced the convergence decision-making process within India and have led the GOI and the ICAI to favour convergence vis-à-vis full adoption despite the International Accounting Standards Board (IASB) recommending full adoption of IAS/IFRS in India, in line with its agenda of global accounting harmonisation.

Deliberations on convergence with IAS/IFRS in India commenced partly due to increased levels of foreign direct investments after the opening up of the economy in 1991 as well as to a rise in the number of domestic companies who were either buying foreign companies or entering into joint ventures with foreign companies. The commencement of the IFRS–US GAAP convergence project in 2002 and the Securities and Exchange Commission's proposal in the US to permit the filing of IFRS-compliant financial statements without reconciliation statements between US GAAP and IFRS in 2007 also contributed to the decision for convergence with IFRS within India (ICAI, 2007). India's participation in and membership of several global forums such as the United Nations Conference on Trade and Development, Organisation for Economic Co-operation and Development, International Organisation of Securities Commissions and G-20 conferences also provided further impetus to the decision-making process (Krishnan, 2016). Another key event that was influential was the mandatory adoption of IFRS by the European Union in 2005.

In 2006, the ASB (Ind) prepared a concept paper to facilitate discussion of the matter of formal IAS/IFRS convergence with various stakeholders including the GOI, NACAS and regulatory authorities. Accordingly, in October 2006, the ASB (Ind) formed a task force convened by its chair which included representatives from the ICAI, representatives from industry (e.g. the Federation of Indian Chamber of Commerce and Industry (FICCI) and the Confederation of Indian Industry (CII)), representatives from the financial system, including a representative of the RBI, and representatives of the International Accounting Standards Committee Foundation and the IASB (ICAI, 2007).

The concept paper was published by the ICAI in October 2007. In this paper, the ICAI provided the following definition of convergence:

> To design and maintain national accounting standards in a way that financial statements prepared in accordance with national accounting standards draw unreserved statement of compliance with IFRSs.
>
> *(ICAI, 2007: 12)*

The ICAI recognised the need for variation between Indian domestic accounting standards (Ind AS) and IFRS. There were several reasons for the ICAI's decision to not fully adopt IAS/IFRS and these were discussed in the 2007 concept paper. The ICAI highlighted the importance of maintaining consistency with legal and regulatory requirements within Ind AS. Ind AS 21 Consolidated Financial Statements, Ind AS 25 Interim Financial Reporting and Ind AS 31 Financial Instruments are a few examples of domestic accounting standards framed to suit the legal position in India, rather than following IAS/IFRS. For example, under Ind AS 21, 'control' was defined according to criteria listed in the Companies Act 1956, which was different from the definition provided under IAS 27 Consolidated and Separate Financial Statements. Ind AS 25 and Ind AS 31 were also identified as having similar differences to corresponding IAS due to legal requirements in India.

The influence of markets, in particular the use of the fair value approach in IFRS, was also raised as problematic for convergence. According to the concept paper, markets in India were not sufficiently developed to determine reliable fair values of various assets and liabilities (ICAI, 2007). This point has been validated by a member of the industry:

> There is a dire need for developing professional elite services such as valuation. There should be valuation standards in India without which there will be no uniformity in the reports presented and fair value system will be a failure.
>
> *(Krishnan, 2016: 172)*

Discussions in the concept paper and information collected from interviews with members of industry by the author seem to indicate that both the ICAI and Indian industry held the opinion that Indian markets were not equipped to adopt the fair value system successfully (Krishnan, 2016).

The level of preparedness was also raised as being problematic. The ICAI in its concept paper identified and discussed difficulties that industry might encounter if IAS/IFRS were to be fully adopted without any amendments or modifications. For example, Ind AS 15 *Employee Benefits* took into account the Indian context in relation to employee benefits. Ind AS 15 allowed the deferment of expenditure upon termination of services in response to structural changes within Indian industry rather than following IAS 19, which did not allow this treatment. This would have been problematic for Indian companies.

Finally, conceptual differences were raised as being potentially problematic for convergence. Ind AS 29 and IAS 37 *Constructive Obligations* were cited as an example of this. IAS 37 mandates the creation of a provision on the basis of a constructive obligation that would require the provision to be recognised at an early stage. Restructuring of an enterprise is cited as an example wherein a liability cannot crystallise in its early stages due to which an early recognition of provision would be inappropriate. Conceptual differences discussed in the concept paper seem to suggest that ICAI had differences of opinion with the IASB on the timing of recognising the provision as well as the judgement of related determining factors. These differences seem to arise as a result of choice rather than the influence of compelling legal and economic factors (Krishnan, 2016).

Following the concept paper, the ICAI in 2007 announced its decision to converge Ind AS with IFRS. This decision was followed by an official notification from the MCA in 2008, declaring the intention to achieve convergence by 2011 (Krishnan *et al.*, 2017).

The ICAI proposed the promulgation of Ind AS which would be based on IAS/IFRS but would reflect the socio-economic context of India. These standards, it was argued, would be accepted as being compliant with IFRS, because although IAS 1 stipulated compliance with all the requirements of IFRSs, the IASB had accepted in its 2006 *Statement of Best Practice: Working Relationships between the IASB and other Accounting Standards-Setters* that adding disclosure requirements or removing optional treatments would not of itself create non-compliance with IFRS (ICAI, 2007: part 2, para 1.12).

This confirmed that the exclusion of optional treatments or addition of disclosure requirements to suit the local context did not imply non-compliance with IAS/IFRS. This explanation provided by the ICAI implied that the ICAI saw the newly developed Ind AS being globally recognised as IFRS compliant, despite some differences between the Ind AS and IAS/IFRS. This was, however, not necessarily accepted by all. For example, some arguments were presented that, due to the differences between Ind AS and IAS/IFRS, financial statements prepared according to Ind AS would be unlikely to be acknowledged as IFRS compliant by the global investor community (Krishnan, 2016).

In 2009, the government established a core group to engage with key stakeholders in relation to the convergence process for Ind AS. The group was led by the Secretary of the MCA at the time. Two subgroups were formed to support the core group. The first subgroup was led by the chair of NACAS and was formed of members of professional accounting bodies such as the ICAI, professional auditing firms such as Deloitte, and GOI representatives from various state regulatory authorities. This subgroup identified issues on regulatory and legislative amendments that would be required to achieve IFRS convergence (Krishnan, 2016).

The second subgroup focused on industry and was led by the director of Infosys, one of the largest multinational companies (MNC) in India. This subgroup included representatives of chief financial officers of major MNCs and representatives of industrial associations such as FICCI and CII. This subgroup dealt with concerns of industry regarding convergence as well as the level of preparedness of industry (Krishnan, 2016).

However, despite these steps, India was not able to meet its 2011 deadline for IFRS convergence. The factors identified by the ICAI in its concept paper did indeed lead to delays in the convergence of Ind AS with IAS/IFRS (*The Economic Times*, 2011). Furthermore, in December 2010, FICCI formally requested the MCA to postpone the planned implementation of IFRS in April 2011 (MCA, 2011).

FICCI argued that a delay was needed for several reasons. One reason related to unworkable deadlines. They argued that business entities needed more time to get accustomed to the new standards and regulations. Another issue related to ambiguity. FICCI argued there was a lack of clarity in relation to the preparation of financial statements. For example, they argued that it was not clear whether financial statements were expected to be prepared according to IFRS or Schedule VI of the Companies Act 1956. If a dual set of financial statements was needed, this would increase costs to business. In addition, proposed changes to the Companies Act 1956 were also being discussed, for example with the Companies Bill 2011 and the Draft Code Bill 2011, and FICCI argued that until these had been fully debated and the outcome of the amendments determined, it would not be possible to prepare clear and unambiguous implementation plans for convergence. The process of ongoing revisions to IFRS, for example in relation to financial instruments, investments, loans, accounting for income taxes and revenue recognition, were further cited as reasons to support FICCI's request for a delay in the convergence timetable (*The Economic Times*, 2011).

FICCI also raised the issue of tax as another reason for calling for a delay to the convergence process. In India, tax accounting standards had been promulgated at this time and these were independent of Indian GAAP and the extant Ind AS. FICCI highlighted that this whole issue needed to be reviewed before convergence could be progressed.

Such delays in the convergence process when explored through theoretical and conceptual perspectives of transnational communication and power relations revealed issues such as disagreements on timing and terms of convergence arising due to differences in the priorities of actors involved in the process. For example, the idea of transnational communication helps analyse interactions between global and local actors involved in the decision-making process (Djelic and Sahlin-Andersson, 2006; Samsonova, 2009; Krishnan 2016). The concept of resource dependencies between decision makers (Casciaro and Piskorski, 2005; Djelic and Quack, 2010) enables further analysis of such negotiations through the lens of power imbalance between actors (Mir and Rahman, 2005; Krishnan, 2018). Power dynamics between decision makers have been explored by analysing the institutional agendas of actors representing different institutional fields including India (Phillips *et al.*, 2000; Krishnan, 2018).

In February 2011, despite the outstanding taxation issues, the MCA officially published 35 Ind AS which they stated were converged, and which the IASB agreed were substantially converged, with IAS/IFRS (MCA, 2011; ICAI, 2018). However, the deadline of preparing financial statements according to these Ind AS by April 2011 was not met due to pending taxation and legislative issues raised by industry and in 2011 the MCA made an announcement that a new deadline of April 2013 was set for IFRS convergence (ICAI, 2012). This, too, was delayed. In June 2014, the union minister for finance at the time proposed mandatory implementation of Ind AS in the period 2016–2021. The MCA then published a new roadmap for convergence in February 2015 in which most companies were required to adopt Ind AS by 2017–2018 and specialist companies, for example those in banking and insurance, were given until 2020–2021 to adopt Ind AS 8 (Krishnan, 2016).

A total of 39 Ind AS had been issued as of November 2018 by the MCA. This was followed by actual implementation of the Ind AS by those Indian companies required to do so, within the time frame outlined above (ICAI, 2018). In practice, the IASB has now agreed that Ind AS are substantially converged with IAS/IFRS (ICAI, 2018).

Interactions between the ICAI and the IASB

As well as working towards convergence with IAS/IFRS, the ICAI also played a significant role in influencing IAS/IFRS through ongoing negotiations with the IASB in relation to specific standards. For example, the valuation of agricultural assets under IAS 41 was considered to be unsuitable in the Indian context and was considered one of the hurdles to convergence in India (Krishnan *et al.*, 2017).

The ICAI, along with other professional accounting bodies representing different nation states holding the same view on valuation of agricultural assets, discussed the issue at meetings conducted by the Asian-Oceanian Standard Setters Group (AOSSG). The decision to form a working group specifically to address issues in IAS 41 was made by the AOSSG at its third meeting in Tokyo in 2010. China, Hong Kong, India, Indonesia, Korea and Malaysia were members of this working group which was led by India and Malaysia[9] (AOSSG, 2011; Krishnan *et al.*, 2017).

In 2011, the working group further discussed the issues surrounding IAS 41 and submitted a proposal to the IASB requesting amendments in IAS 41. This proposal was accepted by the IASB in June 2013. In June 2014, the IASB issued proposed amendments to IAS 41. These have been applicable since January 2016. The corresponding Ind AS 41 has only minor variations from IAS 41 such as the use of terminology (Krishnan, 2016; Krishnan *et al.*, 2017). Thus, India and other countries have been able to successfully influence IAS/IFRS where these were considered problematic. We see here the interaction and influence of the ICAI on the IASB.

Future directions

As discussed in this chapter, there has been some research on accounting developments within India post-independence covering the promulgation of accounting regulations within the Companies Act 1956, professionalisation of accounting within India and the process towards adoption of IAS/IFRS within India. However there remains huge scope for further accounting research on India, which still remains relatively under-researched.

Building on existing research, further research using a political economy approach and exploring the socio-economic and political context of India on accounting including the role of the state would be of particular interest. This includes tracing accounting developments both pre-independence and post-independence.

In the pre-independence period more detailed studies of professionalisation within India in an imperial context including exploration of links between accounting professions within different jurisdictions within the British Empire would help us further understand professionalisation during this period. Some research on India in the pre-independence period has been started, for example Sian and Verma (2017), but more research within this time period is warranted. Particular issues of interest include the role of the British government in accounting development in this period, the role and interactions of British professional accounting bodies in relation to Indian professionalisation, both chartered bodies and others, and the development of professional associations of Indian accountants. Research into the British Empire and research in different imperial contexts would be of value as these have received much less attention.

Research on legal accounting developments post-independence within India, for example the accounting changes within the Companies Act 1956 in 1974 and 1988 and the promulgation of the Companies Act 2013, would be interesting in relation to India due to the importance of such regulation in the country. Research encompassing both the changes to the Companies Act and its enforcement would be of particular interest to highlight the role of the State and the socio-economic and political context on accounting and actual practices that are adopted.

More recent episodes in the professionalisation of accounting would be a fruitful area of research, too. Topics of particular interest would be the linkages between the Indian accounting institutes, the ICAI and the ICWAI, and professional accounting institutes in other countries, as recently interactions between professional accounting bodies of different countries have been developing and increasing in importance.

The interactions between the ICAI and ICWAI and how these affect the accounting landscape is another area of interest as these interactions have been important in shaping accounting in India. In addition, the impact of changes in economic direction on accounting post-1991 is a topic that would be of interest. The entry of global, international accounting firms and the impact of these on the existing accounting firms in India are areas that have not been explored in any depth.

The development of Indian accounting standards and the progress of the adoption of IFRS within India, particularly in relation to the involvement of the state and other key actors within the socio-economic context, is worthy of further research. A key aspect is exploring the role of the state vis-à-vis the socio-political and economic context in the country to gain an understanding of the decision-making process that precedes the actual implementation of IFRS. Particularly, the impact of decision-making processes for convergence and the impact of such processes on the success or failure of IFRS implementation would enhance our understanding of the IFRS convergence movement spearheaded by the IASB and its role in achieving global accounting harmonisation. This includes consideration of how the ICAI and other professional accounting bodies may influence the processes and decisions of the IASB of the ICAI. In these areas, qualitative methodologies would be particularly helpful in explicating the influence of the state and socio-economic factors in relation to the issues identified above.

Extant literature on convergence with international accounting standards can be broadly classified into four categories: drivers of convergence with international accounting standards (Briston, 1978; Abdelsalam and Weetman, 2003), benefits and disadvantage of convergence with international accounting standards (Biddle and Saudagaran, 1991; Peng and Bewley, 2010), compliance with international accounting standards (Weetman *et al.*, 1998; Tsalavoutas, 2011) and convergence as a decision-making process (Mir and Rahman, 2005). Some research on the last of these has been undertaken in relation to India (Krishnan, 2018) but the other strands of research have not. Several reports on the potential effects of IFRS adoption of financial statements in India have been published by the Big Four audit firms. However, academic research on this and other issues surrounding IFRS convergence in India is limited (Krishnan, 2016).

The development of Indian capital markets in terms of being equipped to adopt the fair value system has been raised in relation to India and would also be an interesting area of research.

Capital markets have a long history within India. The Bombay Stock Exchange (now known as the BSE) can trace its roots back to 1875 and the setting up of the Native Share and Stock Brokers Association. The Bombay Stock Exchange was the first stock exchange to be granted permanent recognition post-independence under the Securities Contract Regulation 1956 and is the major regional stock exchange in India. As such, it has influenced other regional stock exchanges within India (Machiraju, 1995). In addition to regional stock exchange, a national stock exchange was established in 1992, gaining formal recognition as a stock exchange by the regulator, the Securities and Exchange Board of India, in 1993. The National Stock Exchange (NSE) offers trading facilities nationally and since 2015 has increased cooperation with the London Stock Exchange (NSE, 2018).

In addition to the stock exchanges, there has been a significant inflow of Foreign Direct Investments (FDI) into India in response to the opening up of Indian markets after 1991. FDI in India averaged US$1,328.99 million from 1995 until 2018.[10]

Family businesses, too, are important in India. The majority of private sector entities in India are family run businesses that account for a market capitalisation of US$839 billion (Credit Suisse, 2018). A few of the major family run businesses in India are the Tata Group, Birla Group, Reliance Industries, Dabur, Bajaj, Jindal and Hindalco. However, these businesses are stated to have independent CEOs who run day-to-day operations and large executive councils at group level to provide strategic direction (Krishnan, 2016). The impact of the capital markets and business structures and the interactions between these and accounting developments and standards within India, especially in a changing economic context, are topics that would enhance our understanding of the linkages between these areas and accounting. We would suggest that quantitative studies as well as qualitative studies would be important in adding to our understanding of accounting in India, for example in the area of capital markets, corporate structure and convergence.

Notes

1 Report of the Company Law Committee, 1952, pp. 16–20, Government of India.
2 Companies Act 1956, Government of India.
3 Companies Act 1956 as amended in 1965, Government of India.
4 Companies Act, 1974, Government of India.
5 Companies Act, 1988, Government of India.
6 Report of the Company Law Committee, 1952.
7 Report of the Parliamentary Committee on the Chartered Accountants Bill, 1948, Government of India; Report of the Company Law Committee, 1952, Government of India; Report of the Company Law Amendment Committee, 1957, Government of India.
8 All domestic companies whose securities trade in a public market other than the SME Exchange are required to use Ind AS.
9 At meetings conducted by National Standard Setters in 2010, professional accounting bodies of other countries such as Brazil, Taiwan, Canada, France, Sudan and South Africa also extended their support to drafting a proposal requesting the IASB to review IAS 41.
10 https://tradingeconomics.com/india/foreign-direct-investment (accessed 25 January 2019).

References

Abdelsalam, O. and Weetman, P. (2003). Introducing International Accounting Standards to an emerging capital market: Relative familiarity and a language effect; the case of Egypt. *Journal of International Accounting Auditing and Taxation*, 12(1), 63–84.

Annisette, M. (2000). Imperialism and the professions: The education and certification of accountants in Trinidad and Tobago. *Accounting, Organizations and Society*, 25(7), 631–659.

AOSSG (2011). Letter to IASB on short-term revision to IAS 41. Asian-Oceanian Standard Setters Group www.aossg.org/docs/WG/Agriculture/Letter_to_IASB_on_short-term_revision_to_IAS41_20_Nov_2011.pdf (accessed 25 Jan 2019).

Bakre, O. M. (2010). Imperialism and professionalisation: The case of accountancy in Jamaica, in Poullaos, C. and Sian, S. (Eds.), *Accountancy and Empire*. New York: Routledge, 144–167.

Biddle, G. C. and Saudagaran, S. M. (1991). Foreign stock listings: Benefits, costs, and the accounting policy dilemma. *Accounting Horizons*, 5(3), 69–80.

Briston, R. J. (1978). The evolution of accounting in developing countries. *International Journal of Accounting*. 14(1), 105-120.

Carnegie, G. D. and Edwards, J. R. (2001). The construction of the professional accountant: The case of the Incorporated Institute of Accountants, Victoria (1886). *Accounting, Organizations and Society*, 26(4/5), 301–325.

Carnegie, G. D. and Parker, R. H. (1999). Accountants and empire: The case of co-membership of Australian and British accountancy bodies, 1885 to 1914. *Accounting, Business & Financial History*, 9(1), 77–102.

Casciaro, T. and Piskorski, M. J. (2005). Power imbalance, mutual dependence and constraint absorption: A closer look at resource dependency theory. *Administrative Science Quarterly*, 50(June), 167–199.

Chakravorty, D. K. (1994). *Development of Corporate Reporting in India*. New Delhi: Venus Publishing House.

Chander, S. (1992). *Corporate Reporting Practices in Public and Private Sectors*. New Delhi: Deep & Deep Publications.

Chua, W. F. and Poullaos, C. (1993). Rethinking the profession–state dynamic: The case of the Victorian charter attempt, 1885–1906. *Accounting, Organizations and Society*, 18(7/8), 691–728.

Chua, W. F. and Poullaos, C. (1998). The dynamics of 'closure' amidst the construction of market, profession, empire and nationhood: An historical analysis of an Australian accounting association, 1886–1903. *Accounting, Organizations and Society*, 23(2), 155–187.

Chua, W. F. and Poullaos, C. (2002). The Empire strikes back? An exploration of centre-periphery interaction between the ICAEW and accounting associations in the self-governing colonies of Australia, Canada and South Africa, 1880–1907. *Accounting, Organizations and Society*, 27(4/5), 409–445.

Cieslewicz, J. K. (2014). Relationships between national economic culture, institutions, and accounting: Implications for IFRS. *Critical Perspectives on Accounting*, 25(6), 511–528.

Credit Suisse (2018). Research Institute – The CS Family 1000 in 2018. www.credit-suisse.com/media/assets/corporate/docs/about-us/research/publications/the-cs-family-1000-in-2018.pdf (accessed 28 January 2019).

Das Gupta, N. (1977). *Financial Reporting in India*. New Delhi: Sultan Chand & Sons.

Djelic, M. L. and Quack, S. (Eds.), (2010). *Transnational Communities: Shaping Global Economic Governance*. Cambridge: Cambridge University Press.

Djelic, M.-L. and Sahlin-Andersson, K. (2006). Introduction – A world of governance: The rise of transnational regulation, in Djelic, M.-L. and Sahlin-Andersson, K. (Eds.), *Transnational Governance: Institutional Dynamics of Regulation*. Cambridge: Cambridge University Press, 1–30.

ICAI (2007). *Concept Paper on Convergence with IFRSs in India*. New Delhi: Institute of Chartered Accountants of India.

ICAI (2012). President's message, Institute of Chartered Accountants of India. www.icai.org/post.html?post_id=8828 (accessed 27 May 2018).

ICAI (2018). *Indian Accounting Standards (IFRS Converged): Successful Implementation – Impact Analysis and Industry Experience*. New Delhi: Institute of Chartered Accountants of India.

IMF (2019) India at a glance. www.imf.org/en/Countries/IND (accessed 22 May 2019).

Johnson, T. J. (1973). Imperialism and the professions: Notes on the development of professional occupations in Britain's colonies and the New States, in Halmos, P. (Ed.), *Professions and Social Change (Sociological Review Monograph 20)*. Keele: University of Keele, 281–309.

Johnson, T. J. and Caygill, M. (1971). The development of accountancy links in the Commonwealth. *Accounting and Business Research*, 1(2), 155–173.

Joshi, V. and Little., I. M. D. (1994). *India: Macroeconomics and Political Economy, 1964–1991*. Washington, DC and New Delhi: World Bank and Oxford University Press.

Joshi, V. and Little, I. M. D. (1996). *India Economic Reforms 1991–2000*. New Delhi: Oxford University Press.

Kapadia, G. P. (1972). *History of the Accountancy Profession in India, Volume 1*. New Delhi: The Institute of Chartered Accountants of India.

Krishnan, S. (2016). *IFRS and IPSAS convergence in India: Transnational perspectives.* Unpublished PhD thesis. Alliance Manchester Business School.

Krishnan, S. R. (2018). Influence of transnational economic alliances on the IFRS convergence decision in India: Institutional perspectives. *Accounting Forum*, 42(4), 309–327.

Krishnan, S., Samsonova-Taddei, A. and Stapleton, P. (2017). IFRS Convergence in India – Glimpses of the two-way interactive dynamics of the decision-making process. Paper presented to the Critical Perspectives on Accounting Conference, 3–5 July 2017, Quebec.

Kulke, H. and Rothermund, D. (1990). *A History of India.* London and New York: Routledge.

Kumar, D (Ed.) (1982). *The Cambridge Economic History of India, Volume 2.* New Delhi: Cambridge University Press.

Machiraju, H. R. (1995). *The Working of Stock-Exchanges in India.* New Delhi: New Age International Publishers.

MCA (2011). Press release, Ministry of Corporate Affairs. www.mca.gov.in/MinistryV2/press_release. html (accessed 25 September 2012).

Mir, M. Z. and Rahman, A. S. (2005). The adoption of international accounting standards in Bangladesh. *Accounting, Auditing & Accountability Journal*, 18(6), 816 –841.

NSE (2018), History and milestones. www.nseindia.com/global/content/about_us/history_milestones. htm (accessed 7 December 2018).

Parker, R. H. (1989). Importing and exporting accounting: The British experience, in Hopwood, A. (Ed.), *International Pressures for Accounting Change.* Hertfordshire: Prentice Hall International; and London: ICAEW.

Peng, S. and Bewley, K. (2010). Adaptability to fair value accounting in an emerging economy: A case study of China's IFRS convergence. *Accounting, Auditing and Accountability Journal*, 23(8), 982–1011.

Phillips, N., Lawrence, T. B. and Hardy, C. (2000). Inter-organizational collaboration and the dynamics of institutional fields. *Journal of Management Studies*, 37(1), 23–43.

Poullaos, C. (2010). The self-governing dominions of South Africa, Australia and Canada and the evolution of the imperial accountancy arena during the 1920s, in Poullaos, C. and Sian, S. (Eds.), *Accountancy and Empire.* New York: Routledge, 10–52.

Poullaos, C. (2016). Canada vs Britain in the imperial accountancy arena, 1908–1912: Symbolic capital, symbolic violence. *Accounting, Organizations and Society*, 51, 47–63.

Richardson, A. (2010). Canada between empires, in Poullaos, C. and Sian, S. (Eds.), *Accountancy and Empire.* New York: Routledge, 53–76.

Rothermund, D. (1993). *An Economic History of India from Pre-Colonial Times to 1991.* London: Routledge.

Samsonova, A. (2009). Local sites of globalisation: A look at the development of a legislative framework for auditing in Russia. *Critical Perspectives on Accounting*, 20(4), 528–552.

Sian, S. (2006). Inclusion, exclusion and control: The case of the Kenyan accounting professionalisation project. *Accounting, Organizations and Society*, 31(3), 295–322.

Sian, S. (2011). Operationalising closure in a colonial context: The Association of Accountants in East Africa, 1949–1963. *Accounting, Organizations and Society*, 36(6), 363–381.

Sian, S. and Verma, S. (2017). Ornamentalism and the construction of affinities: Accountancy in imperial India from 1900 to 1932. Accounting and Accountability Research Group Working Paper. Queen Mary, University of London.

Spear, P. (1978). *A History of India, Volume 2.* New Delhi: Penguin Books.

Susela, S. D. (2010). The Malaysian accountancy profession and its imperial legacy (1957–1995), in Poullaos, C. and Sian, S. (Eds.), *Accountancy and Empire.* New York: Routledge, 99–123.

The Economic Times (2011). Government deferred IFRS implementation. Available at http://articles. economictimes.indiatimes.com/2011-02-26/ (accessed 7 June 2011.

Tomlinson, B. R. (1993). *The Economy of Modern India, 1860–1970.* Cambridge: Cambridge University Press.

Tsalavoutas, I. (2011). Transition to IFRS and compliance with mandatory disclosures: What is the signal? *Advances in Accounting, Incorporating Advances in International Accounting*, 27(2), 390–405.

Tyrrall, D., Woodward, D. and Rakhimbekova, A. (2007). The relevance of International Financial Reporting Standards to a developing country: Evidence from Kazakhstan. *The International Journal of Accounting*, 42(1), 82–110.

Uche, C. U. (2002). Professional accounting development in Nigeria: Threats from the inside and outside. *Accounting, Organizations and Society*, 27(4/5), 471–496.

Verma, S. (2010). The influence of empire on the establishment of the Institute of Chartered Accountants of India after independence, in Poullaos, C. and Sian, S. (Eds.), *Accountancy and Empire*. New York: Routledge, 192–214.

Verma, S. and Gray, S. J. (2006). The setting up of the Institute of Chartered Accountants of India: A first step in creating an indigenous accounting profession. *Accounting Historians Journal*, 33(2), 131–156.

Verma, S. and Gray, S. J. (2009). The development of Company Law in India: The case of the Companies Act 1956. *Critical Perspectives on Accounting*, 20(1), 110–135.

Weetman, P., Jones, E. A. E., Adams, C. A. and Gray, S. J. (1998). Profit measurement and UK accounting standards: A case of increasing disharmony in relation to US GAAP and IASs. *Accounting and Business Research*, 28(3), 189–208.

Wilmott, H. (1986). Organising the profession: A theoretical and historical examination of the development of the major accountancy bodies in the UK. *Accounting, Organizations and Society*, 11(6), 555–580.

Wolpert, S. (1997). *A New History of India*. New York: Oxford University Press Inc.

Yapa, P. W. S. (2010). The imperial roots of accounting closure: The case of Sri Lanka. In Poullaos, C. and Sian, S. (Eds.), *Accountancy and Empire*. New York: Routledge, 124–143.

4

APPLYING IFRS IN RUSSIA

*Viatcheslav I. Sokolov, Natalia V. Generalova, Iurii N. Guzov
and Svetlana N. Karelskaia*

Introduction

In 2011, International Financial Reporting Standards (IFRS) took legal effect in Russia, following enactment in the Federal Law of 2010. Since 2012, Public Interest Entities (PIEs) and other companies forming a group have been required to prepare their consolidated financial statements in accordance with these standards. PIEs include not only listed companies but also companies the shares of which are federal property, belong to banks, insurance companies, pension funds, clearing companies, credit organisations and state corporations, as described by a list validated by the government. Individual financial statements of all Russian companies, including PIEs are prepared according to national standards. All companies have the right to prepare individual financial statements according to IFRS in addition to local standards. The regulatory changes resulted from an extensive transformation of the Russian form of government, along with the national accounting system as part of the regulatory framework.

Since the end of the 1980s, the country has been transforming from a centrally planned economy into a market economy: Russian public enterprises have been privatised, private property has evolved, joint ventures have been created with capital from different countries, based on control, risk and profit sharing; later, multinational corporations came to Russia; a financial market has emerged and started processing foreign exchange transactions and various financial instruments; Russian entities have been listed on Russian and foreign stock exchanges; consolidated groups of companies (holding structures) have been set up.

Such changes have called for a reform of the accounting system that was an instrument of centralised control in the Soviet Union, where accountants collected statistics and economic data for the government, and therefore were required to follow strictly all statutory accounting rules (Combs *et al.*, 2013: 34). Statutory regulation relieved the accountant of any decision making by establishing strict accounting rules with a description of all possible aspects (Enthoven *et al.*, 1992). IFRS were chosen as the basis for the reform of accounting in the late twentieth century.

Research into IFRS recognition in Russia is interesting not only of itself, but also because Russia used to be the centre of the socialist camp, where the countries forming the camp had similar accounting rules. These countries have gradually adopted IFRS. In the meantime, other BRICS countries (Brazil, Russia, India, China, South Africa) chose an accelerated adoption of, or convergence with, IFRS to meet the ongoing capital requirements, the need to maintain high economic growth rates and to maintain leadership among emerging markets (Kim, 2016: 345). Russia became the last BRICS country to introduce the IFRS in its jurisdiction. It chose to retain its national accounting standards by harmonising Russian Accounting Standards (RAS) used for individual and consolidated reporting with the IFRS. This process of harmonisation in Russia was implemented in an overwhelming environment of strict regulation in both the economy and accounting.

This chapter discusses the introduction and evolution of IFRS application in Russia by referencing current scholarship, published either in Russian or in English. It points in particular to the considerable volume of research published in Russian. The chapter shows how Russia has reformed its accounting system, adapting it for a market economy, and it systematises the information about legal acts and government programmes underlying the reform of accounting and introduction of IFRS in Russia.

The stages of IFRS implementation in Russia were determined using the chronological dominance method. This method was partially used in Generalova *et al.* (2016), where the authors reviewed the main stages of accounting reform in Russia from 1992–2014. This chapter extends the time period covered by the research and adjusts the dates of historical stages.

Literature review

The specifics of Russian accounting in the soviet period have been considered in several papers (e.g. Smirnova *et al.*, 1995; Alexander, 2013). A number of publications discussed the first steps of accounting reform as part of the transformation of the Russian economy in the 1990s (Richard, 1995; Sokolov and Kovalev, 1996).

More recently, there have been several papers on the application of IFRS in Russia. Alon (2013), Garanina and Kormiltseva (2013) and Kim (2013) attempted to identify the effect of IFRS adoption in the country based on empirical data. Kim (2016) continued the research she started and sought to separate adoption of IFRS from simultaneous transformation of accounting in Russian entities. The author has identified the general effect of the introduction of IFRS, although she did not establish how it was directly affected by changes in the legislation. Combs *et al.* (2013) discovered the negative effect of traditions that had evolved in the soviet time on the adaptation of the national accounting system and its convergence with IFRS, which consisted of the need for reform through accounting regulations, the need for the law to establish control and uniformity of accounting treatment.

There have been only 37 research papers in English on the implementation of IFRS in Russia in the international information systems Scopus and Web of Science from 2004 to 2018 (as of 14 July 2018). A spark of interest for this question appeared in 2013 when six papers were published and in 2016 with nine papers. More than half of all publications are written by Russian authors. In Russian-language publications, the implementation of IFRS is a very popular topic.

Figure 4.1 represents an analysis of information about IFRS-related Russian-language publications in Russia, the number of which has consistently increased over the years under review. The difference in the number of publications can be explained by the 'local character' of the question and also by the language barrier. Foreign researchers may not have the facility to work with the numerous regulatory documents in Russian. It is no surprise that most publications on this matter in English have been written by Russians: access is limited by the language barrier. Since the Russian Academic Citation Index (RACI)[1] was introduced in 2006, the data for previous years are not sufficiently representative. The data for 2017 and 2018 are not fully

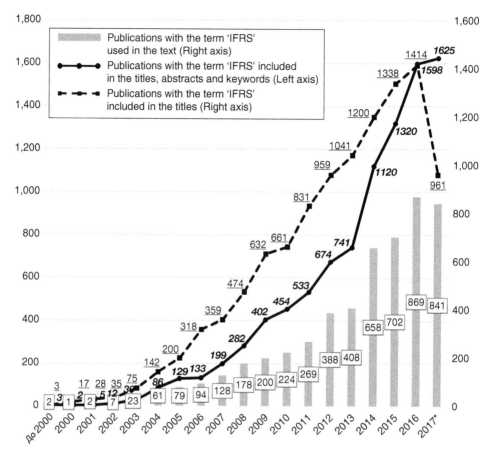

Figure 4.1 IFRS-related publications in Russia

Source: Calculations by the authors based on RACI as at 14 July 2018.

Note: * 2017 data are incomplete.

representative either, since not all publications have been included in the index, as the publishing houses print them with a slight delay. The first wave of publications appeared in 2009–2011, i.e. during the preparation for the introduction of IFRS in Russia, the standards and first comments were published in 2011–2012, and from 2012 to the present day has been the period of IFRS practical application by Russian companies and educational institutions that researchers have started to analyse in their publications.

Based on RACI as at 14 July 2018, we identify three characteristics. First, 515 phrases containing the term 'IFRS' were used as keywords for 3,277 articles; second, the term 'IFRS' was included in the titles of 1,312 publications; and third, the term 'IFRS' was used in the text of 10,816 publications. Key subject matters of IFRS-related research in Russia are: analysis of the differences between IFRS and RAS (Makarevich, 2001; Khorin, 2006), application of IFRS in Russian entities (Shneidman, 2001; Zolotareva and Tregubov, 2012), issues of IFRS translation (Generalova *et al.*, 2010) and legal issues of IFRS application (Sigidov and Nastenko, 2013; Baranenko and Busygina, 2014).

National specifics of Russian accounting

Accounting in Russia has always developed, and is still developing, at the government's initiative and under its control. Throughout the entire history of the country, it has been based practically on the same principles determined by the nature of its economy and people's mentality. The Russian accounting system has acquired the following specific features (Enthoven *et al.*, 1992; Kuter and Sokolov, 2012):

1   Supremacy of state-owned property: the state is the owner of all or almost all property existing in the country. Hence the need for a single body regulating the accounting procedures and organisation of the accounting function.
2   Supremacy of administrative relations: obligations to regulators always have a higher priority than obligations to third parties. This determines the Russian understanding of accounting as an obligation rather than as a management tool.
3   Supremacy of control: the goal of accounting is to control business processes rather than collect information about them. RAS have historically sought to describe the accountant's control activities rather than the financial statements.
4   Supremacy of regulations: all actions of the employees are determined by the regulator's instructions. The purpose of accounting is not to describe the financial position and financial result, but to observe the rules. Unified national rules determine the chart of accounts, the templates of accounting documents, the procedures for cash storage and payment, etc.
5   Supremacy of form over substance: the appearance of documents, their correlation, rules and sequence of their completion form an integral part of accounting; procedure is a higher priority than contents. In practice, it means that accounting does not recognise undocumented facts: no document means no fact – change the document and you can change the fact itself.

Russian accounting evolves by constantly borrowing ideas from abroad and transforming them in accordance with its principles (Bychkova *et al.*, 2008; Kuter and Sokolov, 2012).

Reasons for introducing IFRS in Russia

Russia abandoning the soviet economic system and adopting market relations has revealed the weaknesses in the soviet accounting model. It was based on a chart of accounts, which was the same for all enterprises and regulated the accounting treatment for all transactions permitted in the country. However, the market gave rise to new facts, and the old system had to be replaced or transformed. The reformation process continues to date. It is based on the application of IFRS principles and norms. The implementation of IFRS in Russia commenced for both objective and subjective reasons. The objective reasons were as follows (Generalova *et al.*, 2016):

1   Cross-border capital-raising required that the investors were provided with understandable financial statements comparable to financial statements from other markets.
2   Investors, such as banks and stock exchanges, required Russia to provide them with understandable financial statements.
3   New transactions that did not exist in Russia previously called for new accounting treatments that already existed within IFRS.
4   Multinational corporations that opened their affiliated societies in Russia needed to consolidate them.

Subjective reasons related to the keenness to promote IFRS:

1   Together with foreign business, the Big Six (now the Big Four) came to Russia and started to develop the market for their services by promoting and offering to Russian entities and regulators the implementation of IFRS as the best existing accounting system.
2   International qualifications, such as the Association of Chartered Certified Accountants and the Chartered Institute of Management Accountants, were interested in a broader application of IFRS in Russia, which would expand the market for their educational services.
3   The younger generation of Russian accountants, and most importantly accounting teachers, regarded IFRS as an excellent career lift (McGee, 2005; Bychkova *et al.*, 2008; Sokolov, 2016).

Stages of IFRS implementation in Russia

Acquaintance with diverse GAAP (1985–1991)

During the perestroika, private capital was legalised in the USSR along with foreign capital. At the same time, the country permitted the issuance of corporate securities. Transnational organisations, first among them the United Nations Conference on Trade and Development (UNCTAD),[2] have organised several workshops for Russian accountants on recognising capital-related transactions (Smirnova *et al.*, 1995). They helped to develop a chart of accounts that included recognition of capital, foreign currency, leasing and accrual-based recognition of revenue (Richard, 1995).

Looking for a baseline (1991–1997)

During this period, Russia did not express an intention to adopt International Accounting Standards (IAS). It was on the lookout for 'baselines' – standards to refer to while building a new accounting system. It considered IAS, US GAAP, and German and French accounting standards. The understanding that changes were required was shared by the entire accounting community, since the new market economy required a suitable accounting and reporting system. On 23 October 1992, the Russian Parliament adopted the government programme for the transition of the Russian Federation to an internationally accepted accounting and statistics system in accordance with the development needs of a market economy. In the same year, it adopted the first national standards, which had never previously existed in Russia. These were Accounting Policy, Construction Contracts, Recognising Entities' Assets and Liabilities Denominated in Foreign Currencies. It adopted the Federal Law *On Accounting* on 21 November 1996. The Russian Parliament (Federal Law, 1996) determined the setup of accounting functions at both public and private organisations. The law reiterated the rules that existed in the Soviet Union, which was natural since the Russian legislation did not take IAS into account; the economy suffered from hyperinflation and lack of qualified experts and generally from a lack of people who understood English.

At the same time, major multinational corporations opened businesses in Russia: for example, Procter and Gamble, Unilever, Philip Morris and General Motors. These multinational corporations required IAS or US GAAP for consolidation accounting within the group. Russian industrial colossi looking for funding were also forced to prepare financial statements in accordance with GAAP (metals and oil) or IFRS (other companies). These companies prepared financial statements according to IFRS in addition to Russian standards. Such financial statements were prepared and audited by the Big Six that had opened their offices in Russia by 1991 (Garanina and Kormiltseva, 2013; Alexander and Alon, 2017).

Official focus on IFRS (1998–2003)

Russian accounting turned towards IAS in 1998, when the government adopted the *Programme for Reforming the Accounting System in Alignment with International Accounting Standards*, which clearly and unequivocally set the course for IAS and subsequently IFRS: 'The reform of the accounting system's purpose is to align the national accounting system with the requirements of a market economy and international accounting standards'.[3] To achieve that purpose, this document formulated three objectives of the reform:

> 1) to create a system of accounting and reporting standards providing users with useful information, especially investors; 2) ensure correlation between the accounting reform in Russia and the main global trends of standards harmonisation; 3) provide methodological support to entities in understanding and implementing the reformed model of accounting.
>
> *(Resolution of the Russian Federation Government 1998: Section 1)*

The Programme achieved a considerable upgrade of the accounting framework. In addition to 4 existing Accounting Rules, 16 more were developed for such accounting areas as contingent liabilities, deferred tax, government grants, events after the end of the reporting period, etc. A new Chart of Accounts was adopted (Richard, 1995). As a result, a new nomenclature emerged similar to that generally accepted in international practice, and new accounting items appeared (Shneidman, 2001). Another interesting feature of 'Programme-1998' was the goal 'to re-focus regulation from accounting to reporting'. Historically, in the Soviet Union, little attention was paid to reporting, least of all to disclosures, since there were no other users of such information than the state that controlled all the companies directly (Alexander and Alon, 2017). Russia's pivot towards IFRS was largely influenced by the adoption of IFRS in the European Union.

Building the IFRS application infrastructure (2004–2011)

In 2004, Programme-1998 was superseded by the *Concept of Mid-Term Development of Accounting and Reporting in the Russian Federation* (Order of the Ministry of Finance of the Russian Federation 2004). The reason for that was the slow progress of transition to IFRS, including the absence of a relevant implementation mechanism and supporting institutions in Russia. There was no proper translation into Russian, the IFRS statements were virtually outside of the Russian legal framework and were audited 'optionally' or 'if necessary', there was a lack of IFRS experts (accountants, auditors, teachers) (Generalova *et al.*, 2010). The key provision of the Concept was the separation of national and international standards: consolidated financial statements were prepared only under IFRS, and individual financial statements only under RAS (Generalova *et al.*, 2016).

Legal acknowledgement of IFRS in Russia (2012)

The obligation to prepare consolidated financial statements in accordance with IFRS was established in the Federal Law *On Consolidated Financial Statements* (Federal Law, 2010). The law came into effect in 2012 and compelled all listed entities, banks, insurance companies, pension funds and major public companies to prepare consolidated financial statements in accordance with IFRS (Alon, 2013). IFRS are applied only in their translation into Russian and after they have been approved by the Ministry of Finance, which has the right to omit certain provisions of IFRS that do not comply with the Russian Law *On Accounting* (Federal Law, 2011). However, the Ministry of Finance has not made any omissions to date. Russia acknowledges only the texts of the inherent part of standards and interpretations, as amended (Generalova *et al.*, 2016). Therefore, the Russian Federation has not officially acknowledged the application guidance, illustrative materials, basis for conclusions and other parts of standards and interpretations that were included in the original version published by the International Accounting Standards Committee Foundation.

The TACIS programme

The EU has actively assisted with the transition of Russian accounting to IFRS. To this end and within the TACIS programme,[4] the EU initiated the reform of accounting and reporting that was carried out in 2000–2007 in three stages by KPMG (stage 1) and PwC and other Russian audit firms (stages 2 and 3). In the course of this programme, the parties developed RAS based on IFRS, which largely represented a translation of IFRS. They also conducted training seminars and wrote manuals on IFRS (The TACIS programme). However, these materials have not been used in the Russian Federation. TACIS programmes in Russia were wound up after the audit conducted by the European Court of Auditors. Its report stated that the following errors had been made in the course of the programmes: insufficiently specific goals of the programme, poor management, unsatisfactory financial discipline, and lack of appropriate control over spending (Browne, 2006).

Application of IFRS by Russian companies

Russian companies started to implement IFRS long before their official enforcement in Russia. At the end of the 1990s, major Russian companies, which were not required by law to prepare IFRS financial statements, started to apply IFRS to prepare consolidated financial statements proactively. These Russian companies used IFRS statements voluntarily because the emerging market relations required them to raise capital through international and Russian markets. In 1998 the government required Gazprom,[5] Transneft[6] and United Energy System,[7] the biggest Russian corporations with state ownership, to prepare IFRS financial statements.[8] In 2003 a similar requirement was imposed on all banks (Letter of the Bank of Russia, 2003).

Below is information in order to characterise the adoption of IFRS in the Russian environment. This information is calculated on the basis of ratings of the biggest Russian companies in terms of turnover, as prepared by the rating agency Expert RA[9] (hereafter 'Expert Rating'). To date this rating is the only source of comprehensive data on this question in Russia. It contains listed (inside and outside Russia) as well as non-listed companies. The rating is based on turnover, as this is the best indicator for the scale of business activity of companies and is related to indicators of gross domestic product (GDP). This rating has been used because in Russia a stock exchange listing held by a company is not of itself a criterion for application of IFRS. The majority of companies which prepare their financial statements according to IFRS are not listed companies, and, in the period under review, not all listed companies prepared their financial statements in accordance with IFRS; many used US GAAP.

Figure 4.2 shows the number of Russian companies applying IFRS across 2005–2017, based on Expert Rating. Since there is no information about the periods preceding 2005, this year was taken as the starting point. Prior to 2015, the rating comprised only 400 companies; thus, all our calculations are based on those 400 companies. Total revenue of the companies included in the 2017 rating was RUB66,555.07 billion, or 77.25 per cent of Russian GDP in 2016 (RUB86,148.60 billion in current prices[10]). This allows us to recognise these data as indicative of the situation in the country as a whole.

As shown in Figure 4.2, the percentage of companies using IFRS was practically the same for the TOP-100 and for the TOP-400 companies. The increase between 2005 and 2017 was 2.92 times and 3.02 times, respectively. Year on year, the number of Russian companies using IFRS was growing on average by 11 per cent of 400 and by 10 per cent of 100. In general, changes in these two indicators were correlated; however, across the population, the number of companies using IFRS grows by 1 per cent faster. The years 2007, 2009 and 2017 were exceptions from the general trend. In 2007, the TOP-100 list in Expert Rating lost one company due to the changes in certain companies' ranking by sales volume. In 2009, seven of the TOP-400 companies ceased to issue financial statements under IFRS, which could be explained by the influence of the economic crisis. In 2017, an insignificant number of companies dropped out from both TOP-100 and TOP-400 due to changes in their rankings. The TOP-400 group was renewed by 10 per cent, adding over 40 companies that were not in the rating in 2013, and the TOP-400 group grew by 2 per cent, adding two companies. In the meantime, the total share of companies which prepared their financial statements according to IFRS amounted to 13.25 per cent in 2005 and 40 per cent in 2017. The corresponding figures for the top 100 companies amounted to 25 per cent in 2005 and 40 per cent in 2017. This confirmed that the decision not to demand IFRS statements from all companies, but to focus only on PIEs, was correct.

In 2011, the number of companies that prepared IFRS statements exceeded 30 per cent of the ranked population. By then, almost 50 per cent of the TOP-100 applied IFRS. Since the European Union has required consolidated IFRS statements, the number of Russian companies applying IFRS grew due to those that gave up US GAAP and started using IFRS (such as OAO BALTIKA Breweries (a subsidiary of Carlsberg) in 2005, OAO Magnitogorsk Integrated Iron-and-Steel Works in 2008, RUSAL (Russian Aluminium) and Polimetal in 2011).

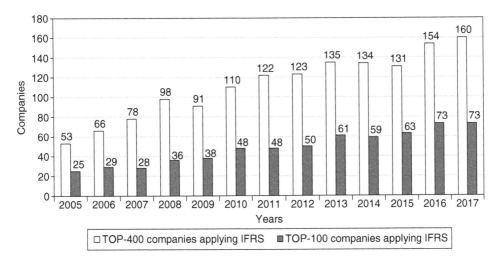

Figure 4.2 Number of largest Russian companies (by revenue) using IFRS

Source: Calculations by the authors based on Expert Rating (accessed 18 June 2018).

The popularity of IFRS in a country is largely determined by its application in various industries. Table 4.1 provides additional details underlying the graph shown in Figure 4.2, disclosing information about the largest Russian companies by revenue included in Expert Rating that applied IFRS in 2005–2017, with breakdown by industry.

The banking sector shows the biggest stability, which is typical practically for all countries, not only for Russia. Thus, a large share of major Russian companies reporting under IFRS (41.5 per cent in 2005 and 20 per cent in 2017) are lending institutions, which are required to do so by the Bank of Russia. However, their share in the total number of companies has been shrinking in the period covered by the study. They are well ahead of the runner-up, the oil and gas industry with 8.1 per cent, followed by machine building and electric power with 6.9 per cent each. A positive movement in the application of IFRS in the largest companies is the increase in 'other industries' by 18 per cent over 2005–2017, which is a sign of the growing use of IFRS in Russia.

As demonstrated in Figure 4.2 and Table 4.1, the introduction of legal requirement for IFRS statements did not have a significant impact on the major Russian companies. However, it legitimised the existing practice. The reasons why companies chose to apply IFRS were revealed by a survey conducted in 2016 by the joint efforts of the *IFRS in Practice* journal and Baker Tilly Rusaudit, an audit and consulting firm. The study summarised the answers given by representatives of 300 companies categorised into six groups by the amount of revenue (Skoromnikova, 2016).

Skoromnikova (2016: 37) found that the main factor driving company groups to issue IFRS statements is the shareholders' requirements (35 per cent in large companies and 49 per cent in smaller companies). Other reasons vary for different groups of companies. The second reason for entities using IFRS is the creditors' requirements (24 per cent with revenue greater than RUB50 billion per year, 29 per cent with revenue RUB15–30 billion per year) and investors' requirements for those with a turnover of RUB6–15 billion per year (24 per cent). For other groups of companies, the second most important reason could be legislative requirements. Therefore, legal considerations have become an essential driver for companies with lower income to prepare IFRS statements (20 per cent with a revenue of less than RUB3 billion, 27 per cent with RUB3–6 billion), as well as for those with revenues of RUB30–50 billion per year (27 per cent). However, this study confirms that the introduction of statutory requirement to prepare financial statements under IFRS did not lead to significant changes in the practices of Russian companies.

Applying IFRS in Russia – practice

Reporting approaches under IFRS

In Russia, the most broadly practised approach to preparing IFRS statements is through the transformation of data from Russian accounting records. Some companies also introduce parallel accounting based on IFRS, but they are fewer in number. The reason behind this choice of approaches is that transformation is easier to perform than parallel accounting (it does not require software that supports several types of accounting systems, nor specialists); quite often, there is no need for parallel accounting, since the accounting data are analysed under RAS, while IFRS statements are 'imposed', and therefore prepared on an annual or quarterly basis. Another argument in favour of transformation is that it can be performed by third parties. Sometimes the transformation approach is used in combination with parallel accounting. For example, the register of property, plant and equipment is kept under RAS and under IFRS (an element of

Table 4.1 Expert Rating companies using IFRS in 2005–2017 in percent, with breakdown by industry

Indicators	2005	2006	2007	2008	2009	2010	2011	2012	2013	2014	2015	2016	2017
RAEX-600 companies preparing IFRS statements by industry, total. The total includes, by industry:	100	100	100	100	100	100	100	100	100	100	100	100	100
Banks	41.5	36.4	33.3	30.6	29.6	27.3	25.9	21.1	20.7	24.6	23.7	24.7	20.0
Machine building	9.4	9.1	6.4	6.1	8.8	6.4	7.1	7.3	8.2	9.0	6.9	7.1	6.9
Oil and gas	3.8	4.5	3.9	3.1	3.3	2.7	3.6	3.3	6.7	6.0	6.9	7.1	8.1
Retail	11.3	10.6	5.1	8.2	4.4	6.4	8.9	6.5	6.7	6.7	6.9	5.8	5.6
Insurance	0	0	0	2.0	3.3	3.6	3.6	3.3	5.9	5.2	5.3	3.9	3.8
Transport	7.5	10.6	11.6	8.2	6.6	6.4	7.1	8.1	7.4	6.7	6.9	5.2	5.0
Chemical and petrochemical	3.8	3.0	6.4	3.1	5.5	6.4	8.9	8.1	7.4	7.5	7.6	6.5	6.3
Ferrous metals	7.6	4.6	5.1	7.1	6.6	4.5	6.3	5.7	5.2	5.2	6.1	5.8	6.3
Electric power	1.9	3.0	5.1	5.1	13.2	11.8	13.4	13.0	8.9	6.0	5.3	7.1	6.9
Other (less than 5 companies per industry)	13.2	18.2	23.1	26.5	18.7	24.5	15.2	23.6	22.9	23.1	24.4	26.6	31.2

Source: Calculations by the authors based on Expert Rating (accessed 18 June 2018).

parallel accounting), while other areas of accounting are adjusted at the level of reported indicators (transformation).

Many Russian companies make a disclosure of the respective approach in their financial statements, such as in this excerpt from the consolidated IFRS statements of mining and metallurgical company Norilsk Nickel:

> BASIS FOR PREPARATION
> Statement of compliance with IFRS
>
> …
>
> The Group entities maintain their accounting records in accordance with the statutory accounting and reporting laws of the countries where the Group entities are incorporated and registered. The accounting principles existing in the countries where Group entities are registered may significantly differ from the generally accepted principles and procedures under IFRS. The financial statements of such entities were adjusted for the purpose of presentation of IFRS consolidated financial statements.
>
> *(translation from Russian; Norilsk Nickel, 2017: 13)*[11]

The use of software also varies depending on the entity's scale and type of business. Excel spreadsheets are still broadly used for transformation, due to their simplicity and popularity, enabling various specialists to perform the work. Major companies use such software as SAP and Oracle.

Differences between IFRS and RAS

The conceptual difference between IFRS and RAS consists in the reporting purpose. It in turn gives rise to other differences: application of professional judgement, valuation (fair value, discounting, etc.), impairment of assets, supremacy of content over form, etc. IFRS are aimed at providing the investors with accurate and potentially necessary information. Meanwhile, in accordance with the national specifics outlined above, RAS aims no so much to inform as to control and keep safe property, mostly government property. Russian accounting records are kept for the management and for taxation purposes; therefore financial and management accounting are united and integrated. Particular differences arising from the details of various IFRS and RAS have been described in a rather comprehensive manner in *Comparative Analysis of IFRS and RAS* issued by KPMG (600 pages), with similar generalisation made by other audit firms of the Big Four (Ernst & Young, 2011; PwC, 2015; KPMG, 2016) and analysed in academic papers (Khorin, 2006; Sokolov, 2016).

Challenges of applying IFRS in Russia

Along with success, the application of IFRS in Russia constantly faces various challenges. Their main source is the conflict between IFRS and the Russian accounting and legal tradition. Accounting rules cannot be in conflict with the law. The Russian code-based law system is accompanied by a system of accounting rules based on detailed rules and on the chart of accounts. The common law system underlying the IFRS allows certain regulatory freedom based on general accounting principles. An alien law system in the sphere of accounting regulation cannot be adequately implemented in practice, and is neither accepted nor supported by the people who establish or follow such regulations. In this lies the root of all issues relating to the implementation of IFRS. The 'true and fair view' concept is a good example. Under Russian law, 'present fairly' means 'in compliance with'. Another source of problems lies in the specifics of the Russian economy. Here, the owners manage their businesses directly, i.e. from the IFRS perspective all Russian entities are either small and medium-sized entities or government enterprises, the latter requiring special regulation. The IFRS were designed to inform owners that are not directly involved in business management, in order to protect their interests (Richard, 2005: 16).

Another issue is that of translation into Russian. IFRS have been translated into Russian several times, but even the latest translation agreed with International Accounting Standards Board is far from perfect. The main problem is that the Russian language is not analytical. It does not have a strict word order, it is too homonymous, and the words have no clear hierarchy. Thus, the Russian words corresponding to the terms 'possible' and 'probable' mean the same degree of probability, 'liabilities' and 'obligation' are translated with the same word, and 'accounting' and 'bookkeeping' are indistinguishable in Russian. Russian accountants, professors and students have a very poor command of English, and most of them do not speak English at all. Therefore, the intent of IFRS guidelines can be distorted in practice. In universities, students first study the traditional Russian accounting, and then the IFRS separately, without synthesising their knowledge of the two systems.

Future directions

IFRS have become an integral part of the global economy in the context of globalisation, ensuring smooth operation of its mechanisms. Russia did not become an exception from the general trend – its modern accounting theory and practice develops harmoniously with global trends, and while it is developing the national accounting system, the IFRS are implemented more broadly and faster, giving Russian businesses access to global capital markets, and allowing investors to benchmark information about Russian entities against similar indicators reported by entities from other countries.

The sphere of implementation of IFRS in Russia is widening. Today significant work is being done in order to elaborate new Russian standards of accounting for the state sector.[12] All standards are created on the basis of International Public Sector Accounting Standards (IPSAS). New Russian Standards of Accounting are elaborated and current ones are reviewed with a view to harmonising them in accordance with IFRS. The plan is to adopt 14 new standards and review three current ones in the period from 2018 to 2020. Among new ones, there is a standard for financial instruments and extraction of natural resources.[13] Future research could address public sector accounting in accordance with IPSAS, and the introduction of new or revised IFRS.

Notes

1 The Russian Academic Citation Index (RACI) is a publicly available tool measuring and analysing the publishing activity of researchers and organisations in ELIBRARY.RU – Russia's largest electronic library of research papers containing over 26 million scientific articles and publications, including electronic versions of over 5,300 Russian scientific and technical journals. https://elibrary.ru/defaultx.asp (accessed 14 July 2018).
2 United Nations Conference on Trade and Development (UNCTAD) is a body of the United Nations General Assembly. The Conference was established in 1964. Its head office is in Geneva. At the moment, the Conference includes 194 countries. UNCTAD decisions are passed in the form of resolutions and serve as guidelines.
3 Resolution of the Russian Federation Government 1998: Section 1 (in Russian).

4 The TACIS programme (Technical Assistance to the Commonwealth of Independent States and Georgia) was initiated by the EU in December 1990. Its goal was to assist with economic reforms and development in the CIS and Georgia. http://europa.eu/rapid/press-release_MEMO-92–54_en.htm (accessed 1 June 2018).

5 Gazprom, (1998) Financial report. www.gazprom.com/investors/disclosure/reports/1998/ (accessed 1 July 2018).

6 Transneft, Financial statements on IFRS. www.en.transneft.ru/investors/year_reports/?re=en (accessed 1 July 2018).

7 United Energy System has been liquidated since the reform of the electric energy sector. www.fsk-ees. ru/shareholders_and_investors/company_overview/company_history/ (accessed 1 July 2018).

8 Decree of the Government of the Russian Federation from 17.07.1998 № 968 (in Russian).

9 Rating of 600 major Russian companies ranked according to the volume of sales (https://raexpert.ru/rankingtable/top_companies/2017/tab01). Rating is issued by rating agency Expert RA using a methodology approved by PricewaterhouseCoopers. https://raexpert.ru/rankingtable/top_companies/2017/tab01 (accessed 18 June 2018).

10 National accounting of the Russian Federation. Site of the State Statistics of the Russian Federation, Russian GDP за 2016 г. www.gks.ru/wps/wcm/connect/rosstat_main/rosstat/ru/statistics/accounts/# (accessed 15 July 2018).

11 Financial statements are in Russian, company website is www.nornickel.ru (accessed 29 January 2019).

12 Standards of Financial Accounting for the State Sector. Official site of the Ministry of Finance of Russia, Order of the Ministry of Finance of the Russian Federation (2017). № 85n Programme for Drafting Federal Accounting Standards for 2017–2019 (in Russian), dated 7 June 2017. www.minfin.ru/ru/perfomance/budget/bu_gs/sfo/ (accessed 15 July 2018).

13 Organisation of Drafting of Standards. Official site of the Ministry of Finance of Russia, Order of the Ministry of Finance of the Russian Federation (2018). № 83n Programme for Drafting of Federal Accounting Standards for 2018–2020 (in Russian), dated 18 April 2018. www.minfin.ru/ru/perfomance/accounting/development/setup/, www.minfin.ru/ru/document/?id_4=114488 (accessed 1 September 2018).

References

Alexander, D. (2013). The Soviet Accounting Bulletin, 1973–1983. *Accounting and Management Information Systems*, 12(2), 345–378.

Alexander, D. and Alon, A. (2017). Layering of IFRS and dual institutionality of accounting standards in Belarus. *Accounting in Europe*, 14(3), 261–278.

Alon, A. (2013). Complexity and dual institutionality: The case of IFRS adoption in Russia. *Corporate Governance: An International Review*, 21(1), 42–57.

Baranenko, S. P. and Busygina, A. V. (2014). Challenges and outlook for implementing International Financial Reporting Standards. *Economy and Society: Modern Development Models*, 8–1, 70–83. (Published in Russian).

Browne, A. (2006). The times gone east: How 7bn EU cash melted away with the Cold War. *The Times*, April 21, www.thetimes.co.uk/edition/news/gone-east-how-7bn-eu-cash-melted-away-with-the-cold-war-c7pjlvc7mgj (accessed 1 July 2018).

Bychkova, S., Enthoven, A. and Sokolov, Y. (2008). Historical Accounting Developments in Russia annals: Current transition towards international accounting standards. *12th World Congress of Accounting Historians, July 20–24, 2008, Istanbul, Turkey. Congress Proceedings*, 2, 1768–1775.

Combs, A., Samy, M. and Myachina, A. (2013). Cultural impact on the harmonisation of Russian Accounting Standards with the International Financial Reporting Standards: A practitioner's perspective. *Journal of Accounting and Organizational Change*, 9(1), 26–49.

Enthoven, A. J., Sokolov, J. V. and Petrachkov, A. M. (1992). *Doing Business in Russia and the Other Former Soviet Republics: Accounting and Joint Venture Issues*. Montvale: Institute of Management Accountants.

Ernst & Young (2011). *Applying IFRS*; collective of authors, 3 volumes, translated from English. Ed. 6, revised and amended. Moscow: United Press. (Published in Russian).

Federal Law (1996). *On Accounting*. № 129-FZ dated 21 November 1996. (In Russian). http://legalacts.ru/doc/federalnyi-zakon-ot-21111996-n-129-fz-o/ (accessed 1 September 2018).

Federal Law (2010). *On Consolidated Financial Statements*. № 208-FZ dated 27 July 2010. (In Russian). www.minfin.ru/ru/search/?q_4=208-%D1%84%D0%B7&pub_date_from_4=&pub_date_to_4=&page_id_4=0&source_id_4=6# (accessed 1 September 2018).

Federal Law (2011). *On Accounting*. № 402-FZ dated 6 December 2011. (In Russian). www.minfin.ru/ru/search/?q_4=402-%D1%84%D0%B7&source_id_4=6# (accessed 1 September 2018).

Garanina, T. A. and Kormiltseva, P. S. (2013). The effect of International Financial Reporting Standards (IFRS) adoption on the value relevance of financial reporting: A case of Russia. *Accounting in Central and Eastern Europe*, 13, 27–60.

Generalova, N. V., Pyatov, M. L. and Smirnova, I. A. (2010). Applying IFRS: Language-related and terminological issues. *Bukh. 1C*, 3, 36–40. (Published in Russian).

Generalova, N., Soboleva, G. and Sokolova, N. (2016). Adoption of IFRSs in Russia: 22 years of accounting reforms. *Journal of Eastern Europe Research in Business and Economics*, 1, 1–10.

Khorin, A. N. (2006). Market-oriented financial statements: A balance of corporate capital. *Accounting*, 14: 39–44; 16, 50–57. (Published in Russian).

Kim, O. (2013). Russian accounting system: Value relevance of reported information and the IFRS adoption perspective. *The International Journal of Accounting*, 48(4), 525–547.

Kim, O. (2016). The IFRS adoption reform through the lens of neoinstitutionalism: The case of the Russian Federation. *The International Journal of Accounting*, 51(3), 345–362.

KPMG (2016). Comparative analysis of IFRS and RAS. https://assets.kpmg.com/content/dam/kpmg/pdf/2016/06/ru-ru-ifrs-vs-russian-gaap-2012.pdf (accessed 1 July 2018).

Kuter M. and Sokolov V. (2012). Russia, in *A Global History of Accounting, Financial Reporting and Public Policy: Eurasia, the Middle East and Africa*. Sydney: Emerald Group Publishing Limited.

Letter of the Bank of Russia (2003). 181-T On Methodological Recommendations 'On Order of Preparation and Presentation of Financial Statements by Credit Organisations'. Vestnik Banka Rossii 72 (in Russian), dated 25 December 2003. http://legalacts.ru/doc/pismo-banka-rossii-ot-25122003-n-181-t/ (accessed 1 September 2018).

Makarevich, M. E. (2001). Comparative analysis of recognition of property, plant and equipment in financial statements: PBU 6/01 and IFRS 16. *International Accounting*, 10, 6–14. (Published in Russian).

McGee, R. W. (2005). International accounting education and certification in the former Soviet Union. *International Journal of Accounting, Auditing and Performance Evaluation*, 2(1–2), 19–36.

Order of the Ministry of Finance of the Russian Federation (2004). № 180 Concept of Mid-Term Development of Accounting and Reporting in the Russian Federation (in Russian), dated 1 July 2004.

PwC (2015). RAS and IFRS: Similarities and differences. www.pwc.ru/en/ifrs/publications/assets/rar-versus-ifrs-2015.pdf (accessed 1 July 2018).

Richard, J. (1995). The evolution of the Romanian and Russian accounting charts after the collapse of the communist system. *European Accounting Review*, 4(2), 305–322.

Richard, J. (2005). Les trois stades du capitalisme comptable français, in Capron, M. (Ed.), *Les normes comptables internationales, instruments du capitalisme financier*. Paris: La Découverte, 89–119. (Published in French.)

Shneidman, L. Z. (2001). How to use International Financial Reporting Statements. *Accounting*, 11, 73–78. (Published in Russian.)

Sigidov, Y. I. and Nastenko, D. A. (2013). Topical issues of preparing consolidated financial statements. *International Accounting*, 9, 2–13. (Published in In Russian.)

Skoromnikova, T. (2016). The practice of IFRS application in Russia in 2014–2016: Research findings. *IFRS in Practice*, 1, 32–39. (Published in Russian.)

Smirnova, I. A., Sokolov, J. V. and Emmanuel, C. R. (1995). Accounting education in Russia today. *The European Accounting Review*, 4(4), 833–846.

Sokolov V. (2016) Russia: Can IFRS be considered accounting? in Bensadon D. and Praquin, N. (Eds.), *IFRS in a Global World: International and Critical Perspectives on Accounting Essays in Honor of Professor Jacques Richard*. Cham, Heidelberg, New York, Dordrecht, London: Springer, 187–200.

Sokolov, J. V. and Kovalev, V. V. (1996). In defense of Russian accounting: A reply to foreign critics. *The European Accounting Review*, 5(4), 743–762.

Zolotareva, G. I. and Tregubov, E. A. (2012). Issues related to reporting in integrated aerospace structures. *Accounting, Analysis and Audit: Theory and Practice*, 9, 48–57. (Published in Russian.).

5

IFRS AND FAIR VALUE ACCOUNTING IN CHINA

Songlan (Stella) Peng and Kathryn Bewley

Introduction

China has provided a rich opportunity for accounting researchers. As a large, populous nation with a long, complex history, China's evolution from a feudal system, to a purist Communism regime, to a global trading nation has created a wide array of political, economic and social changes that profoundly affected the nature and use of accounting information within China. In addition, China's desire to engage with other nations in trading and investment has led to its outwardly focused attention on the accounting practices of developed nations. These complex conditions serve as driving factors in the emergence and acceptance of accounting concepts and have driven the implementation of consequential accounting practices within China.

This chapter outlines existing research related to China's adoption of International Financial Reporting Standards (IFRS) and acceptance of the fair value accounting (FVA) measurements that IFRS encompass. We start with a brief summary of research outlining the distinct stages of China's IFRS adoption and application of FVA, followed by an analysis of the insights from existing research findings about the consequences of IFRS adoption and FVA application in practice, and a discussion of research findings related to the factors affecting or impeding its adoption and convergence with international accounting practices. Throughout, the chapter identifies promising lines of enquiry for future academic study.

Stages of IFRS adoption and FVA development in China

IFRS adoption

Research on accounting evolution in China notes that an important shift occurred after the 1978 economic reforms of Deng, in the period of significant change when China became increasingly open to international influences (Ezzamel *et al.*, 2007). Table 5.1 provides a summary of the main accounting regulations in force at each stage discussed below, highlighting the changing application of fair value measurements over this period.

The first set of accounting standards after the 1978 reform, titled *Accounting Regulations for Sino-Foreign Joint Ventures*, came into effect in 1985. Another important change arose as two stock exchanges were opened, the first in Shanghai (1990) and the second in Shenzhen (1991).

Table 5.1 Overview of accounting regulations in China and level of fair value use

Year	Accounting regulations in force	Level of fair value use
Pre-Stage 1: Pure historical cost period (prior to 1992)		
1985	Accounting Regulation for Sino-Foreign Joint Ventures, effective July 1, 1985.	Carrying value of assets should not be adjusted, regardless of whether market value changes. Requires disclosure of net realisable value and potential loss on inventory.
Stage 1: Historical cost period with restrictive fair value use (1992–1996)		
1992a	Accounting Standards for Business Enterprises (the original 'Basic Standard').	Carrying value of assets should not be adjusted unless otherwise prescribed.
1992b	Accounting Regulations for Foreign Investment Enterprises, supersedes 1985 Accounting Regulation for Sino-Foreign Joint Ventures.	Carrying value of assets should not be adjusted except for rare circumstances with the consent of the responsible government authority.
1992c	Accounting System for Experimental Joint Stock Limited Enterprises	Carrying value of assets should not be adjusted except for rare circumstances at a government prescribed rate. Disclosure of the market value for short-term and long-term investments is required if they are available.
Stage 2: Initial introduction of FVA (1997–2000)		
1998	Accounting System for Joint Stock Limited Enterprises, supersedes the 1992c.	Requires fair-value-based allocation and disclosure of fair value under certain circumstances. Use of fair value is not required in asset impairment tests. The regulations are silent on fair value as a measurement basis.
1997–2000	10 Chinese Accounting Standards (CAS), effective during 1997–2000.	Fair value measurement is required in three standards: debt restructuring (1999), non-monetary transactions (1999) and investments (2000). Fair value use in asset impairment tests is not required.
Stage 3: Suspension of fair value accounting (2001–2005)		
2001	Accounting System for Business Enterprises, supersedes the 1998 Accounting System and the 1992b.	Same as the prescriptions in CAS (2001–2005). Fair value measurements are not allowed under any circumstances.
2001–2005	16 CAS, including 6 new and 10 revised from 1997–2000 CASs.	Fair value measurements are not allowed under any circumstances.
Stage 4: Revised FVA (2006–)		
2006	Accounting System for Business Enterprises, consisting of a new 'Basic Standard' Accounting Standard for Business Enterprises that supersedes the 1992a, plus 38 specific standards that supersede the 2001 Accounting System and all previous CAS.	Of the 38 CAS issued, direct use and indirect use of fair value are allowed or required in 25 standards.

The fast development of joint ventures and listed firms on these stock exchanges created immediate needs for accounting regulation over the firms. As detailed in Peng and Smith (2010), from 1992 through 2006, China's Ministry of Finance prescribed a series of four accounting regulations applicable to these firms, referred to hereinafter as the 1992, 1998, 2001 and 2006 Regulations, respectively. Each set replaced the previous one and was considered to bring China into greater conformity with the IFRS in force at the time (Peng *et al.*, 2008).

The first stage (the 1992 Regulations) extended from 1992 to 1996, and was considered a revolutionary change in Chinese accounting since it introduced a market-oriented accounting model, shifting the focus away from providing information for a central government-planned economy and towards the needs of a socialist market economy (Chen *et al.*, 2002; Peng *et al.*, 2008). In 1992, a Basic Standard called *Accounting Standards for Business Enterprises* (Table 5.1, 1992a) and two sets of accounting standards were issued: *Accounting Regulations for Foreign Investment Enterprises* (Table 5.1, 1992b) and the *Experimental Accounting System for Joint Stock Limited Enterprises* (Table 5.1, 1992c). The 1992a Basic Standard is similar to the conceptual framework in Western accounting standards, and the two sets of accounting standards regulate joint ventures and listed firms, respectively. The 1992b Regulation directly replaces the 1985 accounting regulation mentioned previously, and the 1992c Regulation is the first regulation applied to Chinese firms trading on the two new stock markets.

The second stage of standards development from 1997 to 2000 (the 1998 Regulations) involved the issue of the *Accounting System for Joint Stock Limited Enterprise* (which replaced the 1992b and 1992c Regulations) and 10 new specific Chinese Accounting Standards (CAS) during the period.

The third stage of development, extending from 2001 to 2006 (the 2001 Regulations), is defined by the issue of the *Accounting System for Business Enterprises*, which replaced the 1998 Accounting System, as well as the issue of 16 CAS, which consisted of six newly issued CAS, five revised CAS and five original CAS.

The fourth stage of development, starting from 2006 (the 2006 Regulations), is defined by the issue of a revised Basic Standard and 38 revised or newly issued CAS on 15 February 2006. The revised Basic Standard replaced the 1992 Basic Standard (Table 5.1, 1992a). The 38 CAS replaced the 2001 Accounting System and the 16 previously issued CAS, and formally ends the parallel co-existence of the Accounting System and the CAS that existed during the second and third stages.

Fair value accounting standards development

Since the start of its economic reforms, the application of China's FVA accounting standards transitioned from virtually no fair value use at all during Stage 1 (as of 1996) to limited use of fair value in Stage 2 (1997–2000), to abrupt suspension of fair value use in Stage 3 (2001–2005) and finally to aggressive reintroduction of fair value in Stage 4 (2006–). Such a degree and pace of change in a fundamental accounting principle is unusual for developed economies (Peng and Bewley, 2010) but, during the reform process, FVA was a notable impediment to the full adoption of IFRS and hence received special attention from both standard setters and accounting academia.

Before Stage 1, China's accounting systems were pure historical cost accounting regimes, with very limited fair value requirements in the standards. Chinese standards explicitly required that the carrying value of an asset should not be adjusted, regardless of the market value of the assets. Although measuring assets at fair value was strictly prohibited at this stage within the financial statements proper, joint ventures were allowed to disclose market values for certain assets in the notes to the statements.

During Stage 1, the 1992 Regulations continued to emphasise historic cost, but did start to permit more exceptions in rare instances. For example, some enterprises, such as joint ventures or foreign investment enterprises, were allowed to accrue inventory impairment or bad debt allowances, but the adjustments had to use a government-approved rate. The standards also started to require limited disclosure of fair value information in the financial statement notes.

Over the period from 1997 to 2000 (Stage 2), China's Ministry of Finance began to take aggressive steps to introduce FVA standards into the new CAS by issuing requirements that were consistent with the current FVA approach in effect in the IFRS at that time. However, this resulted in some highly publicised, widespread accounting scandals involving abuse of the FVA standards.

The degree of abuse forced China's Ministry of Finance to hastily revise existing fair value standards in 2001. The use of fair value was fully suspended during Stage 3, the period from 2001 to 2005, and carrying value was required to be used in all circumstances where fair value had been required.

During Stage 4 starting in 2006, the new 2006 Regulations reintroduced fair value by introducing standards which permitted or required FVA in a wide range of areas. The 2006 Regulations included FVA requirements parallel to those in IFRS, and were considered to have achieved substantial convergence. Yet there remained some critical differences (Peng and Bewley 2010), to be discussed later.

In parallel with the accounting standards issued as Chinese GAAP (generally accepted accounting principles), China also instituted key legal and regulatory structures that were perceived to be essential supports for IFRS and FVA. These included the China Securities Regulation Commission (CSRC) regulation *Form and Content of Information for Disclosure by Companies with Securities Issued to the Public* and other regulations issued by the CSRC, and the *Accounting Law of the People's Republic of China* issued in 1995 and revised in 2000 by the State Council of China (Peng *et al.*, 2008).

As China's accounting regulations evolve over time, research updating the documentation of developments in China's accounting standards will be a valuable contribution to the literature, and can provide an important basis for designing future studies on IFRS convergence and FVA implementation.

Literature assessing convergence with IFRS

Convergence can be assessed based on two indicators of a country's ability to adapt to IFRS: the extent to which IFRS are adopted in official standards (i.e. *de jure* convergence), and the extent to which the adopted IFRS have been effectively implemented in practice (i.e. de facto convergence).

De jure convergence: standard adoption

Peng and Smith (2010) apply process theory to study China's adoption of IFRS, through analysing the progression of convergence. By examining 159 key measurement items in 4 successive adoption stages of Chinese accounting regulations, the study documents that significant progress towards convergence occurred, with convergence levels increasing from 20 per cent through 35 per cent, 49 per cent to 77 per cent in the 1992, 1998, 2001 and 2006 Regulations, respectively. The study further examines whether the convergence happens through direct import or progressive adoption. The results show that 84 of the 159 IFRS items examined are directly imported, 55 items involve some progressive change during the 4 stages, and 20 items are not adopted in China. Further analysis shows that direct import occurs for items either reflective of traditional Chinese accounting practice or ones that addressed situations not considered or not relevant under the previous accounting model. Progressive changes were observed on items substantially different from traditional practice. Overall, the study concludes that a combination of staged implementation and direct import has proven to be practical and effective in converging Chinese accounting regulations with IFRS.

Related to the convergence of FVA in China with IFRS, Peng and Bewley (2010) provide a content analysis of China's 2006 Regulations. The findings show China has extensively adopted FVA derived from IFRS but identifies nine divergences in FVA adoption. Official reasons provided by Chinese standard setters to support China's divergence relate to the need to conform to its special circumstances and reduce opportunities for manipulation of accounting information. Officials also point to aspects of IFRS that are impractical to adopt in China, and argue that the International Accounting Standards Board (IASB) should consider revising these standards. Given that these reasons relate to fundamental characteristics of the Chinese economic and political environment, the study concludes that the divergence appears unlikely to be bridged in the near future.

De facto convergence: implementation in practice

China's listed firms can issue two types of shares: A-shares and B-shares. A-shares are sold only domestically to locals and denominated in local currency. B-shares are denominated in foreign currencies and sold only to foreign investors. Firms issuing A-shares must comply with Chinese accounting regulations; firms issuing B-shares must comply with IFRS. Prior to 2006, firms issuing both A- and B-shares were required to provide a reconciliation schedule between the IFRS-based numbers and CAS[1]-based numbers (Haw *et al.*, 1998; Abdel-Khalik *et al.*, 1999). This requirement provides a unique opportunity to examine the de facto convergence of CAS with IFRS during this period (e.g. Lin and Chen, 2005), and research on this topic during 1992 to 2006 is discussed below. In 2006, Chinese accounting standard setters claimed that the reconciliation from Chinese numbers to IFRS numbers was no longer necessary and stopped requiring the reconciliation, since CAS had by that time been substantially converged with IFRS.

Both Chen *et al.* (1999) and Chen *et al.* (2002) found there to be a significant difference between the CAS-based and IFRS-based net incomes of Chinese listed firms. Chen *et al.* (1999), by examining firms following the 1992 Regulations, found the reported earnings determined under Chinese GAAP to be 20–30 per cent higher on average than earnings reported under IFRS. After restatement from IFRS to Chinese GAAP, 15 per cent of the B-share companies changed from a reported profit to a reported loss. Analysis of the findings suggests that the differences between the two sets of earnings are caused by differences in accounting standards and financial rules, opportunistic applications of Chinese GAAP, and unusual market-wide events. Chen *et al.* (2002) examined the 1998 Regulations and found that, despite the Chinese government's efforts to harmonise the accounting standards in this stage, there was no evidence that the gap between Chinese and IFRS earnings was eliminated or significantly reduced. The authors conclude that the reasons for the continued earnings gap after the 1998 Regulations included a lack of adequate supporting infrastructure, manifested in excessive earnings management and low-quality auditing.

Peng *et al.* (2008) extend Chen *et al.* (1999) and Chen *et al.* (2002) by evaluating the level of and improvement in the convergence of Chinese listed firms' accounting practices with IFRS since promulgation of the 2001 Regulations. Using the 1999 and 2002 annual reports of Chinese listed firms that issue both A- and B-shares, the study uses three measures to assess de facto harmonisation: a compliance index, defined as the percentage of specific regulations applicable to a firm with which that firm complied; a consistency index, which is a measure of the uniformity in a firm's accounting choices for the same transactions in the two different sets of financial statements it prepares under CAS and IFRS; and a comparability index, which measures the comparability between two sets of accounting standards by comparing specific items presented in the financial statements, such as net income and owners' equity. The findings indicate a high level of compliance with Chinese accounting standards in both 1999 and 2002, but the compliance with IFRS appears consistently lower than the compliance with the Chinese standards. The consistency indices indicate a moderate level of consistency in accounting treatments between Chinese and IFRS-based annual reports in both 1999 and 2002, implying that there was an improvement in the consistency of application of accounting methods in the 2002 Chinese and IFRS-based annual reports as compared to the 1999 annual reports. Comparability index values in 1999 and 2002 show that net income is higher under Chinese standards than under IFRS in these years, consistent with the findings of Chen *et al.* (2002) for 1998. Both the mean and the percentile comparability index values suggest a reduction in the earnings gap and the convergence of net incomes as reported in firms' CAS-based and IFRS-based annual reports from 1999 to 2002.

Chen and Cheng (2007a) examined whether the reduced earnings gap is associated with improved corporate governance, which is expected to facilitate the effective implementation of internationalised standards. The study assesses improvements in board independence, audit committee, institutional stockholdings and statutory audit. The results show that the reformed corporate governance has not made a significant contribution towards harmonisation of earnings measurement.

Chen and Cheng (2007b) and Chen and Zhang (2010) evaluate the CSRC's regulatory enforcement in 2001 on the harmonisation of accounting practices. A 2001 regulation issued by the CSRC prohibits a firm from providing different accounting estimates based on its Chinese-based reports and its IFRS-based reports for the same business transactions and events. Chen and Cheng (2007b) find that this regulation significantly reduced the earnings gap between the two standards. The Chen and Zhang (2010) study also reveals a decline in the earnings gap between IFRS-based and Chinese-based earnings; however, the findings do not attribute the gap reduction to the convergence of Chinese GAAP with IFRS, but to the implementation of the CSRC's 2001 mandatory compliance policy and the effectiveness of audit committees in ensuring that firms made the same accounting choices under IFRS and Chinese accounting standards.

Lin and Chen (2005) examined the value relevance of the requirement to reconcile CAS-based accounting numbers and IFRS-based numbers. The study showed the reconciliation of earnings and book values from CAS to IFRS to be partially value relevant, mainly to stock prices in the B-share market, while the earnings reconciliation is generally not value relevant to stock returns in either the A- or the B-share market.

A few studies, instead of focusing on the reconciliation schedule from CAS to IFRS, investigate the value relevance of A-shares and B-shares, respectively, to see if IFRS accounting numbers are superior to Chinese accounting numbers. However, the findings from these studies are mixed. Haw *et al.* (1998) found the accounting information reported under CAS to be more strongly associated with stock returns than the information reported under IFRS. In contrast, Abdel-Khalik *et al.* (1999) found accounting earnings and A-share prices not to be correlated, but earnings and B-share prices are correlated. Lin and Chen (2005) found earnings and book values of owners' equity determined under Chinese accounting standards to be more relevant accounting information for the purpose of determining the prices of A- and B-shares, suggesting that during the study period accounting numbers based on domestic accounting standards, in contrast to IFRS, were more value relevant in the Chinese stock market. Eccher and Healy (2000) found the IFRS-based earnings information to be no more value relevant than that of the CAS earnings. The authors argue that one explanation for the failure of IFRS data to dominate Chinese GAAP data is the absence of effective controls and infrastructure in China to monitor the additional reporting judgement available to managers under IFRS.

Further evidence related to the impact of IFRS adoption on contracting uses of accounting information is provided by Ke *et al.* (2016). This study examines the effect of the 2006 Regulations on managerial pay-for-accounting performance sensitivity of publicly listed Chinese firms, and found that the sensitivity significantly declined after the 2006 Regulations for central-government-controlled firms. The findings suggest that China's new 2006 Regulations reduce the stewardship usefulness of financial reporting.

Several extant studies also provide insights into the impact of IFRS adoption on the other aspects of accounting information quality. Wu *et al.* (2014) examined the effects of harmonisation and convergence with IFRS on the timeliness of earnings. The study finds evidence that the 2006 accounting standard convergence does not achieve the initial expectation that the timeliness of earnings recognition would be improved, as the timeliness is found to be lower in the post-2006 period than in the pre-2006 period. However, the authors point out the results should be interpreted with caution given the relatively small sample size for each of the years under study. Ahsan (2015) found increases in the audit report lag after the adoption of 2006 Regulations, indicating a loss of timeliness.

Ke *et al.* (2015) provide evidence that the weak institutional environment in China results in the Big Four audit firms providing lower-quality audits to companies that are listed only in China (A-share companies), based on findings that the Big Four assign their less experienced partners to companies that are listed only in China compared with clients cross-listed in Hong Kong (companies issuing both A- and B-shares). The Big Four also are less likely to issue modified audit reports, and charge lower audit fees for clients that are listed only in China.

In an exploratory study of earnings management, Cang *et al.* (2014), using Chinese capital market data from 2003 to 2009, found that the adoption of IFRS overall did not facilitate analysts serving as an external monitoring function to lower the level of earnings management. The reason for this may be that the use of fair value creates many new opportunities for managers to engage in earnings management.

Taken together, these studies show that, with a few exceptions to reflect China's unique national institutional factors, Chinese accounting regulations demonstrated an increasing level of convergence in form (*de jure* convergence); however, findings on convergence in practice (de facto convergence) are inconclusive and the *de jure* convergence in standards may not lead to de facto convergence in practice. This line of research also raises many important fundamental questions that warrant further study, related to the objectives and usefulness of accounting information and the impact of conforming local accounting standards to international norms.

Literature assessing FVA implementation in practice

To examine the convergence of fair value accounting in China with IFRS in practice, Peng and Bewley (2010) also provide an analysis using Chinese listed firms' 2007 and 2008 annual reports. The results show an apparent reluctance by Chinese listed firms to use FVA in long-term non-financial asset valuation and a lack of explanation in the notes about the method they used to construct the fair value measures. The study also finds that seemingly subtle divergence in standards can produce a significant impact on implementation in practice. The findings reveal that few firms choose FVA when historic cost valuation is an allowed option, leaving their reports with little fair value information other than for financial instruments, and resulting in FVA implementation outcomes in China that may differ considerably from IFRS reporting in other countries.

Qu and Zhang (2015) investigated the value relevance of earnings and book value over 20 years of institutional transition in China, from 1991 to 2010, and explored the suitability of FVA in the emerging capital market by dividing data into five time spans: 1991–1992, 1993–1998, 1999–2000, 2001–2006 and 2007–2010. The study provides evidence that the implementation of 2006 Regulations has improved the overall value relevance of financial information, but China's attempt to converge with IFRS and the consequent application of FVA does not contribute to the improvement of value relevance of earnings and book value. However, the results and conclusions should be interpreted with caution due to the small sample size of fair-value-applied firms and non-fair-value-applied firms.

Evidence of the opportunistic nature of Chinese firms' asset impairment accruals, and the effects of the new 2006 Regulations in reducing 'big bath' reporting by loss firms is provided by Chen et al. (2009). They studied the regulatory incentives for earnings management, using Chinese listed firm data for 2003 to 2006 and manual collection of impairment reversal information from annual reports. The study finds the impairment reversals are mainly driven by companies' earnings management incentives, to meet the bright line set by the CSRC regulations and reduce or avoid the possibility of trading suspension or de-listing. Such opportunistic reversals are negatively related to stock value. Zhang et al. (2010) further examined the impact of the 2006 Regulations' new prohibition on the reversal of long-lived asset impairments by contrasting write-off recognition and reversal across the pre- and post-prohibition GAAP regimes. They showed that firms listed on Chinese stock exchanges recognised fewer impairment charges after announcement of the new standard and before the effective date than in the pre-announcement periods. Also, firms with substantial previous write-downs reversed more impairment charges to achieve their earnings targets in the transition period, suggesting opportunistic use of FVA in practice.

He et al. (2012) showed that the new FVA for trading securities in the 2006 Regulations fails to generate the intended benefits of improved transparency, and, worse, the new FVA for debt restructuring creates new opportunities for earnings management. The results also show that these unintended consequences are more severe for firms with weak corporate governance and those in provinces with weaker institutions, suggesting that FVA abuses are more likely to occur in firms in which financial accounting plays a stronger contracting role than information role, and in which the institutional environment is incompatible with IFRS.

Peng and Bewley (2010) present evidence that, under FVA, volatility of market prices in China affects the stability of reported financial information, potentially undermining both its relevance and reliability. Zhang et al. (2012) also provide evidence that FVA has produced significant volatility in the Chinese capital market that has favoured the Chinese elite but has negatively affected ordinary investors in China. By studying two examples of large Chinese companies, one a manufacturer and the other in the financial services industry, the authors support this argument by showing that, despite increasing operating profits during 2008, net profit fell due to decreases in prices of cross-holding shares that produced large losses. Zhang et al. (2012) report that the Secretary of the CSRC acknowledged that, market wide, one-third of the increases in profits of listed companies in 2007 came from fair value changes in the cross-holding shares of other listed companies.

These findings indicated to China's government that a large number of listed firms were complying with accounting regulations only in appearance. Poor corporate governance and immature capital markets were considered to be part of the problem. Further, a lack of specific guidance on how to accrue for asset impairment, how to determine net recoverable amount, and how to apply techniques to estimate present value of estimated future cash flows created problems in accounting practice, making it hard for regulators to distinguish between the inadvertent misuse and the deliberate abuse of asset impairment accruals.

Overall, the findings of these studies show that further research on the value relevance of FVA implementation is needed to help uncover the impact of this information in China. These prior studies explore the use of FVA in potentially opportunistic ways, rather than to improve quality and usefulness of financial information, posing questions that can be further illuminated by future research. The existing research identifies unique institutional features of the Chinese capital market environment that can provide a rich field for further theory-grounded studies by academic researchers.

Literature assessing factors driving/impeding IFRS and FVA adoption: discussion and critique of convergence

Research on accounting in China can provide 'insights into the wider institutional and social positioning of financial accounting', as called for in Hopwood (2000: 763) and Zhang and Andrew (2016). This section outlines literature taking a critical perspective on the institutional, political and social environments that can act as drivers of China's IFRS adoption and FVA implementation, and contrasting aspects that can impede convergence or challenge its fundamental appropriateness. These studies provide critical perspectives on China's IFRS and FVA adoption in a broader socio-political context.

Peng and Bewley (2010) showed that the initial adoption of IFRS and FVA at Stages 1 and 2 appeared to be associated with the increasing awareness by Chinese officials of problems caused by using only historical-cost-based reporting. For example, many obsolete inventories and uncollectible receivables were held on the books, and short- or long-term investments could accumulate huge gains or losses in the market that were not reported until the investments were disposed of. Meanwhile, FVA was gaining support internationally from leading standard setters (Financial Accounting Standards Board and IASB, for example), major market regulators (SEC for example) and accounting academia (Barth, 1994) and started being implemented in China during Stage 2 on an experimental basis. However, this study points out that such FVA implementation within the historical and socio-economic context of China has not been accompanied by the necessary changes in capital and other market infrastructure – the embryonic stage of China's capital markets, the limitations in corporate governance, and the inadequate knowledge and skill needed for Chinese accounting practitioners to implement a valuation method developed in a Western-developed economy context may impede IFRS and FVA adoption. The study concludes that these factors may be too deeply imbedded to change.

Bewley *et al.* (2018) conducted an in-depth analysis of factors that shape China's IFRS and FVA adoption by applying a theoretical frame based on social movement literature. By comparing the institutional factors between China's first unsuccessful attempt to adopt FVA and its second successful attempt, the study finds that motivations to adopt FVA in China are attributable more to political and social factors than to economic factors. The re-adoption of FVA in Stage 4 was not a result of significant changes of economic factors, but collective efforts of elite national and international groups with shared interests, as well as the mobilisation of critical financial, legal, personnel and institutional resources, and specific actions to frame and legitimise FVA standards.

Through different analytical approaches and theories, a few other studies provide similar observations. Baker *et al.* (2010) examined the difference between CAS and IFRS in accounting for business combinations, in which IFRS allows only the fair-value-based allowance method, while China allows the pooling of interest method, and concludes that divergence is driven more by the politico-economic factors rather than a desire to serve the needs of capital markets.

Ezzamel *et al.* (2007) provide evidence that the political ideology of China's national leaders plays an important role in the convergence of Chinese accounting standards with IFRS, and the transition from pure historic cost-based measurements to more market-oriented fair value measurements and disclosures. The ideological shift of national leaders from an emphasis on class struggle to an emphasis on economic development can be interpreted as a political opportunity that supported the ideological shift of Chinese standard setters away from an emphasis on historical cost and towards FVA.

Zhang *et al.* (2012) point out that FVA is used as a tool for government and powerful elites in China to enhance their political and economic power, rather than to advance public interest. By adopting a perspective of neoliberalisation,[2] the authors argue that Chinese share prices can never reflect 'fair values', as these depend on a free market in which all parties are 'knowledgeable' and 'willing', and where transactions happen at 'arm's length'. In the Chinese context, FVA can only ever exist in name – as a symbol of China's commitment to global capitalism. To this end, China's adoption of IFRS requires an embrace of so much more than comparable accounting techniques. It requires a commitment to the ongoing neoliberalisation of China which is disconnected from the underlying political and economic architecture that is operating within China. The study also criticises the Split Share Structure Reform[3] that the Chinese government has been implementing since 2005, contending that this reform has affected share prices, and correspondingly influenced the 'fair values' of shares in China. In reality, the Chinese market is a creation of the state and its reforms – yet the illusion of free markets and fair values has been sustained. The authors contend that the illusion sustained by FVA is critical to the neoliberalisation of China.

Several studies also explored strategies that China uses to converge with international accounting practices at the same time as it strives to maintain its independence by retaining some accounting regulations that are not converged with IFRS. By examining the convergence of Chinese accounting standards for foreign invested firms with IFRS, Ezzamel and Xiao (2015) argue that the reference to 'Chinese characteristics' plays an important role in this process in suiting the various interests of actors seeking to produce new accounting regulations. Chinese characteristics are seen as a signifier that carved out a space for local networks to attain their identity and retain some measure of independence from global networks, shaped the construction of each accounting regulation for foreign invested firms into an attractive package, and influenced the adaptation and transformation of those elements of Western accounting that arrived into China. In turn, IFRS became part of the discursive field on accounting regulation that helped mediate the shifts in the interpretation of Chinese characteristics over time. Peng and Bewley (2010) and Bewley *et al.* (2018) also provide evidence that communications at the elite official level, actively seeking seats in international organisations such as IASB and hosting academic and regulatory conferences on a regular basis, are among strategies used by China to voice its position and seek mutual understandings.

In a review of the research on proponents of and opponents to FVA adoption in China, Zhang and Andrew (2016) identified a series of academic studies that support FVA adoption, with arguments that include technical strength, development of market economy and globalisation of accounting standards. Also, government and media discourse are cited that support the adoption. The main opponents and resistance to FVA adoption include the lack of appropriate market conditions for FVA in China and criticism of neoliberal reforms that do not enhance social and economic welfare nor deliver on promises of environmental improvements and greater political liberties.

Future directions

To provide a reasonably succinct overview of the broad array of existing research on China's accounting in this brief chapter, we chose to focus only on IFRS adoption and the implementation of fair value measurement. Even with this seemingly narrow focus, however, a vast array of research questions and approaches arises. In the literature reviewed above, we outline several ongoing streams of enquiry that could be extended by new research projects. Promising paths forward include more critical views of the evolving CAS, further empirical studies of the consequences of adopting international-based accounting standards on company reporting and on market valuations, and motivations driving the choice of accounting methods within China's unique institutional, political and social environment.

Accounting is often assumed to be a neutral technical system for capturing economic information and one that hence can be taken for granted. But empirical examples of the consequences of accounting choices and various approaches used in standardising the output of accounting practices has fostered deeper considerations of the objectives and conceptualisations of accounting. Studies of the conceptual basis of accounting show that within differing practical contexts, accounting presents a wide variability. Contextual differences arise across different companies, industries or political systems, and over time even within fairly static contexts. Within these factors, competing perspectives and conflicts give rise to the kinds of tension that many different research approaches can thrive upon. Technical analysis of differences in the underlying conceptual frameworks of accounting standards in use around the world reveals the true subjectivity of the fundamental basis of accounting (Scott, 2002). Thus, technical analysis of the differences between accounting standards and valuation methods form a critical perspective for understanding international variations in accounting practices.

Further, an understanding of the drivers of acceptance of particular accounting methods and their economic consequences for society can enhance future accounting standard setting and practice. Research approaches applying political, social and institutional theories have found many opportunities to generate theorised descriptions of events and conditions that have arisen in China's accounting practices over time.

Finally, empirical studies have sought to use the contrasting conditions appearing between China and the developed world, and within China over its rapid emergence to a modernised global trading economy, to examine the value relevance of accounting information to investors and its impact on managers of firms.

Many research areas remain untapped, however. For example, the social movement analytical framework used in Bewley *et al.* (2018) can be used for research analysing future developments in IFRS-based standard-setting initiatives in non-Western societies. Extending the research findings from China to the challenges of international standardisation more broadly can lead to new insight in countries that struggle to maintain their own unique identity in the face of dominant international powers. Another example could be studies exploring accounting's use in colonisation as a means of enabling dispossession of indigenous peoples, providing insights into new directions to address the emerging need for reconciliation of diverse social groups in modern nations (Annisette and Neu, 2004; Buhr, 2011).

Finally, taking a very broad view of the fundamental role that accounting has played throughout human history, deeper consideration of the socio-political causes and consequences of changes in accounting practices would be a fruitful avenue for future thought and enquiry

(Robson, 1992). Theoretical study of the nature of accounting itself could expand our understanding of what drives the demand for standardisation, what determines whether accounting practices gain general acceptance and what is the essential power that accounting yields in human development.

Key challenges for future research will arise from data availability constraints. While the modernisation of capital markets is leading to greater availability of economic data for research, qualitative research will face continuing challenges. In particular, interview data that may be useful to understand the behind-the-scenes deliberations, trade-offs and politicking that one would expect to observe in such a complex field as accounting may be difficult to obtain. Cultural factors also could present challenges in seeking candid, personal perspectives from participants in the field. Considering the Chinese tradition of being seen to obey authorities it may be difficult to elicit perspectives that are not in line with accepted views.

New research approaches that can provide robust, controlled comparisons of capital markets data, supplemented by qualitative assessments of narratives provided by company personnel, both within their published reports and through other media such as the internet and news outlets, can help us to peer behind the curtains and enhance our understanding of the forces behind corporate accounting information-reporting decisions. Qualitative research exploring the perspectives of other stakeholders in the accounting field can also be a fruitful line of international accounting research.

Notes

1 Chinese Accounting Standards (CAS) has two meanings in this chapter. The CAS refer to specific Chinese Accounting Standards, while CAS is also used as a generic term for Chinese accounting regulations since 1985.
2 Neoliberalism is an ideology and policy model that emphasises the value of free market competition, with ideological roots in the classical liberalism of the nineteenth century, which championed economic laissez-faire and the freedom (or liberty) of individuals against the excessive power of government (source: www.britannica.com/topic/neoliberalism, accessed 4 December 2018).
3 The Split Share Structure refers to the special share-ownership structure of Chinese listed companies. Under the structure, only about one-third of the shares in domestically listed firms float on the stock markets, which creates a large volume of non-tradable state-owned and legal-person shares. The structure puts public investors in an inferior position relative to the actual controllers in making corporate policies and disposing of the firm's profits and assets. In 2005, the Chinese government introduced the Split Share Structure Reform (SSSR) to transform non-tradable state shares into freely floating shares so that the markets could be more efficient. This reform is expected to reduce information asymmetry and better protect investors. However, the large-scale transformation of restricted shares to floating shares caused much volatility in stock prices, making the use of fair value to measure financial instruments a problematic practice.

References

Abdel-Khalik, A. R., Wong, K. A. and Wu, A. (1999). The information environment of China's A and B shares: Can we make sense of the numbers? *The International Journal of Accounting*, 34(4), 467–489.

Ahsan, H. (2015). The new Chinese Accounting Standards and audit report lag. *International Journal of Auditing*, 19(1), 1–14.

Annisette, M. and Neu, D. (2004). Accounting and empire: An introduction. *Critical Perspectives on Accounting*, 15(1), 1–4.

Baker, C. R., Biondi, Y. and Zhang, Q. (2010). Disharmony in international accounting standards setting: The Chinese approach to accounting for business combinations. *Critical Perspectives on Accounting*, 21(2), 107–117.

Barth, M. E. (1994). Fair value accounting: Evidence from investment securities and the market valuation of banks. *The Accounting Review*, 69(1), 1–25.

Bewley, K., Graham, C. and Peng, S. (2018). The winding road to fair value accounting in China: A social movement analysis. *Accounting, Auditing and Accountability Journal*, 31(4), 1–29.

Buhr, N. (2011). Indigenous peoples in the accounting literature: Time for a plot change and some Canadian suggestions. *Accounting History*, 16(2), 139–160.

Cang, Y., Chu, Y. and Lin, T. W. (2014). An exploratory study of earnings management detectability, analyst coverage and the impact of IFRS adoption: Evidence from China. *Journal of Accounting and Public Policy*, 33(4), 356–371.

Chen, C. J. P., Gul, F. A. and Su, X. (1999). A comparison of reported earnings under Chinese GAAP vs. IAS: Evidence from the Shanghai Stock Exchange. *Accounting Horizons*, 13(2), 91–111.

Chen, J. J. and Cheng, P. (2007a). Corporate governance and the harmonization of Chinese accounting practices with IFRS practices. *Corporate Governance*, 15(2), 284–293.

Chen, J. J. and Cheng, P. (2007b). The impact of regulatory enforcement on harmonization of accounting practices: Evidence from China. *Journal of Contemporary Accounting and Economics*, 3(1), 58–71.

Chen, J. J. and Zhang, H. (2010). The impact of regulatory enforcement and audit upon IFRS compliance: Evidence from China. *European Accounting Review*, 19(4), 665–692.

Chen, S., Sun, Z. and Wang, Y. (2002). Evidence from China on whether harmonized accounting standards harmonizes accounting practices. *Accounting Horizons*, 16(3), 183–197.

Chen, S., Wang, Y. and Zhao, Z. (2009). Regulatory incentives for earnings management through asset impairment reversals in China. *Journal of Accounting, Auditing and Finance*, 24(4), 589–620.

Eccher, E. and Healy, P. M. (2000). The role of international accounting standards in transitional economies: A study of the People's Republic of China. Working paper, MIT Sloan School of Management and Harvard Business School.

Ezzamel, M. and Xiao, J. Z. (2015). The development of accounting regulations for foreign invested firms in China: The role of Chinese characteristics. *Accounting, Organizations and Society*, 44, 60–84.

Ezzamel, M., Xiao, J. Z. and Pan, A. (2007). Political ideology and accounting regulation in China. *Accounting, Organizations and Society*, 32(7–8), 669–700.

Haw, I.-M., Qi, D. and Wu, W. (1998). Value-relevance of financial reporting disclosures in an emerging capital market: The case of B-shares in China. Working paper, The Chinese University of Hong Kong.

He, X., Wong, T. J. and Young, D. (2012). Challenges for implementation of fair value accounting in emerging markets: Evidence from China. *Contemporary Accounting Research*, 29(2), 538–562.

Hopwood, A. (2000). Understanding financial accounting practice. *Accounting, Organizations and Society*, 25, 763–766.

Ke, B., Lennox, C. and Xin, Q. (2015). The effect of China's weak institutional environment on the quality of Big 4 audits. *The Accounting Review*, 90(4), 1591–1619.

Ke, B., Li, Y. and Yuan, H. (2016). The substantial convergence of Chinese accounting standards with IFRS and the managerial pay-for-accounting performance sensitivity of publicly listed Chinese firms. *Journal of Accounting and Public Policy*, 35(6), 567–591.

Lin, Z. J. and Chen, F. (2005). Value relevance of international accounting standards harmonization: Evidence from A- and B-share markets in China. *Journal of International Accounting, Auditing and Taxation*, 14, 79–103.

Peng, S. and Bewley, K. (2010). Adaptability to fair value accounting in an emerging economy: A case study of China's IFRS convergence. *Accounting, Auditing and Accountability Journal*, 23(8), 982–1011.

Peng, S. and Smith, J. van der L. (2010). Chinese GAAP and IFRS: An analysis of the convergence process. *Journal of International Accounting, Auditing and Taxation*, 19(1), 16–34.

Peng, S., Tondkar, R. H., Smith, J. van der L. and Harless, D. W. (2008). Does convergence of accounting standards lead to the convergence of accounting practices? A study from China. *The International Journal of Accounting*, 43(4), 448–468.

Qu, X. and Zhang, G. (2015). Value-relevance of earnings and book value over the institutional transition in China: The suitability of fair value accounting in this emerging market. *International Journal of Accounting*, 50(2), 195–223.

Robson, K. (1992). Accounting numbers as 'inscription': Action at a distance and the development of accounting. *Accounting, Organizations and Society*, 17(7), 685–708.

Scott, W. R. (2002). An international comparison and evaluation of financial accounting concepts statements. *Canadian Accounting Perspectives*, 1(2), 163–184.

Wu, G. S., Li, S. and Lin, S. (2014). The effects of harmonization and convergence with IFRS on the timeliness of earnings reported under Chinese GAAP. *Journal of Contemporary Accounting and Economics*, 10(2), 148–159.

Zhang, E. and Andrew, J. (2016). Rethinking China: Discourse, convergence and fair value accounting. *Critical Perspectives on Accounting*, 36, 1–21.

Zhang, R., Lu, Z. and Ye, K. (2010). How do firms react to the prohibition of long-lived asset impairment reversals? Evidence from China. *Journal of Accounting and Public Policy*, 29, 424–438.

Zhang, Y., Andrew, J. and Rudkin, K. (2012). Accounting as an instrument of neoliberalisation? Exploring the adoption of fair value accounting in China. *Accounting, Auditing and Accountability Journal*, 25(8), 1266–1289.

6

CONVERGENCE WITH IFRS IN MALAYSIA

Mazni Abdullah and Marizah Minhat

Introduction

We discuss the issues and challenges of the movement to convergence with International Financial Reporting Standards (IFRS) in Malaysia. In reviewing some previous studies of IFRS in Malaysia, we point to directions for future research.

It is widely suggested in the literature that IFRS offer several advantages to the countries that have adopted them or have converged their own standards with IFRS. The advantages include increased transparency and comparability of financial statements, enhanced quality of financial reporting and increased capital market efficiency. However, the standards issued by the International Accounting Standard Board (IASB) have been largely influenced by the institutional characteristics of developed economies. Hence, converging with IFRS in a developing country like Malaysia is not without issues and challenges.

In the case of Malaysia, effort to converge the local accounting standards with IFRS started in 2005. In 2008, the country declared its aim to achieve full convergence with IFRS by 1 January 2012. Nevertheless, full convergence was delayed to 2018 due to several outstanding issues that will be discussed later in this chapter (*The Star*, 2015; *Borneo Post*, 2015). This indicates that the IFRS convergence is hardly a straightforward journey for a developing country like Malaysia.

Overview of financial reporting and disclosure regulation in Malaysia

Historically, Malaysia was under British colonial influence from the eighteenth century until it gained independence in 1957. With this historical background, the regulation of financial reporting and disclosures in Malaysia has, to a large extent, been influenced by the UK. This influenced the development of the Companies Act and accounting standards.

Prior to the establishment of the Malaysian Accounting Standards Board (MASB) in 1997 accounting standards were issued by two accounting bodies, namely the Malaysian Institute of Accountants (MIA) and the Malaysian Institute of Certified Public Accountants (MICPA). MICPA is a local professional accounting body that was formed in 1958, whereas MIA, established under the Accountants Act 1967, is a regulatory body that regulates and develops the accounting profession in Malaysia. The accounting standards that were jointly issued by the MICPA and MIA were known as Malaysian Accounting Standards (MAS).

The MASB was established under the Financial Reporting Act 1997 with the main object-ives of developing and issuing accounting standards in Malaysia. The accounting standards developed by MASB were based on the International Accounting Standards (IAS) with addi-tional guidance and illustrations to enhance understanding and also to ensure compliance with local laws and regulations. Accounting standards issued by the MASB were recognised as 'approved accounting standards'. The adoption of MASB standards was effective from 1 July 1999. Under this reporting framework the application of MASB standards has the force of law. Compliance with approved accounting standards is required in Section 244 of the Companies Act 2016 (formerly known as the Companies Act 1965).

The enforcement of MASB standards was entrusted to three regulatory agencies, namely the Securities Commission, the Central Bank of Malaysia (Bank Negara) and the Companies Com-mission of Malaysia (CCM). The MIA as an accounting regulatory body has also formed the Financial Statements Review Committee (FSRC) to ensure that accountants in Malaysia adopt and comply with the approved accounting standards.

Apart from the requirement to comply with MASB's approved accounting standards, finan-cial reporting and disclosure practices of listed companies in Malaysia are also governed by the Companies Act 2016, the Securities Commission Act 1993, the Bursa's Listing Requirements and the CCM.

The Malaysian Institute of Corporate Governance was also formed to deal with corporate governance issues in Malaysia and to promote awareness of corporate governance principles to all corporate participants and investors (Liew, 2007). The Malaysian Code on Corporate Gov-ernance (MCCG), which was introduced in 2000, was developed based on the UK's 'Cadbury Code' and the *Hampel Report* (Mat Zain and Subramaniam, 2007). To enhance good govern-ance and disclosure practices among Malaysian companies, the MCCG was revised several times, and the latest revision took place in 2016.

In brief, corporate reporting and disclosure practices in Malaysia were not only governed through legal rules (e.g. the Financial Reporting Act 1997 and Companies Act 2016) but also guidance (e.g. then MCCG). This regulation strategy mirrors that in the UK.

Convergence with IFRS

The initiative to converge with IFRS in Malaysia began in 2005 when the MASB standards were renamed as Financial Reporting Standards (FRS), and the numbering of the standards was matched to those of the IFRS (for example, FRS 1 referred to IFRS 1, and FRS 101 referred to IAS 1) (MIA, 2005). Since 2006 the FRS have been made identical to IFRS on a per standard basis (MASB, 2007). To reduce the burden of compliance on private entities that would result from complex IFRS,[1] the MASB introduced the Private Entity Reporting Standards (PERS)[2] in 2006. Hence, from 2006, there was a two-tier financial reporting framework: the FRS frame-work and the PERS framework.

In 2008, Malaysia declared its intention to achieve full convergence with IFRS by 1 January 2012 and the MASB continued to adopt the IFRS in stages based on the full convergence time-line (MASB, 2008). The MASB described 'full convergence' as 'full compliance' with IFRS, meaning that the FRS had to be made identical to the IFRS both in terms of their content (i.e. verbatim) and timing of implementation. According to the MASB, the word 'convergence' is used rather than 'adopting' because the issuance of standards in Malaysia involves due process that might take around nine to 15 months and requires compliance with local legislation.

Subsequent to the full convergence announcement in 2008, MASB issued a new accounting framework on 19 November 2011. This was named the Malaysian Financial Reporting Standards

(MFRS) framework, which is fully compliant with the IFRS framework (MIA, 2012a). The new MFRS framework became effective for annual reporting periods beginning on or after 1 January 2012, and applied to all non-private entities except entities within the scope of MFRS 141 *Agriculture* or IC Interpretation 15 *Agreements for the Construction of Real Estate*.[3] Effectively this exemption applied to companies involved in real estate and agricultural activities. These exempted companies were referred to as 'Transitioning Entities' (TEs), where they were allowed to apply the previous FRS framework. In this regard, entities involved in property development and the agriculture sector can continue applying FRS 201 *Property Development Activities* and FRS 204 *Accounting for Aquaculture* respectively until 2017.[4] The TEs were finally mandated by law to comply with the MFRS framework for annual reporting periods beginning on or after 1 January 2018 (MASB, 2016).

In light of this, as of 1 January 2012, there were three sets of MASB-approved accounting frameworks in Malaysia: (1) MFRS framework; (2) FRS framework; and (3) PERS framework (MIA, 2012a). PERS were later replaced with the Malaysian Private Entity Reporting Standards (MPERS) in 2014. MPERS is applicable to all private entities effective for annual reporting beginning on or after 1 January 2016. Principally, MPERS mainly match word for word the IFRS for Small and Medium-Sized Entities (SMEs) issued by the IASB, except for the requirements relating to property development activities, income tax and some terminology changes.

In summary, due to the issues on MFRS 141 *Agriculture* and IC Interpretation 15 *Agreements for the Construction of Real Estate*, full convergence with the IFRS, which was initially announced to be achieved by 1 January 2012, was delayed to 1 January 2018. This means that all listed companies (including their subsidiaries, associates and companies jointly controlled by them) and non-listed companies that have applied FRS became compliant with the MFRS framework for financial statements beginning on or after 1 January 2018.

Issues and challenges of IFRS convergence in Malaysia

Previous studies have suggested that many countries envisaged and experienced various challenges in adopting the IFRS (e.g. Larson and Street, 2004; Jermakowicz and Gornik-Tomaszewski, 2006). The most common challenges identified were complexity of certain standards, lack of technical expertise of preparers and auditors, underdeveloped local capital markets, insufficient guidance for first-time application of IFRS, lack of practical knowledge on application of standards, cost of convergence and problematic fair value accounting.

Interestingly, some have suggested that the convergence path for Malaysia was comparatively less challenging than the paths of other countries attempting convergence or adoption for the first time. The rationale for this argument was that most of the provisions of IFRS had already been incorporated into local accounting standards, hence converging the local standards to IFRS was less burdensome for Malaysia (MIA, 2008).

That said, Malaysia's experience in IFRS convergence was not without challenges. Apart from the above common challenges, there were three areas that are unique in the context of Malaysia. These refer to (1) the application of MFRS 141 *Agriculture*, (2) the IC Interpretation 15 *Agreements for the Construction of Real Estate*, and (3) the accounting for Islamic financial instruments, which have not been given adequate attention but matter significantly to Malaysia as a pioneer country in Islamic finance. These issues are discussed in detail below.

Application of MFRS 141 Agriculture (identical to IAS 41)

In Malaysia, companies involved in agricultural activities had been using historical cost accounting. This practice was in opposition to IAS 41, which requires companies to fair value all types of biological assets.[5] In this regard, the preparers have voiced their concerns about the absence of active markets for some biological assets, lack of expertise and additional costs involved in order to determine the fair value of biological assets.

Given that Malaysia is one of the largest producers and exporters of palm oil and natural rubber in the world, the adoption of IAS 41 was likely to have a substantial impact on the industry, particularly the plantation companies. The MASB had raised this concern to the IASB, requesting the IASB improve the requirements in IAS 41 and also enhance them for bearer biological assets (MASB, 2010). The MASB had been in discussion with the IASB since 2008, and, finally, the issue of IAS 41 was added to IASB's Agenda Consultation 2011 and ranked as one of the IASB's high priority projects (MASB, 2016). Consequently, an Exposure Draft ED/2013/8 *Agriculture: Bearer Plants* was issued by IASB for public comment on 26 June 2013, and accordingly the amendments to IAS 41 and IAS 16 for bearer plants were issued on 30 June 2014. Following the amendments of the standards by the IASB, the MASB issued the *Agriculture: Bearer Plants* (Amendments to MFRS 116 and MFRS 141) in September 2014 and it became effective for annual reporting periods beginning on or after 1 January 2016 (MASB, 2016).

Given that the effective date for the real estate companies to apply MFRS 15 was 1 January 2018, the MASB had decided that the mandatory effective date to apply the MFRS framework for both agriculture and real estate companies should be the same (MIA, 2014). This was to avoid the TEs (both agriculture and real estate companies) having to use different frameworks for the year 2016 that may have confused the users. In view of this, the TEs were required to apply the MFRS framework for annual reporting periods beginning on or after 1 January 2018 (MASB, 2016).

Application of IC Interpretation 15 Agreements for the Construction of Real Estate

IC Interpretation 15 *Agreements for the Construction of Real Estate* (IC 15) is identical to the international interpretation of IFRIC 15 (International Financial Reporting Interpretations Committee) issued by the IASB in 2008. In Malaysia, the primary business model of the real estate industry is based on the 'sell and build' concept where most houses are sold before they are built.

If Malaysia were to adopt the IC 15 (IFRIC 15), it would significantly affect the real estate industry, as the IC 15 requires that the profits only be recognised on completion of the projects as opposed to the existing practice (i.e. the percentage of completion method or over time). In this regard, the Real Estate and Housing Developers' Association Malaysia had raised a concern to MASB on the implementation of IC 15 (MASB, 2011). It was argued that the proposed accounting treatment did not reflect the 'sell and build' business model in Malaysia.

Given that the exposure draft on *Revenue from Contracts with Customers* was initially planned for issue by the IASB in mid-2010, the MASB had decided to defer the effective date of IC 15 from 1 July 2010 to 1 January 2012 (MASB, 2011). This deferment was intended to allow the deliberations on the implementation of IC 15 to continue. It also enabled the examination of the proposed standard on *Revenue from Contracts with Customers* with stakeholders. Following the issuance of IFRS 15 *Revenue from Contracts with Customers*[6] by the IASB in May 2014, the MASB also issued MFRS 15 *Revenue from Contracts with Customers* in September 2014 with the same effective date as IFRS 15, i.e. effective for annual reporting periods beginning on or after 1 January 2017 (MASB, 2016). In light of this, in January 2015 the Financial Reporting Standards Implementation Committee (FRSIC) of MIA issued a guideline to apply MFRS 15, named 'FRSIC Consensus 23 Application of MFRS 15 *Revenue from Contracts with Customer on Sale of*

Residential Properties' (MIA, 2015). According to the guideline by FRSIC, a revenue arising from the sale of property under development can be recognised over time in accordance with paragraph 35(c) of MFRS 15 so long as the contracts with customers are governed by Schedule G and Schedule H of the Housing Development Act 1966.

However, in 2015 the MASB decided to defer the effective date to 1 January 2018 given that the effective date to adopt IFRS 15 *Revenue from Contracts with Customers* had been deferred by the IASB. As a result of this deferral, the real estate companies were permitted to continue applying FRS 201 *Property Development Activities* until 2017. The real estate companies were mandated to apply the MFRS framework effective 1 January 2018 and at the same effective date FRS 201 *Property Development Activities* was replaced by MFRS 15 *Revenue from Contracts with Customers*.

Financial Reporting Standards for Islamic financial instruments

Another important issue in Malaysia's context is the progress in addressing issues associated with accounting and reporting for Islamic financial instruments. The strong influence of Islam in Malaysia has led to the development of local Islamic Capital Markets, Islamic Financial Institutions (IFIs) and Islamic financial instruments. Malaysia is known globally as the market leader for *Sukuk* (i.e. Islamic structured securities) and has the world's largest market for these financial instruments (Ali, 2012). *Murabahah*-based instruments are more commonly used by IFIs and corporate firms compared to other Islamic instruments (Minhat and Dzolkarnaini, 2016).

In principle, Islamic financing instruments do not contain interest (i.e. *riba*), which is prohibited. For example, a *murabahah*-based financing envisages that an Islamic bank will purchase an asset (e.g. property) and sell it onward to a consumer for a profit. In principle, this has to be a genuine and real trading (i.e. buy and sell) activity, whereby the parties in the transaction will bargain on a margin of profit (or mark-up) over the known cost of the underlying asset. This means that the buyer–seller relationship in *murabahah*-based trading is supposed to be distinguishable from the straightforward lender–borrower relationship that forms interest-based conventional bank financing.

However, in applying IFRS 9 *Financial Instruments* (an equivalent of MFRS 9), profit earned by a bank under a *murabahah* contract could be viewed as being akin to interest, and therefore would be accounted for as interest revenue. This 'substance over form' approach dismisses the real trading notion envisaged for *murabahah*. It also portrays *murabahah*-based trading as if it is tantamount to an interest-based lending activity. It is questionable whether the intended 'Islamic' trading element of *murabahah*-based financing is fairly reported if it is treated as akin to interest-based borrowing (Minhat and Dzolkarnaini, 2018).

The view of the MASB is that the MFRS framework can be applied to IFIs in the same way that they apply to conventional financial institutions (MIA, 2012b). However, as illustrated above, an improper accounting treatment denies the distinctive characteristics of Islamic financial instruments and the need for IFIs to be seen as following Shariah (i.e. Islamic law) requirements. Treating Islamic financial instruments as akin to interest-based financing is surely against the will of Muslim stakeholders. This poses a question on whether adapting the IFRS is proper in accounting for Islamic financial instruments.

Studies of IFRS in the context of Malaysia

This section provides a review of selected previous studies,[7] grouped under several themes, in the context of Malaysia.

Drivers of, and barriers to, IFRS convergence

Following the announcement by the MASB of its intention to achieve full convergence with IFRS, several studies have been conducted to examine the drivers of, and barriers to, IFRS convergence in Malaysia (e.g. Tan *et al.*, 2007; Yapa *et al.*, 2011; Phang and Mahzan, 2013). Findings from previous studies suggest that coercive isomorphism from stakeholders is the main driver of IFRS convergence in Malaysia (e.g. Yapa *et al.*, 2011; Phang and Mahzan, 2013). Studies also point out that the main internal barriers to IFRS convergence include inadequate knowledge and skills to apply new standards, lack of IFRS training, lack of communication and dissemination of IFRS knowledge to stakeholders, and inadequate time to understand new standards.

Challenges and benefits of IFRS adoption

Survey questionnaires were employed by prior studies to examine the perceptions of accounting practitioners in Malaysia on these aspects (e.g. Jaafar Sidik and Abd Rahim, 2012; Joshi *et al.*, 2016). These studies have generally reported that the complexity of the new standards, difficulty in digesting the standards and costly adoption are among the challenges faced by the respondents. Despite these challenges, the prior studies reported that the respondents supported IFRS adoption and perceived that the new standards help to improve comparability and transparency in reporting.

Impact of IFRS adoption

Several studies have examined the impact of IFRS adoption in Malaysia (e.g. Yaacob and Che-Ahmad, 2012a, 2012b; Wan Ismail *et al.*, 2013; Marzuki and Abdul Wahab, 2016). The findings of these studies generally suggest that (1) higher quality of reported earnings is associated with IFRS adoption, (2) IFRS have enhanced earnings conservatism, and (3) audit fees and audit delay have increased after IFRS adoption.

Compliance with IFRS disclosure

Many previous studies in Malaysia have examined the extent of compliance with IFRS mandatory disclosure requirements and factors that are associated with the level of compliance (e.g. Carlin *et al.*, 2009; Othman and Ameer, 2009; Abdul Rahman and Hamdan, 2017; Abdullah *et al.*, 2015). The findings of these studies vary depending on the sample size, the nature and number of standards they examined and the subjectivity involved in scoring the disclosure levels.

Overall, studies documented low levels of compliance with IFRS disclosure requirements in Malaysia, while findings on the factors associated with compliance levels are mixed. Given that compliance with IFRS is mandatory, the findings of low levels of compliance with IFRS pose a question as to the effectiveness of regulatory enforcement in Malaysia.

Studies also highlight that auditors sometimes issue an unqualified or clean audit report despite incidence of non-compliance with accounting standards (e.g. Abdullah *et al.*, 2013). Based on interviews with auditors, Abdullah *et al.* (2017) suggest that materiality and true and fair view could be the reasons for issuing a clean audit report despite non-compliance with accounting standards.

Value relevance of accounting information under IFRS

The value relevance of IFRS-based accounting information is currently under-studied in Malaysia and findings are somewhat inconclusive. For example, a study that was based on a property-sector sample found that under the IFRS regime, only book value is value relevant for decision making whereas earnings are not (Kadri *et al.*, 2009). A study using a larger sample size found that both book value and earnings are value relevant under the IFRS regime (Lau, 2010).

Another study finds no evidence that mandatory IFRS disclosure levels are value relevant (Abdullah *et al.*, 2015). According to Abdullah *et al.* (2015) there are plausible reasons to suggest that compliance with IFRS disclosure requirements may not affect the market value of companies in Malaysia. First, the dominance of family-controlled firms in Malaysia serves as a conduit for the market to be informed more efficiently through private communication channels rather than (IFRS-based) public disclosure. Second, the net effect of a disclosure on a firm's value may be negligible due to the market's mixed reaction (i.e. positive and negative effects). Third, high non-compliance levels, especially for standards that attract high proprietary costs, means relevant information remains undisclosed. Future research in this area should consider the distinctive characteristics of Malaysia's capital market to shed more light on the relevance of IFRS-based disclosure.

A summary of these prior studies is presented in Table 6.1.

Table 6.1 Summary of prior studies of IFRS in the context of Malaysia

Author(s)	Objective(s)	Sample	Key findings
Abdul Rahman and Hamdan (2017)	Examine compliance with mandatory accounting standard (FRS 101) by Malaysian companies.	105 companies listed on Bursa Malaysia in 2009 (from ACE market category).	Overall disclosure compliance score with FRS 101 is high (92.5 percent). Firm size positively influences compliance with mandatory disclosure requirements.
Abdullah *et al.* (2017)	Explore the reasons why an unqualified audit report was issued despite significant non-compliance with IFRS disclosure requirements.	A semi-structured interview with 11 auditors in Malaysia.	The interview findings suggest that non-compliance with IFRS disclosure requirements does not lead to qualification of audit reports on the basis of materiality and true and fair view override.
Fitriany *et al.* (2017)	Examine the impact of the adoption of IFRS on asymmetric information and cost of equity, and whether the impact of the adoption depends on the quality of public governance and the number of analysts following.	Listed companies in ASEAN countries (Indonesia, Malaysia, Singapore, Thailand, Philippines); data 2001–2014.	(1) IFRS adoption reduces asymmetric information and cost of equity. (2) Better public governance and higher analyst following strengthen the reduction of cost of equity due to IFRS adoption.

Author(s)	Objective(s)	Sample	Key findings
Joshi et al. (2016)	Examine the perceptions of professional accountants on issues associated with IFRS adoption in ASEAN countries.	The survey includes accountants from Singapore (30), Malaysia (25) and Indonesia (31).	Respondents agreed that (1) their countries benefited from IFRS adoption and (2) government, media and professional accounting bodies play a significant role in the IFRS adoption process.
Marzuki and Abdul Wahab (2016)	Examine the impact of IFRS convergence and institutional factors on conditional conservatism in Malaysia.	1,760 firm-year observations (2004–2008).	(1) IFRS enhances conditional conservatism. (2) After IFRS convergence, family firms and firms with *Bumiputra* directors are more conservative whereas firms with richest-men connection are less conservative.
Abdullah et al. (2015)	Examine the influence of family control on compliance with the mandatory disclosure requirements of 12 IFRS and the value relevance of compliance level.	221 companies listed on Bursa Malaysia (Main Board) as at 31 December 2008.	(1) Family control is negatively related to disclosure. (2) Compliance levels are not value relevant. (3) Low levels of compliance for standards involving high proprietary costs and standards that are different or absent from earlier Malaysian GAAP.
Adznan and Nelson (2015)	Examine the financial instruments disclosure practices (MFRS 7) among Malaysian listed companies.	391 companies listed on Bursa Malaysia.	Overall mean score for financial instrument disclosure is 80.76%. Audit committee independence and external audit are significantly associated with the disclosure.
Phang and Mahzan (2013)	Identify external drivers and internal barriers of IFRS convergence in Malaysia.	Distribute 859 questionnaires to Malaysian public listed companies (usable for analysis: 150).	(1) Coercive forces from stakeholders especially regulators are the main factor that influence preparedness of IFRS. (2) Inadequate knowledge and skills and time to understand new standards are the main internal barriers of IFRS implementation.
Wan Ismail et al. (2013)	Examine the impact of IFRS adoption on earnings quality of Malaysian firms.	4,010 firm-year observations (2002–2009).	(1) IFRS adoption is associated with higher quality of reported earnings (lower earnings management). (2) Earnings reported during the period after IFRS adoption are more value relevant.

continued

Table 6.1 Continued

Author(s)	Objective(s)	Sample	Key findings
Jaafar Sidik and Abd Rahim (2012)	Examine the benefits and challenges of FRS adoption in Malaysia.	Distribute 200 questionnaires to Malaysian accountants (usable for analysis: 159).	(1) The respondents perceive that IFRS improves comparability and leads to greater reporting transparency. (2) The challenges of IFRS include the complex nature of standards, difficulty in digesting new standard and cost.
Yaacob and Che-Ahmad (2012a)	Examine the impact of FRS 138 *Intangible Assets* on timely issuance of audit report.	2,440 firm-year observations (2005–2008).	A significant increase in audit delay after the adoption of FRS 138.
Yaacob and Che-Ahmad (2012b)	Examine the impact of audit fees/pricing after IFRS adoption.	3,050 firm-year observations (2004–2008).	A significant increase in audit fees after the adoption of IFRS.
Yapa *et al.* (2011)	Examine the socio-economic impacts of the adoption of IFRS in Singapore, Malaysia and Indonesia.	Interview 28 accounting professionals: Singapore (9), Malaysia (11), Indonesia (8).	(1) IFRS is more established in Singapore compared to Malaysia and Indonesia. (2) The application of fair value requirements of IFRS standards is problematic. (3) The main concerns include inadequate IFRS training and lack of competent staff.
Lau (2010)	Examine the value relevance of financial reporting in Malaysia for the three reporting periods (pre-MASB, MASB and IFRS).	5,517 firm- year observations (1993–2007).	(1) IFRS is value relevant for decision making among investors. (2) Book value and earnings are value relevant for the three reporting periods (pre-MASB, MASB, IFRS regimes).
Carlin *et al.* (2009)	Assess the level of compliance and disclosure quality of FRS 136 *Goodwill*.	36 companies listed on Bursa Malaysia as at 2006.	There was substantial non-compliance with basic disclosure requirements of FRS 136 (e.g. 61.1 percent of the observed companies did not disclose the growth rate used in estimating recoverable amount for an impairment testing).
Kadri *et al.* (2009)	Examine the effect of changes in financial reporting regime on (1) value relevance of book value and earnings and (2) the relationship between earnings and operating cash flow.	59 property companies listed on Bursa Malaysia as of 30 April 2008 (2002–2007).	(1) The change of financial reporting regime affects the value relevance of the book value, but not earnings. (2) The change of financial reporting regime does not affect the relationship between earnings and operating cash flow.

Author(s)	Objective(s)	Sample	Key findings
Othman and Ameer (2009)	Examine the market risk disclosure practices under FRS 132 *Financial Instruments: Disclosure and Presentation*.	429 public listed companies. Annual reports for the financial year ending 2006/2007.	(1) The extent of compliance with FRS 132 varied among the companies. (2) Interest rate disclosure was the most mentioned compared to credit risk among the market risks categories.
Tan *et al.* (2007)	Examine the impact of the implementation of FRS on Malaysian companies.	Distribute 888 questionnaires to Malaysian listed companies (received and usable for analysis: 67); and interview audit partners and regulators (total: 7 respondents).	(1) The main problem in the implementation process was the lack of communication to financial analyst and investors on the impact of FRS on financial statements. (2) The most difficult standards to apply include FRS 139 and FRS 2.

Future directions

First, the internationalisation of financial reporting standards has undoubtedly introduced challenges based on convergence or adoption in Malaysia. Most of the challenges identified so far in research studies have been based on the perceptions of accountants and auditors. Challenges as perceived by various groups of stakeholders might be different, but are largely unknown. Therefore, it is suggested that future studies revisit the issue by surveying the perceptions of different groups of stakeholders such as financial analysts, institutional investors, lenders and regulators. Considering different perspectives will enable researchers to gauge a holistic view of the challenges associated with IFRS adoption in order to formulate a meaningful feedback to improve regulation if need be.

Second, it is also observed that, while some research has used surveys, questionnaires or interviews, to gather perceptions on IFRS convergence or adoption, most studies have used quantitative research approaches based on accounting data or market data to examine IFRS-related issues. The issues examined include compliance with the IFRS and impact of the IFRS on stakeholders. There is a view that the quantitative research approach is rather limited in its ability to explain the 'why' aspect of an observation. The extant literature on IFRS can be enriched exploring further the 'why' aspect through using qualitative research approaches that may involve interviews, case studies and other methodologies.

Third, it is also inferred from the findings of previous studies that adequate and effective training has to be in place to support the introduction of new standards. In this regard, to what extent the principle of fair value accounting, particularly MFRS 9, has been understood and properly applied by companies has yet to be explored. Furthermore, future research can also explore the impact of MFRS 141 and MFRS 15 on the plantation and real estate industries in Malaysia. It would also be interesting to know how the plantation companies and 'sell and build' property companies in Malaysia cope with the requirements imposed by the MFRS.

Fourth, exploring the challenges and issues associated with applying the IFRS to accounting for Islamic financial instruments is an interesting avenue for future research. This research agenda is particularly relevant to Malaysia, which has been promoting the use of Islamic financing to support the government's ambitious plan for economic growth. The Islamic Financial Services Board estimated that the Islamic finance industry grew annually at a rate of 17 per cent between 2009 and 2013. Failing to accommodate the need to account for Islamic financial instruments as non-interest-bearing instruments risks the reputation of the industry and regulators as stakeholders are becoming more sophisticated. Therefore, research to pre-emptively tackle this issue is important to address reputational risk.

Finally, the adoption of IFRS to account for Islamic financial instruments remains a subject of interesting debate and research. Effective deliberation on this topic requires competency in accounting, finance and Islamic finance. The risk of 'capture' for commercial interest is possible if competency and integrity are lacking. To what extent the voice of experts at MASB has been considered in deliberating the accounting rules for Islamic financial instruments at international level is questionable. These instruments are generally accounted for as interest-based instruments, and often regarded as interest-based instruments in legal and commercial disputes. Taking Malaysia as a pioneer of the Islamic finance industry, Malaysian regulators are responsible for leading and steering the current practice to the right direction. In our view, this is the greatest challenge to be shouldered by MASB going forward to protect the public interest.

Notes

1 A private entity is defined in the Companies Act 2016 (section 2) as a private company that; (a) is not required to prepare or lodge any financial statements under any law administered by the Securities Commission Malaysia or Bank Negara Malaysia; and (b) is not a subsidiary or associate of, or jointly controlled by, an entity which is required to prepare or lodge any financial statements under any law administered by the Securities Commission Malaysia or Bank Negara Malaysia.
2 Fundamentally, PERS were MASB standards issued by the MASB prior to 1 January 2005. PERS were much simpler than FRS because the standards were not affected by revisions and requirements of IFRS. The private entities have the option to apply in its entirety either the PERS or FRS, which is mandatory for non-private entities, if they deemed the FRS framework to be more appropriate for them.
3 MFRS 141 and IC Interpretation 15 are identical to IAS 41 and IFRIC 15 issued by the IASB.
4 The TEs were initially expected to apply the MFRS framework beginning on or after 1 January 2013 (MASB, 2011). The rationale for delaying the adoption date for TE was to accommodate possible changes in IAS 41 and IC 15. Nevertheless, the mandatory effective date for the TEs to apply the MFRS framework has been deferred several times, i.e. from the first deferment date of 1 January 2013 to 1 January 2017 and then to 1 January 2018.
5 That said, there are special conditions for rebuttal of the fair value presumption where fair value cannot be measured reliably.
6 IFRS 15 superseded IAS 18 *Revenue*, IAS 11 *Construction Contracts*, IFRIC 15 and related interpretations.
7 Our review covers empirical studies that are either open access or accessible via Google Scholar and ResearchGate as at 28 February 2018. We used the following keyword searches; IFRS, FRS, MFRS, Malaysia.

Reference

Abdul Rahman, A. and Hamdan, M. D. (2017). The extent of compliance with FRS 101 standard: Malaysian evidence. *Journal of Applied Accounting Research*, 18(1), 87–115.
Abdullah, M., Evans, L., Fraser, I. and Tsalavoutas, I. (2015). IFRS mandatory disclosures in Malaysia: The influence of family control and the value (ir) relevance of compliance levels. *Accounting Forum*, 39, 328–348.
Abdullah, M., Sapiei, N. and Ismail, N. (2017). Unqualified audit report and non-compliance with IFRS: Interview evidence. *Pertanika Journal of Social Science and Humanities*, 25(S), 185–198.
Abdullah, M., Sulaiman, N., Sapiei, N. and Minhat, M. (2013). Some observations on mandatory disclosure practices of Malaysian public listed companies. *Middle East Journal of Scientific Research*, 17(9), 1228–1236.

Adznan, S. and Nelson, S. P. (2015). Financial instruments disclosure practices: Evidence from Malaysian listed firms. *Asian Journal of Accounting and Governance*, 6, 37–48.

Ali, H. (2012). The future of Islamic finance. *Accountants Today*, 25(3), 60–62.

Borneo Post (2015). Malaysia to fully converge with IFRS in 2018. *Borneo Post*, 1 December 2015, www.theborneopost.com/2015/12/01/malaysia-to-fully-converge-with-ifrs-in-2018/ (accessed 30 November 2017).

Carlin, T. M., Finch, N. and Laili, N. H. (2009). Goodwill accounting in Malaysia and the transition to IFRS: A compliance assessment of large first year adopters. *Journal of Financial Reporting & Accounting*, 7(1), 75–104.

Fitriany, U. S., Farahmita, A. and Anggraita, V. (2017). Economic consequences of IFRS adoptions around the ASEAN countries. *International Journal of Economics and Management*, 11(S2), 529–551.

Jaafar Sidik, M. H. and Abd Rahim, R. (2012). The benefits and challenges of financial reporting standards in Malaysia: Accounting practitioners' perceptions. *Australian Journal of Basic and Applied Sciences*, 6(7), 98–108.

Jermakowicz, E. K. and Gornik-Tomaszewski, S. (2006). Implementing IFRS from the perspective of EU publicly traded companies. *Journal of International Accounting, Auditing and Taxation*, 15, 170–196.

Joshi, M., Yapa, P. and Kraal, D. (2016). IFRS adoption in ASEAN countries: Perceptions of professional accountants from Singapore, Malaysia and Indonesia. *International Journal of Managerial Finance*, 12, 211–240

Kadri, M. H., Abdul Aziz, R. and Ibrahim, M. K. (2009). Value relevance of book value and earnings: Evidence from two different financial reporting regimes. *Journal of Financial Reporting and Accounting*, 7(1), 1–16.

Larson, R. K. and Street, D. (2004). Convergence with IFRS in an expanding Europe: Progress and obstacles identified by large accounting firms' survey. *Journal of International Accounting, Auditing and Taxation*, 13, 89–119.

Lau, C. K. (2010). The value relevance of financial reporting in Malaysia: Evidence from three different financial reporting periods. *International Journal of Business and Accountancy*, 1(1), 1–19.

Liew, P. K. (2007). Corporate governance reforms in Malaysia: The key leading players' perspectives. *Corporate Governance: An International Review*, 15(5), 724–740.

Marzuki, M. M. and Abdul Wahab, E. A. (2016). Institutional factors and conditional conservatism in Malaysia: Does international financial reporting standards convergence matter? *Journal of Contemporary Accounting & Economics*, 12, 191–209.

MASB (2007). MASB Releases exposure draft to amend 10 accounting standards. www.masb.org.my (accessed 1 July 2008).

MASB (2008). Malaysia's convergence with IFRS in 2012. www.masb.org.my (accessed 6 September 2009).

MASB (2010). Comment letter on IASB's exposure draft: Fair value measurement (ed.) request for input on application in emerging and transition economies. www.masb.org.my/pdf.php?pdf=cl (accessed 17 December 2017).

MASB (2011). Frequently asked questions on Malaysia's convergence with IFRS in 2012. www.masb.org.my/pages.php?id=75 (accessed 17 December 2017).

MASB (2016). Implementation of MFRSs. www.masb.org.my/pdf.php?pdf=2016 (accessed 17 December 2017).

Mat Zain, M. and Subramaniam, N. (2007). Internal auditor perceptions on audit committee interactions: A qualitative study in Malaysian public corporations. *Corporate Governance: An International Review*, 15(5), 894–908.

MIA (2005). MASB moves closer to convergence with their planned renaming of MASB standards. *Accountants Today*, 18(2), 49.

MIA (2008). Full Convergence with IFRS in 2012. *Accountants Today*, 21(10), 22–23.

MIA (2012a). First steps towards IFRS convergence. *Accountants Today*, 25(1), 29–31.

MIA (2012b). MASB on convergence. *Accountants Today*, 25(3), 12–13.

MIA (2014). Circular No. MF15/2014. www.mia.org.my/enews/2014/09/03/circular_no_mf_152014.html (accessed 30 November 2017).

MIA (2015). FRSIC Consensus 23 Application of MFRS 15 *Revenue from Contracts with Customers* on Sale of Residential Properties. www.mia.org.my/v2/.../frsic/consensus/.../mia_frsic_consensus-23-2015.p (accessed 17 December 2017).

Minhat, M. and Dzolkarnaini, N. (2016) Islamic corporate financing: Does it promote profit and loss sharing? *Business Ethics: A European Review*, 25(4), 482–497.

Minhat, M. and Dzolkarnaini, N. (2018) Has the Islamic finance industry prospered with integrity? *The Malaysian Reserve*, 27 August 2018, https://themalaysianreserve.com/2018/08/27/has-the-islamic-finance-industry-prospered-with-integrity/ (accessed 27 August 2018).

Othman, R. and Ameer, R. (2009). Market risk disclosure: Evidence from Malaysian listed firms. *Journal of Financial Regulation and Compliance*, 17(1), 57–69.

Phang, S. Y. and Mahzan, N. (2013). The response of Malaysian public listed companies to the IFRS convergence. *Asian Journal of Business and Accounting*, 6(1), 95–120.

Tan, L. L, Lazar, J. and Othman, Radiah (2007). Adoption of Financial Reporting Standards (FRSs): Impact on Malaysian companies. Working paper, Malaysian Accountancy Research and Education Foundation. www.academia.edu/6500604/Adoption_of_Financial_Reporting_Standards_FRSs_Impact_on_Malaysian_Companies_ADOPTION_OF_FINANCIAL_REPORTING_STANDARDS_FRSs_IMPACT_ON_MALAYSIAN_COMPANIES_PREPARED_BY_TAN_LAY_LENG (accessed 30 November 2017).

The Star (2015). Malaysian firms to adopt global reporting standards by 2018. *The Star*, 7 December 2015, www.thestar.com.my/business/business-news/2015/12/07 (accessed 30 November 2017).

Wan Ismail, W. A., Kamarudin, K. A., van Zijl, T. and Dunstan, K. (2013). Earnings quality and the adoption of IFRS-based accounting standards: Evidence from an emerging market. *Asian Review of Accounting*, 21(1), 53–73.

Yaacob, N. M. and Che-Ahmad, A. (2012a). Adoption of FRS 138 and audit delay in Malaysia. *International Journal of Economics and Finance*, 4(1), 167–176.

Yaacob, N. M. and Che-Ahmad, A. (2012b). Audit fees after IFRS adoption: Evidence from Malaysia. *Eurasian Business Review*, 2(1), 31–46.

Yapa, P. W. S., Joshi, M. and Kraal, D. (2011). The socio-economic impacts of the adoption of IFRS: A comparative study between the ASEAN countries of Singapore, Malaysia and Indonesia. www.researchgate.net/publication/264854114_The_SocioEconomic_Impacts_of_the_Adoption_of_IFRS_a_comparative_study_between_the_ASEAN_countries_of_Singapore_Malaysia_Indonesia (accessed 15 February 2018).

7

THE ACCOUNTING ENVIRONMENT AND ALIGNMENT WITH IFRS IN VIETNAM

Nguyen Cong Phuong

Introduction

Vietnam is a developing country in Southeast Asia. It adopts Marxist-Leninist ideology serving as guidance for its activities and promoting the nation's traditions. The country was greatly influenced during the twentieth century by strong countries, such as France, the former Soviet Union, the United States and China, due to its relations with the latter regarding ideology, politics and the economy. The economic and accounting system under the centrally planned economy was adopted from the former Soviet Union's model. Economic reforms started in 1986 have changed the country's economic system, moving from a planned economy towards a market-oriented one while preserving the state's strong control. The country has also made great strides in opening up its economy and integrating into the global economy.

In response to the important changes in the accounting environment, an accounting reform was carried out in 1995 that established an accounting system moving towards a private capitalist accounting model. Through the issuance of accounting standards by 2005, Vietnamese accounting has converged with the International Accounting Standards Board's (IASB) standards (the 2003 version), which aims towards the Vietnamese state's desire to integrate its economy into the global economy. At the same time, Vietnam retains the Uniform Accounting System (hereafter UAS), which originated in the era of central planning, for maintaining the traditional control function of accounting. Its retention also reflects the relative weakness of the accounting profession. The co-existence of accounting standards and UAS differs from the approaches of most countries in the world. Up to now, this approach has seemed to be appropriate for the achievement of Vietnam's goals. However, due to the different politico-economic context and accounting tradition, when the accounting standards based on an Anglo-Saxon philosophy that focuses on a principles-based approach are used in a mixed economy known as 'a market economy under socialist orientation' some problems emerge (Phuong and Nguyen, 2012; Phan *et al.*, 2018). The chapter also shows how the Vietnamese regulators find a way to overcome the challenges. The chapter concludes with a discussion on directions for future research.

Politics, the economy and their effect on the environment of accounting

In the past, Vietnam adopted a Marxist-Leninist ideology and a Leninist political framework from the former Soviet Union. Traditionally, the Communist Party's influence over the planning process is reinforced by its control of all-important managerial positions in the economy, from the state planning bureaucracy to state-owned enterprises (McCormick, 1998; Bergeret, 2002). Despite gradually moving towards a market economy from 1986, Vietnam is still a communist country and the Communist Party of Vietnam (CPV) always plays a supreme and pervasive role in society. Although the CPV should not take the role of the government in the state's leadership system, in reality, however, the Party maintains its central role in controlling all organisations of government, politics and society as a whole. In the context of moving towards a market economy, one of the biggest challenges that the CPV faces is how to 'maintain a balance between political ideology and economic legitimacy, or how to boost economic development while keeping its absolute power and comprehensive leadership' (Tu Anh, 2014a). The CPV therefore uses the state sector as means to control and lead the economy under a 'socialist orientation'. This ideology is emphasised in the Constitution of the Socialist Republic of Vietnam which states that 'the state economic sector has played a leading role, arranging the foundation for institutions' (Article 19, 51, The National Assembly of Vietnam, 1992, 2013). The reform process, regulation and control over the economy have therefore been shaped by this ideology.

Vietnam's economy is characterised by the state's strong control; a large state-owned enterprise (SOE) sector (about 28.8 per cent of GDP,[1] in comparison with 10 per cent in the world,[2]) has grown strongly over the past decades and has gradually integrated with the international economic system. The SOEs have played a leading role in the economy, arranging the foundation for institutions to ensure a socialist society. SOEs have often been prioritised by the government, using 60 per cent of national capital resources (Anh, 2006; Tho, 2009). They have often been in the spotlight over poor governance and lack of accountability, inefficiency and massive corruption, as indicated by the World Bank's *Report on the Observance of Standards and Codes* (World Bank, 2013: 2): 'Overall, the corporate governance of many SOEs remains poor, with weaknesses in terms of transparency.' Consequently, to maintain the so-called 'socialist orientation', the SOE sector must occupy the central place in the government's economic development strategy, play the leading role in the economy and stabilise the macroeconomy, while at the same time ensuring a harmonious society as well as sustainable development of Vietnam's economy (Tu Anh, 2014b). Economic policies and strategies, including accounting regulation, have therefore emphasised the regulation of the state economic sector, and the implications of this regulation for this sector.

Like other developing economies, Vietnam's financial market is characterised by a credit-based system in which most of the financing resources are provided by bankers, accounting for 68.1 per cent in 2016 (National Financial Supervisory Commission, 2016). Vietnam's equity market is immature and small in scale. Since its establishment in July 2000, at the end of 2015, there were 686 companies listed on two stock exchanges with a total capitalisation of 32.4 per cent GDP (National Financial Supervisory Commission, 2016). The capital market is embryonic, has a large proportion of individual investors who are slow to react to fundamental changes in the market because of an irrational attachment to a perceived value, and a small number of major investors that hold large amounts of shares (Vo Thanh Tri and Le Xuan Sang, 2012: 8). The commercial bankers are the major investors (holding around a 76 per cent share in 2015) while the government's giant financial corporations such as the Social Security of Vietnam, State Capital Investment Corporation, and Depository Insurance of Vietnam hold around 15 per cent

(Huong and Thuy, 2016). The stock market is characterised by weak equity outsiders, strong market speculation and weak form efficiency (National Financial Supervisory Commission, 2017). A small number of institutional investors that hold a large number of shares may make the market dependent on those investors and consequently there is large-scale market manipulation. According to Xiao *et al.* (2004), the weaknesses of the capital market have influenced the demand for, and supply of, accounting information in Vietnam. The accounting system emphasises, therefore, the government's information needs rather those of other users, as recognised in the UAS (Ministry of Finance, 1995: 5, 2006: 7).

In Vietnam there is an ongoing process of largely integrating the economy into the regional and the global economies. The country has made important commitments to trade liberalisation under various bilateral and multilateral agreements.[3] The gradual integration with the world market has become a central pillar of Vietnam's economic policy. Important changes in Vietnam's legal framework have arisen through becoming a member of the World Trade Organization (WTO), implementing the US–Vietnam Bilateral Trade Agreement liberalisation commitments, being part of the ASEAN Free Trade Area and meeting the emerging obligations of the Asia-Pacific Economic Cooperation (APEC) and the Comprehensive and Progressive Agreement for Trans-Pacific Partnership. All of these have brought important changes in Vietnam's legal framework, requiring adjustment to be suitable for the underlying values of the 'international standards' such as free trade, fair competition, non-discrimination, finance and accounting. Under pressure from international institutions to create a non-discriminatory and level playing field as well as an effective legal framework for the performance of enterprises, the Vietnamese Accounting Standards (VAS), which were primarily based on the International Accounting Standards (IAS) at that time (up to 2003), were issued from 2001 to 2005.

As stated in the opening remarks of the Vietnam Development Forum 2014,[4] Vietnam's continuous efforts to build a more competitive economy have required continued attention to institutional reform and international integration, including accounting development. With integration and an increasingly sophisticated economy, demand for formal economic institutions has increased. The government of Vietnam has set out purposes for reforms. Vietnam's 2011–2020 Socio-Economic Development Strategy (SEDS) concentrates on structural reforms, environmental sustainability, social equity and emerging issues of macroeconomic stability. In addition to the SEDS, the five-year Socio-Economic Development Plan (SEDP) for 2011–2015 concentrated on three critical restructuring areas: the banking sector, state-owned enterprises and public investment. The SEDP for 2016–2020, approved in April 2016, recognises slow progress on certain SEDP reform priorities and stresses the need to accelerate these institutional reforms over the next period to achieve targets set out in the 10-year SEDS. Following the SEDS and SEDP, an accounting development strategy to 2020, Vision 2030, was also issued by the government in 2013 (Prime Minister, 2013). This strategy continues to recognise accounting 'as an important part of the state's economic and financial management instruments', as recognised since 1995 (Ministry of Finance, 1995: 5, 2006: 7). Due to the demands from the World Bank, International Finance Corporation and foreign investors, among others, Vietnam is on the way to filling the gap between VAS and IFRS and it is expected that full adoption of IAS/IFRS will be implemented by 2020 for listed firms first.

In the past three decades of transition towards a market economy, Vietnam is 'only partly market driven, retaining non-market capitalist forms of ideology' (Phuong and Richard, 2011). In harmony with the rhythm of economic reform, the ideology of the Vietnamese Communist Party (VCP) has been systematically translated into distinguishing economic institutions and governance policies for the economy. The leading role of SOEs and strong control of the state-party in the socio-economy make the Vietnamese economy different from a traditional mixed economy (e.g. that seen in France in the 1960s). As a result, the SOEs have received favourable treatment, including accounting regulation from the state-party in order to maintain their important role in improving economic legitimacy for the VCP.

Gradualist mixed approach to regulating accounting

One of the classifications of accounting systems is based on whether a country adopts a UAS, characterised by specific accounting features or accounting standards (Nobes, 1998; Xiao *et al.*, 2004). Xiao *et al.* (2004) provide a framework to explain the differences between the two approaches and the impact of the factors on the demand for, and supply of, UAS and accounting standards. The standards-based approach prevails in the Anglo-Saxon countries while the UAS-type approach persists in the Continental Europe. However, it is necessary for some countries to use both approaches to set accounting regulations. China and Vietnam are two of them. According to Xiao *et al.* (2004), the co-existence of UAS and accounting standards in a country can be explained by the political influence, equity market and accounting tradition. The experience of China with a similar political and social context had shown Vietnam that the co-existence of a UAS and accounting standards may be appropriate for the country where there is strong control by the state-party over a socio-economy, an immature capital market, SOEs in a lead role and a weak accounting profession.

Indeed, faced with pressures exerted by the main commercial partners and international organisations, while aiming to maintain the state's central role in regulating and controlling a socio-economy, the regulators have been careful in their approach to regulating accounting and find ways to combine the two approaches for the development of accounting. As a result, the Vietnamese accounting system is characterised by the co-existence of a UAS and accounting standards. On the one hand, accounting reforms and developments in Vietnam that started in 1995 have maintained the traditional control function of accounting that originated in the era of central planning. This control function has a macroeconomic effect in leading to a prescriptive UAS (including a uniform plan of accounts, basic rules for recording, recognition and measurement, and rigid formats of financial statements). The latter allows the state to continue to meet the requirements of political and macroeconomic control. On the other hand, the emergence of the capital market, although it is still immature, and especially the pressures from the international business community motivate experimentation with accounting standards. With the technical and financial assistance of the Euro-TapViet project, the World Bank and the Asian Development Bank, Vietnam issued 26 accounting standards from 2001 to 2005 that were based largely on the 2003 version of IAS. The appearance of VAS that are based on IAS is of public interest since Vietnam only needs an 'IAS label'. This label would express Vietnam's desire to move towards globalisation and would provide the international community with a promise of financial transparency.

The Uniform Accounting System and Vietnamese Accounting Standards

Uniform Accounting System

As a result of accounting reform responding to the market-oriented economic reform, the UAS that adapted the former 'socialist' accounting system and moved towards a private capitalist accounting model was issued in 1995. After issuance of the 26 VAS by 2005 (see below), the UAS was amended in 2006 and was further amended in 2014 (entitled 2006 UAS and 2014 UAS) to update rules of recognition and measurements according to VAS/IFRS. All types of enterprises in Vietnam are required to follow the UAS and other prevailing Vietnamese decisions and circulars. Legally, the 2014 UAS provides guidance on VAS over the application and adoption of accounting standards for all types of enterprises. Consisting of basic rules for recording, recognition and measurement, including a chart of accounts and rigid formats of financial statements, the UAS is an explanation of how accounts are applied to typical economic transactions and how financial statements are prepared. It focuses less on disclosure. While the third version of the UAS was recently issued[5] to bring up to date many principles/rules adopted from the IAS/IFRS, the 26 VAS are not revised and updated. This results in some conflicts between VAS and the UAS within some areas in terms of fair value.

Vietnamese Accounting Standards

Vietnam issued 26 accounting standards from 2001 to 2005, which were adopted from and primarily based on the IASB standards prevailing at the time of issuance (up to 2003). Though some modifications were made to reflect the local regulations and environment of accounting, none of the IASB's amendments to IAS or the new IFRS have been updated or adopted. Key differences between IAS/IFRS and VAS include terminology, applied methods and presentation scope due to the continuing changes and amendments of IFRS. The VAS financial statements are the statutory and primary financial statements. Although the VAS are applicable to all forms of enterprises, in fact, they are mainly applicable to listed companies and, in particular, many of those companies prefer to apply the UAS rather the VAS to prepare their financial information (Phuong, 2012). Some Vietnamese companies prepare IAS/IFRS financial statements for the purpose of reporting to foreign investors. However, those financial statements compliant with IAS/IFRS are supplementary financial statements, not a substitute for financial statements prepared using VAS.

In response to international pressures, Vietnam has carried out the first stage of a two-stage model to follow IAS/IFRS adoption.[6] However, for a second stage, institutional reforms in Vietnam have not been advanced enough to provide the adequate accounting infrastructure (for example, a developed equity market, good corporate governance, legal protection of investors and a strong accounting profession) following IAS/IFRS to drive up the financial reporting quality.

Issues of accounting regulation aligned with IAS/IFRS

A different politico-economic context

Faced with situations of uncertainties and international institutional pressures about the approach to regulating accounting, the Vietnamese regulators have sought standards of the IASB that are viewed as being more legitimate and have 'mimicked' them, regardless of these standards' efficiency in Vietnam's context. As discussed in the literature, the accounting standards of the IASB are controversial. Besides the potential benefits for the country such as attracting foreign domestic investment, the different political, cultural and governance challenges associated with adopting IAS/IFRS are far more difficult to deal with than the technical accounting issues, and will likely prevent the achievement of Vietnam's goal. These VAS, aligned almost entirely with the international accounting standards at that time (version 2003) and the adoption of IFRS in the future (from 2020), when used in a mixed economy known as 'a market economy under socialist orientation' result in some problems. The differences in the political ideologies, cultures and business practices between the Anglo-Saxon nations and Vietnam have to be considered, and that requires flexibility. Vietnam's legal system is based on code law. As such, unlike in common law countries such as the US and UK, state agencies and creditors (especially banks) are the main users of financial information, rather than shareholders. Apart from that, the IFRS are more principle driven than the rule-driven Vietnamese traditional accounting (see below). Therefore, the full adoption of IAS/IFRS may not be suitable to Vietnam's socio-economic context where the objectives of Vietnamese accounting are characterised by the requirements of strongly political and macroeconomic control (see Ministry of Finance, 1995: 5, 2006: 7) and accounting tradition is in the code-based system. Indeed, IAS/IFRS focus on the needs of investors in equity while Vietnamese government emphasises macroeconomic accounting information; adoption of IAS/IFRS means that the needs of the state and enterprises play a role subordinate to the needs of the investors in equity. This issue has not been fully resolved in the short term.

The literature notes that there is a continuing discussion, focusing on whether the global accounting standards (IAS/IFRS) are the best choice for developing countries like Vietnam, with mainly small businesses and strong macroeconomic control (Hopper, 2012; Perera, 2012). These debates resulted from the evident fact that there exists a trade-off between the costs and benefits of adopting internationally compliable standards. On one hand, setting the VAS fully compliant with IAS/IFRS, as one of the many requirements for achieving appropriate financial regulation in the framework of fulfilling the conditions of international integration, has given Vietnam a lot of political advantages but maybe not many economic advantages due to the limited number of big companies in Vietnam aspiring to attract foreign investments. On the other hand, for the small and medium-sized enterprises, which account for more than 96 per cent of Vietnamese companies, it has been a significant cost to adopt the VAS aligning with IAS/IFRS because of the need to train internal staff or hire outside consultants with higher accounting services fees.

Accounting tradition

The embrace of an accounting system based on an Anglo-Saxon philosophy, which focuses on a principles-based approach, is only possible if accompanied by a gradual transformation of the legitimating structures in the evolving social environment. Despite the institutional changes in Vietnam it is significant that this evolution does not reflect an Anglo-Saxon institutional logic. Consequently, the VAS adapted from IASB standards are not perceived to be more successful for most domestic enterprises since the code-based orientation of the Vietnamese accountants has led them to prefer rules to principles (see also Nguyen *et al.*, 2013). As the VAS contain concepts and principles in line with IASB standards, enterprises often use the UAS to record, recognise and measure transactions and to prepare financial statements. In fact, the VAS contain concepts and principles to guide the professional application of accounting methods based on conventions raised in the context of capitalist and developed countries, whereas the UAS, consisting of a chart of accounts and rigid formats of financial statements, is an explanation of how accounts are applied to typical economic transactions and how financial statements are prepared. The move to IAS/IFRS has involved a change in accounting mindset, as IAS/IFRS are built on a different framework to a traditional accounting system. The implementation of VAS arguably requires a high degree of professional judgement, but the scope of professional judgement is restricted. Lack of knowledge and experience of IAS/IFRS is one among the many challenges of implementing VAS in Vietnam. This is what macro management and accounting practice have been accustomed to doing for a long time in order to comply with accounting rules, which explains how the accounts are applied to typical economic transactions and how the financial statements are prepared.[7] Furthermore, while accounting standards are concepts and principles designed to guide the professional application of accounting methods, Vietnamese accountants have long been accustomed to the rigid rules and the majority of them do not have the competence and experience to make professional judgements concerning choices of accounting policies.[8] As a result, Vietnamese regulators primarily revise the UAS, instead of VAS, with the measurement and recognition rules aligned with the IASB's amendments.

Accounting profession

There are six organisations involved in Vietnamese accounting regulation, including the Management and Supervision of Accounting and Auditing (DMSAA),[9] the Vietnam Accounting Association (VAA), Vietnam Association of Certified Public Accountants (VACPA), the Accounting Standards Steering Committee (ASSC), the Accounting Standards Setting Group (ASSG) and the National Council for Accountancy (NCA). All of them were established by the minister of finance, and the last three organisations were created from 1998 to 2000 to set the Vietnamese accounting standards. Each of the six organisations has its own functions in accounting regulation. However, these agencies are not independent of the government. Except for VAA and VACPA, membership of the other agencies is decided by the Ministry of Finance and the majority consist of accounting and financial specialists from Ministry of Finance departments (Narayan and Godden, 2000). The VAA and VACPA are traditionally weak and are not exercising their role as a professional body. As before, they do not play an active role in regulating accounting. According to the Law on Accounting issued in 2003 and 2015, the Ministry of Finance preserves its responsibility for setting and issuing accounting standards (The National Assembly of Vietnam, 2003, 2015). In order to do that, the Ministry of Finance created the ASSC in 1998[10] and the NCA in 2000[11] alongside the DMSAA. The ASSC is responsible for steering standards setting. The NCA's functions include the development of strategies, policies and other issues concerning auditing and accounting activities. The NCA is the key regulatory body for accounting and auditing arrangements in Vietnam. Its structure and functions are similar to those of accounting regulatory boards in other countries. However, the Department of Management and Supervision of Accounting and Auditing has also been a steering organisation of the NCA since its establishment. It also is in charge of exercising state management on both accounting and auditing activities.

The analysis of the institutional structure for regulation of accounting shows that the Ministry of Finance, through the DMSAA, often has a dominant position. This is because Vietnam lacks strong professional bodies to set and implement accounting standards. On the other hand, this reflects not only its traditional regulatory role, which existed in the planned economy, but its responsibility for tax policy and tax collection. The nature of the regulatory apparatus is actually under state control. The number of representatives of state budget departments in the apparatus allows, therefore, the state to formulate accounting rules in accordance with its interests (collection of tax revenues). This may cause some conflicts of interest between other stakeholders to emerge during the economic reform. It is, therefore, necessary that the responsibility of the accounting administration be made a pre-requisite objective so that the disclosure mechanisms of financial information better meet the interests of the plurality of user groups. However, the weak accounting profession reveals that regulation of Vietnamese accounting by the government may be logical. To play a more active role in standards setting, and in enhancing the professional skills of accountants and auditors, the role of the VAA and VACPA should be strengthened.

Future directions

The co-existence of accounting standards and a UAS in Vietnam reflects a specific circumstance of an economy known as 'a socialist market-oriented economy' where the state-party plays a supreme and pervasive role in leading and controlling a society. This different approach reveals the key role of the state in regulating accounting, aiming at governmental control over enterprises while moving towards (symbolic) convergence with the IASB's standards. Until now, the situation seems to be under control. This may not change even if Vietnam does adopt or adapt the IFRS 'label' in next two years when institutional reforms in Vietnam may be advanced enough to provide the adequate accounting infrastructure. This paper testifies that the process of moving towards convergence with the IASB's standards in this developing country has faced some issues previously evidenced in the literature, due to national particularities such as the politico-economic system and accounting tradition. It suggests that the requirements of strongly political and macroeconomic control help explain challenges in adopting the IASB's standards in Vietnam. Further, this finding reinforces the analysis of Ball *et al.* (2000) and extends Nobes (1998) and Xiao *et al.* (2004) by showing that political factors have strongly influenced the nature of the accounting system in a developing economy, especially in a socialist country such as Vietnam.

While changes in legal and policy documents in Vietnamese accounting is made, it takes longer to change the social values and beliefs needed for effective implementation of new regulations based on IASB's standards. This is due to the specific accounting environment of Vietnam, which is considered different from the institutional setting in which the IFRS were developed. As suggested in the literature review, the development of accounting systems in a country is largely a function of environmental factors (Gray, 1988; Doupnik and Salter, 1995; Nobes, 1998). It implies that researchers should adopt an institutional framework and culture of accounting to study insight into the challenges of adopting IASB's standards. The accounting framework developed by Gernon and Wallace (1995) is an example. This is important because it allows researchers to examine contextual issues, such as social, organisational and professional environments, that influence the implementation of IFRS in a country. Moreover, it is seen that the IFRS may not really be appropriate for Vietnam at the current time. Vietnamese regulators need to explore and apply lessons from past experiences of developing countries and transition economies such as China and Eastern Europe, but must also be prepared to learn and adapt institutions to the practical needs of Vietnam with its unique political, economic and social institutions. Academic research can inform and provide feedback into a dynamic regulation process in several ways. First, research explores lessons from implementing IFRS in developing countries from which Vietnam can learn. Second, academic research is able to provide insights in assessing the successes and failures of the implementation of IFRS in developing countries. Such insights should be taken into account by regulators interested in adapting IFRS to the country.

Notes

1 According to the General Statistics Office, SOEs contribute 34.35 per cent GDP in 2008 and 28.8 per cent in 2016. In 2015 SOE assets were at 80 per cent of GDP. http://vietnamnews.vn/economy/271002/soe-assets-at-80-of-gdp.html#5MVwZ58BPHJ4klDy.97.
2 See Bruton *et al.* (2015: 92).
3 Vietnam signed with the ASEAN Free Trade Area in 1995; joined APEC in 1998; signed Free Trade Agreements with the United States, Japan, Chile, South Korea, the Eurasian Economic Union and the European Union; became a member of the WTO in late 2006 and of the Asian Economic community

in late 2015; and signed the Comprehensive and Progressive Agreement for Trans-Pacific Partnership in 2016.
4 Held by Ministry of Planning and Investment and the World Bank on 5 December 2014. www.mpi. gov.vn/en/Pages/tinbai.aspx?idTin=619&idcm=133.
5 Circular No. 200/2014/TT-BTC dated 22 December 2014.
6 This model is noted by Tyrrall *et al.* (2007).
7 Interview in *Stocks Investment*, 12 April 2009, with Mr Dang Van Thanh, former director of the Department of Accounting Policies, Ministry of Finance and now president of the Vietnam Association of Accountants and Auditors.
8 Interview in *Stocks Investment*, 10 August 2008, with Mr Bui Van Mai, director of the Department of Accounting Policies at the time.
9 Before 2018, its name was the Department of Accounting Policy.
10 Decision No. 1563/1998 QD-BTC dated 30 October 1998.
11 Decision No. 276/QD-BTC dated 28 March 2000.

References

Anh, N. T. (2006). Fiscal risks from the perspective of state-owned enterprises in Vietnam, in *Paper Under Sponsorship of Ministry of Finance of Vietnam*. Presented at APEC Finance Ministers' Meeting, Hanoi (in Vietnamese).
Ball, R., Kothari, S. P. and Robin, A. (2000). The effect of international institutional factors on properties of accounting earnings. *Journal of Accounting and Economics*, 29(1), 1–51.
Bergeret, P. (2002). *Paysans, Etat et marchés au Vietnam: Dix ans de coopération agricole dans le bassin du Fleuve rouge*. Karthala Editions. www.karthala.com/1157-paysans-etat-et-marches-au-vietnam-978284 5861923.html.
Bruton, G. D., Peng, M. W., Ahlstrom, D., Stan, C. and Xu, K. (2015). State-owned enterprises around the world as hybrid organizations. *The Academy of Management Perspectives*, 29(1), 92–114.
Doupnik, T. S. and Salter, S. B. (1995). External environment, culture and accounting practice: A preliminary test of a general model of international accounting development. *The International Journal of Accounting*, 30(3), 189–207.
Gernon, H. and Wallace, R. O. (1995). International accounting research: A review of its ecology, contending theories and methodologies. *Journal of Accounting Literature*, 14, 54–106.
Gray, S. J. (1988). Towards a theory of cultural influence on the development of accounting systems internationally. *Abacus*, 24(1), 1–15.
Hopper, T. (2012). *Handbook of Accounting and Development*. Edward Elgar Publishing.
Huong, N. T. T. and Thuy, N. T. T. (2016). Vietnam's securities market: 16 years of establishment and development (2000–2016). *Nomura Journal of Asian Capital Markets*, 1(1), 31–39. www.nomura foundation.or.jp/wordpress/wp-content/uploads/2016/10/NJACM1-1AU16-09_Vietnam.pdf (accessed 18 July 2018).
McCormick, B. L. (1998). Political change in China and Vietnam: Coping with the consequences of economic reform. *The China Journal*, 40, 121–143.
Ministry of Finance (1995). *Enterprise Accounting System*. Ministry of Finance, Hanoi, Vietnam (in Vietnamese).
Ministry of Finance (2006). *Enterprise Accounting System*. Ministry of Finance, Hanoi, Vietnam (in Vietnamese).
Narayan, F. B. and Godden, T. (2000). *Financial Management and Governance Issues in Vietnam*. Asian Development Bank, Manila.
National Financial Supervisory Commission (2016). Financial market overview report in 2016. http://nfsc.gov.vn/sites/default/files/bctq2016_final.pdf (in Vietnamese) (accessed 25 July 2018).
National Financial Supervisory Commission (2017). *Report on Economic and Financial Situation in 2017, Outlook for 2018*. Document for government meeting in December 2017. http://nfsc.gov.vn/sites/default/files/bccp2017m12_final.pdf (in Vietnamese) (accessed 25 July 2018).
Nguyen, L., Hooper, K. and Sinclair, R. (2013). Conservatism versus change in the Vietnamese accounting field. *Corporate Ownership & Control*, 11(1), 471–482.
Nobes, C. (1998). Towards a general model of the reasons for international differences in financial reporting. *Abacus*, 34(2), 162–187.
Perera, H. (2012). Adoption of international financial reporting standards in developing countries, in *Handbook of Accounting and Development*. Edward Elgar Publishing: Cheltenham, 95–107.

Phan, D., Joshi, M. and Mascitelli, B. (2018). What influences the willingness of Vietnamese accountants to adopt International Financial Reporting Standards (IFRS) by 2025? *Asian Review of Accounting*, 26(2), 225–247.

Phuong, N. C. (2012). *Global Economic Integration and Developing Vietnamese Accounting from 1995: Reality, Challenges and Prospects.* Working paper, College of Economics, University of Danang: 1–93.

Phuong, N. C. and Nguyen, T. D. K. (2012). International harmonization and national particularities of accounting: Recent accounting development in Vietnam. *Journal of Accounting & Organizational Change*, 3(8), 431–451.

Phuong, N. C. and Richard, J. (2011). Economic transition and accounting system reform in Vietnam. *European Accounting Review*, 20(4), 693–725.

Prime Minister (2013). Decision N. 480/QD-TTg on approval of accounting-auditing development strategy to 2020, vision 2030, 18 March 2013. http://congbao.chinhphu.vn/noi-dung-van-ban-so-480-qd-ttg-3778?cbid=1633 (in Vietnamese).

The National Assembly of Vietnam (1992). *The 1992 Constitution of the Socialist Republic of Vietnam* (amended 25 December 2001), Hanoi, Vietnam (in Vietnamese).

The National Assembly of Vietnam (2003). *Law on Accounting,* No *03/2003/QH11.* Hanoi, Vietnam (in Vietnamese).

The National Assembly of Vietnam (2013). *The 2013 Constitution of the Socialist Republic of Vietnam.* Hanoi, Vietnam (in Vietnamese).

The National Assembly of Vietnam (2015). *Law on Accounting No 88/2015/QH13.* Hanoi, Vietnam (in Vietnamese).

Tho, T. V. (2009). Vietnamese gradualism in reforms of the state-owned enterprises: The first phase of Doi Moi, in Ichimura, S., Sato, T. and James W. (Eds.), *Transition from Socialist to Market Economies.* Palgrave Macmillan: London.

Tu Anh. V. T. (2014a). The political economy of industrial development in Vietnam: Impact of state–business relationship on industrial performance, 1986–2013, in Page, J. and Tarp, F. (Eds.), *The Practice of Industrial Policy: Government–Business Coordination in Africa and East Asia.* Oxford: Oxford University Press, 167–190.

Tu Anh, V. T. (2014b). WTO accession and the political economy of state-owned enterprise reform in Vietnam. GEG working paper 2014/92. www.geg.ox.ac.uk/sites/geg.bsg.ox.ac.uk/files/GEG%20WP_92%20WTO%20Accession%20and%20the%20Political%20Economy%20in%20Vietnam.pdf (accessed 15 January 2016).

Tyrrall, D., Woodward, D. and Rakhimbekova, A. (2007). The relevance of International Financial Reporting Standards to a developing country: Evidence from Kazakhstan. *The International Journal of Accounting*, 42(1), 82–110.

Vo Thanh Tri and Le Xuan Sang (2012). Restructuring the financial system of Vietnam: Problems and orientation of solutions. Presented at the 2012 Spring Economic Forum: *Vietnam's economy in 2012: Strong restructuring the economy* (in Vietnamese).

World Bank (2013). Report on the Observance of Standards and Codes: Corporate governance country assessment for Vietnam. http://documents.worldbank.org/curated/en/695081468129601987/Vietnam-Report-on-the-Observance-of-Standards-and-Codes-ROSC-corporate-governance-country-assessment (accessed 8 November 2018).

Xiao, J. Z., Weetman, P. and Sun, M. (2004). Political influence and coexistence of a uniform accounting system and accounting standards: recent developments in China. *Abacus*, 40(2), 193–218.

8

THE ADOPTION OF IFRS IN EIGHT SOUTH ASIAN COUNTRIES

The institutional context

Muhammad Jahangir Ali, Kamran Ahmed and Mohammad Zakaria Masud

Introduction

The purpose of this chapter is to assess the corporate reporting environments and adoption of IFRS in the countries of the South Asian Association for Regional Cooperation (SAARC). SAARC was established in 1985 by seven countries, these being Bangladesh, Bhutan, India, Maldives, Nepal, Pakistan and Sri Lanka. The objective was to develop regional cooperation and enhance economic growth in South Asia (SAARC, 2018). Afghanistan joined SAARC in 2005. According to the Asian Development Bank (ADB, 2018) most South Asian countries achieved on average 6.7 per cent economic growth in 2017 except for Sri Lanka, Afghanistan and Maldives. Since the adoption of liberal economic policies nearly two decades ago foreign direct and indirect investments have increased significantly. The capital markets are now open for international investors in local companies. However, transparency, higher levels of disclosure, quality accounting and audit practices are important if investors are to make informed decisions (Assenso-Okofo *et al.*, 2011). The environmental factors that influence accounting and reporting practices in South Asian countries (for example, Ashraf and Ghani (2005) on Pakistan; Ali and Ahmed (2007) on India, Pakistan and Bangladesh) have also not been widely reported. However, these analyses of South Asia have not covered the financial reporting practices in the other five SAARC countries, namely, Afghanistan, Bhutan, Maldives, Nepal and Sri Lanka. The gap in our knowledge is filled here by looking at all eight SAARC countries to describe and explain the comprehensive corporate reporting environments and the extent of IFRS adoption in these countries. In this way, the chapter makes a substantial contribution to the international accounting literature.

SAARC – an outline

India is the largest of the SAARC countries with a total population of 1.3 billion and is likely to become the most populous nation by 2028 (BBC, 2018). The GDP (gross domestic product) growth rate of India has been stable for the past decade and was 6.89 per cent in 2017 (World Bank, 2017). India was part of the British Empire for approximately 200 years until August 1947 when India and Pakistan were divided into two independent nations (Ali and Ahmed, 2007). Pakistan is the second largest nation in South Asia and it covers an area of 796,095 km² and its total population is 193 million (BBC, 2018). According to the World Bank, the GDP growth rate in Pakistan was 4.6 per cent in 2017, lower than India's. Bangladesh (formerly known as East Pakistan) was a part of Pakistan but gained its independence in 1971. The country is densely populated with 162 million people living in an area covering 143,998 km² (BBC, 2018). The GDP growth rate of Bangladesh was 7.30 per cent in 2017 (World Bank, 2017). Like India, Sri Lanka was ruled by the British for about 150 years and became an independent country in 1948. The country's total area is 65,610 km², comprising 21.2 million people (BBC, 2018). In 2017, Sri Lanka had the lowest GDP growth rate and this was 3.1 per cent due to the adverse weather conditions (World Bank, 2017).

Unlike other South Asian countries, Nepal was not a colony of another country. However, it was a buffer state between China and India (Lawoti and Hangen, 2013). Its area and population are about 147,181 km² and 31 million. The Word Bank reports shows that Nepal's economic growth reached 7.85 per cent in the 2017 financial year due to the influx of investment. Bhutan, which is located between India and China, is one of the smallest of the SAARC nations, followed by Maldives. The total area of Bhutan is 38,364 km² and its population is about 750,000. The GDP growth rate in Bhutan was 7.36 per cent in 2017 and this was in fact the second highest among the SAARC countries. Factors contributing to this rate are the developments being made in hydroelectricity, tourism and agriculture (World Bank, 2017). Maldives has an area of only 298 km² and it is the home of 324,000 people. The GDP growth rate in Maldives was 6.19 per cent in 2017 and the important sectors of its economy are tourism, fishing and shipping (World Bank, 2017). The eighth member nation of SAARC is Afghanistan, whose total area and population are 652,864 km² and 31.6 million, respectively (BBC, 2018). Afghanistan had the lowest annual GDP growth rate (2.59 per cent) in 2017 and this was due to the adverse weather conditions, and the ongoing political uncertainty and violence that started in 2001 (World Bank, 2017).

Financial reporting regulations in SAARC countries

The corporate reporting practices implemented in the SAARC countries are influenced by their respective Companies Acts, Securities Exchange Acts and Income Tax Laws. The most important legal framework for financial reporting practices in these countries is their respective Companies Acts (Ali and Ahmed, 2007). According to these statutes, companies should keep appropriate accounting records and prepare their financial statements, including income statement, statement of changes in equity, cash flow statement and statement of financial position. Doing this provides a true and fair view at the end of the reporting period, during which an annual independent audit will be conducted, and notes prepared for accounts following local or the IASB's (International Accounting Standards Board's) standards. Table 8.1 summarises the sources of financial reporting regulations in SAARC countries.

The first Indian Companies Act was passed by the British government in 1913 and was modelled on the British Companies Act of 1908 (Marston, 1986). The Companies Act 1913 provided requirements for the preparation of corporate financial statements. This act was amended in 1956 and 2013. After the partition in 1947, Pakistan adopted the Indian Companies Act 1913 and passed the Companies Ordinance in 1984. More recently, the Act has been amended by Pakistan's parliament as the Companies Act 2017. Like Pakistan, Bangladesh also embraced the Indian Companies Act 1913, which governs the financial reporting practices of companies. The Act was amended in 1994 to cater for the changing regulatory requirements for reporting

Table 8.1 Sources of corporate reporting regulations in South Asian countries

Country	Company law	Securities exchange law	Income tax law
Afghanistan	Corporation and Limited Liability Companies Law, 2018	–	Income Tax Law, 2005
Bangladesh	Companies Act, 1994	Securities and Exchange Commission Act, 1987	Income Tax Ordinance, 1984
Bhutan	Companies Act, 2016	–	Income Tax Act, 2001
India	Companies Act, 2013	Securities and Exchange Board Act of India, 1992	Income Tax Act, 1961
Maldives	Companies Act, 1996	Securities Act, 2006	Business Profit Tax Act, 2011
Nepal	Companies Act, 2017	Securities Act 2063, 2007	Income Tax Rule 2058, 2000
Pakistan	Companies Ordinance, 1984	Securities and Exchange Commission Act, 1997	Income Tax Ordinance, 1979
Sri Lanka	Companies Act, 2007	Securities Exchange Act, 1987	Inland Revenue Department Act No. 38 of 2000

entities (Ali and Ahmed, 2007). The Companies Act No. 7, which came into effect in 2007 in Sri Lanka, contains accounting and reporting requirements for companies operating in the country. The chief regulatory requirement of Nepal is the Companies Act 2006. The first amendment was recently passed by the Nepal parliament in 2017. The first Companies Act of the Royal Kingdom of Bhutan came into force in 1989, being subsequently amended in 2000 and 2016 (ILO, 2018). The Companies Act of Maldives was enacted in 1996. In Afghanistan, the Corporation and Limited Liability Companies Law 2018 requires companies to comply with applicable standards developed by the IASB in the preparation of their financial statements.

The second regulation regarding corporate reporting in South Asian countries is the Securities Exchange Act (Ali and Ahmed, 2007). Its principal function is to standardise securities contracts and enforce equal access of disclosure of information to investors. The Securities Exchange Board of India (SEBI) Act was enacted on 30 January 1992 (amended in 2017) and it functions to protect investors' interests. The Securities Exchange Commission of Pakistan (SECP) Act was passed by the parliament in 1997 and came into force in 1999. The SECP requires that all listed companies comply with the Companies Act 2017 and IAS/IFRS in preparing their financial statements (KPMG, 2017). The purpose of this law is to develop efficient regulatory systems to protect investors and reduce systematic risk (SECP, 2018). The Bangladesh Securities Exchange Commission (BSEC) was established in 1993 to, first, protect the interests of investors in securities and, second, develop securities markets. The BSEC provides corporate reporting guidelines for companies listed on the Dhaka Stock Exchange (DSE) (Ali and Ahmed, 2007). In Sri Lanka the Securities Exchange Commission (SECS) came into effect in 1987, and was subsequently amended in 1991, 2003 and 2009. Its purpose is to protect investors' interests and develop an efficient capital market (SECS, 2018). The SECS regulates listed companies' accounting and disclosure practices. The Securities Board of Nepal (SEBON) has been operating since 7 June 1993. The Securities Act 2063, 2007 provides required guidelines for listed companies including the preparation of financial statements (SEBON, 2018). In Maldives, the Securities Act was promulgated in 2006 and its purpose is to govern securities business (CMDA, 2006). There is yet no Securities Exchange Act in Afghanistan or Bhutan due to the non-existence of stock exchanges in these two SAARC countries.

It is argued that the taxation of a country will influence its accounting practices (Al-Akra *et al.*, 2009). Tax laws are required to record revenues and expenses for tax purposes. In the SAARC countries taxes are calculated using audited income statements and balance sheets. Furthermore, companies operating in these countries are required to reconcile accounting profit and tax income to estimate taxable income (Ali and Ahmed, 2007).

Due process of accounting standards setting in SAARC countries

Reporting entities in the SAARC countries need to comply with standards developed by the local standard setters or the International Accounting Standards Board (IASB). Statutes on company law and business operations in the South Asian region require listed companies to prepare general-purpose financial statements, which must provide a true and fair view of the financial performance and financial position of the firm. However, Companies Acts do not specify the measurement methods and disclosure of elements of financial reporting (Ali and Ahmed, 2007). Therefore, listed companies must prepare their financial statements to national accounting standards/IASB's standards.

Bodies responsible for setting accounting standards

Professional bodies are involved in setting accounting standards in the SAARC countries and these bodies were developed around the British model (Ali and Ahmed, 2007). Among the SAARC countries, Bangladesh, India, Pakistan and Sri Lanka have strong professional bodies due to their large economies compared to Afghanistan, Bhutan, Nepal and Maldives. The accounting standard-setting body in India is the Institute of Chartered Accountants of India (ICAI), which is the second largest professional body of chartered accountants in the world. It was established in 1949 to regulate the chartered accountancy profession in India (ICAI, 2018a). In total, ICAI has 282,193 members of which 92,089 are fellows and 190,104 are associates (ICAI, 2018a). In Pakistan, the Institute of Chartered Accountants of Pakistan (ICAP) was formed in 1961 and it also participates in establishing regulations for several important industries. The total membership of ICAP is 7,585 including 4,444 associate members and 3,141 fellow members (ICAP, 2018). Following Bangladesh's liberation from Pakistan, The Institute of Chartered Accountants of Bangladesh (ICAB) was formed in 1973 in order to regulate the accounting profession in that country (ICAB, 2018). It has 1,544 members of whom 1,035 are fellows and 509 are associate members. The Institute of Chartered Accountants in Sri Lanka (CA Sri Lanka) was set up in 1959 and plays an important role in developing the accounting and finance profession in that country (CA Sri Lanka, 2018). The total number of fellow and associate members is 5,600. The institute is also known as one of the largest tertiary education providers, having approximately 44,000 students (CA Sri Lanka, 2018). The Institute of Chartered Accountants of Nepal (ICAN) was founded in 1997 and had 1,159 members in 2018 (ICAN, 2018). There is no institute of chartered accountancy or association to license statutory auditors in Bhutan. This is due to the paucity of private sector development and having an insignificant economy (World Bank, 2009a). CPA Afghanistan is the sole body that regulates the accountancy profession in Afghanistan. There is a lack of qualified accounting and audit professionals and only 16 accounting and audit firms are listed with the Afghanistan Investment Support Agency (AISA) (World Bank, 2009b).

Standard-setting process in SAARC countries

The growing acceptance of IFRS suggests IASB is a model for transnational standard setting (Lloyd *et al.*, 2007). However, a question is raised about how the legitimacy and accountability of the transnational standard-setting bodies are established and maintained outside the sovereignty of democratic states (Richardson and Eberlein, 2011). An important issue here is to evaluate the due process of setting accounting standards by domestic standard setters over and above what the IASB prefers. On this theme, most of the SAARC countries follow a formal process of setting accounting standards, except for Afghanistan, Bhutan and Maldives. However, unlike, Afghanistan and Bhutan, Maldives incorporates the adoption or endorsement of IFRS with different regulations (IFRS Foundation, 2018a). The degree of formalities followed by SAARC countries varies in the standard-setting process, as described below.

The ICAI (2018b: 91) in its first edition of *Impact Analysis and Industry Experience of Ind AS (IFRS Converged)* explained the standard-setting process. The Accounting Standards Board (ASB) of ICAI formulates accounting standards in India. Similar to most other countries, the standard-setting process in India began by identifying the broad area that accounting standards encapsulated. The ASB, which includes industry associations, regulators, financial institutions, and academic and professional bodies, forms a study group to prepare a preliminary draft. The ASB considers the draft and circulates it to the ICAI Council members and 12 specified outside bodies, for example, Comptroller and Auditor General, Securities and Exchange Board of India, etc. Based on feedback issued by these bodies, an exposure draft is prepared by the ASB for public comment. To make the standard-setting process more transparent, a paperless online submission and public viewing of comments was introduced (ICAI, 2018b). Thereafter, the ASB finalises the Indian domestic accounting standard (Ind AS) by accommodating all the relevant comments and submits it to the ICAI Council for approval. The National Advisory Committee on Accounting Standards (NACAS) of the Ministry of Corporate Affairs reviews the standard once the ICAI Council finalises it. The NACAS recommends the standard, if not otherwise, to the central government for notification in the *Gazette* so that it is then legally authoritative.

Similar to India, in Bangladesh, the Technical and Research Committee (TRC) of the ICAB is in charge of identifying any relevant matter concerning accounting standards. The TRC reviews national and international pronouncements on a regular basis to initiate the process. Once the issue is identified, it conducts a technical review concerning adoptability and acceptability of the issue. It follows the due process of preparing an exposure draft, receiving comments from relevant interest groups and the public before referring the proposed standard for approval to the ICAB Council.

The CA Sri Lanka develops financial reporting standards (SLFRS) based on IFRS after modifications and promulgates them by legislation. The CA Sri Lanka starts the process by preparing exposure drafts for public comment. To identify the impact of the proposed standards, unlike in other SAARC countries, CA Sri Lanka conducts round-table discussions with company chief financial officers and prepares the draft with all the comments and forwards its views to the Sri Lanka Accounting and Auditing Standards Monitoring Board. Once finalised, SLFRS are translated into both the Sinhala and Tamil languages. To make it legally authoritative, those two versions along with an English translation are gazetted and published as required by the Accounting and Auditing Standards Act No. 15 of 1995.

In Pakistan, the SECP is responsible for adopting IFRS standards by notification in the official government *Gazette* to make it legally authoritative. The process starts with identification and consideration of any issues on adoption by the Accounting Standards Committee (ASC) of the ICAP. The ASC then forwards the matter to the Professional Standards and Technical Advisory Committee (PS&TAC) (IFRS Foundation, 2018a) and shares the matter with the ICAP Council. An evaluation of the relevant adoption and implementation issues concerning the proposed matter is conducted by the PS&TAC. The Coordination Committee of the ICAP refers any amendment in local regulations necessitated by the proposed matter to the SECP and/ or the State Bank of Pakistan (SBP) (ICAP, 2017). The PS&TAC and the Council reconsider the matter after obtaining a satisfactory resolution from SECP and/or SBP. Finally, the ICAP Council decides and recommends the proposed standard to SECP and to SBP (if it concerns banks and other financial institutions). The adoption decision is finalised by SECP and SBP (IFRS Foundation, 2018a). To further consolidate corporate reporting in Pakistan, the ICAP formed the ASB in March 2017 (ICAP, 2017: 20).

Nepal adopts new or amended IFRS standards involving different bodies in the process, including accountants, regulatory bodies, the business community, academics and other interested groups (IFRS Foundation, 2018b). The Accounting Standards Board (ASB) of Nepal is the body responsible for setting accounting standards and conducting public meetings if required. Part of its remit is to also consult with the advisory council concerning major projects, work priorities and agenda decisions. Technical matters are also discussed in meetings that are open to public observation. The development procedures for Nepal Financial Reporting Standards (NFRS) begin by identifying a specific topic or issue, then this is followed by a review of relevant issues in line with the conceptual framework (IFRS Foundation, 2018b). Before consulting on the topic with the ASB members, delegated staff members need to study the national accounting requirements and practices so that the issue can be discussed with national regulators. The issue is then presented before the ASB members and the advisory group to include it (or not) in the ASB's agenda. Once the issue is included in the agenda, an advisory group and expert team work on the project to advise the ASB. A discussion document and exposure draft with different opinions voiced by ASB members are then published seeking public comments (AOSSG, 2014). Once all the comments and opinions are considered, conclusions are reached concerning the desirability of holding a public hearing and conducting a field test. A favourable conclusion leads to an approved standard getting at least seven votes from ASB members before sending it to the ICAN for pronouncement. The ICAN determines the effective dates (IFRS Foundation, 2018a).

Adoption of IFRS in SAARC countries

For listed companies in India, the SEBI permits an alternative method for parent entities to prepare and submit their consolidated financial reports either in accordance with IFRS or the Companies Act 1956, which is specified in section 211(3C). Reporting entities need to declare that their financial statements have been prepared following IFRS. Separate financial statements need to be submitted to the stock exchange following Indian GAAP (generally accepted accounting principles) (IAS plus, 2018). India decided to adopt IFRS in 2011 but this proved to be unsuccessful. On 5 January 2015, a road map was announced by the Indian Ministry of Corporate Affairs, which emphasised the convergence of Ind AS with IFRS. Under the new rules, except in banking, insurance and non-banking finance companies, if a company has a net worth of Rs5,000 million or more (approximately US$69 million), it must comply with Ind AS (which is converged with IFRS) to prepare and lodge its financial statements. This has been a requirement since April 2016. Further, if a listed company's net worth is less than Rs5,000 million, then it is required to comply with Ind AS converged with IFRS as of the beginning of April 2017 (IAS plus, 2015). However, IFRS are not permitted for unlisted companies (IAS Plus, 2018).

Listed companies in Pakistan need to comply with IFRS. The majority of IFRS and IAS are adopted by Pakistan, except, first, IFRS 1, IFRS 7, IFRS 9, IFRS 14, IFRS 15, IFRIC 4 and IFRIC 12; and second, IAS 39 and IAS 40. Currently Pakistan is considering adopting IFRS 9 for listed companies. Financial institutions are required to comply with (IAS 39, IAS 40 and IFRS 7) the recognition and measurement requirements of the State Bank of Pakistan. For other standards, listed companies comply with their own measurement and disclosure requirements. Like Bangladesh and India, IFRS are not permitted for unlisted companies in Pakistan. The SECP in Pakistan has approved the adoption of the International Financial Reporting Standard for Small and Medium-Sized Entities (IFRS for SMEs). The adoption became effective for annual financial periods beginning on or after 1 January 2015 (IAS Plus, 2018).

The ICAB issues accounting standards for the reporting entities. Bangladesh has adopted all the IFRS which are known as Bangladesh Financial Reporting Standards (BFRS). IAS are referred to as Bangladesh Accounting Standards except for IFRS 9, which is currently under review (IAS plus, 2018). Regarding Sri Lanka, IFRS are required for all listed companies, and entities also need to declare their compliance with IFRS. Some unlisted companies need to follow IFRS (IAS plus, 2018). In Nepal, local listed companies need to state that financial statements have been prepared following IFRS and unlisted companies are permitted to follow IFRS (IAS Plus, 2018). IFRS are permitted for listed companies in Maldives. For domestic listed companies, audit reports need to mention that the financial statements have been prepared following IFRS. IFRS are also permitted for domestic unlisted companies (IAS Plus, 2018). Since Afghanistan does not as yet have a stock exchange, IFRS are not applicable in this country. However, all companies need to employ IFRS to prepare their financial statements. In Bhutan, there is no requirement for companies to follow IFRS (IAS Plus, 2018).

Enforcement of and compliance with accounting standards

Scholars argue that useful standards themselves must be enforceable, either implicitly or explicitly (Sunder, 1997: 167). This is because enforcement can confirm the quality of financial information (Kothari, 2000: 92). Even the best standard will be inconsequential in the absence of adequate enforcement (Hope, 2003: 238). British colonial rule left the major countries of the SAARC region with the legacy of a common legal environment. Prior research argues that common law countries have better disclosure practices (Nobes and Parker, 2010), and hence financial reports published in these countries tend to be more transparent (although relative higher transparency does not necessarily mean perfect compliance with the disclosure requirements of accounting standards). As discussed previously, most of the SAARC countries adopted the IFRS developed by the IASB. However, the IASB lacks any direct enforcement power. Wulandari and Rahman (2004) (as cited in Al-Akra *et al.* 2009), suggested a combination of preventive and punitive measures to make enforcement effective. In the SAARC region, as in many other countries, government agencies and professional bodies are responsible for enforcing financial disclosure rules, particularly punitive measures. Table 8.2 lists the bodies having jurisdictional authority in different SAARC countries and the responsibility for enforcing accounting standards (IFRS Foundation, 2018a).

The Companies Act in most SAARC countries requires companies to file accounts with the Registrar of Companies. The Registrar oversees the level of compliance in preparation and presentation of financial statements. In Pakistan, the Enforcement and Monitoring division of SECP carries out this responsibility for all listed companies. In Sri Lanka, the Sri Lanka Accounting and Auditing Standards Monitoring Board is responsible for monitoring compliance of all specified business enterprises (SLAASMB, 2018). In Maldives, companies are required to deliver

Table 8.2 Bodies responsible for implementing IFRS in SAARC countries

Country	Enforcement bodies
Afghanistan	Da Afghanistan Bank (the Central Bank of Afghanistan)
Bangladesh	The Institute of Chartered Accountants of Bangladesh
Bhutan	Accounting and Auditing Standards Board of Bhutan
India	The Institute of Chartered Accountants of India
Maldives	Capital Market Development Authority
Nepal	Accounting Standards Board, Nepal
Pakistan	The Institute of Chartered Accountants of Pakistan
	Securities and Exchange Commission of Pakistan
Sri Lanka	The Institute of Chartered Accountants of Sri Lanka

copies of their financial statements and audit reports to the Registrar. However, the Registrar's office does not have enough technical expertise and so the Registrar is not well positioned to perform his role effectively (World Bank, 2000: 73).

The professional accountancy bodies of these countries initiate enforcement and ensure compliance, directing their members to examine compliance issues with accounting standards while conducting audits. The Financial Reporting Review Board of ICAI and the Compliance and Monitoring Committee of ICAB act to identify non-complying firms/auditors so that appropriate measures can be implemented. ICAP conducts a process of quality control review for all listed firms to impose proper punishment on non-complying entities. ICAN established an independent Quality Assurance Board in 2015 for mandatory quality assurance reviews (IFAC, 2018) of companies listed on the securities exchange, banks, insurance companies and public sector undertakings. Although the accounting practices of SAARC countries are influenced by British colonial precedents, when compared to developed countries the extent of standard enforcement and compliance is lower and the actions against non-complying entities are rarely evident in this region (ADB, 2013).

The role of the South Asian Federation of Accountants in improving corporate reporting in SAARC countries

The South Asian Federation of Accountants (SAFA), a forum of professional accountancy bodies in the SAARC region, works towards positioning, maintaining and developing the accountancy profession in the region. It works closely with international accountancy bodies like IASB and IFAC and other regional accountancy bodies.

The SAFA promotes integrated reporting in the SAARC region and is collaborating with the International Integrated Reporting Council. It circulates different exposure drafts and consultation papers produced by IFAC/IASB to its member bodies, and shares the views expressed by one member body with other bodies, to make them more suitable for the region. SAFA's award for the best-presented annual reports under different categories promotes high-quality reporting practices according to the international framework that member countries adhere to. Moreover, the recognition of best corporate governance disclosure (through the SAARC Anniversary Award) and integrated reporting practice (through the Integrated Reporting Award) promotes high-quality reporting practices in the region.

In establishing professional accountancy bodies, SAFA is assisting Afghanistan, Bhutan and Maldives through its technical expertise and in obtaining financial support (SAFA, 2017). With an objective to develop the accountancy profession in the SAARC region, SAFA stated several action plans in its annual activity report for 2017. One priority target is regional harmonisation of the accountancy profession with a focus on issues like education, accounting, auditing and professional/ethical standards. Launching the SAFA Virtual Knowledge and Training Centre for e-learning is one step taken to achieve this particular objective. Arranging seminars, technical workshops and international conferences are routine aspects of SAFA annual plans and programmes. Considering all the steps taken by SAFA, it seems SAFA's actions are more about knowledge sharing and building awareness than developing accounting standards.

The role of capital markets in improving corporate reporting in SAARC countries

Many studies support the fact that a well-developed capital market attracts capital for economic development (Levine and Zervos, 1998), ensuring investors' confidence (Assenso-Okofo *et al.*, 2011), and promotes good accounting and disclosure practices (Adhikari and Tondkar, 1992). Considerable progress has been made in the capital markets of the SAARC region during the last 25 years. Most of the countries in this region operate structured and regulated capital markets. Moreover, studies also found market size and the level of market development are considerably different from country to country (ADB, 2013).

The largest capital market in the SAARC region is that of India with more than 7,600 listed companies (Statistica, 2017) traded mostly in two major nationwide stock exchanges and 21 regional stock exchanges. Total trading is split approximately 80 : 20 between the Bombay Stock Exchange (BSE) and the National Stock Exchange (NSE) (ADB, 2013). One study on stock market development and economic growth in the SAARC countries shows market capitalisation is the most representative indicator of capital markets' growth (Muktadir-Al-Mukit *et al.*, 2014). Market capitalisation in India is worth approximately US$4.27 trillion (BSE, 2018; NSE, 2018). BSE and NSE are the world's tenth and eleventh largest stock exchanges, respectively (*The Hindu*, 2018). The Securities and Exchange Board of India is the single securities regulator and it regulates securities markets including mutual funds.

The Dhaka Stock Exchange and Chittagong Stock Exchange are the two stock exchanges in Bangladesh and are regulated by the BSEC. The market is of significant size with 307 listed companies and market capitalisation, worth approximately US$85 billion (DSE, 2018; CSE, 2018a). Similar to Bangladesh, Pakistan's capital market operates under the jurisdiction of the SECP and with three stock exchanges: Islamabad Stock Exchange, Karachi Stock Exchange and Lahore Stock Exchange. The number of listed companies in Pakistan is 836 with market capitalisation being worth approximately US$71 billion (PSX, 2018). For Sri Lanka, the Colombo Stock Exchange is the only stock exchange and it has 298 listed companies and market capitalisation worth nearly US$18.08 billion (CSE, 2018b). The country's capital market is regulated by the Securities Exchange Commission Sri Lanka. Similar to Sri Lanka, the only stock exchange in Nepal is the Nepal Stock Exchange with 211 listed companies and market capitalisation of approximately US$12.57 billion (NEPSE, 2018). The Securities Board of Nepal regulates the securities market including mutual funds. The Ministry of Finance has day-to-day involvement in the management and operations of the exchange (ADB, 2013).

Regarding the smallest SAARC countries, Bhutan operates a very small capital market with only 21 listed companies and market capitalisation is worth about US$730 million (RSEB, 2018). The only stock exchange in Bhutan is the Royal Securities Exchange of Bhutan and it is regulated by a department under the auspices of the Royal Monetary Authority. Like Bhutan the capital market in Maldives is very small. The number of listed companies on the Maldives

Stock Exchange is 9, the level of market capitalisation is approximately US$899 million (MVSE, 2018) and the capital market is regulated by the Capital Market Development Authority. It can be stated here that the basic features of the capital markets in SAARC countries include requirement for prospectuses, corporate disclosure, prohibition of market abuse, governance codes and accountancy standards. SAARC markets are closed to foreign companies, open to foreign brokers for the purpose of setting up local subsidiaries, and there is only limited interest in treating the SAARC region as a worthwhile investment destination by its member countries (ADB, 2013).

Future directions

Our chapter has traced the institutional context within which all the SAARC countries have moved towards adopting the majority, or all, of the IFRS/IAS (Bhutan is the exception). Prior research has indicated either no, or very little, evidence of any punitive measures taken by the regulators against any listed companies for non-compliance with accounting standards. It is encouraging that SAFA is working to improve the financial reporting quality through discussions, seminars and training opportunities, and providing prizes for preparing the best annual reports. It is expected that financial reporting practices will be improved after adoption of the whole set of IFRS by 2021 in the region. Full adoption will provide opportunities to evaluate the success of the project.

Our study is descriptive in nature, in setting out the historical influences and development of accounting regulation in moving towards IFRS and it provides avenues for future research. The detail provided in this chapter will help in understanding the financial reporting regulations within SAARC countries. Future research likely to be conducted will use annual report data to test whether the adoption of IFRS in these countries has any influence on accounting earnings quality, harmonisation of reporting practices in terms of presentation and contents both cross country and over time, firm performance and valuation, taxation, cost of financing and flow of capital into this region. It would be worthwhile to assess whether firms belonging to business groups and family firms are better off in adopting IFRS and whether compliance with IFRS is greater for these firms compared with firms not belonging to family or business groups (standalone). Future research is also likely to be conducted in investigating the role of corporate governance in improving financial reporting quality in SAARC countries. The empirical research in the region is interesting because SAARC countries have been experiencing significant economic growth during the last three decades due to the availability of a skilled labour force at relatively low wages. Therefore, the findings of future research are likely to be informative to international investors planning to transfer their resources in SAARC countries.

References

All URLs were checked for access in November 2018.

ADB (2013). Development of capital markets in member countries of the South Asian Association for Regional Cooperation. Asian Development Bank. IDEAS Working Paper Series from RePEc. www.adb.org/sites/default/files/publication/31110/development-capital-markets-saarc-member-countries.pdf.
ADB (2018). *South Asia: Economy*. Asian Development Bank. www.adb.org/data/south-asia-economy.
Adhikari, A. and Tondkar, R. H. (1992). Environmental factors influencing accounting disclosure requirements of global stock exchanges. *Journal of International Financial Management & Accounting*, 4, 75–105. doi:10.1111/j.1467-646X.1992.tb00024.x.
Al-Akra, M., Ali, M. J. and Marashdeh, O. (2009). Development of accounting regulation in Jordan. *The International Journal of Accounting*, 44(2), 163–186.

Ali, M. J. and Ahmed, K. (2007). The legal and institutional framework for corporate financial reporting in South Asia. *Research in Accounting Regulation*, 19, 175–205.

AOSSG (2014). Report on standard setting capacity in Nepal: Building regional capacity initiative. Asian-Oceanian Standard Setters Group. www.aossg.org/docs/news/.

Ashraf, J. and Ghani, W. I. (2005). Accounting development in Pakistan. *The International Journal of Accounting*, 40, 175–201.

Assenso-Okofo, O., Ali, M. J. and Ahmed, K. (2011). The development of accounting and reporting in Ghana. *The International Journal of Accounting*, 46(4), 459–480.

BBC (2018). India country profile. www.bbc.com/news/world-south-asia.

BSE (2018). Bombay Stock Exchange Limited. www.bseindia.com.

CA Sri Lanka (2018). The Institute of Chartered Accountants in Sri Lanka. www.casrilanka.com/casl/.

CMDA (2006). Capital Market Development Authority. www.cmda.gov.mv/docs/securities_act_english.

CSE (2018a). Chittagong Stock Exchange. http://cse.com.bd/market/historical_market.

CSE (2018b). Colombo Stock Exchange. www.cse.lk/home/listByAlphabetical.

DSE (2018). Dhaka Stock Exchange limited. www.dsebd.org/recent market_information.php.

Hope, O. (2003). Disclosure practices, enforcement of accounting standards, and analysts' forecast accuracy: An international study. *Journal of Accounting Research*, 41(2): 235–272.

IAS Plus (2015). Roadmap for application of IFRS converged standards in India released, notification to follow 'shortly'. Deloitte. www.iasplus.com/en/news/2015/01/india.

IAS Plus (2018). Use of IFRS by jurisdictions. Deloitte. www.iasplus.com/en/resources/ifrs-topics/use-of-ifrs.

ICAB (2018). The Institute of Chartered Accountants of Bangladesh. www.icab.org.bd/icabweb/web-GeneralContent/view/14245.

ICAI (2018a). The Institute of Chartered Accountants of India. www.icai.org.

ICAI (2018b). Indian Accounting Standards (IFRS converged): Successful Implementation, Impact Analysis and Industry Experience (1st Ed.), ICAI: New Delhi. https://resource.cdn.icai.org/50820indas40481b.pdf.

ICAN (2018). The Institute of Chartered Accountants of Nepal. www.ican.org.np/new/.

ICAP (2017). ICAP annual report. www.icap.org.pk/wp-content/uploads/annualreports/ICAP-annualreport-2017.pdf.

ICAP (2018). The Institute of Chartered Accountants of Pakistan. www.icap.org.pk /icap/about-icap/.

IFAC (2018). International Federation of Accountants. www.ifac.org/about-ifac/membership/country/nepal.

IFRS Foundation (2018a). International Financial Reporting Standards Foundation. www.ifrs.org.

IFRS Foundation (2018b). International Financial Reporting Standards Foundation – Nepal. www.ifrs.org/use-around-the-world/use-of-ifrs-standards-by-jurisdiction/nepal/.

ILO (2018). International Labour Organization: Promoting jobs, protecting people. www.ilo.org/wcmsp5/groups/public/@dgreports/@dcomm/documents/meetingdocument/wcms_113995.pdf.

Kothari, S. P. (2000). The role of financial reporting in reducing financial risks, in Rosengren, E. S. and Jordan, J. S. (Eds.), *The Market in Building an Infrastructure for Financial Stability*. Federal Reserve Bank of Boston Conference Series No. 44, 89–102.

KPMG (2017). A brief on the Companies Act, 2017. https://home.kpmg.com/pk/en/home/insights/2017/07/a-brief-on-the-companies-act–2017.html.

Lawoti, M. and Hangen, S. (2013). *Nationalism and Ethnic Conflict in Nepal: Identities and Mobilization after 1990*. Routledge Contemporary South Asia series. London: Routledge, 58.

Levine, R. and Zervos, S. (1998). Stock Markets, Banks, and Economic Growth. *The American Economic Review*, 88(3), 537–558.

Lloyd, R., Oatham, J. and Hammer, M. (2007). *Global Accountability Report*. London: One World Trust.

Marston, C. (1986). *Financial Reporting in India*. London: Croom Helm.

Muktadir-Al-Mukit, D., Uddin, M., Islam, M. and Arif, M. (2014). Stock market development and economic growth: Evidence from SAARC countries. *ANVESHAK-International Journal of Management*, 3(1), 45–58.

MVSE (2018). Maldives Stock Exchange. https://stockexchange.mv/.

NEPSE (2018). Nepal Stock Exchange Limited. www.nepalstock.com.

Nobes, C. W. and Parker, R. H. (2010). *Comparative International Accounting*, 11th ed. Hemel Hempstead: Prentice Hall.

NSE (2018). National Stock Exchange. www.nseindia.com/index_nse.htm.

PSX (2018). Pakistan Stock Exchange Limited. www.psx.com.pk.

Richardson, A. and Eberlein, B. (2011). Legitimating transnational standard-setting: The case of the International Accounting Standards Board. *Journal of Business Ethics*, 98(2), 217–245.

RSEB (2018). Royal Securities Exchange of Bhutan. www.rsebl.org.bt/index.

SAARC (2018). The South Asian Association for Regional Cooperation. http://saarc-sec.org/about-saarc.

SAFA (2017). Annual activity report. South Asian Federation of Accountants. www. esafa.org.

SEBON (2018). The Securities Board of Nepal. http://sebon.gov.np/content/introduction.

SECP (2018). The Securities Exchange Commission of Pakistan. www.secp.gov.pk/about-us/vision-and-mission/.

SECS (2018). The Securities Exchange Commission of Sri Lanka. www.sec.gov.lk.

SLAASMB (2018). Sri Lanka Accounting and Auditing Standards Monitoring Board. http://slaasmb.gov.lk/.

Statistica (2017). Number of companies listed in NSE and BSE across India from FY 2000 to FY 2017. www.statista.com/statistics/731969/india-number-of-companies-listed-in-nse-and-bse/.

Sunder, S. (1997). *Theory of Accounting and Control*. Cincinnati, OH: South-Western Publishing.

The Hindu (2018). BSE in the top 10 league as market cap vaults to $1.6 trillion. www.thehindubusinessline.com/markets/stock-markets.

World Bank (2000). Country financial accountability assessment – Republic of Maldives. http://site resources.worldbank.org/SOUTHASIAEXT/Resources/.

World Bank (2009a). Bhutan: Report on Observance of Standards and Codes (ROSC), accounting and auditing. http://documents.worldbank.org/curated/en/202401468017438110/pdf/495770ESW0BT0 P1C0Disclosed081171091.pdf.

World Bank (2009b). Afghanistan: Report on Observance of Standards and Codes (ROSC), accounting and auditing. http://documents.worldbank.org/curated/en/532691467994629084/Afghanistan-Report-on-Observance-of-Standards-and-Codes-ROSC-accounting-and-auditing.

World Bank (2017). The World Bank. https://data.worldbank.org/country.

Wulandari, E. R. and Rahman, A. R. (2004). A Cross Country Study on the Quality, Acceptability, and Enforceability of Accounting Standards and the Value Relevance of Accounting Earnings. Singapore: OECD Working Paper.

9

USEFULNESS OF ACCOUNTING INFORMATION TO PROFESSIONAL INVESTORS IN AN IFRS ENVIRONMENT

The case of China

Guoqiang Hu, Hui Lin and Jason Zezhong Xiao

Introduction

Examination of users' information needs has mainly been undertaken in developed economies. In contrast, there is little study of users' information needs in emerging and transition economies (Ionaşcu *et al.*, 2014). This chapter addresses three questions: (1) Is accounting information useful in professional users' investment decision making relative to other information? (2) What role does accounting information play in professional investors' investment decision making (confirmative vs predictive)? (3) How do professional investor characteristics affect their perception of the usefulness of accounting information?

We examine these questions in the context of China because China is the largest emerging and transitional economy, one of the largest recipients of inward investment and one of the largest outward investors. Its domestic stock markets, while growing rapidly in terms of the number of listed firms, have experienced major turbulence on several occasions since their inception in the early 1990s. One of the main reasons for the occurrence of such upheavals is the existence of information asymmetry. To alleviate this problem, it is important to study and understand users' information needs.

We focus on Chinese professional investors because they are more sophisticated than private investors in China, but are less sophisticated and less experienced than their counterparts in developed markets (Hu *et al.*, 2003a; Mei *et al.*, 2009).

Background

The economy

China's gross domestic product (GDP) rose to over US$12.238 trillion in 2017. It has been the largest economy in the world by monetary purchasing power since 2014 according to the International Monetary Fund (IMF, 2014). Although the GDP growth is expected to slow down to between 6 and 7 per cent or even below 6 per cent in future years according to the *Report on the Work of the Government* (The State Council, 2018), it is comparatively high and indicates that China will continue to be a major contributor to the world economy.

Despite rising trade protectionism, China is likely to continue to adopt an open-door policy. An important vehicle of this policy is the Belt and Road Initiative which aims to strengthen the link between China and the global economy through developing the economic belt along the historic Silk Road and building up a new marine Silk Road. In parallel, China has created several regional or international organisations such as the Asia Infrastructure Investment Bank. China has also launched a campaign to internationalise its currency so that the renminbi (RMB) will become an international currency. RMB-denominated assets can then be used as an investment vehicle internationally and RMB will be used to settle transactions internationally.

The stock market

Since the establishment of the Shanghai Stock Exchange (SHSE) and Shenzhen Stock Exchange (SZSE) in the early 1990s, the Chinese stock market has grown rapidly. At the end of 2017, there were 3,485 listed firms, with a total market value of more than RMB56.7 trillion (about US$8.7 trillion). According to Zeng (2018), by the end of 2016 there were nearly 1.2 billion securities investors, of which only 326,200 were institutional investors.

Despite the rapid growth of the stock market, the level of securitisation in China is still low compared with more mature markets (Zeng, 2018) but continues to grow. One recent development is to connect the Chinese stock exchange with overseas stock exchanges (such as Hong Kong and London) so that investors can purchase securities traded at the overseas markets via qualified Chinese securities brokers and vice versa, in addition to allowing qualified foreign institutional investors (QFII) and Renminbi-qualified foreign institutional investors (RQFII) to operate in China.

The securities investment consulting industry

By June 2018, there were 2,753 professional financial analysts (including buy-side and sell-side analysts) working in 121 securities corporates and 8 securities investment consultant corporates in China.[1] According to the China Stock Market and Accounting Research database, 1,648 sell-side analysts issued 44,071 research reports on 2,494 A-share listed firms (81.72 per cent of the number of A-share listed firms) in 2016. The average analyst followed 1.51 firms and issued 26.74 research reports.

The Securities Association of China (SAC) was founded on 28 August 1991 as a nationwide self-disciplinary organisation. SAC is a not-for-profit social institutional legal-person function under the guidance and supervision of the China Securities Regulatory Commission (CSRC) and Ministry of Civil Affairs of China. To regulate the financial analysts' behaviour, the SAC established the Securities Analysts Committee on 5 July 2000. This was a milestone in the development of China's financial analyst industry. Under the leadership of the SAC, the Committee aims to enhance self-regulation and research and establish relevant self-regulatory rules and practice standards, and boost the practice quality of securities analysts, facilitate exchanges among securities analysts, and protect their interests.

China's securities investment funds (SIF) industry emerged in the early 1990s. The publication of *Temporary Measures for the Administration of Securities Investment Fund* by the Securities Committee of the State Council (SCSC) on 14 November 1997 is a milestone for the development of China's SIF industry.[2] The CSRC began to regulate the industry in 1997, and the first batch of SIF companies was founded in March 1998, such as Guotai Asset Management and China Southern Asset Management. By March 2018, there were 116 public fund management companies in China, with 12.37 trillion RMB assets (about $1.82 trillion) which is about 15 per cent of China's 2017 GDP and 5,085 funds.[3] The public funds industry employed 19,072 qualified people by 2016. Meanwhile, 17,988 managers in private SIF operated 46,010 private SIF products amounting to RMB8.25 trillion (about $1.21 billion) and employed about half a million qualified workers at the end of 2016.[4] To strengthen the management of the SIF industry, the Asset Management Association of China was founded on 6 June 2012. Before that, the CSRC was the main regulator of the SIF industry.[5]

Despite these developments, some problems remain. For example, Zeng (2018) argues that the securities investment consulting firms are still too small, their use of technology is lagged and there is a lack of high-end specialists resulting in an overall low level of analysis capacity. This means that there will be a need for many more qualified financial analysts, especially high-end specialists.

The regulation of, demand for, and supply of accounting information

All Chinese listed firms are required to publish an annual report within four months after the end of a fiscal year, an interim report within two months after the end of the first half of a fiscal year and quarterly reports within one month following the end of the first and third quarters.

All annual reports are required to be audited by a qualified CPA firm, and even interim reports are audited if the firm intends to distribute profits, transfer reserves into share capital or use reserves to make up for losses in the next half of the fiscal year. The directors and executives of the listed firms are required to certify that these publicly disclosed reports are true, complete and reliable and there is no false statement. Together, these reporting requirements help improve the quality of information disclosed by Chinese listed firms.

Nevertheless, China's financial markets continue to suffer from weak information systems and the resulting low quality of accounting information (Piotroski and Wong, 2011). The results from numerous country reports and surveys show that transparency of accounting and financial information in China continues to lag behind many developed and developing countries (e.g. WEF, 2018). Stock prices in China are more susceptible to crash (Piotroski and Wong, 2011), with stronger momentum effects and higher synchronised stock price movements (Gul *et al.*, 2010). These characteristics are closely related to the weak information environments in China's stock markets.

Several institutional factors exist to attenuate the demand for and supply of information in China's capital market (Piotroski and Wong, 2011). On the demand side, because of the highly concentrated ownership in Chinese listed firms, the demand for accounting information in a listed firm is significantly weaker than that of a US firm with diffuse ownership. As the predominant non-controlling shareholders in Chinese listed firms, retail investors have limited resources for, and little experience in, using financial accounting information (Xu and Wang, 1999), and tend to be sensitive to short-term sentiment effects (Choi *et al.*, 2012). This reduces their demand for and use of financial information. Additionally, in the current institutional environment in China, the demand for high-quality external auditing is also lower because of the highly concentrated ownership, large likelihood of a government bailout, and relationship-based transactions.

On the supply side, given the use of bright-line accounting-based rules by the China Securities Regulatory Commission to screen firms for rights offerings and delisting, Chinese listed firms have strong incentives to manage earnings (Chen and Yuan, 2004; Haw *et al.*, 2005).

Moreover, compared to an oligopolistic market structure such as the US, the Chinese audit market is much more dispersed (Guan *et al.*, 2016).[6] The fierce competition of audit market, together with ineffective enforcement of laws (Allen *et al.*, 2005), makes it more likely that an audit firm will yield to managerial pressure and thus provide low audit quality. Also, information intermediaries such as financial analysts and media are not fulfilling a key informational role in China (Piotroski and Wong, 2011), further lowering the supply of information.

In summary, the institutional arrangements in China affect the demand for and supply of high-quality information, and thus restrict the usefulness of accounting information. Nevertheless, the continuing improvements prompt us to investigate the usefulness of accounting information to market investors in China. For example, Chinese regulators stipulated a new set of accounting standards in 2006, largely based on IFRS, and over 23 of them require or permit the use of fair value measurement or disclosures. However, it is not clear whether investors have a strong demand for forward-looking accounting information in China.

Literature review

Accounting information is found to be a critical source in the process of financial analysts' decision making since the establishment of capital markets (Hope, 2003). Although accounting information remains important in the decision-making process of investors, its value to users is declining (Hail, 2013). Recent studies confirm that non-financial information, as a useful supplement to financial information, can improve the accuracy of analysts' forecasts and decrease forecast dispersion (Orens and Lybaert, 2007).

Prior studies of financial analysts' information needs are mainly conducted in developed countries. Evidence from these studies may not be generalised to emerging economies due to differences in institutions, information environments and the development of capital market. Generally, developed markets emphasise the importance of strategic and forward-looking information (both financial and non-financial) for decision making (Orens and Lybaert, 2007). But in emerging economies, the information environment is very different, even though they implement the same IFRS (Soderstrom and Sun, 2007).

The current literature confirms that there is a close connection between accounting information and financial analysts' activities in China. Some studies find that disclosure of listed companies' management earnings forecasts will improve the quality of analysts' forecasts (Li and Xiao, 2015). Other studies demonstrate that high quality accounting information improves the accuracy of analysts' forecasts (Wu and Hu, 2015).

Apart from accounting information, some studies focus on the role of non-financial information in analysts' forecasts. Since the CSRC encourages listed companies to publish a Corporate Social Responsibility Report (CSR report), many studies examine whether the report improves financial analysts' forecasts. Li and Zhang (2014) show that high-quality CSR reports enhance the accuracy of analysts' forecasts, especially in firms with lower transparency. Zhang *et al.* (2017) demonstrate that the disclosure of a CSR report can decrease the error and dispersion of analysts' forecasts. This evidence shows that non-financial information serves as a good supplement to financial information.

Some research focuses on the ability of Chinese securities analysts to analyse and use information. Based on a questionnaire survey, Hu *et al.* (2003a) found the development level of securities analysts in China to be lower than that of their counterparts in developed countries, and annual reports remain the most important sources of information for most securities analysts in China. In addition, Hu *et al.* (2003b) found that securities analysts use far more accounting information than management information in decision making and, in the use of accounting information, securities analysts pay more attention to earnings information. For access to information, Tan and Cui (2015) found that if the analysts do field research about the firm, the accuracy of the analysts' earnings forecasts decreases with a more optimistic attitude towards the future of the firm. In contrast, Hu *et al.* (2008) found that when analysts conduct more company-level surveys and have more access to firms' indirect information, they have better job quality.

Analysts' attributes influence their needs and information preferences during decision making. Cai and Yang (2013) indicate that securities analysts (sell-side) prefer the contextual type of non-fundamental information about the company when making recommendations or earnings forecasts, while institutional investors (including buy-side analysts and portfolio managers) focus on both the core information, which reflects the intrinsic value and fundamentals of the companies, and the broader contextual information. Hu *et al.* (2008) found analysts' educational background to have a positive impact on their analytical abilities while their work experience improves their job quality.

Apart from analyst attributes, corporate characteristics can influence the behaviour of analysts as well. For example, Huang and Wright (2015) found that state shareholding is negatively related to the quality of consensus analysts' earnings forecasts for listed companies in China.

Survey evidence from China

Survey implementation and descriptive data

We used a questionnaire survey to explore the perceived importance of different information resources available to financial analysts when they provide investment advice or make investment decisions. We also asked about the respondents' perceptions of the main role of accounting information in professional investors' investment decision making: confirmative or predictive. The formal survey was carried out during July and December 2015 as a web version through www.mikecrm.com by CFA China and two securities firms, and by email to 116 securities firms and 95 investment funds.

We received 186 responses. Untabulated results show that most of the respondents work as buy-side analysts (63.44 per cent) and sell-side analysts (36.56 per cent). Analysts are the main respondents (67.74 per cent), followed by departmental managers (19.35 per cent), chief analysts (11.29 per cent), senior executives (0.54 per cent) and others (1.08 per cent). We categorise departmental managers and senior executive as top managers. The respondents are mostly male (70.43 per cent) and with a higher degree (92.47 per cent of respondents having a Master or even PhD degree), while the minority of respondents (15 per cent) have an accounting-related educational background (e.g. accounting, auditing or finance). The average working years of respondents as financial analysts are 6.33, with the median being 5. More than 75 per cent of respondents have worked as financial analysts for fewer than 10 years.

Is accounting information useful in professional users' investment decision making relative to other information?

Using prior literature (e.g. Vergoossen, 1993), we have identified the seven information sources available to financial analysts in making investment decisions (see Table 9.1). The first item represents accounting information while the remainder concern non-accounting information.

Column 10 in Table 9.1 shows that all the averages are significantly larger than 3 (moderately important) at the 1 per cent level, suggesting that accounting and non-accounting information are important for investors to make decisions. Respondents view the accounting information

Table 9.1 Perceived importance of information when analysts provide investment advice or make investment decisions

	Extremely important (5)		Very important (4)		Moderately important (3)		Slightly important (2)		Not at all important (1)		5 + 4		Mean	SD	T test (=3)
	No.	%	No.	%	No.	%	No.	%	No.	%	No.	%			
Accounting information disclosed publicly by the company	139	74.73	29	15.59	8	4.30	0	0	10	5.38	186	90.32	4.54	0.99	21.21***
Non-accounting information disclosed publicly by the company	120	64.52	40	21.51	16	8.60	0	0	10	5.38	186	86.03	4.40	1.03	18.50***
Information on the company's industry	108	58.06	59	31.72	10	5.38	3	1.61	6	3.23	186	89.78	4.40	0.91	20.86***
My understanding of the company's management quality	95	51.08	62	33.33	17	9.14	3	1.61	9	4.84	186	84.41	4.24	1.02	16.54***
Information on the whole macroeconomy	56	30.11	85	45.70	33	17.74	6	3.23	6	3.23	186	75.81	3.96	0.95	13.83***
Information I obtained by myself but that is not disclosed publicly by the company	48	25.81	71	38.17	44	23.66	9	4.84	14	7.53	186	63.98	3.70	1.13	8.42***
Information through quantitative/technical analysis according to market data	26	13.98	57	30.65	76	40.86	18	9.68	9	4.84	186	44.63	3.39	1.00	5.33***

Notes:
Respondents indicated the level of importance with the above information on a scale of 1 (not at all important), 2 (slightly important), 3 (moderately important), 4 (very important) and 5 (extremely important).
★ ≤0.10; ★★ ≤0.05; ★★★ ≤0.01, in two-tailed tests.

disclosed publicly by the company as the most important information with the mean being 4.54. Of the respondents, 90.32 per cent ranked the accounting information as very or extremely important. Respondents also ranked the non-accounting information disclosed publicly by the company (e.g. company's strategy) and the information on the company's industry as the second and third most important information respectively, with a mean of 4.40 for both. The fourth is the personal understanding of the company's management quality, followed by the information on the whole macroeconomy and the information that the respondent obtains personally that is not disclosed publicly by the company. Respondents ranked the information through quant-itative/technical analysis according to market data as the least important in all seven information sources.

The findings concerning the perceived importance of accounting information to professional investors' decisions are consistent with the findings of earlier studies based on developed coun-tries (e.g. Vergoossen, 1993) and are interpreted as follows. The gradual improvement of institu-tions and regulations in China in recent years has strengthened the quality of and thus the usefulness of accounting information to market investors. Gul *et al.* (2010) found the greater level of foreign shareholdings and high quality of audit to be negatively related to the synchro-nicity of stock prices in China. Evidence from surveys also shows that overall transparency in China's stock markets has been improving over the last decade in response to better regulation, stronger enforcement actions and increasing demand from foreign investors (e.g. WEF, 2011). In addition, in spite of a very short history, the securities analyst industry in China has grown exponentially. Compared with the individual investors, professional investors have a stronger demand for accounting information.

These results appear broadly consistent with the perceptions of financial analysts in developed markets in the 1970s–1980s, but are out of step with the current international trend that the usefulness of accounting information is declining while that of non-accounting information is on the increase. These comparative results are justifiable because there is less non-accounting information available in China, so financial analysts rely more on accounting information. It is probably also because Chinese financial analysts are less familiar with how to use non-accounting information. Another reason is that accounting information is more regulated than non-accounting information. In a country like China with a strong preference for statutory control and uniformity (Gray, 1998; Xiao *et al.*, 2004), financial analysts would trust regulated account-ing information more.

What role does accounting information play in professional investors' investment decision making (confirmative vs predictive)?

An objective of financial accounting is to provide decision-useful information that can assist in the assessment of the amounts, timing and uncertainty of future cash flows and the prediction of returns on economic resources.

This led us to examine the main role of accounting information perceived by investors. The results reported in Table 9.2 show that over three-quarters of respondents think that accounting information plays both confirmative and predictive roles when they provide investment advice or make investment decisions. Another 15 per cent of respondents perceive that accounting information is mainly used to predict the enterprise's future value. The results indicate that accounting information, particularly forward-looking information, plays an important role in investment decisions.

Table 9.2 The role of accounting information in providing investment advice or making investment decisions

	No.	Percentage of total (186)
Accounting information is mainly used to confirm previous investment advice or decision (defined as Confirm = 1)	10	5.38
Accounting information is mainly used to predict the enterprise's future value (defined as Predict = 1)	28	15.05
Accounting information is used to both confirm previous investment advice or decisions, and predict the enterprise's future value (defined as Both = 1)	146	78.49
Accounting information is used neither to confirm previous investment advice or decisions, nor to predict the enterprise's future value	2	1.08

How do professional investor characteristics affect perceived usefulness of accounting information?

Finally, we investigate the impact of financial analyst attributes on the importance of accounting information through model (1). We first construct the variable *Importance_Most* to capture the importance level of accounting information perceived by the respondents. *Importance_Most* equals 1 if analysts ranked accounting information as extremely important, and 0 otherwise. We also create two variables to capture analysts' perceptions on the relative importance of accounting information versus non-accounting information. In particular, *Importance_More* equals 1 if the rating of accounting information is above the mean rating of non-accounting information, and 0 otherwise. *Importance_Relative* is the difference between the rating of accounting information and non-accounting information.

The independent variables include *BuySide*, *Manager*, *YofEXP*, *Gender*, *HighDegree* and *AccBackground*. *BuySide* equals 1 if the analysts are buy-side analysts, and 0 otherwise. *Manager* equals 1 if the analysts assume managerial positions such as board director, senior executive or department managers, and 0 otherwise. *YofExp* is the working years of the respondent as a financial analyst. Gender equals 1 if analysts are male, and 0 otherwise. *HighDegree* equals 1 if the analysts have a Master or doctoral degree, and 0 otherwise. *AccBackground* equals 1 if the analysts have accounting education background, including accounting, auditing or finance, and 0 otherwise.

$$Importance\_Most/Importance\_More/Importance\_Relative =$$
$$\alpha_0 + \alpha_1 BuySide + \alpha_2 Manager + \alpha_3 YofEXP + \alpha_4 Gender + \alpha_5 HighDegree + \alpha_6 AccBackground$$
$$+\varepsilon \ (1)$$

Table 9.3 summarises the logit and OLS regression results. Column 1 shows that the coefficient of *BuySide* is significant and positive, suggesting that buy-side analysts are more likely than sell-side analysts to rank accounting information as most important. The results of models (2) and (3) show that the coefficient of *BuySide* is significantly positive for both *Importance_More* and *Importance_Relative*. This indicates that buy-side analysts perceive accounting information as more important than non-accounting information. In contrast, sell-side analysts think that non-accounting information is more important, which is consistent with the findings from other researchers' questionnaire surveys and content analysis of analysts' research reports (e.g. Breton and Taffler, 2001; Orens and Lybaert, 2007).

Generally, sell-side analysts work in a research department of an investment bank/ brokerage that offers investment advice to external clients (e.g. institutional investors), while buy-side analysts work for investment firms (i.e. investment funds) at the investors' own account. Compared with buy-side analysts, sell-side analysts, as financial intermediaries, have more incentives and ability to search more non-accounting information sources. This weakens the relative importance of accounting information versus other information. On the one hand, as trading commissions from institutional investors are the primary source of revenue and performance of research departments at investment banks/brokerage in China (Gu *et al.*, 2013), sell-side analysts have incentives to cater to the needs of institutional investors through searching more information. On the other hand, in a relationship-based system such as China, sell-side analysts tend to maintain a good relationship with managements of listed firms to obtain privileged access to listed firms' private information or to obtain business contracts with institutional investors (Gu *et al.*, 2013). For example, sell-side analysts in China initiate more site visits, as important information sources, than those in well-developed markets (Cheng *et al.*, 2016).

Turning to the effect of analysts' positions, Table 9.3 shows that the coefficient of *Manager* is significant and negative for all three proxies for the importance of accounting information. This suggests that compared with general financial analysts, top managers view non-accounting

Table 9.3 The impact of analyst attributes on the importance of accounting information

	Logit	*Logit*	*OLS*
	1	*2*	*3*
		Importance	
	Most	*More*	*Relative*
BuySide	0.738★	0.900★★	0.201★★
	(1.86)	(2.11)	(2.08)
Manager	−0.877★	−0.949★	−0.393★★★
	(−1.74)	(−1.71)	(−3.13)
YofEXP	0.053	0.099★	0.033★★★
	(1.12)	(1.82)	(2.90)
Gender	−0.406	−0.050	0.073
	(−1.00)	(−0.12)	(0.75)
HighDegree	1.512★★	1.295★	0.537★★★
	(2.41)	(1.93)	(3.17)
AccBackground	−1.022★★	−1.252★★★	−0.236★
	(−2.25)	(−2.66)	(−1.91)
_cons	−0.419	−0.484	−0.246
	(−0.53)	(−0.58)	(−1.18)
N	186	186	186
Pseudo R²/Adj_R²	0.073	0.087	0.097

Significance:
★ ≤0.10; ★★ ≤0.05; ★★★ ≤0.01, in two-tailed tests.

information as more important than accounting information. Because of intense competition, top managers who take charge of the development of a department or whole company face higher pressure and need to have a broader view of a group of securities within or across sectors. As a result, they have to pay more attention to macro-level and industry-level information, rather than firm-specific financial information. The complexity of management tasks also reduces the time left to devote to the analysis of financial information in detail. In addition, top managers are more likely to have private interactions with the managers of listed companies than general analysts. This helps top managers to obtain other private information.

The results reported in Table 9.3 also indicate that analysts with longer working years (*YofExp*) consider accounting information as more important than non-accounting information. The results are consistent with the findings of Orens and Lybaert (2010). This may be because analysts with more experience can conduct more-sophisticated information searches than novices. In addition, the results also show that analysts' perceptions on the importance of accounting information is significantly and positively related to their level of education (*High-Degree*). Compared with analysts with a lower academic degree, analysts with a higher degree may have a higher level of knowledge and skills to perform analyses of financial statements. However, the coefficient of *AccBackground* is significantly and negatively related to the importance level of accounting information perceived by analysts. We do not find a significant impact of analysts' gender on the importance of accounting information.

We also test the impact of analysts' attributes on the role of accounting information through running a second logit model (2). The dependent variables are *Confirm*, *Predict* and *Both*, respectively. *Confirm* equals 1 for analysts who think accounting information only as having a confirmative role in decision making, and 0 otherwise. *Predict* equals 1 for analysts who believe the main role of accounting information is predictive, and 0 otherwise. In addition, *Both* equals 1 if analysts view that accounting information has both confirmative and predictive roles, and 0 otherwise.

$$Confirm/Predict/Both = \alpha_0 + \alpha_1 BuySide + \alpha_2 Manager + \alpha_3 YofEXP + \alpha_4 Gender + \alpha_5 HighDegree + \alpha_6 AccBackground + \varepsilon \ (2)$$

Table 9.4 reports the regression results. We find that for all proxies for analyst attributes, only *BuySide* has a significantly negative association with *Predict*, while being significantly positive related to *Both*. This indicates that buy-side analysts believe that accounting information plays both confirmative and predictive roles. In contrast, sell-side analysts think the predominant role of accounting information is predictive. This further supports the results on the relative important of accounting information perceived by buy-side and sell-side analysts above.

Future directions

Our literature review and field survey have gained a number of insights into the information needs of Chinese professional investors and their perceived usefulness of accounting information. They also generate some findings that require confirmation by further investigation. Other future research avenues relate to future changes to the Chinese economy, the capital market, the professions of financial analysts and fund managers, and accounting and auditing regulations.

Researchers could investigate further why buy-side and sell-side analysts have different perceptions of the importance of accounting vs non-accounting information and the role of accounting information. Interviews and case studies may be useful in such research. A more detailed and thorough examination of the institutional context may also help uncover the underlying reasons.

Table 9.4 The impact of analyst attributes on the role of accounting information

	1	2	3
	Confirm	*Predict*	*Both*
BuySide	1.030	−1.196★★★	0.711★
	(1.24)	(−2.61)	(1.82)
Manager	−1.393	0.404	−0.121
	(−1.20)	(0.67)	(−0.23)
YofEXP	0.056	0.025	−0.015
	(0.69)	(0.47)	(−0.33)
Gender	0.426	0.435	−0.555
	(0.52)	(0.89)	(−1.29)
HighDegree	0.031	−0.088	0.041
	(0.03)	(−0.11)	(0.06)
AccBackground	0.405	0.163	−0.407
	(0.48)	(0.29)	(−0.86)
_cons	−4.183★★	−1.576	1.429
	(−2.54)	(−1.57)	(1.64)
N	186	186	186
Pseudo R	0.048	0.051	0.029

Significance:
★ ≤0.10; ★★ ≤0.05; ★★★ ≤0.01, in two-tailed tests.

It is important to gain a better understanding of how professional investors (including financial analysts) actually use non-accounting information and how they integrate accounting and non-accounting information. Not only will this reveal why non-accounting information is seen to be useful, but it also helps companies improve the provision of non-accounting information and integrated information.

Research into the future information needs of financial analysts and their perceived usefulness of accounting information versus non-accounting information would benefit from taking into account China's drive to economic globalisation, the future development of the capital market and the future development of the securities investment consulting industry.

The future scale and growth of the Chinese economy gives China an important role to play in global governance in general and in the setting of accounting, auditing and finance standards in particular. China's increasing attention to GDP quality means more emphasis on social and environmental protection and sustainability. As a result, more social and environmental information will be produced, and professional investors and financial analysts will make greater use of that information in the future. Future research may further investigate the effect of more detailed non-accounting information (e.g. information on enterprise social responsibility) on investors' decisions.

Uneven marketisation and economic conditions will cause the demand for and supply of accounting information and the quality of accounting and auditing to continue to vary across different regions of China. Reporting companies, auditors, professional investors and financial analysts in different regions will continue to face different information environments. Future research could investigate the effect of information environments on analysts' decisions.

China's initiatives towards greater globalisation create many opportunities for Chinese firms to operate in foreign countries and thus generate a great demand for an international convergence of accounting and finance standards and practice. They also create a need for Chinese professional investors including financial analysts to understand foreign accounting and finance systems and be able to use accounting and non-accounting information produced by companies in other countries relating to the Belt and Road Initiative. Equally important is the need for them to understand foreign culture and ways of doing business.

The growing stock market will create a considerable need for more qualified financial analysts and more information-based investment consulting opportunities. The various initiatives to increase the level of securitisation and connect the Chinese stock exchanges with international stock exchanges require Chinese (foreign) stock brokers, professional investors and financial analysts to be able to understand and use the rules and regulations of foreign (Chinese) regulators and standards setters and the information (whether accounting or non-accounting) produced under them.

It will take a long time to overcome the problems in the securities analyst industry, such as the crisis of confidence, the shortage of qualified Chartered Financial Analysts, the small scale of securities investment consulting firms, and their lagged use of technology. Therefore, the quality of accounting information is particularly important because many financial analysts will continue to have a limited ability to discover new information and make the most of accounting and other information provided to them.

An important trend is the integration of securities investment research and consulting services with foreign exchange, futures, bonds, options, financing securities services, and a combination of investment consulting with macroeconomic information services (Zeng, 2018). This requires financial analysts to possess a broad range of knowledge and the skills of integrating different domains of knowledge. It also means that they need information from a greater variety of sources, not only accounting information, but also information about industries and macroeconomies. As a result, the relative importance of accounting information may be reduced.

Another significant trend is the increasing use of hi-techs such as AI, WeChat, big data, business analytics, blockchains and the internet for securities investment analysis and consulting (Zeng, 2018). Such uses will integrate traditional accounting information and non-accounting information with large databases across the internet, to form platforms that enable securities analysts to find and compare investment opportunities, discover patterns of securities price trends, and make more informed predictions. The use of these technologies will also enable financial analysts to provide more user-tailored information and solutions and enable sophisticated users themselves to simulate investment opportunities and trading strategies. This in turn will raise the demand for more standardised corporate reporting on the one hand, to increase the credibility of accounting information, while on the other hand the demand for more customised or customisable information will also be raised, to meet the varied information needs of different users (Jensen and Xiao, 2001).

An important factor that will continue to influence the use of accounting information by professional investors and financial analysts is *guanxi* or social ties. In the absence of strict legal enforcement and lax ethical considerations, it is likely that many financial analysts provide inaccurate forecasts and dishonest recommendations for self-interest. When there is a social tie between financial analysts and the reporting companies they follow, the financial analysts may produce optimistic earnings forecasts and/or investment recommendations (Firth *et al.*, 2013; Gu *et al.*, 2013; Huyghebaert and Xu, 2016). This implies that financial analysts can misuse or abuse accounting information. However, there is limited empirical evidence on the effect of *guanxi* on financial analysts' behaviour in the extant literature. In addition, future research will benefit from considering both analyst forecasts and their securities recommendations (Chen *et al.*, 2017).

New accounting and auditing regulations/standards will cause changes to the information environment for professional investors and thus create new opportunities for researching the changes to their information needs and informational behaviour. For example, in 2016, Chinese regulators stipulated an auditing standard on the communication of key audit issues in the audit report. It would be interesting and important to see how the audit report based on this standard affects how professional investors use and perceive the reported key audit issues and whether the key audit matters disclosed change the accuracy of financial analysts' forecasts and stock recommendations.

Acknowledgements

We acknowledge with appreciation the financial support from the ICAEW Charitable Trusts for funding the project 'Fair Value Accounting in China: The Effects of Institutional Factors on Its Adoption, Implementation and Usefulness' (published as Xiao and Hu, 2017) from which we have drawn the empirical data used in this paper. Guoqiang Hu and Jason Xiao also acknowledge financial support from the National Natural Science Foundation of China (71502122) for the project 'The Managerial Discretion in Fair Value Estimates and Its Consequences and Governance: A Study Based on the OBS Information on Employee Equity Incentives'.

Notes

1 Data from the SAC website: www.sac.net.cn.
2 The SCSC was founded to enhance the supervision of China's security market in 1992. In April 1998, the SCSC was incorporated into the CSRC.
3 Data from the Asset Management Association of China (AMAC) website: www.amac.org.cn.
4 Data from the *2016 Report of China's Securities Investment Fund Industry Development* published by the AMAC.
5 The AMAC is also subject to operational guidance, supervision and administration by the operational competent authority, CSRC and Ministry of Civil Affairs of the People's Republic of China.
6 The 10 largest audit firms audit only 20–30 per cent of Chinese listed firms (Gul *et al.*, 2010).

References

Allen, F., Qian, J. and Qian, M. (2005). Law, finance and economic growth in China. *Journal of Financial Economics*, 77(1), 57–116.

Breton, G., and Taffler, R.J. (2001). Accounting information and analyst stock recommendation decisions: A content analysis approach. *Accounting and Business Research,* 31(2), 91–101.

Cai, Q. F. and Yang, K. (2013). Who is 'catching at shadow'? Institutional investors vs securities analysts: An empirical study based on the information preference of informed investors of A-share. *Journal of Financial Research*, 6, 193–206 (in Chinese).

Chen, C., Jin, Z., Rui, O. and Su, X. (2017). Impairment of Ethical Considerations and Distortion of Information by Financial Analysts. China–Europe International Business School working paper.

Chen, K. and Yuan, H. (2004). Earnings management and resource allocation: Evidence from China's accounting-based regulation of rights issues. *The Accounting Review*, 79(3), 645–665.

Cheng, Q., Du, F., Wang, X. and Wang, Y. (2016). Seeing is believing: Analysts' corporate site visits. *Review of Accounting Studies*, 21(4), 1245–1286.

Choi, J. J., Jin, L. and Yan, H. (2012). What does stock ownership breadth measure? (June 30, 2012). SSRN: https://ssrn.com/abstract=1571694 or http://dx.doi.org/10.2139/ssrn.1571694 (accessed 25 January 2019).

Firth, M., Lin, C., Liu, P. and Xuan, Y. (2013). The client is king: Do mutual fund relationships bias analyst recommendations? *Journal of Accounting Research*, 51(1), 165–200.

Gray, S. J. (1988). Towards a theory of cultural influence on the development of accounting systems international., *Abacus*, 24(1), 1–15.

Gu, Z., Li, Z. and Yang, Y. G. (2013). Monitors or predators: The Influence of institutional investors on sell-side analysts. *The Accounting Review*, 88(1), 137–169.

Guan, Y., Su, L., Wu, D. and Yang, Z. (2016). Do school ties between auditors and client executives influence audit outcomes? *Journal of Accounting and Economics*, 61(2–3), 506–525.

Gul, F., Kim, J. and Qiu, A. (2010). Ownership concentration, foreign shareholdings, audit quality, and stock price synchronicity: Evidence from China. *Journal of Financial Economics*, 25(3), 425–442.

Hail, L. (2013). Financial reporting and firm valuation: Relevance lost or relevance regained? *Accounting and Business Research*, 43(4), 329–358.

Haw, I., Qi, D. and Wu, D. (2005). Market consequences of earnings management in response to security regulations in China. *Contemporary Accounting Research*, 22(1), 95–140.

Hope, O. -K. (2003). Disclosure practices, enforcement of accounting standards, and analysts' forecast accuracy: An international study. *Journal of Accounting Research*, 41(2), 235–272.

Hu, Y. M., Lin, T. W. and Li, S. Q. (2008). An examination of factors affecting Chinese financial analysts' information comprehension, analyzing ability, and job quality. *Review of Quantitative Finance and Accounting*, 30(4), 397–417.

Hu, Y. M., Lin, W. X. and Wang, W. L. (2003a). Information sources, focus areas, and analysis tools for security analysts. *Journal of Financial Research*, 12, 52–63 (in Chinese).

Hu, Y., Yao, Y., Chen, Y., Wang, W. L. P. and Lu, W. (2003b). The ability of Chinese securities analysts to analyze and use information. *Accounting Research*, 11, 14–20 (in Chinese).

Huang, W. and Wright, B. (2015). Analyst earnings forecast under complex corporate ownership in China. *Journal of International Financial Markets, Institutions & Money*, 35, 69–84.

Huyghebaert, N. and Xu, W. (2016). Bias in the post-IPO earnings forecasts of affiliated analysts: Evidence from a Chinese natural experiment. *Journal of Accounting and Economics*, 61(2–3), 485–505.

IMF (2014). Estimates for 2014 nominal GDP. International Monetary Fund. www.imf.org/external/pubs/ft/weo/2014/02/weodata/weoselgr.aspx (accessed 20 August 2018).

Ionaşcu, M., Ionaşcu, I., Săcărin, M. and Minu, M. (2014). IFRS adoption in developing countries: The case of Romania. *Accounting and Management Information Systems*, 13(2): 311–350.

Jensen, R. and Xiao, Z. (2001). Customized financial reporting, networked databases and distributed file sharing. *Accounting Horizons*, 15(3), 202–222.

Li, W. J. and Zhang, L. (2014). Non-financial disclosure and analyst forecast accuracy: Empirical evidence on corporate social responsibility disclosure from Shenzhen Stock Exchange. *The Theory and Practice of Finance and Economics*, 35(191), 69–74 (in Chinese).

Li, X. Z. and Xiao, T. S. (2015). Are management earnings forecasts useful for analyst forecast revisions? *Nankai Business Review*, 18(2), 30–38 (in Chinese).

Mei, J., Scheinkman, J. A. and Xiong, W. (2009). Speculative trading and stock prices: Evidence from Chinese A-B share premia. *Annals of Economics and Finance*, 10, 225–255.

Orens, R. and Lybaert, N. (2007). Does the financial analysts' usage of non-financial information influence the analysts' forecast accuracy? Some evidence from the Belgian sell-side financial analyst. *International Journal of Accounting*, 42(3), 237–271.

Orens, R. and Lybaert, N. (2010). Determinants of sell-side financial analysts' use of non-financial information. *Accounting and Business Research*, 40(1), 39–53.

Piotroski, J. D. and Wong, T. J. (2011). Institutions and information environment of Chinese listed firms, in Fan, J. and Morck, R. (Eds.) *Capitalizing China*. Chicago University Press, Chicago.

Soderstrom, N. S. and Sun, K. J. (2007). IFRS adoption and accounting quality: A review. *European Accounting Review*, 16(4), 675–702.

Tan, S. T. and Cui, X. Y. (2015). Can the filed research of listed companies improve the accuracy of analysts' forecasts? *The Journal of World Economy*, 4, 126–145 (in Chinese).

The State Council (2018). Report on the work of the government (2018). The State Council of the People's Republic of China. http://en.people.cn/n3/2018/0403/c90000-9445262.html (accessed 25 January 2019).

Vergoossen, R. G. A. (1993). The use and perceived importance of annual reports by investment analysts in the Netherlands. *European Journal Review*, 2(2), 219–244.

WEF (2011). The Global Competitiveness Report 2011–2012. World Economic Forum, www.weforum.org/reports/global-competitiveness-report-2011-2012.

WEF (2018). The global competitiveness report 2018. World Economic Forum, www.weforum.org/reports/the-global-competitveness-report-2018 (accessed 26 December 2018).

Wu, X. H. and Hu, G. L. (2015). Uncertainty, conservatism and analyst forecasts. *Accounting Research*, 9, 27–34 (in Chinese).

Xiao, J. Z. and Hu, G. (2017). Fair value accounting in China: Implementation and usefulness. ICAEW Charitable Trusts www.icaew.com/-/media/corporate/files/technical/research-and-academics/fair-value-report-web-final.ashx (accessed 3 January 2019).

Xiao, Z., Weetman, P. and Sun, M. L. (2004). Political influence and co-existence of a uniform accounting system and accounting standards in China. *Abacus*, 40(2), 193–218.

Xu, X. and Wang, Y. (1999). Ownership structure and corporate governance in Chinese stock companies. *China Economic Review*, 10(1),75–98.

Zeng, Q. Z. (2018). *A Report on the Securities Investment Consulting Industry*. Baidu Wenku (in Chinese). https://wenku.baidu.com/view/f56095401611cc7931b765ce05087632311274fe.html.

Zhang, Z. Y., Hu, Y. Y. and Ji, L. (2017). Does corporate social responsibility assurance reduce the deviation of analyst earnings forecasts? *Journal of Audit & Economics*, 5: 85–95 (in Chinese).

PART II

The accounting profession in emerging economies

10

ACCOUNTING COMPETENCIES IN ROMANIA

Cătălin N. Albu and Nadia Albu

Introduction

The changing roles and competencies affecting the accounting profession in general represent a major area of interest at the global level (Carter *et al.*, 2015; ACCA, 2016a, 2016b; ICAS and FRC, 2016). Influences such as increasingly intensifying developments in information technologies (IT), regulation or deregulation activities or generational changes lead to an adaptation of services and activities provided by accountants. The competencies of the accounting professionals reflect a behaviour, the ability to apply knowledge, skills and professional values, to undertake the required tasks to be performed (IFAC, 1998; CGA, 2009). Professional bodies prescribe the necessary skills and competencies for their members, and then should play an important educational role in providing and maintaining them. For example, the International Accounting Education Standards Board (IAESB, 2014) defines the intellectual, interpersonal and communication, personal and organisational competence areas and related professional skills that are expected from professional accountants, which should be integrated with technical competencies and professional values and ethics. However, the competencies required from professional accountants are closely related to the roles they are expected to play (e.g. information provider, decision supporter, bookkeeper, controller, etc.). Moreover, these roles, and hence competencies, are influenced by broader organisational, cultural and institutional factors, and may vary significantly between and across different professional contexts.

In addition to these wide-ranging challenges, the accounting profession in the post-socialist Central and Eastern European (CEE) countries witnessed many changes in the advent of the reforms moving these countries from a totalitarian regime to a market economy. Professional bodies were created or re-created, new forms of business and economic models emerged, new institutions, laws and regulations were introduced, or existing ones were modified. All these triggered significant changes in the roles that accountants are expected to assume by business entities, governments and society at large, and in the competencies they should possess. Additionally, the accounting profession in such countries faces institutional and cultural differences relative to its Western counterparts, shaping the process of change in the profession, its magnitude and pace.

To organise our analyses and indicate several broad directions for future research, we view the accountants' competencies as being influenced by (1) State–profession boundaries and efforts for professionalisation, (2) the role and image of accountants in society, and (3) the changes in the economic, technological, social and organisational context. These factors impact the demand for professional competencies and the role accountants are expected to play in organisations and society, both at a certain moment in time and longitudinally. In this chapter, we mobilise existing research and our knowledge of one of the CEE countries (i.e. Romania) to illustrate the changes in the accounting profession's competencies, highlight what is known and identify several future research opportunities. Given the institutional similarities of transitioning countries, our arguments may inform research on the accounting profession in other emerging economies, particularly in the post-socialist ones.

State–profession boundaries and efforts for professionalisation

Understanding the development of the profession and the arrangements between various local actors, as well as identifying the local sites of professionalisation, is crucial for the way competencies and skills are constructed and reproduced in contexts such as those in CEE, since professional bodies' 'histories, allegiances and struggles' influence the activity and expertise of the profession (Cooper and Robson, 2006: 416).

Historically, accounting during the socialist regime represented an instrument of control by and for the State, being mainly restricted to bookkeeping (Bailey, 1995; Seal *et al.*, 1996). Accountants were certified, trained and controlled by the State, worked for the State (or for State-owned enterprises), and their status and activities involved limited skills. Accounting was viewed as a reporting tool fulfilling the macroeconomic needs of the centralised State. The State provided accountants 'a sufficiency of skills for the efficient operation of the standardised accounting system', to be 'a personification of the conservative and rule-bound bureaucrat' (Bailey, 1988: 12).[1]

After the fall of their socialist regime, CEE countries transitioned from a centrally planned towards a market-based economy. It would be reasonable to assume that, almost 30 years into the transition, these countries have institutions that are comparable to the ones in the Western world, especially since most of these countries have also joined the European Union. However, we argue that the professional culture and identity still persisting from the socialist mindset (Swaan and Lissowska, 1996; Ekiert and Hanson, 2003), the volatile economic context, the unfamiliar tools and methods that were implemented and the political instability affecting these countries shape the development of the accounting profession and their corpus of expertise, thus creating spaces for further reflection and investigation (Brock, 2016).

One of the main attributes of a profession in the sociology of professions literature consists in acquiring the skills needed by the respective professionals (Yee, 2001), based on theoretical knowledge and requiring training and education. In a functioning market economy, the profession responds in terms of qualifications and skill development to the market needs. However, the institutional arrangements characterising a market economy (i.e. functioning capital markets, trading activities, financial institutions) are only nascent in transition economies, may function inefficiently and are unknown to many participants in the economic life (Bailey, 1995). Additionally, the state remains an important actor in the professionalisation process, unless other professionalisation sites are developed.

The transition towards the market economy involves the development of the accounting profession within and by local professional bodies, assumed to be more or less independent from the State. These professional bodies were created (or, in most CEE countries, re-created) in the region of the early 1990s (King *et al.*, 2001). Due to various scope limitations, intra-professional disputes appeared in some countries, when new professional bodies were created to cover specific areas such as statutory audits. Moreover, local professional bodies interact with international bodies, transnational organisations and big accounting firms, this interaction shaping the professionalisation of the field for accountants.

The Romanian case illustrates very well the complexity of this professional field. The accounting profession was re-created in the country via CECCAR (Corpul Experților Contabili și Contabililor Autorizați din România) in 1994. However, in 1999, at the request of the World Bank and the International Monetary Fund (King *et al.*, 2001), the Chamber of Financial Auditors of Romania (Camera Auditorilor Financiari din România) was created. Albu (2013a) explores the pressures and mechanisms of change, and discusses how the professional bodies responded, both in terms of organisation and knowledge base, to the external coercive pressures of the World Bank, and the mimetic pressures resulting from the desire to become a member of the International Federation of Accountants (IFAC). This last objective resulted in collaborations with foreign professional bodies and in some mimetic actions in terms of organisation and curriculum. However, this mimetism was at a general level and merely intended to obtain IFAC membership, and did not involve real rapprochement with the accession and curriculum requirements of international bodies.

One of the examples provided by Albu (2013a) to illustrate the limited mimetic actions of the Romanian professional bodies is the absence of corporate governance and sustainability topics from their curricula, while these represent important developments to the professional field for international bodies. This is an illustration of the inertia of local professional bodies, and of their difficulty in keeping up the pace of pushing new accounting tools, concepts, methods and norms down (in terms of competencies) towards the individual professional. Moreover, the insufficient involvement of local professional bodies in these new areas has encouraged the development of alternative fields of professionalisation, which in Romania include, besides the big accounting firms, already identified in the international literature as important (e.g. Cooper and Robson, 2006), the subsidiaries of multinational corporations and the global professional bodies (Albu, 2013a). These professionalisation sites are connected to the Western world and represent laboratories for developing new competencies that are more aligned to the trends recognised in the profession at the international level.

Seal *et al.* (1996) investigated the efforts of professionalisation in the Czech Republic in the early years of transition. They discuss how the accounting professional bodies were created in that setting, their relationship with the State, the emerging role of the big accounting firms, the role of academia and the changing boundaries in terms of expertise. Additional developments occurred in the decades following the fall of the socialist regime, of course. Therefore, the topics investigated in these early studies and the questions about the pace and extent of change in the profession are still relevant, as the complexity of the transition period and the impact the national states still have on the local accounting professions in post-socialist contexts continue to provide ample opportunities for research on the sites of professionalisation.

In line with these remarks, a potentially fruitful stream of future research is the profession–State relationship, and its impact on the competencies body of the profession. The boundaries between the profession and the State are generally characterised by political aspects and power issues (Yee, 2012), but in transitional contexts these issues are even more visible and worthy of investigation. Seal *et al.* (1996) mention 'the battle over competency' along with collaborations in education, such as inviting officials from the accounting regulator (i.e. the Czech Ministry of Finance) to provide training for the members of the profession. What may have seemed a transitory activity in the 1990s might have, however, a longer period of impact on the profession in CEE countries, as we observe the same arrangements manifesting even currently in the Romanian context (Albu and Albu, 2018). We further suggest that this state–profession intertwining in education influences the role socially ascribed to the professions, along with the associated competencies. This situation facilitates the maintenance of the 'accounting for the state' view held by management of local entities, who mainly expect tax competencies from Romanian accountants (Albu and Albu, 2018) (see the later point on the social image of accountants in CEE countries). We thus encourage researchers to further investigate this strong relationship in terms of local accountants' professional identity, struggles, competency development and impact on the new professional roles (as Apostol and Pop (2018) investigate from the tax consultancy point of view). Sociological and behavioural theories might be particularly helpful here, to add to the growing body of research on the recent evolutions within the accounting profession.

Additionally, the focus of most research conducted so far in CEE countries has focused more on individual professional bodies, and less on the relationships between them (Samsonova-Taddei and Humphrey, 2014). Given the current cooperation and, to some extent, competition between local professional bodies, and between them and the global/regional ones, further attention should be given to how they contribute to competency and identity formation in local contexts. Global professional bodies such as the Association of Chartered Certified Accountants (ACCA) have made a notable impact in many CEE countries (Albu, 2013a), competing for members with the local professional bodies, but also working with them for capacity building. The local professional bodies' histories and strategies of managing their membership could be envisaged as potential areas of research, as it would greatly complement prior work conducted by, among many others, Ballas (1998) or Evans (2018) in other settings.

Another stream of research concerns the other sites of professionalisation. Although the role played by the big accounting firms in the post-socialist countries has already been investigated (Cooper et al., 1998), additional research is necessary to understand how these international firms open spaces for the profession, introduce new services, balance the competencies of accountants and non-accountants (Lander et al., 2013), impact the regulatory activities at the local level, or develop identities and skills. Local firms that are members of such international networks are very large employers on the local markets and are viewed as important actors in the regulatory fields. However, their activities are conditioned by the current state of development of the accounting and auditing market in emerging economies, including their employees' competencies. Moreover, their role in competency development may overlap, complement or compete with the training provided by the professional bodies and universities. Big accounting firms open training academies, provide advanced training for professional certification or have particular career development expectations (in terms of anticipated education and qualifications) of their staff. Future research may also investigate these shifts in the accounting education field.

Furthermore, the role played by the subsidiaries of multinational entities in developing accounting competencies could prove fruitful for future research. These entities are vectors of improvements in reporting, auditing and corporate governance mechanisms, acting as facilitators of the transfer of knowledge from their parent entities to the local context. Skill acquisitions and behavioural change in post-socialist contexts are complicated processes in the absence of appropriate incentives and institutions (Swaan and Lissowska, 1996). Subsidiaries thus represent an appropriate field to investigate change, given the availability of Western models as targets for imitation and the internal incentives for change. Moreover, given various professional segments and subgroups (local versus international, small versus big), the role of institutional entrepreneurship arising in movements between segments might be investigated (e.g. how former big-firm employees, or accountants working in multinationals, spread knowledge when they move towards smaller firms or local companies).

The role and image of accountants in society

The social image of a professions plays a role in attracting people to it and influences the inter-action of professionals with other social actors (Brouard *et al.*, 2017). The caricature aspect of social image is reflected by stereotypes. Moreover, social images (including stereotypes) usually associate some competencies to the respective professionals, including accountants. Accounting professional bodies continuously investigate the current and future roles of their members, and discuss and attempt to predict changes, in order to design appropriate paths for the development of adequate competencies. For example, by identifying the drivers of change in the accounting profession and the challenges this profession faces, ACCA (2012) lists the public perception and attractiveness of the profession, the definition of the scope of the accountant's role and the social expectations ascribed to the profession as important factors impacting the profession in both the short and the long term.

The traditional stereotype associated with the accounting profession is that of bookkeeper, as a trusted, honest, uncreative and uncommercial professional. By contrast, the modern stereotype is that of a creative, business-focused and opportunistic business professional (Carnegie and Napier, 2010). Both stereotypes have positive and negative attributes (Carnegie and Napier, 2010). Richardson *et al.* (2015) identify four subtypes, representing positive (scorekeeper and guardian) and negative (bean counter and entrepreneur) interpretations of the two basic stereo-types. In terms of competencies and skills, the modern stereotype needs communication and soft skills, a high level of technical expertise, social skills and a commercial attitude. These compe-tencies also result as a must from the studies investigating the changes and expected develop-ments in the profession (ICAS and FRC, 2016). Quite expectedly, international professional bodies, along with large accounting firms, actively support the promotion of the modern stereo-type (Warren and Parker, 2009).

Given the historical background of the accounting profession of post-socialist countries, it is expected that the bean counter/bookkeeper stereotype still dominates, despite certain develop-ments. For example, Tobór-Osadnik *et al.* (2013) discuss how *homo sovieticus*, a personality type shaped by the thinking and attitude specific to a totalitarian system (such as submission to authorities, lack of individuality, not making important decisions, expecting authorities to show the way, etc.), still persists in the accounting profession. Prior research in Romania illustrates how this stereotype is still influential, despite some developments that have occurred over time. By surveying Romanian professional accountants, Istrate (2009) finds that attention to details, rigour, patience and correctness characterise this social group, with many of these attributes describing accountants in the socialist times as well. Investigating in more depth, Albu (2013b) finds that this image mainly pertains to accountants working in small and medium-sized entities (SMEs), dealing with taxation and a lot of documentary paperwork. This image of the account-ing professional is held by both management of SMEs and the accountants working in such entities themselves (social identity) (Albu, 2013b). Accountants fulfil different roles in larger companies and in big accounting firms, including counselling, analysis and support for decision making, while their related stereotypes have more positive nuances and are closer to the modern image. These roles, reflected in job offers by such depictions as 'consultant', 'first partner to the manager', 'business partner' (Albu *et al.*, 2011) trigger a different set of competencies from accountants, including critical thinking, communication, analysis and business acumen.

Survey-based studies reveal that the most prominent role played by accountants in Romania is bookkeeping, despite roles such as financial analyst, internal consultant, accounting system designer and change agent also increasing over time (Albu, 2013b). Technical competencies are the ones most expected from Romanian accountants, but soft skills and a broader business understanding are also required. Albu (2013b) further investigates the association between competencies and roles, and finds a significant correlation of technical competencies with control and audit roles, project management, financial reporting and tax management; knowledge of the organisation and soft competencies are positively and significantly correlated with roles such as strategic support, risk management, information analysis, communication with stakeholders and shareholders, project management, financial management and tax management.

Most studies in Romania (for example Albu *et al.*, 2011; Albu, 2013b) or elsewhere in the region (Král and Šoljaková, 2016; Král *et al.*, 2017, among others) testify to the changes in the professional role and competencies in CEE countries, incorporating in their development some of the features of the profession of Western countries. We already know, therefore, that, slower or quicker, to a smaller or a larger extent, the Western model of the accounting professional is being followed in the CEE region as well. We also observe in the same region, on the other hand, remnant influences from the socialist times (Tobór-Osadnik *et al.*, 2013). However, most of the existing studies perform radiography at a specific moment, on a specific group of accounting professionals, therefore leaving space for in-depth longitudinal studies. For example, it would be interesting to know how the actual change from one role to another occurred, and how various subgroups with different roles and levels of skills share the professional space, work together or create boundaries. Further research similar to work conducted in East Germany (e.g. Evans *et al.*, 2016) could also investigate the current status of female accountants or auditors resulting from a historically downgraded, feminised occupation existing under the socialist regime in former Soviet Bloc countries. Anecdotal evidence exists about the high percentage of female partners of large accounting, auditing and advisory firms in the local offices in some CEE countries such as Romania, or the almost absolute predominance of female accountants and auditors in some lower tier firms. The consequences of such situations could be further explored and contrasted with the more male-dominated accounting settings of more developed countries.

Significant ideological and practical modifications to the socialist accounting systems of CEE countries occurred over a relatively short period of time (about 30 years), requiring fast and essential adaptation to the new regimes. In this uneasy context, it would be interesting to study the extent to which the accounting professionals who were trained under, or right after the fall of, the socialist regime have changed or adapted over time. Alternatively, are the professionals fulfilling the new roles ascribed to accountants young people trained under the new regime(s)? If the latter, how does this affect the hierarchy in the professional space in the CEE countries? The professional literature mostly refers to gender discrimination in the profession (Brock, 2016), or to the replacement of accountants by non-accountants if they do not adapt their skills (Lander *et al.*, 2013). But we also wonder whether there is any space for age discrimination in emerging economies as well, to the extent some professionals do not keep up with the expectations in their environment. Are there any power conflicts between more and less experienced professionals, because of hierarchy, skills or (perceived) higher value of international certifications and qualifications versus national ones? How do management of various types of entities perceive these subgroups and their competencies? What role does the battle for talent play in this context? Moreover, it would be interesting to know how accounting professionals displaying different images or having skills and roles work together (Taylor and Scapens, 2016).

Changes in the economic, technological, social and organisational environment

Changes in the economic environment, especially privatisation, the establishment of subsidiaries by multinational corporations and the arrival of the big accounting firms, created new roles and competency demands for professional accountants in the CEE region. These changes were accompanied by the arrival of Western accounting norms and tools. While the change process offered and still offers many opportunities for conducting research on the role and competencies of accounting professionals, few CEE studies investigate this issue.

For example, Albu *et al.* (2011) and Albu and Albu (2009) investigate, in the Romanian context, the impact of these changes on accountants, especially that of International Accounting Standards/International Financial Reporting Standards (IAS/IFRS) and Enterprise Resource Planning (ERP) systems, as models pertaining to global organisations. By applying job-offer analysis, Albu *et al.* (2011) investigated the demand for accounting competencies in Romanian accountants, and found the adoption of ERP systems or IFRS to be associated with hybrid accounting positions (i.e. positions requiring both financial and managerial accounting competencies). Similarly, Albu and Albu (2009) analysed via interviews the changes of the roles and competencies of professional accountants in business in the context of IFRS and ERP adoption. Their findings mirror those in the international literature. In the first case, hybridisation results from IFRS reporting becoming the job of controllers, while in the second case, because ERP leads to efficiencies and fewer accountants are involved in the accounting process.

These cases also illustrate some of the local features, such as the very limited exposure to IT in most Romanian entities before ERP implementation, but confirm that the ERP systems bring efficiencies in the accounting function. However, the idea that IT tools narrow the role of accountants should not be presumed. As such, Albu *et al.* (2015) found that the ERP system implemented has actually introduced new roles for accounting in a Romanian SME that had not developed much internal accounting before the implementation. The ERP system provided more in-depth analyses and details about the firm's activities and expanded accountants' roles. Even if the ERP adoption and implications for accountants were extensively investigated, emerging economies may still provide such examples of unexpected changes in or unintended consequences for the accountant's roles and competencies. For example, will the adoption of such advanced IT systems or software by entities having extensive means contribute to the growth of such entities, exceeding the growth of entities that have not adopted such systems, and with effects on the role of accountants? Will this move increase the attractiveness of international IT certifications to accounting professionals in emerging (CEE) countries, and if so, with what consequences for the traditional professional bodies?

Additionally, other recent IT developments such as big data, audit analytics, Robotic Process Automation or the advent of artificial intelligence are expected to significantly impact the accounting profession (ACCA, 2016b, 2017). Such studies anticipate that technology will replace many entry-level roles of the profession and will challenge some of the traditional accounting activities performed, while at the same time providing multiple opportunities for new services and activities by accounting professionals (such as analysing data, communicating with shareholders, engaging in internal and external advisory, etc.). Moreover, the boundaries between accounting and other professions blur following IT implementation, and skills from various areas, including IT skills and communication, management, marketing or human resources, will be needed by accountants if they wish to maintain a strong position in this field. Given the recognised importance of IT as both a challenge and an opportunity for the accounting profession (ACCA, 2012), as well as the uneven exposure to technology in different entities and across various subgroups of accountants, and the variety of professionals' reactions to these developments, especially in developing countries, more studies are needed in this area to understand how accountants' roles and competencies are shaped, changed or replaced by the new technologies. Moreover, in such fields where the necessary competencies pertain only loosely to the accounting profession, or where new organisational positions appear vaguely related to accounting, it would be interesting to investigate how accountants maintain, or not, an important role.

Another related question is whether, and to what extent, the skills and competencies formed inside the profession (e.g. by professional bodies) create a versatile accounting professional, or if the personal attributes and/or other sites of professionalisation help accountants reinvent themselves and survive in an IT-led/dominated environment. This topic is of importance given the role of professional bodies in supporting their members and, in case of turbulence, creating new spaces for services and activities. However, prior research (e.g. Greenwood *et al.*, 2002) finds that, although professional bodies may support innovation and change in activities and services, the backing is minimal if there are limited changes to the accession and training curricula. Additionally, it would be interesting to study the extent to which the public perception of accounting and accountants will change (for the better) by association with the latest IT developments. Will management of local or international businesses acting in emerging economies seize the opportunity of challenging the accounting profession to respond to these developments and augment their roles? Will the tax-oriented, bookkeeping image of post-socialist accountants working in local SMEs change, to become more involved in the decision-making processes, or will the introduction of new IT systems furthermore divide different subgroups of accountants? To what extent will the implementation of new IT systems improve internal reporting and, by extension, corporate governance practices of CEE entities, and with what consequences for the competencies of accounting professionals in these markets?

Related to the point above, emerging economies have witnessed the creation on their territories of new organisational forms such as the Shared Service Centres. Primarily motivated by efficiency considerations, but also raising several challenges (Kastberg, 2014), these entities impact accounting professionals (as pointed out by, for instance, Herbert and Seal (2012)), among other professions. For example, types of services that are different to the ones usually performed by accountants are executed in such entities, attracting young eager professionals to/via an international working environment and by offering fast(er) career development opportunities. Nevertheless, anecdotal evidence points to, for example, the difficult interaction between various stakeholders of the auditing process, as manifested in the context of such organisational forms. Critical studies could thus investigate the extent to which, in practice, such organisational innovations have delivered on their promises of cost savings and service enhancements (Richter and Brühl, 2017).

Future directions

Existing studies point towards both change and inertia processes characterising the accounting profession in CEE countries, in terms of roles and competencies alike. We suggest the existence of the extreme cases of the bookkeeper role (having technical-, tax- and rule-oriented competencies), contrasted with that of the modern, Western-aligned professional (involving particular expertise in Western standards and models, communication, and critical thinking) as indicated in literature, and we suggest that many situations exist in between. These examples testify to the existence of several subgroups in the accounting profession in developing countries, evolving at different paces.

This provides, in our opinion, a very rich background for conducting research on accounting competencies in such economies. Research informed by local institutional challenges is needed, and not merely replicating studies performed in developed contexts, nor researching if Western professional roles and competencies manifest in emerging economies. We already know that, to some extent, these Western influences exist in CEE (Seal *et al.*, 1996; Albu *et al.*, 2011; Král and Šoljaková, 2016; Král *et al.*, 2017). Given the findings of existing studies, now would probably be a good time to further investigate how the socialist past still influences professional behaviour

and competencies, how it blends with Western influences to create the modern local professional, and how the local arrangements, actors and institutions shape the accounting professionalisation field. It would be interesting, for example, to study the ethical behaviour of accounting
professionals acting in CEE countries (Brouard *et al.*, 2017), in an environment characterised by
fast development of firms, lower investor protection and a discrepancy between the formal
existence of accountability mechanisms and their actual performance ('sleeping accountability')
(Veselý, 2013). Would these professionals give in to potential pressures from management and
owners of local firms to be more lenient in considering not-so-clear situations, to the unlawful
benefit of these interested parties more easily than their Western counterparts, given the lower
status of accounting in CEE countries, inherited from socialist times? Would such (if any)
behaviour impact the accountants' professional competences and roles assumed within the businesses? How are professional bodies assisting their members in addressing such ethical issues,
other than some formal ethics modules included in the standard training?

Finally, we underline the importance of extending the background of future research and the
framing of research questions on competencies to include other fields that are important for
understanding accountants' work and their competencies, such as the small business literature
(for accountants working in, or with, small businesses) or studies on knowledge-intensive firms
(for research on accounting firms and their employees). We suggest that future research may in
turn look at how the socialist past still influences professional behaviour and competencies, how
it blends with Western influences to create the modern professional, and how the local arrangements, actors and institutions shape the accounting professionalisation field.

In conducting such research, we encourage prospective authors to obtain or mobilise an in-
depth knowledge of the institutional environment of the CEE countries (Albu *et al.*, 2017).
Given the region's fast pace of changes, multiple influences and differing developments in areas
such as accounting systems, capital markets developments and adherence to various international
standards and organisations, academic papers would therefore benefit from the use of alternative
approaches to the 'positivistic' ones (Hoque, 2018) such as naturalistic, institutional or critical
theories. To clarify, we are not excluding the 'positivistic' ones, such as agency theory, in
researching the context of CEE countries, but the explanatory power of such analyses may be
less strong than in more developed countries, given the smaller scale of the countries, the less
strict reporting environment (in terms of enforcement mechanisms, for example) and the less
developed accounting profession (in terms of independence from state institutions).

With respect to research strategies and data analysis, we believe that surveys, interviews, case
studies and other methods generally classified as qualitative ones (Hoque *et al.*, 2017; Libby and
Thorne, 2017) would produce the most relevant results given the nature of the research questions of interest (i.e. very context-dependent and formulated mostly in terms of how? and why?
than what?) (Riahi-Belkaoui, 2017). As such, in-depth case studies could be conducted in local
and multinational firms to study, for example, the various mutations affecting the accounting
profession in CEE countries. Large questionnaire-based surveys could be administered to
accounting professionals, managers, students or other stakeholders, with a view to understanding
the perceptions of such parties regarding the accounting profession in general (e.g. whether and
why the profession is perceived as being attractive, and with what consequences on the profession itself), or on some particular aspects (e.g. the preferred or envisaged roles of accounting
professionals, or to what extent some accounting services such as advisory or audit are valued by
firms in CEE countries, influencing the accountants' set of skills and competences).

We conclude the wide array of research themes and approaches that could be investigated in
the under-researched context of CEE countries, and encourage colleagues to intensify their
efforts in putting together well-designed studies of the intricacies characterising accounting in

general, and the accounting profession in particular, in this region. The recent interest of established international publishers and journals in quality research covering emerging economies (such as this *Companion*, or the special section of *Accounting in Europe* (A in E, 2017) dedicated to corporate reporting in CEE) seems highly encouraging for prospective authors who wish to disseminate research conducted in this region.

Note

1 The socialist period unfortunately stopped further developments in the accounting profession in the region initiated after the First World War. The Body of Expert and Licensed Accountants of Romania (ro. Corpul Experților Contabili și Contabililor Autorizați din România – CECCAR) was created in 1921 and had achieved significant development until it was dismantled by the socialist regime in 1945.

References

A in E (2017). Special Section: Central and Eastern Europe. *Accounting in Europe*, 14(3), 249–387.
ACCA (2012). *100 Drivers of Change for the Global Accountancy Profession*. London: Association of Chartered Certified Accountants.
ACCA (2016a). *Professional Accountants – The Future: Drivers of Change and Future Skills*. London: Association of Chartered Certified Accountants.
ACCA (2016b). *Professional Accountants – The Future: Generation Next*. London: Association of Chartered Certified Accountants.
ACCA (2017). *The race for relevance*. Technology opportunities for the finance function. London: Association of Chartered Certified Accountants.
Albu, C. N. and Albu, N. (2009). How does organizational change affect the accountant's role? An institutional approach on two Romanian settings. *Accounting and Management Information Systems*, 8(1), 40–52.
Albu, C. N., Albu, N., Faff, R. and Hodgson, A. (2011). Accounting competencies and the changing role of accountants in emerging economies: The case of Romania. *Accounting in Europe*, 8(2), 153–182.
Albu, C. N., Albu, N., Dumitru, M. and Dumitru, V. (2015). The impact of the interaction between context variables and Enterprise Resource Planning systems on organizational performance: A case study for a transition economy. *Information Systems Management*, 32(3), 252–264.
Albu, N. (2013a). Exploring the recent evolution of the accounting profession in Romania: An institutional approach. *Accounting and Management Information Systems*, 12(4), 537–552.
Albu, N. (2013b). *A Romanian Perspective on the Image and Role of the Accounting Profession*. Bucharest: Editura ASE.
Albu, N. and Albu, C. N. (2018). State's Institutional Work in the Accounting Regulatory Space: Insights from an Emerging Economy. EAA 2018 Congress, working paper.
Albu, N., Albu C. N. and Filip, A. (2017). Corporate reporting in Central and Eastern Europe: Issues, challenges and research opportunities. *Accounting in Europe*, 14(3), 249–260.
Apostol, O. and Pop, A. (2018). 'Paying taxes is losing money': A qualitative study on institutional logics in the tax consultancy field in Romania. *Critical Perspectives on Accounting*, in press, https://doi.org/10.1016/j.cpa.2018.05.001.
Bailey, D. (1988). *Accounting in Socialist Countries*. London: Routledge.
Bailey, D. (1995). Accounting in transition in the transitional economy. *European Accounting Review*, 4(4), 595–623.
Ballas, A. A. (1998). The creation of the auditing profession in Greece. *Accounting, Organizations and Society*, 23(8), 715–736.
Brock, D. M. (2016). Professionals and their workplaces in emerging markets: A research agenda. *International Journal of Emerging Markets*, 11(3), 460–472.
Brouard, F., Bujaki, M., Durocher, S. and Neilson, L. C. (2017). Professional accountants' identity formation: An integrative framework. *Journal of Business Ethics*, 142(2), 225–238.
Carnegie, G. D. and Napier, C. J. (2010). Traditional accountants and business professionals: Portraying the accounting profession after Enron. *Accounting, Organizations and Society*, 35(3), 360–376.
Carter, C., Muzio, D. and Spence, C. (2015). Scoping an agenda for future research into the professions. *Accounting, Auditing & Accountability Journal*, 28(8), 1198–1216.

CGA (2009). *CGA Competency Framework*. Certified General Accountants Association of Canada.

Cooper, D. J. and Robson, K. (2006). Accounting, professions and regulation: Locating the sites of professionalization. *Accounting, Organizations and Society*, 31(4–5), 415–444.

Cooper, D. J., Greenwood, R., Hinings, B. and Brown, J. L. (1998). Globalisation and nationalism in a multinational accounting firm: The case of opening new markets in Eastern Europe. *Accounting, Organizations and Society*, 23(5–6), 531–548.

Ekiert, G. and Hanson, S. E. (2003). *Capitalism and Democracy in Central and Eastern Europe: Assessing the Legacy of Communist Rule*. Cambridge: Cambridge University Press.

Evans, L. (2018). Shifting strategies: The pursuit of closure and the 'Association of German Auditors'. *European Accounting Review*, 27(4), 683–712.

Evans, L., Detzen, D. and Hoffmann, S. (2016). 'The Lives of Others': Gender and the Audit Profession in the Context of German Reunification. 39th Annual Congress of the European Accounting Association, Maastricht, the Netherlands.

Greenwood, R., Suddaby, R. and Hinings, C. R. (2002). Theorizing change: The role of professional associations in the transformation of institutionalized field. *Academy of Management Journal*, 45(1), 58–80.

Herbert, I. P. and Seal, W. B. (2012). Shared services as a new organisational form: Some implications for management accounting. *The British Accounting Review*, 44(2), 83–97.

Hoque, Z. (2018) (Ed.). *Methodological Issues in Accounting Research*. London: Spiramus Press Ltd.

Hoque, Z., Parker, L. D., Covaleski, M. A. and Haynes, K. (2017) (Eds.). *The Routledge Companion to Qualitative Accounting Research Methods*. New York: Routledge, 542.

IAESB (2014). *International Education Standard (IES) 3: Initial Professional Development – Professional Skills*. International Accounting Education Standards Board. New York: IFAC.

ICAS and FRC (2016). *Auditor Skills in a Changing Business World*. The Institute of Chartered Accountants of Scotland and Financial Reporting Council, London.

IFAC (1998). Competence-Based Approaches to the Professional Preparation of Accountants. Discussion paper, International Federation of Accountants, New York.

Istrate, C. (2009). Despre cum este văzută contabilitatea dinăuntrul şi dinafara profesiei, in *Informarea financiar-contabilă în condiţii de criză: 15 ani de la implementarea noului sistem contabil în România* (pp. 124–137), [How accounting is perceived from within and outside the profession, in *Finance and Accounting Reporting Under Crisis: 15 Years Since the Implementation of the New Accounting System in Romania*]. Ed. Univ. A. I. Cuza, Iaşi.

Kastberg, G. (2014). Framing shared services: Accounting, control and overflows. *Critical Perspectives on Accounting*, 25(8), 743–756.

King, N., Beattie, A., Cristescu, M. M. and Weetman, P. (2001). Developing accounting and audit in a transition economy: The Romanian experience. *European Accounting Review*, 10(1), 149–171.

Král, B. and Šoljaková, L. (2016) 'Development of controllers' professional competence: The case of the Czech Republic'. *Economy and Sociology*, 9(1), 86–100.

Král, B., Mikołajewicz, G., Nowicki, J. and Šoljaková, L. (2017). Professional competences of controllers: The case of Poland. *European Financial and Accounting Journal*, 12(2), 17–40.

Lander, M. W., Koene, B. A. S. and Linssen, S. N. (2013). Committed to professionalism: Organizational responses of mid-tier accounting firms to conflicting institutional logics. *Accounting, Organizations and Society*, 38(2), 130–148.

Libby, T. and Thorne, L. (2017). (Eds.) *The Routledge Companion to Behavioral Accounting Research*. New York: Routledge.

Riahi-Belkaoui, A. (2017). The new context of the accounting profession (September 15, 2017). SSRN: https://ssrn.com/abstract=3037598 or http://dx.doi.org/10.2139/ssrn.3037598.

Richardson, P., Dellaportas, S., Perera, L. and Richardson, B. (2015). Towards a conceptual framework on the categorization of stereotypical perceptions in accounting. *Journal of Accounting Literature*, 35, 28–46.

Richter, P. C. and Brühl, R. (2017). Shared service center research: A review of the past, present, and future. *European Management Journal*, 35(1), 26–38.

Samsonova-Taddei, A. and Humphrey, C. (2014). Transnationalism and the transforming roles of professional accountancy bodies: Towards a research agenda. *Accounting, Auditing & Accountability Journal*, 27(6), 903–932.

Seal, W., Sucher, P. and Zelenka, I. (1996). Post-socialist transition and the development of an accountancy profession in the Czech Republic. *Critical Perspectives on Accounting*, 7(4), 485–508.

Swaan, W. and Lissowska, M. (1996). Capabilities, routines, and Eastern European economic reform: Hungary and Poland before and after the 1989 revolutions. *Journal of Economic Issues*, 30(4), 1031–1056.

Taylor, L. C. and Scapens, R. W. (2016). The role of identity and image in shaping management accounting change. *Accounting, Auditing & Accountability Journal*, 29(6), 1075–1099.

Tobór-Osadnik, K., Wyganowska, M. and Kabalski, P. (2013). International Financial Reporting Standards vs. *homo sovieticus* personality: The case of Poland. *International Journal of Business and Social Research*, 3(6), 17–35.

Veselý, A. (2013). Accountability in Central and Eastern Europe. *International Review of Administrative Sciences*, 79(2), 310–330.

Warren, S. and Parker, L. (2009). Bean counters or bright young things? Towards the visual study of identity construction among professional accountants. *Qualitative Research in Accounting and Management*, 6(4), 205–223.

Yee, H. (2001). The concept of profession: A historical perspective based on the accounting profession in China. Accounting History International Conference, Deakin University, working paper, http://citeseerx.ist.psu.edu/viewdoc/download?doi=10.1.1.195.6579&rep=rep1&type=pdf (accessed 1 September 2018).

Yee, H. (2012). Analyzing the state-accounting profession dynamic: Some insights from the professionalization experience in China. *Accounting, Organizations and Society*, 37(6), 426–444.

11

THE ACCOUNTANCY PROFESSION AND EMERGING ECONOMIES

Reflections on the case of Syria at the margins of the global order

Rania Kamla, Habiba Al-Shaer, Sonja Gallhofer and Jim Haslam

Introduction

Accounting research has highlighted the complex and ambiguous or ambivalent consequences of globalisation as it interacts with accounting and the profession (Annisette, 2000, 2004; Caramanis, 2002; Arnold, 2005; Cooper and Robson, 2006; Gallhofer and Haslam, 2006, 2007). Such research has revealed how globalisation, with its international governance institutions and arrangements (including the World Bank, International Monetary Fund (IMF) and international trade agreements) often results in promoting – or even imposing – narrow capitalistic, Anglo-American accounting practices and thought in non-Western and emerging contexts. In these contexts, local professional accountancy bodies act mainly as promoters or facilitators of UK- and US-based qualifications, standards, training and education (Bakre, 2004, 2005, 2007; Gallhofer et al., 2009, 2011; Kamla et al., 2012; Aburous, 2016).

Despite these advances in the literature, critical and contextual explorations of the development of the accountancy profession and the socialisation of professional accountants outside Western contexts are still underdeveloped. Especially scarce are insights into the professional development and socialisation of accountants in the Arab world. In this chapter we focus on the accounting–globalisation interrelationship in Syria, an Arab country that prior to the outbreak of extreme violence in 2011 was seeking increased economic liberalisation and aspiring to gain a larger stake in the global economy after a long period of isolation and animosity with the West. We elaborate on how, before the violent events of more recent times, Syrian accountants were mobilising debates and shaping their professional identity vis-à-vis the new role of the accountancy profession they envisaged in the era of globalisation. We consider future research possibilities, including reflecting in this context on the terrible and tragic events impacting Syria in recent times.

The chapter is organised as follows. First, we provide a socio-economic and historical appreciation of the Syrian context and the development of the accountancy profession in Syria.

Second, we review how Syrian accountants were shaping debates and positioning themselves within the new open market environment, highlighting the main challenges faced by Syrian accountants and how they negotiated these challenges. Third, we consider future research possibilities, including after reflecting on the unrest in Syria.

Syria and the accountancy profession: an historical review

The Syrian context

Appreciating the development of the accountancy profession in Syria entails understanding Syria's historical, socio-economic, political and cultural context. Post-independence from France in 1946, Syria pursued a socialist, Pan-Arab agenda as defence against neo-imperialism, aligning itself closely with the Soviet Union (Fisher, 2005). Arab nationalism in particular became a significant feature of Syria's political identity, especially after the creation of Israel in Palestine in 1948 and the subsequent annexation of the Syrian Golan Heights by Israel in 1967. Syria and Syrians at that time prided themselves as socialist, anti-imperialist and anti-Zionist. However, for many Syrians, especially since the 1970s, there was a realisation that these pan-Arab and socialist slogans were merely rhetorical, used by the State to control debate and hinder public criticism (Mogannam, 2018).[1]

The socialist and nationalist sentiments led to State control over the main industries, engendering a large public sector controlling the main areas of Syria's economy and infrastructure (Quilliam, 1999). As Syria's Arab neighbours, who had closer relations with the West, moved towards the open market and liberalisation of their economies, it was difficult for Syria to sustain a socialist and nationalised economy, especially after the collapse of the Soviet Union (Wieland, 2006; Mogannam, 2018). Syria's conflict with the West and sanctions imposed on it by the US meant that Syria's liberalisation was mainly linked to Russia, China and Iran (Mogannam, 2018). Especially since the 1990s, major 'modernisation' efforts were manifested in all sectors of the economy, and private investment was promoted in previous State monopolies, such as education and banking (Gallhofer *et al.*, 2011). Although the privatisation of the Syrian economy was gradual, the material reality for Syrians was difficult, very similar to the experience of their Arab neighbours in Jordan, Lebanon or Egypt, who aligned their market reforms with the West and programmes of the IMF (Mogannam, 2018).

Especially since the 2000s, Syrians began to witness an even smaller elite (often a political elite or those aligned with the regime) who benefited from the booming private sector, getting richer while the majority of the population struggled to meet their daily requirements. A shrinking clan of the national bourgeois class was established in the supposedly socialist state (Wieland, 2006). The withdrawal of the welfare state that accompanied privatisation and the collapse of the industrial and agricultural sectors as the State withdrew subsidies meant a significant decline in the living standards of Syrians and a sharp rise in unemployment, especially youth unemployment (Wieland, 2006; Mogannam, 2018). In 2006, it was estimated that 30 per cent of Syrians were unemployed and that a similar percentage of the population lived below the poverty line. The majority of those employed earned low salaries with many professional Syrians having to hold as many as three jobs at a time to survive (Wieland, 2006). Meanwhile, globalisation and technological advancement exposed Syrians to the luxurious lifestyles and corruption of elites inside and outside Syria, exacerbating the significant social and economic divide between the haves and have-nots in the country (Wieland, 2006). Many commentators link the popular uprising that swept Syria in 2011 to the above-mentioned economic factors (Mogannam, 2018).

The Syrian national and collective habitus is influenced by a history of anti-colonialism against the West; Arab defeat and humiliation against Israel in 1948 and 1967; Pan-Arab and socialist sentiments that dominated the 1950s–1970s; state corruption, unemployment and financial hardship accompanied by political and economic isolation and economic liberalisation linked substantively to Russia and China. Islam also has a significant influence on Syrians. Indeed, with the receding influence of socialism and pan-Arabism, combined with troubled relations with the West, Syria was opened to increased Islamic influence, especially through funded missions by Saudi Arabia and other Gulf States (Wieland, 2006; Kamla *et al.*, 2012).

Accounting and the accountancy profession

The development of the accountancy profession followed the political and economic developments in Syria. Under French colonial rule, significant Western influence was evident in the socio-political and cultural spheres of Syria where aspects of the French accounting system were introduced (Qadi, 1996).[2] Generally, the socialist experience constituted an important chapter of Syria's history, and accounting practice and the accountancy profession substantively developed in this context (Kamla *et al.*, 2012). Accounting before the 1990s was strongly geared towards macroeconomic planning and public ownership of productive resources, with the first Syrian Unified Accounting System (UAS) issued by the state in 1978 (Kamla *et al.*, 2012). During that period, the professional accountancy body – the Association of Syrian Certified Accountants (ASCA) – did not have much influence.

Increased economic liberalisation and associated private sector expansion did not lead to substantive accounting regulations for private sector organisations (Meri, 1997; OBG, 2008). Syria established a State-supported accountancy body in 1958 – ASCA. This was modelled on the UK-influenced Egyptian body (Gallhofer *et al.*, 2011). A small private sector and State control over key industries meant that ASCA's role was limited, with little influence. ASCA, until the 1990s, had no permanent residence, no full-time members, no authority to enforce standards and no role in certification or examination of public accountants (these duties were consigned to State bodies, notably the Ministry of Supplies and Institute of Financial Auditing and since 2009 to the Ministry of Finance) (Gallhofer *et al.*, 2011). It was not until the 1990s and 2000s, with the growth of a stock exchange, a greater connection with global markets and the establishment of accounting standards, that ASCA began to gain some control and its membership started to expand. ASCA endorsed International Accounting Standards (IAS) in 2001. There were no Syrian accounting standards previously and the newly developed ones in 2001 mirrored those of the International Accounting Standards Committee/International Accounting Standards Board without much adaptation (Gallhofer *et al.*, 2011).

ASCA, perceiving increased opportunities for accountants in a more open market environment, played a role as a significant advocate for liberalisation (Gallhofer *et al.*, 2009, 2011). In 2005, as Syria began talks with the EU regarding a trade agreement, including for the services sector, ASCA sought to lobby the Parliament and the Ministry of Finance to change its status from an association to a syndicate (mirroring the status of the medical and engineering professions historically linked to the public sector in Syria). Despite ASCA's support for increased liberalisation of the economy, many local Syrian accountants associated with ASCA at the time were concerned with the increased influence of large accountancy firms in Syria and the lack of protection of local, small companies in the country (Gallhofer *et al.*, 2011). ASCA did not succeed in changing its legal status to a syndicate but Law 33 of 2009 stipulated that while the Ministry of Finance held the authority to qualify auditors, all qualified auditors should become members of ASCA in order to practise auditing, boosting ASCA's membership and funding.

Oversight of the profession, however, was entrusted to the newly established Accountancy and Auditing Board (AAB), a governmental body chaired by the Minister of Finance with members from academia, the government, the business sector and ASCA (Globaltrade, 2018). To date, ASCA still lacks prestige among Syrian accountants, with Syrians that have the financial means opting for Western-based qualifications, especially US CPA, rather than those issued by ASCA. ASCA's main role remains on the margins, carrying out seminars and International Financial Reporting Standards (IFRS) training (Kamla, 2018).[3]

Globalisation: Syrian professional accountants at the crossroads between globalism and isolation

The historical, political and socio-economic conflicts shaped much of Syrian accountants' national and professional identity, resulting in ambiguity, contradiction and fragmentation as we will show below. Publications by Gallhofer *et al.* (2009, 2011), Kamla *et al.* (2012) and Kamla (2012, 2014, 2018) reveal significant dimensions of tensions, ambiguity and contradictions associated with the globalisation–accounting interrelationship as expressed by Syrian accountants.[4]

A main contradiction in Syrian accountants' narratives is related to how they welcomed globalisation, open-markets and Western IAS/IFRS in their professional field, perceiving these as beneficial and inevitable (if acknowledging some negative impact at least in the short term). Meanwhile, Syrian accountants bemoaned and cautioned against Western influence and globalisation vis-à-vis cultural and social aspects of their lives. They often expressed a significant de-coupling between their professional and social lives and identities. One Syrian accountant, an owner of a small auditing firm and a prominent member of ASCA, expressed enthusiasm towards the expanding new role of auditors in Syria, contrasting this with the marginalisation of the profession under socialism:

> Auditors in Syria used not to be highly regarded [in the socialist area], as they used to be seen as those who deal with capitalists and aristocrats … but things are changing now.
>
> *(cited in Gallhofer et al., 2009: 356)*

While aware of their possible negative consequences, Syrian accountants hoped that liberalisation measures would provide, in the long term, an opportunity for Syrians to share some of the benefits of international trade and technology. While on the one hand this enthusiasm can be explained in relation to self-interest in expanding work opportunities for accountants and auditors as the private sector grew, it was shared by all participants in the study including academics, as they perceived these efforts as a beginning of change to the isolationist era and re-integration with the global economy. IAS/IFRS were professed as a significant step forward and a pre-condition to moves in this direction. A lecturer at Damascus University explained:

> Whether we like it or not we cannot keep on being isolated from the rest of the world, especially if we want to have a Stock Exchange and if Syrian companies desire to get listed on other … exchanges, they need to adopt IASs. We cannot only be concerned with our national environment, we should join the international community. When we talk about IASs, we talk about harmonisation of accounting practices globally … are we going to stay isolated from the world? Until when are we going to be afraid of how globalisation is going to affect us, rather than being part of it? … I am one of those strongly encouraging usage of IASs.
>
> *(cited in Gallhofer et al., 2011: 383)*

It is usual for accountants in emerging economies to perceive IAS/IFRS as promoting high quality accounting, facilitating open and transparent markets (Lehman, 2005; Gallhofer *et al.*, 2011). Syrian accountants to this extent repeated this rhetoric and seemed on the surface little concerned with the Western nature of IFRS. Indeed, as in the literature, Syrian accountants advocated the full adoption of IFRS quoting demands by multinationals, financial markets and ostensibly foreign investors (Aburous, 2016). However, beneath the surface, embedded in the narratives advocating IFRS, were veiled calls for wider change to address both political and economic isolation as well as also internal corruption and state control over the accountancy profession in Syria. While not able to talk openly and directly about corruption or political change in Syria, a practitioner and ASCA member when defending IFRS linked this to transparency and accountability that IAS/IFRS were perceived to bring:

> [T]he country is crippled by isolation and fear of the future. In such an atmosphere, I am afraid you cannot have improvement and development.… The most important thing for development is political and economic stability. If you do not have that, you'll not have development.
>
> *(cited in Gallhofer* et al., *2011: 388)*

Addressing economic isolation dominated the advocacy of IFRS adoption. Previous research would explain such somewhat misguided views as reflecting the significant impact of Western cultural imperialism including education programmes and professional training on accountants, especially young people. Islam (2003), for instance, indicated how Arab countries require, or at least encourage, their auditors today to have UK or US professional qualifications and to train in IFRS. These notions are also often explained in relation to insensitive cultural imperialism that often promotes and enforces narrow capitalistic policies, displacing other possibilities (Annisette, 2000; Lehman, 2005; Kamla *et al.*, 2012). These explanations are valid, especially in previous UK colonies, or in economies close to the West, but how can they explain Syrian accountants' enthusiasm towards them? In socialist and isolated Syria, accounting was mainly perceived as a state macroeconomic tool for planning and control of the economy and, as one young accountant explained, the education system until 2009 focused on educating accountants in relation to the controlled economy:

> I had not heard of IASs until I started working for a major international company. My university lecturers were all graduates of the GDR [German Democratic Republic] or the Soviet Union. International Accounting Standards were not on the menu in Socialist Syria.
>
> *(cited in Gallhofer* et al., *2009: 354)*

In their analysis of the foregoing sentiments, Gallhofer *et al.* (2009, 2011) explained that the lack of critical adoption of Syrian accountants of IFRS is linked to the pressures of globalisation, which have been linked to a general trend to apply Western rules and regulations globally. Globalisation and its instruments, therefore, have the aura of inevitability (Lehman, 2005). This is reflected in Syrian accountants' narratives. But one further dimension seems to be linked to the desire of Syrians for change coupled with significant disillusionment of Syrians with the empty rhetoric that dominated the so-called socialist era where suspicion of the West, its standards and technology was often used to curtail any calls for internal change (see Mogannam, 2018). In this respect, Syrian accountants' embracing of what appeared to be more transparent practices gradually taking away control from the state appear to have been traces of a veiled outcry against what was perceived as the paucity of the state's deliverance to Syrians in the pre-unrest times focused upon. One interviewee, who later went on to be exiled outside Syria due to his opposition to the regime, stressed that there is a need for Syrians to move away from blaming its problems on global imperialism, Israel or the West. There is a need for them to begin to take control of their own destiny:

> We need to put our own internal house in order. We should not get into a pessimistic mood that we cannot do anything. Success stories are few, but they exist.
>
> *(cited in Gallhofer et al., 2011: 391)*

It is important here to note that the interviewee was not at all blinded to the negative impact of neoliberal policies and the erosion of the welfare state on the material realities of Syrians. Various publications by him (as a prominent accountant and economic analyst) before and after leaving Syria, analysed the Syrian revolution in relation to rapid liberalisation of the economy combined with state policies that were mainly concerned with protecting the elite class, with increased unemployment, poverty and inequality. The quote from him, however, reflects the strong senti- ments of many interviewees who insisted that attention needed to be paid to internal socio- economic factors when understanding any aspects of Syria's interrelation with globalisation. Such voices have often been explained in the critical accounting literature, as mentioned earlier, vis-à- vis the impact of cultural imperialism. More multifaceted theoretical explanation is needed.

Meanwhile, many Syrian accountants wanted to reap the benefits that they observed their counterparts in neighbouring Arab countries as having. They observed ways in which account- ants from Jordan and Lebanon, countries preceding Syria in adopting liberalisation measures and international standards, were able to dominate high ranking accounting positions in Syria, with significant financial rewards, displacing local Syrians from these positions. To address this imbal- ance they perceived a need to further open up to Western standards, education and technology, firms (and even Western language) rather than resist them. To this end, even those Syrian accountants that owned small businesses and were threatened by the entry of big firms either welcomed the entry of international global firms or perceived their entry inevitable. An owner of a small auditing firm explained:

> [L]ike it or not, globalisation is happening. So, I don't agree with those opposing … entry of foreign and international corporations to our country. They should have the freedom to operate … and … constitute an incentive for our businesses to develop themselves and have a productive role. They are ahead of us in expertise and organisa- tion. We should benefit from them. We should not close our doors in the faces of foreign companies.
>
> *(cited in Gallhofer et al., 2011: 384)*

The entrance of the large audit firms into Syria did negatively impact on many accountants and small accounting firms in Syria. Instead of creating new job opportunities, the firms brought staff with them from Jordan or Lebanon. Syrians who were able to enter these firms were mainly from certain privileged backgrounds, able to gain Western, especially US, CPA-type qualifica- tions. Also they were fluent in English. Both the English language and Western qualifications acted as proxies for deepening class and gender divisions in the already divided Syrian context (Kamla, 2014). Further, the rise in importance of Western qualifications that intensified with the entry of large audit firms and multinationals to Syria further marginalised the already weak ASCA, in contrast to what ASCA had hoped for, as one young practitioner explained:

I am not a member of the association or a Certified Accountant. I am tempted to become a Certified Accountant as I can see that a number of my colleagues are pursuing this certificate. But to be honest I am tempted to become a (US) CPA or a (British) CA rather than a Syrian CA, as working in an international company it seems that such certificates are more reliable and demanded than the local ones. I do think that if I want to improve my career prospects ... I need to pursue these international certificates.

(cited in Gallhofer et al., 2011: 388)

The foregoing quotes indicated an unrestricted desire by Syrian accountants to join the community of international accountants. Globalisation for them offered an opportunity to have a stake in this international sphere after years of marginalisation and isolation. In understanding these sentiments, it might be useful to understand how Syrians perceived their history and their role in it. They often prided themselves as an outward-looking nation of successful merchants (especially in the cities of Aleppo and Damascus) that historically were the centre of international trade routes (Darke, 2018). Across the centuries commerce dominated Syria, affecting the mentality of the people, who learned to welcome trade as the one constant in their lives in periods of unrest, upheaval, invasions and plagues (Darke, 2018). It was during the colonial period but especially subsequently during the socialist era that Syrians found themselves truly isolated from world trade. Syria, a small nation, found it hard to comprehend its current global marginalisation and political humiliation (Darke, 2018). This sentiment is reflected in the quote below from one interviewee:

Our civilisation has always been about being in contact with the rest of the world and other civilisations passing through our lands. The concept of globalisation is not new for us. Our history and geographical location and religious history as the three religions came from Syria all make us able to adapt to the world.

(cited in Gallhofer et al., 2011: 390)

However, the colonial experience with the West and the subsequent cultural imperialism taught Syrians to be cautious when they welcomed foreign imports, especially of cultural ideas. The quote below reflects sentiments expressed by the majority of Syrian accountants interviewed:

The West wants to spread a new culture instead of the one here.... International organisations are tools to do so. This is why Europe is against the entry of Turkey to the EU. They are afraid of Islamic culture. They want their culture to be dominant by military force or even by other means like these international organisations.

(cited in Gallhofer et al., 2011: 382)

Thus, for Syrians, dealing with these contradictions in their history meant that dealing with the West required a de-coupling between the professional and the social. The professional requires technological advances that are now originating in the West, while valued cultural particularities need to be protected in the process:

Globalisation? I am convinced with one part of it, but not all.... As far as science is considered, it is great. We have suffered for 30 years from isolation. We could not get books or technology. Things are now better thanks to globalisation. Blocking knowledge and education was disastrous.... Globalisation could be useful in transforming knowledge, but it should not impact on our culture, civilisation and religion. This is not accepted.

(cited in Gallhofer et al., 2011: 382)

Future directions

The studies discussed here – they might be collectively termed studies on the Syrian accountancy profession at the margin of globalisation or globalism – were published prior to the major unrest that has impacted Syria so badly in recent times. As well as learning from these studies we need to reflect on the recent crisis context.

Regarding the studies reviewed, capturing a moment in Syria's history as it was shifting from a formally more socialistic to a more neoliberalistic socio-economic positioning, they suggest a number of insights. Dimensions of the voice of Syrian accountants – a voice which can be considered somewhat repressed/silenced in the global context (see Calhoun, 1995; Gandhi, 1998; Loomba, 1998) – are elaborated. The Syrian accountants in this historical context perceived globalisation or globalism in somewhat pragmatic terms. They appreciated it as, in part, a cultural imperialistic force but saw it also as providing positive opportunities of local relevance (e.g. via cross-border interaction/communication, the ending of political and economic isolation, developments in expertise and technology and possibilities for accountancy specifically in terms of joining the global accountancy community).[5]

Such an appreciation of the local perspective reflects the commitment of Gallhofer *et al.* (2011: 378) to appreciate and learn from the other by going 'beyond listening' towards 'engaging' thus promoting 'co-operation and better ways'. Thus, local voices are subjected to a critical hermeneutics whereby they are appreciated, indeed seen as a source for more general critique, but are also challenged and problematised. The studies reviewed reflect an appreciation of the ambivalent and contradictory nature of the interviewees' narrative positions, in relation to which the importance of the national and historical context for understanding Syrian accountants' identity construction was underlined. The papers also highlighted a lack of effective resistance in practical terms to a neoliberal globalisation, which indicates the power of the neoliberal rhetoric (see also Caramanis, 2002; Gallhofer and Haslam, 2007). Linked to the analysis, there is also an argument that academics have a role in problematising and challenging this rhetoric.

Many of the foregoing insights would also appear to be potentially relevant to the case of emerging economies more generally today, including encouraging search for local particularity. The studies reviewed are suggestive of a number of future research possibilities. For instance, how do the global issues that impacted Syria in the context referenced in these studies impact in other contexts? Given, however, the horrendous events impacting Syria that manifested themselves after the publication of the research reviewed in this chapter, it is clearly important to reflect on those events to seek to appreciate what they suggest for future research work.

In part, the unrest in Syria constitutes a brutal reminder of the significance of contextual dynamics and specificities – the specificities of the Syrian context and its interface with the global context, or Syria as different or as differentiated universal (Gallhofer and Haslam, 2003) vis-à-vis a simplifying categorisation such as 'emerging economies'. A major point to re-emphasise here is the need to take context and contextual complexity very seriously.

Reflecting on this in relation to Syria today, there are a variety of critical insights into the context that can seek to deepen appreciation but also problematise and challenge the local views (in accounting research in relation to emerging economies, in this regard, see, for example, Annisette, 2000; Bakre, 2004; Lehman, 2005). This is consistent with the possible mobilising of new emphases in critical hermeneutics and a critical theoretical concern to constantly seek the advancement of theorising.

It is also of interest to develop research argumentation on Syria that reflects the very particular interface Syria has with the global context and its particular position in the global context (both these aspects being dynamic).[6] Constantly advancing an in-depth and critical appreciation of local ideas and perceptions in the context of which they are part is required vis-à-vis the complexity of the global and the local–global interface (see Kamla, 2018). The particular character of Syria's trajectory in context needs to be explored in considerable depth. In relation to the dynamics, what are the specific aspects of the local context and the specificities of a given local–global interface that are of relevance to understanding the trajectory of accountancy? Can we look beyond the current ongoing tragic happenings towards better ways through a further commitment to understanding Syria and its dynamics (its oppressions and interfaces, see Mogannam, 2018) more deeply and critically? How can we forge pragmatic alliances between various constituencies (e.g. academics and local actors), an aspect of what Gallhofer and Haslam (2017) see in terms of the chains of equivalence of Laclau and Mouffe (2001)?

Looking beyond the negative in current times, perhaps Syrian accountants' willingness to themselves be open to others, evident in the pre-crisis studies reviewed, something to promote and to learn from, indicate something deeply embedded in Syrian culture more generally, from which we might also learn – the 'instinctive sense of community and empathy for one another, even for those outside the family' (Darke, 2018: xvi) – a sign of hope, a small bright spark gleaming now faintly against the deep and turbulent darkness of our times.

The recent turbulence is suggestive of the relevance of particular future research focuses, many of which will face different and difficult challenges. What do the developments mean for local accountancy and accountant identities (consider Richardson, 2017)? There is a need vis-à-vis current literature to broaden out the literature on 'local accountancy' (and the studies we have reviewed do reflect an early response to the call made by Richardson (2017) to do just that) but it clearly poses many challenges in this instance. The complex and multifaceted turbulence of Syria, to which multifarious forces contributed and on which there are several perspectives (Mogannam, 2018), can be theorised in relation to accountancy. As we write, it is clearly practically difficult to do this empirically.[7]

Notes

1 Evidence for this is that Syria, supposedly the last standing fortress of socialism and anti-imperialism in the region, had the weakest and least independent workers movement among all Arab states. The state's affiliated unions' main role has often been to organise shows and parties in support of the regime (Allinson, 2015).

2 The commercial law introduced in 1949, for instance, basically followed French law (Qadi, 1996).

3 Especially since Law 33 of 2009 stipulates that the condition for practice is reduced from five years to two years of experience if the candidate has a US CPA or a UK CA (Globaltrade, 2018).

4 The studies referred to relied on interviews of Syrian accountants from all ranks in the period before the revolution in 2002, 2005, 2008 and 2009.

5 Of course, these opportunities have subsequently scarcely been realised in practice.

6 Mogannam (2018: 225–231) suggests the relevance of appreciating what has been Syria's fostering of an 'alternative process of neoliberalisation' with China, Russia and Iran due to historical and ongoing tensions with the West. Such specificities may illuminate intricate complexities of phenomena such as the construction of the identity of the accountant in Syria (and Brouard *et al.* (2017) point to the significance of professionals vis-à-vis the challenges of our times) and of the functioning of accountancy and accounting more generally in Syria. In the pre-crisis context these particularities appear to

have scarcely modified accountancy developments in Syria, which appeared to be substantively refractions of Western influence. The influence of particular variants of neoliberalisation may be part of a detail that can come to be more important in the complex of dynamics and contingencies.

7 We should here note emphatically that a significant number of those accountants interviewed in the pre-crisis studies reviewed had to flee Syria and/or have found themselves jobless (some are unemployed refugees in Europe) as the result of unrest.

References

Aburous, D. (2016). Understanding cultural capital and habitus in corporate accounting: A postcolonial context. *Spanish Journal of Finance and Accounting/Revista Española de Financiación y Contabilidad*, 45(2), 54–179.

Allinson, J. (2015). Class forces, transition and the Arab uprisings: A comparison of Tunisia, Egypt and Syria. *Democratization*, 22(2), 294–314.

Annisette M. (2000). Imperialism and the professions: The education and certification of accountants in Trinidad and Tobago. *Accounting, Organizations and Society*, 25(7), 631–659.

Annisette, M. (2004). The true nature of the World Bank. *Critical Perspectives on Accounting*, 15(3), 303–323.

Arnold P. J. (2005). Disciplining domestic regulation: The World Trade Organisation and the market for professional services. *Accounting, Organizations and Society*, 30(4), 229–330.

Bakre, O. M. (2004). Accounting and the problematique of Imperialism: Alternative methodological approaches to empirical research in accounting in developing countries. *Advances in Public Interest Accounting*, 10, 1–30.

Bakre, O. M. (2005). First attempt at localising imperial accountancy: The case of the Institute of Chartered Accountants of Jamaica (ICAJ) (1950s–1970s). *Critical Perspectives on Accounting*, 16(8), 995–1018.

Bakre, O. M. (2007). The unethical practices of accountants and auditors and the compromising stance of professional bodies in the corporate world: Evidence from corporate Nigeria. *Accounting Forum*, 31(3), 277–303.

Brouard, F., Bujaki, M., Durocher, S. and Neilson, L. C. (2017). Professional accountants' identity formation: An integrative framework. *Journal of Business Ethics*, 142(2), 225–238.

Calhoun C. (1995). *Critical Social Theory: Culture, History and the Challenge of Difference*. Oxford: Blackwell.

Caramanis, C. (2002). The interplay between professional groups, the state and supranational agents: Pax Americana in the age of 'globalisation'. *Accounting, Organizations and Society*, 27(4–5), 379–408.

Cooper D. J. and Robson K. (2006). Accounting, professions and regulation: Locating the sites of professionalization. *Accounting, Organizations and Society*, 31(4–5), 415–444.

Darke, D. (2018). *The Merchant of Syria: A History of Survival*. New York: Oxford University Press.

Fisher, W. B. (2005). *History, Physical and Social Geography of Syria. Europa Regional Surveys of the World Publications 2005*, 51st edn. London/New York: Routledge.

Gallhofer, S. and Haslam, J. (2003). *Accounting and Emancipation: Some Critical Interventions*. London: Routledge.

Gallhofer, S. and Haslam, J. (2006). The accounting–globalisation interrelation: An overview with some reflections on the neglected dimension of emancipatory potentiality. *Critical Perspectives on Accounting*, 17(7), 903–934.

Gallhofer, S. and Haslam, J. (2007). Exploring social, political and economic dimensions of accounting in the global context: The International Accounting Standards Board and accounting disaggregation. *Socio-Economic Review*, 5(4), 633–664.

Gallhofer, S. and Haslam, J. (2017). Some reflections on the construct of emancipatory accounting: Shifting meaning and the possibilities of a new pragmatism. *Critical Perspectives on Accounting*. https://doi.org/10.1016/j.cpa.2017.01.004.

Gallhofer, S., Haslam, J. and Kamla, R. (2009). Educating and training accountants in Syria in a transition context: Perceptions of accounting academics and professional accountants. *Accounting Education: An International Journal*, 18(4–5), 345–368.

Gallhofer, S., Haslam, J. and Kamla, R. (2011). The accountancy profession and the ambiguities of globalisation in a post-colonial, Middle Eastern and Islamic context: Perceptions of accountants in Syria. *Critical Perspectives on Accounting*, 22(4), 376–395.

Gandhi, L. (1998). *Postcolonial Theory: A Critical Introduction*. Edinburgh: University Press.

Globaltrade (2018). Syria tax and accounting standards. www.globaltrade.net/f/business/Syria/Taxes-and-Accounting-Accounting-Standards.html (accessed 23 July 2018).

Islam, M. M. (2003). Regulations and supervision of financial institutions in GCC countries. *Managerial Finance*, 29(7): 17–42.

Kamla, R. (2012). Syrian women accountants' attitudes and experiences at work in the context of globalization. *Accounting, Organizations and Society*, 37(3), 188–205.

Kamla, R. (2014). Modernity, space-based patriarchy and global capitalism: Implications for Syrian women accountants. *Accounting and Business Research*, 44(6), 603–629.

Kamla, R. (2018). Religion-based resistance strategies, politics of authenticity and professional women accountants. *Critical Perspectives on Accounting*. https://doi.org/10.1016/j.cpa.2018.05.003.

Kamla, R., Gallhofer, S. and Haslam, J. (2012). Understanding Syrian accountants' perceptions of, and attitudes towards, social accounting. *Accounting, Auditing & Accountability Journal*, 25(7), 1170–1205.

Laclau, E. and Mouffe, C. (2001). *Hegemony and Socialist Strategy: Towards a Radical Democratic Politics.* London: Verso.

Lehman, G. (2005). A critical perspective on the harmonisation of accounting in a globalising world. *Critical Perspectives on Accounting*, 16(7), 975–992.

Loomba A. (1998). *Colonialism/postcolonialism.* London/New York: Routledge.

Meri, A. R. (1997). *The Role of a Stock Exchange Market in Developing Accounting Systems in Syria.* Unpublished PhD thesis, Damascus University, Damascus.

Mogannam, J. (2018). Syria's anti-imperialist mask: Unveiling contradictions of the left through anti-capitalist thought. *Social Identities*, 24(2), 222–237.

OBG (2008). *Emerging Syria, Emerging Markets Series 2008.* London: Oxford Business Group.

Qadi, H. (1996). *Auditing: The basics*, 3rd edn. Damascus: University Publications.

Quilliam, N. (1999). *Syria and the New World Order.* London: Garnet & Ithaca Press.

Richardson, A. J. (2017). Professionalization and the Accounting Profession in Roslender, R. (Ed.), *The Routledge Companion to Critical Accounting.* London: Routledge.

Wieland, C. (2006). *Syria at Bay: Secularism, Islamism and 'Pax-Americana'.* London: Hurst and Company.

12

THE BRAZILIAN ACCOUNTING PROFESSION AND ACCOUNTING EDUCATION

An historical perspective

Lúcia Lima Rodrigues, Maria Clara Bugarim and Russell Craig

Introduction

This chapter adopts an historical perspective to outline key factors that have influenced the emergence of the accounting profession and accounting education in Brazil. Particular attention is given to highlighting how the evolution of accounting education has been associated with the development of the Brazilian accounting profession. Some current challenges faced by the accounting profession, and by accounting education in Brazil, are also discussed.

Understanding the history of development of accounting education and of the accounting profession in Brazil should be of more than passing interest to accounting scholars. The emerging economy of Brazil offers insights and research opportunities for accounting researchers that are not readily available when using well-developed (and, indeed, emerging) economies as research sites. Brazil possesses some unique features as a site to study the development of accounting. These include its record of importing accounting laws and practices from a well-established country with a long economic history (Portugal). One particularly strong ensuing influence on accounting has been the Portuguese code-law-based system of governing. Other strong features of Brazil as a research site are the high degree of association between accounting education and professional practice (especially after the 1930 revolution) and the influence of the hyperinflationary environment of Brazil in promoting theory and practice with respect to accounting for inflation.

In this chapter, we show that throughout Brazil's history as an emerging economy, politics, business and the accounting profession have been mutually dependent. Some features of the professional development of accounting have survived political and economic change, whereas others have become diluted or have faced new challenges. Two current challenges facing accounting in Brazil are: first, how can the quality of higher education institutions (HEIs) offering accounting education be improved; and, second, how can the limited development of academic research in accounting be expanded and improved?

We begin by contextualising the evolution of accounting education in Brazil. Then we describe the emergence of the Brazilian accounting profession (known as Conselho Federal de

Contabilidade/Conselhos Regionais de Contabilidade (or CFC/CRC system)), before discussing major developments in the evolution of, and some of the main challenges facing accounting education and the accounting profession in Brazil.

Accounting education in Brazil and the creation of the CFC/CRC system

Brazil has been a Portuguese colony since 22 April 1500 when the Portuguese navigator Pedro Álvares Cabral landed on the northeast coast of Brazil, near the present-day city of Porto Seguro. In 1808, the Portuguese Royal Court fled from Portugal to its colony in Brazil to avoid being captured by invading Napoleonic troops. The Royal Court arrived in Bahia on 18 January 1808 and transferred to Rio de Janeiro a month later. There, they transformed the colony into a metropolis from which they could control the Portuguese Empire (Rodrigues and Sangster, 2013).

Almost immediately upon the arrival of the Royal Court in Brazil, Prince João[1] announced several major decisions. These included the opening of Brazilian ports to friendly nations and the creation of a new tax to finance operations of the Royal Court. Prince João also began a programme of establishing the many arms of government that would be needed to administer the Portuguese Empire from Brazil – such as a Royal Treasury in Rio de Janeiro. The Royal Treasury operated its General Controlling Offices (Contadorias Gerais) using double-entry booking (DEB).[2] The administration of the Portuguese Empire from Brazil could not have been conducted effectively without a strong supply of skilled people to fill accounting-related posts in the mercantile community and bureaucracy.

Thus, it was not surprising that on 23 February 1808, Prince João established the Rio de Janeiro School of Commerce (RdJSoC). This school imitated the Lisbon School of Commerce (established in 1759) in structure, operation and curriculum (of arithmetic, algebra, weights and measures, bookkeeping and commerce). Between 1811 and 1821, 199 students enrolled at the RdJSoC and 72 graduated. Similar schools were established to teach commerce (including bookkeeping) in Bahia (1814), Maranhão (1815) and Pernambuco (1821).[3] The accounting technologies of government adopted by D. João VI when establishing the Royal Court in Rio de Janeiro helped to prepare Brazil for independence in 1822 (Rodrigues and Sangster 2013; Araújo et al., 2017. See also Fernandes, 2005). Many practitioners of these accounting technologies of government (which were maintained after independence) were graduates of the accounting programmes offered by the schools referred to above. In 1858, new statutes were issued to establish the Commercial Institute of Rio de Janeiro (CIRdJ) to replace the RdJSoC (Decree 1763).

Brazilian accounting has always been influenced strongly by legislative measures (Rodrigues et al., 2011, 2012) such as by the Commercial Code of 1850.[4] This Code established an obligation to use DEB in the preparation of an annual balance sheet. Understanding this Commercial Code became an essential aspect of the training of accounting students at the CIRdJ.

Several important developments in the professionalisation of accounting and the development of accounting education occurred in the second half of the nineteenth century. In 1860, the Imperial government of D. Pedro II of Brazil approved the first Joint Stock Companies Law (Law 1083) (Ricardino and Iudícibus, 2002; Rodrigues et al., 2011). Article 2 of this law required managers or directors of companies to publish their balance sheets, statements and other documents, and forward them to the government. A few months later, Decree 2679 regulated the financial reporting disclosures required by the government. Article 2 of this decree extended the ambit of the Joint Stock Companies Law to include all 'other companies, civil as well as mercantile'. This decree also required the preparation of standardised balance sheets.[5] The Joint Stock Companies Law was the first step towards the standardisation of financial reporting in Brazil. For the next 80 years, this law guided financial reporting in Brazil (Ricardino and Iudícibus, 2002; Rodrigues *et al.*, 2011).[6]

In 1863, D. Pedro II reorganised commercial education and changed the statutes of the CIRdJ (Decree 3058). Henceforth, the CIRdJ offered a preparatory course and a professional course (Rodrigues *et al.*, 2011). The professional course was extended from two years to four years. Bookkeeping was taught in the third and fourth years. The CIRdJ closed in 1882 because it lacked attractiveness in relation to other courses, had tough course admission criteria and had found it difficult to supply graduates with the abilities sought by commercial employers (Bielinski, 2000).

After the military took control of the Brazilian empire in 1889 (and the country became a republic) Brazil began to rely more on exports, particularly of coffee. The coffee industry expanded considerably. This led to such strong economic development in São Paulo that the financial centre of Brazil gravitated from Rio de Janeiro to São Paulo (Ricardino, 2000). The growth in the coffee industry had a strong positive effect on commerce generally, and for railways, banks, insurance companies and publicly owned firms especially. The ensuing strong demand for bookkeepers and business managers prompted the establishment of two schools in São Paulo to offer accounting programmes that would be recognised for the purpose of certifying accounting professionals. These were the Polytechnic School of São Paulo in 1894 and the Practical School of Commerce in 1902 (Martins *et al.*, 2006).[7] Also in 1902, the Rio de Janeiro Academy of Commerce was founded. In 1905, diplomas issued by the Practical School of Commerce and the Rio de Janeiro Academy of Commerce were officially recognised by Federal Decree 1339. This recognition was a significant milestone in the history of commercial education in Brazil (Machado, 1982).[8]

Some initial hallmarks of the professionalisation of accounting in Brazil soon appeared. In 1912, the first issue of the *Brazilian Review of Accounting* was published. This was superseded in June 1922 by the *Paulista Magazine of Accounting* (Ricardino, 2000). Two professional accounting bodies were established in 1921: the Paulista Institute of Accounting (in São Paulo) and the Brazilian Institute of Accounting (in Rio de Janeiro). In 1924, the first Brazilian accounting congress was held, in Rio de Janeiro. The main topic of debate was 'how to best professionalise accounting' (De Rocchi, 2007; Sá, 2008).

In 1926, technical accounting education was again subject to regulation by the Brazilian government. Decree 17329 established that, in essence, accounting education should be practical and should aim to train specialised accounting technicians. This decree also regulated commercial technical education and obliged officially recognised schools to offer a general degree of four years. Such schools could also offer specialised courses in actuarial studies and auditing (Araújo, 2002: 18).

After the Brazilian Revolution of 1930, the government formed by Getúlio Vargas espoused a corporatist ideology, inspired by the Portuguese tradition of centralised, State-directed, often Catholic-inspired, bureaucratic corporatism (Wiarda, 1978: 31; Rodrigues *et al.*, 2011). The professional regulations issued by the Vargas government provided a framework for establishing and monitoring a chartered accounting profession (Decree 20158). The corporatist State endured in Brazil from 1930 to 1945. During this time accounting was instrumental in helping the government achieve its political commitments to policies of industrialisation and import replacement. Adoption of these policies encouraged the development of accounting. For example, in 1934, enactment of the Water Code (Código de Águas) introduced the principle of 'service at cost' in determining that the price charged for supply of water should recover the current costs of service delivery, including depreciation (Bastos, 2006: 258).

In 1931, consistent with corporatist ideology, Decree 20158 required persons entering the accounting profession to be a graduate of an authorised school and to hold a diploma validated by the Superintendent of Commercial Education. At the time, those who completed a three-year degree received an 'expert accountant' diploma and those who completed a two-year (technical) degree received a 'bookkeeper' diploma. Decree 20158 came at a time when the economy and labour market were growing and government policy in making appointments to public posts was to prefer graduates of recognised commercial schools (Articles 76 and 77, Decree 20158) (Rodrigues *et al.*, 2011). Understandably, in such a setting, the number of graduates in commerce from public and private schools grew considerably. In 1932, the demand for accountants was increased further by the requirement in Decree 21033 that accounting books and documents would only have legal or administrative effect if they were signed by an actuary, 'expert accountant'[9] or by an accountant or bookkeeper.

In 1945, the government mandated that a university degree was required for entry to several occupations, including those in accounting. To facilitate this policy, Decree 7988 established the conditions whereby HEIs could award a four-year bachelor's degree in accounting. One condition was that HEIs offer special courses in general accounting, industrial and agricultural accounting, insurance accounting, governmental accounting, bank accounting and auditing. After 1946, several Brazilian universities responded to the new legislation by creating courses in accounting. The first was the University of São Paulo (Faculty of Economics and Administrative Sciences). In late 1946, it began offering a degree in accounting and actuarial sciences. Rapid growth occurred after 1946 in the number of accounting degrees offered throughout Brazil (Rodrigues *et al.*, 2011).

The government's acknowledgement that practice as an accountant required university-level education was helpful in marshalling support for accounting to be recognised as a profession. Decree-Law 9295 in 1946 created two new regulatory bodies: a Federal Accounting Council (CFC) and Regional Accounting Councils (CRC). These councils still exist: the CFC is the national council of the accounting profession and the CRC is the regional accounting council in each state. The CFC/CRC system requires accountants to be registered in the state in which they practise professionally (Rodrigues *et al.*, 2017). The CFC and CRC are responsible for enforcing legal requirements of the accounting profession. They have broad oversight responsibility. Similar professional councils, accredited by the government, were introduced in other professions too. This move reflected the Brazilian government's policy of creating official agencies to regulate and supervise the professions.

In 1946, Decree 9295 established three levels of practitioners within the accounting profession:

- accountants (*contadores*) – holders of a university degree;
- accounting technicians (*técnicos de contabilidade*) – holders of a commercial high school diploma; and
- bookkeepers (*guarda-livros*) – persons without educational credentials in accounting, but with relevant practical experience.

Accounting education in Brazil after the creation of the CFC/CRC system

The accounting profession in Brazil became official on 27 May 1946. The profession has developed since through the creation of many new educational institutions offering instruction in accounting; and by development of accounting theory through adoption of 'more progressive American ideas' (Machado and Nova, 2008: 3).

In 1951, Vargas was returned to power by popular vote. He continued to emphasise the role of accounting in supporting government activities. The growing specialisation occurred because the development policies of Vargas led to the bachelor's degree in accounting being separated from a bachelor's degree in actuarial studies (Decree 1401, 1951). Nonetheless, the bachelor's degree in accounting retained some actuarial studies subjects.

The post-World War II period in Brazil was characterised by a strong period of inflation that lasted until 1994.[10] High inflation made indexation necessary to preserve the real value of assets and to provide financial statements that better reflected the reality of companies (Rodrigues *et al.*, 2011). In 1947, Decree 24239 required the revaluation of fixed tangible assets, with an off-setting entry to a special equity reserve account.

The decades immediately following World War II witnessed a strong period of change for the accounting profession and for bachelor degrees in accounting. In 1958, during a period of intense change arising from the 'targets plan'[11] of President Juscelino Kubitchek, Law 3384 established a new classificatory profile for professional accountants. Henceforth, there would be only two designations: accountants (*contadores*) and accounting technicians (*técnicos de contabilidade*). The separate category for bookkeepers was abolished. Bookkeepers were now included in the category of accounting technicians.

In 1960, the Federal Education Council (Conselho Federal de Educação – CFE) was created. This body established formal policy guidelines on the standards and bases of national education in Brazil, together with minimum curricula requirements and rules specifying the duration of higher education courses involved in training regulated professions, were established (Law 4024, 20 December 1961). Also in 1961, the first postgraduate degrees in accounting were awarded (Rodrigues *et al.*, 2011, 2012). In 1962, CFE Opinion 397 was responsible for a major change in the teaching of accounting: degrees were divided into 'basic' and 'professional training' cycles. Accounting courses were concentrated in the 'professional training' cycle. They involved instruction in general accounting, commercial accounting, cost accounting, auditing and balance sheet analysis.

The term of office of Goulart as President (1961–1964) was marked by high inflation, economic stagnation and increasingly radical politics. The armed forces staged a *coup d'état* on 31 March 1964 because they believed that change was needed in Brazilian society to thwart the high level of corruption and the threat of a communist government. With increasing inflation rates, accounting techniques involving indexation gradually spread throughout Brazil (Law 4357, 1964). These techniques became more important after 1964, when several economic variables (such as wages and debt) began to be indexed (Rodrigues *et al.*, 2011).

After 1964, the volume of legislation increased rapidly under the military regime. According to Gomes (1978: 8), this 'implied greater tax and accounting controls, both for public agencies and for private companies'. The legislation introduced included the Budget Law (Law 4320, 17 March 1964), the Banking Reform Law (Law 4595, 31 December 1964), the Capital Markets Law (Law 4728, 14 July 1965) and the Administrative Reform Decree-Law (Decree-Law 200, 25 February 1967).

The 1960s heralded a new phase in the development of accounting education (Araújo 2002: 22–23). In 1964, a local version of Finney and Miller's leading North American accounting text, *Introductory Accounting*, was widely adopted. This book was revised and adapted by a team of academics from the University of São Paulo. The book imitated American accounting and was significant because it defined methods of inflation accounting for purposes of presenting a statement of financial position. These contributions from the so-called Brazilian School of Monetary Correction (whose principal exponents were at the University of São Paulo) to inflation accounting have been recognised internationally with approbation, for example, by Doupnik (1986; 1996). Two major academic contributions on inflation accounting were contained in PhD theses awarded by the University of São Paulo to Iudícibus in 1966 and Martins in 1972 (both in Business Administration, specialising in accounting).

The beginning of the modern era of accounting in Brazil is usually dated from about the 1970s: that is, from the time of the development of Brazil's capital market and the introduction of financial system reforms (Niyama and Silva, 2005; Rodrigues *et al.*, 2012). The Capital Markets Law of 1965 created the role of independent auditor. This led, in 1971, to the founding of the Institute of Independent Auditors of Brazil (IAIB).[12] The first fully fledged research-based higher degree programmes in accounting were introduced in 1970 (Master) and 1978 (PhD) by the Faculty of Economics, Administration and Accounting of the University of São Paulo (Peleias *et al.*, 2007). These research-only higher degree programmes stimulated theoretical and scientific advances in accounting knowledge.

Although Brazil was ruled by a right-wing military regime from 1964 to 1985, a democratic environment was gradually restored.[13] Strong impetus for this was provided by Jimmy Carter's election as US president in late 1976. Carter quickly instituted foreign policy settings that impaired the politico-economic sustainability of anti-democratic governments. Carter was strongly opposed to authoritarian anti-communist regimes in Latin America. The ideological shift he made fostered further changes in accounting and auditing. On 15 December 1976, Brazilian Corporation Law (Law 6404) was approved, initiating a new phase in the history of Brazilian accounting. This law improved the quality of published accounting information and facilitated understanding of the financial position and economic performance of companies (Teles, 1989: 52). American influence was strengthened because the new law was similar to the US Corporation Act (Rodrigues *et al.*, 2012). In 1985, Tancredo Neves was elected president of Brazil by the Electoral College, thereby returning political control to civilians. In 1989, Collor de Mello was the first president after the military regime to be elected by direct vote of Brazilians.

In 1992, CFE Resolution 03 set out formal requirements for all bachelor's degrees in Brazil. The bachelor's degree in accounting was to be at least four years' duration for full-time students and five years for part-time students. The resolution also established standards to guide higher education institutions in preparing their curricula for the bachelor's degree in accounting. Courses were grouped into three categories of knowledge: Category I – arts and humanities; Category II – vocational training; and Category III – complementary training activities. Accounting courses were concentrated in Categories II and III (Peleias *et al.*, 2007: 28).

A period of inflationary stability occurred after 1994, following the introduction of the Real Plan (Plano Real) by finance minister Fernando Henrique Cardoso.[14] This plan created a non-monetary currency, the Unidade Real de Valor (URV). The value of one URV was set to approximately one US dollar. This move helped to stabilise inflation. Brazil's annual inflation rate fell from approximately 750 per cent in the first half of 1994 to about 18 per cent in the second half of 1994. The success of the Real Plan helped Cardoso to be elected president of Brazil in 1995 (Rodrigues *et al.*, 2012).

In 1997, the Brazilian Corporation Law (Law 6404) underwent its first major change, with the introduction of new corporate governance rules (especially mechanisms to protect minority shareholders) (Rodrigues *et al.*, 2012).

Between 1991 and 2000, the number of higher degree programmes in accounting increased from 262 to 510 (MEC, 2012). This rapid increase was a source of concern since most of the new HEIs were private (74.7 per cent) and the number of instructors holding a Master or a PhD degree was very low (Coelho, 1999).[15] In 1999, faced with a profusion of newly established private HEIs that offered low-quality bachelor degrees in accounting, the CFC established an entry exam for accounting professionals (Exam of Sufficiency) (CFC Resolution 853). The intent was to maintain a high standard for CFC/CRC members (Rodrigues *et al.*, 2017). The Exam of Sufficiency was suspended between 2005 and 2010 because of complaints that it violated constitutional principles regarding who could become a member of the profession.

Challenges for accounting education and the accounting profession

In the twenty-first century, Brazilian accounting is undergoing significant change as it tries to adapt to the needs of a globalising world. In the field of accounting education, an important change in the undergraduate degree in accounting was prompted in March 2004 when National Curricular Guidelines were established for the bachelor's degree in accounting. In September 2004, these guidelines were changed at the request of the Brazilian Actuarial Institute (IBA) so that the bachelor degree in accounting excluded material that was primarily pertinent to actuaries (Conselho Nacional de Educação/Câmara de Educação Superior – CNE/CES Opinion 269/2004). The IBA's justification was that accounting should not be confused with actuarial studies, since both areas had different foundations (Peleias *et al.*, 2007: 28).

Brazil began to converge national accounting standards with international accounting standards in 2007. President Lula da Silva's government (2003–2011) mandated international accounting standards should be adopted (Lourenço and Braunbeck, 2019). Because of the more complex requirements of these standards, the CFC/CRC moved to require a university degree as a prerequisite for entry to the accounting profession. As was the case in Portugal, where adoption of adapted international accounting standards was a key factor influencing the government to increase the status of the accounting profession from *Chamber* of Accountants to *Order* of Certified Accountants (Guerreiro *et al.*, 2015), similarly in Brazil, the accounting profession negotiated with government for an increase in the social status of the CFC. The CFC argued that the accounting profession had to modernise its rules; had to ensure accounting professionals would now use more complex international accounting standards; and that professional acumen required of individual accountants would be higher.

On 22 May 2006, CFC Ordinance 44 established a national commission to reformulate Decree-Law 9295 of 1946 (the law which established the CFC/CRC system) to align professional performance requirements with present-day needs. Accordingly, on 11 June 2010, Law 12249 amended several provisions contained in Decree-Law 9295/46. The main changes were to:

* require a bachelor degree in accounting for registration as a member;
* clarify that the CFC can issue accounting standards;
* require a pass in the Exam of Sufficiency as a condition to register as an accountant; and
* authorise the CFC to supervise the technical qualifications of its members and the content and delivery of continuing education programmes.

These changes made it clear that the CFC had the lead role in developing accounting standards and in establishing accounting education requirements. Candidates had to attain a mark of at least 50 per cent in the Exam of Sufficiency to be eligible for professional entry. In 2012, the proportion of candidates passing the Exam of Sufficiency was only 24 per cent (Rodrigues *et al.*, 2018).

Currently, the accounting profession has a monopoly on the provision of accounting and accounting-related services in audit, taxation, consultancy and insolvency. The current strength of the accounting profession has arisen, the challenges posed by changes over time in the political, economic and socio-cultural environment in Brazil notwithstanding. Recently, the profession has been focused on addressing the task of adopting and converging international accounting standards. Another challenge has been to decide what to do about the growth of low-quality HEIs. In 2012, 893 HEIs offered a bachelor's degree in accounting. Of these, only 103 were government funded. The proportion of non-government-funded HEIs increased from 72 per cent in 1991 to 88 per cent in 2012. Although an accounting degree was the third most popular choice of first-year enrolments in all HEIs in 2012, accounting was ranked only fifth in numbers of graduating students (MEC, 2012) (Rodrigues *et al.*, 2017). Thus, there is a high student attrition rate. Additionally, the number of higher degree graduates from universities has been very low. As at 30 September 2014, the National Association of Postgraduate Programs in Accounting Sciences (ANPCONT) reported that there were only 3264 Master's degree holders and 275 PhD holders in accounting in Brazil (ANPCONT, 2014). This is a concern because the consequent level of research in accounting is low.

Future directions

Accounting education and the accounting profession in Brazil have been influenced by the ambient social, economic and political context in which they have operated. A strong supply of accountants has long been required to administer state and national tax systems, to maintain economic development, and to sustain political stability. New accounting practices have often been introduced because of prevailing government ideologies (especially of corporatism) and policies that have sought to modernise society and expand commercial activity. The historical institutional analysis undertaken in this chapter has highlighted how ambient economic and political contexts have influenced accounting education and the development of the accounting profession.

In 1945, the government's decision to permit universities to offer a bachelor's degree in accounting and actuarial sciences stimulated the move to seek regulation of accounting, and to create an accounting association. The first degree that promoted the accounting profession specifically was a bachelor's degree in accounting and actuarial sciences. Despite the split of this degree in 1951, it was only in September 2004 that the bachelor's degree in accounting was considered formally as providing insufficient preparation for accountants to engage in actuarial activities. This is evidence of how institutions create path dependence.

When the CFC/CRC system was created in 1946, members of the accounting profession were defined widely to include those who had only practical experience (bookkeepers) and those who possessed a high school diploma (accounting technicians). Thus, in creating the CFC/CRC system, the state accommodated the interests of several rival groups (bookkeepers, accounting technicians and accountants). This was because of the shortage of higher education graduates and because of powerful lobbying by representatives of commercial vocational education institutions. The maintenance of the separate accounting technician category until 2015 damaged the reputation of the accounting profession by lessening the prestige of the accounting profession. However, since 2015, the status of the profession has been enhanced because quality controls for membership are now tighter and better: members must hold a university degree in accounting, must have passed the Exam of Sufficiency and must engage in continuous professional development education.

One of the most important challenges currently facing the Brazilian accounting profession is how to improve the current low pass rate of candidates attempting the professional entrance exam. A principal cause of recent low pass rates has been the proliferation of HEIs offering poor-quality instruction in accounting. The CFC/CRC system is currently exploring how to overcome the low quality of some HEIs, the low quality of some bachelor's degrees in accounting and the low number of teachers holding a Master or a PhD degree in accounting. Future research could explore the development of the accounting profession and of accounting education in emerging economies beyond Brazil by applying an historical institutional analysis lens, as here. This would be beneficial in highlighting national social, cultural, economic and political factors that are likely to confound attempts to harmonise accounting globally.

Notes

1 Due to the mental illness of Queen Dona Maria I of Portugal, her son Prince João ruled in her name, as Regent, from 1799. In 1816, he became King João VI of Portugal.
2 This was not surprising in view of the prescription, in 1761, of double-entry bookkeeping for Portugal's four General Control Offices (Letter of Law, 22 December 1761). In 1834, the role and power of the national Royal Treasury was diminished with the establishment of provincial treasuries (Araújo *et al.*, 2017).
3 For further information regarding the RdJSoC and the features of accounting development in this period, see Araújo and Rodrigues (2013) and Araújo *et al.* (2017).
4 Teles (1989) emphasised the importance of this Code by highlighting its (then) current use in certain legal decisions (see also Bacci, 2002: 53–54).
5 For some examples see Ricardino and Iudícibus (2002).
6 The prescribed standardised balance sheets were adopted until 1940. In that year Law 2627 prescribed different formats.
7 In 1907, the Practical School of Commerce was renamed the Alvares Penteado School of Commerce, in recognition of a donor of an important school building (Polato, 2008).
8 In 1923, graduates of several other schools were also recognised by the state (Decree 4724-A).
9 At the time, this term was used to refer to the person who verified the accounts, who was later known as the 'auditor'.
10 Between 1940 and 1949 Brazil experienced a dramatic increase in the rate of inflation. Prices rose by 215.6 per cent (12.2 per cent per annum, on average) (Munhoz, 1997). In 1964, the inflation rate was 92.1 per cent (Munhoz, 1997).
11 This plan laid out development goals for the country. It sought to develop the transport and communication infrastructure, as well as some key industries, such as agribusiness (machinery, fertilisers and agrochemicals). The plan also marked the beginning of Brazil's automobile industry (Rodrigues *et al.*, 2011).
12 After 1 July 1982, this body became known by the acronym IBRACON.
13 Led by President Geisel (1974–1979) and President Figueiredo (1979–1985).
14 This economic plan introduced a new currency, the Real. This is still in circulation.
15 This concern prompted the CFC/CRC to fund postgraduate and master degrees in accounting for its members, some of them teachers. The CFC/CRC is the only professional association in Brazil to do so (Bugarim, 2015).

References

ANPCONT (2014). *Quantidade de mestres e doutores em contabilidade.* www.anpcont.com.br/site/materia.php?id=31 (accessed 14 October 2014).

Araújo, M. G. A. (2002). *Um estudo sobre os motives de satisfação e insatisfação dos anulos do curso de ciências contábeis da Universidade Federal do Ceará.* Masters dissertation (in accounting control), FEA/USP, São Paulo.

Araújo, W. G. and Rodrigues, L. L. (2013). *As primeiras aulas do comércio do Brasil no se´culo XIX.* Paper presented at the XIV Congresso Internacional de Contabilidade e Auditoria, Lisbon. www.otoc.pt/news/comcontabaudit/pdf/81.pdf.

Araújo, W. G., Rodrigues, L. L. and Craig, R. (2017). Empire as an imagination of the centre: The Rio de Janeiro school of commerce and the development of accounting education in Brazil. *Critical Perspectives on Accounting*, 46: 38–53.

Bacci, J. (2002). *Estudo Exploratório sobre o Desenvolvimento Contábil Brasileiro – uma Contribuição ao Registro de sua Evolução Histórica.* Master's dissertation (in accounting control and strategic management), Fundação Escola de Comércio Álvares Penteado, São Paulo.

Bastos, P. (2006). A Construção do Nacional-Desenvolvimentismo de Getúlio Vargas e a Dinâmica de Interação entre Estado e Mercado nos Setores de Base. *Economia*, 7, 239–75.

Bielinski, A. C. (2000). Educação profissional no século XIX. Curso Comercial do Liceu de Artes e Ofícios: um estudo de caso. www.senac.br/informativo/BTS/263/boltec263e.htm.

Bugarim, M. C. C. (2015). *O exercício profissional e a educação contábil: o caso do Conselho Federal de Contabilidade do Brasil.* PhD dissertation (in accounting), University of Aveiro, Portugal.

Coelho, J. M. A. (1999). Exame de Suficiência: um passo adiante. *Revista Brasileira de Contabilidade*, 28(117), 17–19.

De Rocchi, C. (2007). *Transferência Internacional de Tecnologia Contábil: Um Estudo Comparativo Numa Per-spectiva Geográfico–Temporal.* PhD dissertation, Universidade Federal de Santa Catarina.

Doupnik, T. S. (1986). The evolution of financial statement indexation in Brazil. *Accounting Historians Journal*, 13, 1–18.

Doupnik, T. S. (1996). Brazil: Inflation accounting, in Chatfield, M. and Vangermeersch, R. (Eds.), *The History of Accounting – An International Encyclopedia.* New York, NY: Routledge, 77–79.

Fernandes, G. (2005). Tributação e Escravidão: O Imposto da Meia Siza Sobre O Comércio de Escravos na Provínciade São Paulo (1809–1850). *Almanack Braziliense*, 2, 102–113.

Gomes, J. S. (1978). A profissão contábil no Brasil: uma visão crítica. *Revista Brasileira de Contabilidade*, 27, 6–13.

Guerreiro M. S., Rodrigues, L. L. and Craig, R. (2015). Institutional change of accounting systems: The adoption of a regime of adapted International Financial Reporting Standards in Portugal. *European Accounting Review*, 24, 379–409.

Lourenço, I. and Braunbeck, G. (2019). IFRS adoption in Brazil, in Weetman, P. and Tsalavoutas, I. (Eds.), *Routledge Companion to Accounting in Emerging Economies.* Abingdon, UK: Routledge.

Machado, N. (1982). *O ensino de Contabilidade nos cursos de Ciências Contábeis na cidade de São Paulo.* Master's dissertation (in administration), Escola de Administração de Empresas Ed São Paulo Fundação Getúlio Vargas, São Paulo.

Machado, V. and Nova, S. (2008). Análise comparativa entre os conhecimentos desenvolvidos no curso de graduação em contabilidade eo perfil do contador exigido pelo mercado de trabalho: uma pesquisa de campo sobre educação contábil. *Revista de Educação e Pesquisa em Contabilidade*, 2, 1–28.

Martins, E., Ricardino, A. and Silva, A. (2006). Escola Politécnica: Possivelmente o Primeiro Curso Formal de Contabilidade do Estado de São Paulo. *Revista de Contabilidade & Finanças USP*, 42, 113–122.

MEC (2012). Sinopse da educação superior. http://portal.inep.gov.br/superior-censosuperior-sinopse.

Munhoz, D. G. (1997). Inflação Brasileira: Os ensinamentos desde a crise dos anos 30. *Revista Economia Contemporânea*, 1, 59–87.

Niyama, J. K, and Silva, C. A. T. (2005). Contabilidade e seu ambiente no Brasil. *Brazilian Business Review*, 2, 13–32.

Peleias, I. R., Silva, G. P., Segreti, J. B. and Chirotto, A. R. (2007). Evolução do ensino da Contabilidade no Brasil: uma análise histórica. *Revista de Contabilidade & Finanças*, Ed. Especial, 19–32.

Polato, M. (2008). *A Fundação Escola de Comércio Alvares Penteado (Fecap) e o ensino comercial em S. Paulo (1902–1931).* Master's dissertation (in education), Pontifícia Universidade Católica de S. Paulo.

Ricardino, A. (2000). Short historic retrospective of the development of the Brazilian accounting in the axis Rio de Janeiro/São Paulo. Paper presented at the 8th World Congress of Accounting Historians, Madrid, Spain.

Ricardino, A. and Iudícibus, S. (2002). Primeira Lei das Sociedades Anônimas no Brasil. *Revista de Conta-bilidade & Finanças USP*, 29: 7–25.

Rodrigues, L. L. and Sangster A. (2013). The role of the state in the development of accounting in the Portuguese–Brazilian Empire: 1750–1822. *Accounting History Review*, 23, 161–184.

Rodrigues, L. L., Schmidt, P., Santos, J. and Fonseca, P. (2011). A research note on accounting in Brazil in the context of political, economic and social transformations, 1860–1964. *Accounting History*, 16, 111–123.

Rodrigues, L. L., Schmidt, P., Santos, J. and Fonseca, P. (2012). The origins of modern accounting in Brazil: Influences leading to the adoption of IFRS. *Research in Accounting Regulation*, 24, 15–24.

Rodrigues, L. L., Pinho, C., Bugarim, M. C., Craig, R. and Machado, D. (2017). Factors affecting success in the professional entry exam for accountants in Brazil. *Accounting Education*, 27, 48–71.

Rodrigues, L. L., Pinho, C., Bugarim, M. C., Craig, R. and Machado, D. (2018). Factors affecting success in the professional entry exam for accountants in Brazil. *Journal of Accounting Education*, 27(1), 48–71.

Sá, A. L. (2008). *História geral da contabilidade no Brasil.* Brasília: Conselho Federal de Contabilidade.

Teles, O. S. (1989). O aperfeiçoamento da Contabilidade frente ao desenvolvimento da economia brasi-leira. *Revista Brasileira de Contabilidade*, 68, 16–19.

Wiarda, H. (1978). Corporative origins of the Iberian and Latin American labor relations systems. *Studies in Comparative International Development*, 13, 3–37.

13

THE SOCIO-ECONOMIC CONTEXT OF THE ACCOUNTING PROFESSION IN CAMBODIA

Prem W. Senarath Yapa, Bopta Chan Huot and Sarath Ukwatte

Introduction

In this chapter we map the field of accounting across the political and economic influences experienced by Cambodia. Most professionalisation projects in accounting have followed institutional forms under political and economic development arrangements. These developments are associated with the growth of particular accounting bodies associated with the corporate entrepreneurship of international globalisation (Yapa *et al.*, 2016). As such we argue that the field of accounting cannot simply be understood in terms of professional associations and professionalisation projects but rather that the space of political and economic influences experienced by nations must be explored too. Based on this, this chapter proceeds by discussing the development of accounting in Cambodia. With the introduction of various enactments and laws on accounting and auditing, Cambodian accounting regulation has entered a new phase of co-regulation where accounting standards of the local professional accounting body have been given legal backing. We conclude that more extensive research is needed particularly in examining the effectiveness of implementing accrual accounting to update the literature on how public sector accounting reforms have been directed by the international agencies in less developed countries (LDCs).

Cambodian socio-economic context

Cambodia has become an important player in South East Asia (SEA) and in trade worldwide given its geographic location in the lower Mekong region between Thailand in the west, Vietnam in the east, and Lao PDR in the north. Cambodia was ruled by the French for almost 100 years and became independent in 1954 (Kiernan, 1985). Over the past five years, Cambodia has been one of the fastest-growing economies in Southeast Asia. This economic progress has helped reduce the country's poverty rate from 47.8 per cent in 2007 to 13.5 per cent in 2014 (World Bank, 2018b). Cambodia remains a post-conflict country. Driven by garment exports and tourism, Cambodia sustained an average growth rate of 7 per cent in 2016, ranking sixth in the world. Economic growth reached 6.8 per cent in 2017, according to preliminary estimates. Cambodia is currently expected to remain strong (6.9 per cent in 2018 and 6.7 per cent in 2019), as recovering tourism activity coupled with fiscal expansion compensate for some easing in garment exports and construction growth (World Bank, 2018b).

While Pol Pot[1] and the Khmer Rouge[2] regime might be most widely known in the West as names associated with conflict, Cambodia has experienced a relatively long period of conflict with its neighbours. The government is a multiparty liberal democracy under a constitutional monarchy, established in September 1993. The legal system is primarily one of civil law, being a mixture of French-influenced codes from the United Nations Transitional Authority in Cambodia period, royal decrees and acts of legislature with influences of customary law and remnants of communist legal theory with increasing influence of common law in the recent years. The head of state is King Norodom Sihamoni. Since 2004 the royal government of Cambodia is comprised of the Council of Ministers. The head of government is the Prime Minister. There are two deputy prime ministers and a cabinet. The legislative branch of the government is bicameral, consisting of the Senate (61 seats) and the National Assembly (123 seats). Every five years an election is held. The judicial branch of the government has the supreme council of the magistracy since 1997 – and a system of Supreme Court and lower courts (Cambodian Law on Commercial Enterprises, 2005). Cambodia has adopted the market economy system and this process has been mainly determined by the new Constitution established in 1993. The National Assembly is the only authority to hold legislative power. The National Assembly approves the national budget, state plan, loans, lending, and the creation, changes or annulment of tax. In the mid-1980s, Cambodia embarked on economic reforms. In 1989, private property rights were restored and price control was abolished. State-owned enterprises (SOEs) were privatised and increased incentives were provided to local and foreign private investment. This set the stage for the signing of the Paris Peace Accord in 1991, designed to put an end to the protracted civil wars and to assist the rehabilitation of the economy. After the 1993 general elections, the newly formed royal government of Cambodia began formulating a comprehensive macroeconomic and structural reform and achieved some significant successes in stabilising the economy.

Once Pol Pot was removed from power, the economy was rebuilt with the help of the Vietnamese and many Western countries and assistance from donor agencies such as the World Bank and the Asian Development Bank (ADB). Similarly, accounting and the accounting profession were rebuilt by a small number of remaining professionals. Despite the fact that Cambodia was influenced by communist regimes in the mid-1970s to mid-1980s, internationalism and globalisation created significant change in the Cambodian economy after the 1990s.

In 2004, Cambodia became a member of the World Trade Organization (WTO). Yet Cambodia remains one of the world's least developed countries with a population of about 16 million (World Bank, 2018a), a predominantly rural and agricultural economy, a life expectancy of 68 years and an infant mortality of 35 per 1,000 births (Yapa *et al.*, 2016; World Bank, 2018b). The Cambodian economy continues to expand rapidly and real GDP growth eased to 6.8 per cent in 2017 from 7 per cent in 2016. Cambodia therefore improved with the regional trend, as most developing countries in SEA experienced a growth acceleration in 2016 Following some moderation during the first half of 2017, textile and apparel exports rebounded. The tourism and agriculture sectors experienced initial recovery in the last few years after facing gradual moderation. Growth is projected to remain robust, expanding at 6.9 per cent in 2018. Downside risks to the outlook include erosion of export competitiveness due to rapidly rising real wages, a build-up of vulnerabilities from a prolonged real estate and construction boom, potential election-related uncertainty and periodic jolts to the international trade order in the form of protectionism and escalating trade disputes (World Bank, 2018a).

The Cambodia Securities Exchange (CSX) and stock market regulation

After decades of communist rule and a command economy, Cambodia began the transformation into the free market in the late 1980s. It is now integrating into the regional and world trading framework. In Cambodia, there is no well-developed stock market. In 2005 Cambodia enacted a new company law with assistance from the ADB (ADB, 2005). The law prescribes corporate governance principles to protect and promote international and local investors and follow international best practices in non-listed company and partnership formation. The law applies to partnerships and companies carrying on in Cambodia. A partnership comprises a general partnership (two or more partners) and a limited partnership. A company comprises private limited and public limited as prescribed in the law. Each partnership or company shall file an annual declaration with the Ministry of Commerce (MoC) concerning the status of the partnership or the company.

Overview of the Cambodia Securities Exchange (CSX)

The Cambodia Securities Exchange, also called the Cambodia Stock Exchange (CSX), is a joint venture between the royal government of Cambodia (55 per cent ownership) and the Korean Stock Exchange (45 per cent ownership), The CSX is a private company, under the supervision of the Securities and Exchange Commission of Cambodia (SECC), which was an arm of the Ministry of Economy and Finance (MEF) and was officially established in 2009. The objective of establishing the CSX was to promote Cambodian economic growth to ensure its future economic development plans through raising funds, forming listed companies and issuing its securities such as stocks and bonds to the market. It is clear, as the stock market is developing a new existence in Cambodia, that rigorous laws and regulations need to be created to ensure transparency, professionalism, smooth running and development of the whole market. The listing of a company in the CSX is divided into three steps: (1) a company shall submit an application to CSX to review the listing eligibility; (2) after receiving approval, the company shall submit prospectus reports including disclosure documents and other related documents to the SECC for making an Initial Public Offering (IPO); (3) when the IPO process is complete and approved by the SECC, the company may contact CSX for listing. In short, the first two steps are for the initial public offerings (IPO) process and in the 'primary market', while the third step is for securities trading in the 'secondary market'. For the time being, there are only three SOEs that have officially announced joining the CSX. They are the Phnom Penh Water Supply Authority, Telecom Cambodia and the Sihanoukville Autonomous Port. In addition to these SOEs in the early stage, foreign-owned companies and joint ventures between Cambodia and foreign investors are expected to be listed when the market opens. According to the Director General of the SECC, family-owned companies will soon understand what benefits they can gain by going public, such as getting cheaper and long-term capital through stock exchange. Moreover, listed companies also get a tax incentive of 10 per cent discount on the amount they have to pay before going public. Therefore, it is envisaged that not only three SOEs, but also some private companies in the IPO will take up a listing when the market is open.[3]

Cambodia joined the Association of Southeast Asian Nations (ASEAN) in 1999 and served as ASEAN's chair in 2012. In 2001, the country joined the World Customs Organization. Cambodia has an open and liberal foreign investment regime and actively courts foreign direct investment (FDI). The primary law governing investment is the 1994 Law on Investment. All sectors of the economy are open to foreign investment and the government permits 100 per cent foreign ownership of companies in most sectors. In a few sectors – such as cigarette manufacturing, movie production, rice milling, gemstone mining and processing, publishing and printing, radio and television, wood and stone carving production, and silk weaving – foreign investment is subject to local equity participation or prior authorisation from authorities. There is little or no discrimination against foreign investors either at the time of initial investment or after investment. Some foreign businesses, however, have reported that they are at a disadvantage vis-à-vis Cambodian or other foreign rivals, who engage in acts of corruption or tax evasion or take advantage of Cambodia's poor enforcement of laws and regulations (US Department of State, 2018).[4]

Cambodia's political and economic support for foreign investments has been positive since its market-oriented regime began. According to Cambodia's Amended Law on Investment (1994-Law on Investment) and related sub-decrees, there are no limitations based on shareholder nationality or discrimination against foreign investors except in relation to investments in real property or SOEs. The Law on Investment (1994) and the Amended Law on Investment (1994) state that the majority interest in land must be held by one or more Cambodian citizens. Pursuant to the Law on Public Enterprise (1996), the Cambodian government must directly or indirectly hold more than 51 per cent of the capital or the right to vote in SOEs. Foreign direct investment must be registered with the MoC, and investors must obtain operating permits from the relevant line ministries. If a foreign investor seeks investment incentives as a Qualified Investment Project, he/she must register and receive approval from the Council for the Development of Cambodia or the Provincial-Municipal Investment Sub-Committee. The application to the Council for the Development of Cambodia may be made either before or after registering with the MoC.

The total stocks of foreign direct investment registered capital and fixed assets in Cambodia from 1994 to 2013 were $5.2 billion and $28.14 billion, respectively (ADB, 2016). The average annual foreign direct investment inflow based on fixed assets between 2011 and 2013 amounted to approximately $2.55 billion. Foreign direct investment inflow based on fixed assets decreased by about 11 per cent to $1.22 billion in 2013 (ADB, 2016). Table 13.1 depicts the existing legislative and institutional framework that governs Cambodian accounting and auditing arrangements.

Accounting and accountability policy making

Accounting and financial policies are mainly handled by the Cambodian government. The accounting circulars and regulations (*Prakas*) in Cambodia are issued by the MEF. These regulations may be necessary for the purpose of maintaining uniform standard in the financial reporting of business entities. Table 13.2 provides the main accounting reporting circulars and regulations in Cambodia.

Assurance and auditing standards

With the economic and infrastructure development plans that have been implemented, several other institutional setups have taken place over the past decades in Cambodia to support financial management and scrutiny. Among these institutional developments, the setting up of the National Audit Authority (NAA) is an important achievement in the internationalisation process of Cambodia. Several international financial agencies, such as ADB, and the government of Cambodia set up memorandums of understanding to execute international aid and grants programmes during the past decades.

The National Audit Authority (NAA)

The Law on Audit in Cambodia was passed by the National Assembly on 12 January 2000 at its third plenary session of the second legislature and approved by the Senate on 21 January 2000 at its second plenary session of the first legislature, and was declared to conform with the Constitution by

Table 13.1 Cambodian government's legislative and institutional framework for accounting and auditing services

---

Main governing laws

Law on the Organization and Conduct of the National Bank of Cambodia (1996)

Law on the Foreign Exchange (1997)

Law on Banking and Financial Institutions (1999)

Law on Commercial Regulations and the Commercial Register (1999)

Law on the Chamber of Commerce (1995)

Law on the Chamber of Commerce (1995)

Law on Commercial Enterprises (2005)

Law on Anti-Monetary Laundering and Combating the Financing of Terrorism (2007)

Institutions and their main functions	
Ministry of Economy and Finance (MEF)	*Cambodian Securities and Exchange Commission (CSX)*
Approves accounting and auditing standards	Oversees the Stock Exchange
Supports the ASC and AuSC activities	Administers the Securities Act
National Council of Accounting (NCA)	*Auditor General and Deputy Auditors General*
	Appointed by royal decree for a term of five years
The Kampuchea Institute of Certified Public	on the recommendation of the State and approved
Accountants and Auditors (KICPAA)	by a two-third majority of all members of the
	National Assembly

Ministry of Commerce (MoC)

Registration of foreign direct investments

Maintenance of partnership and company annual declarations

Governing business activities in Cambodia through licensing and inspection

Issuing of three types of licences: Certificate of Origin, Company Registration and Trade Mark Registration

Registrar of Companies

Administers the Companies Act

National Audit Authority (NAA)

Responsible for executing the external audit function of the public sector

National Bank of Cambodia (NBC)

Approves bank auditors

Approves accounting and auditing standards for banks

Determines disclosure requirements for financial institutions

---

the Constitutional Council, except article 40 (MEF, 2005). The purpose of the Law on Audit was to establish an NAA, which is independent in its operations. The NAA is responsible for executing the external audit function of the public sector in Cambodia. The Auditor General is empowered to conduct audits on accounting records, accounts, management systems, operation controls and programmes of government institutions in accordance with generally accepted auditing standards and the government's auditing standards. This law also established the internal audit function in government ministries, institutions and public enterprises.

Table 13.2 Main accounting reporting circulars and regulations

Circulars and Prakas	Issued date
Monthly statement of assets and liabilities on softcopy	23 June 1995
Prakas on adoption and implementation of chart of accounts for banking and financial institutions	25 December 2002
Prakas on international transaction reporting system	6 January 2003
Circular on daily accruals and amortisations for commercial and specialised banks	1 October 2003
Prakas on annual audit of financial statements of banks and financial institutions	29 December 2004
Circular on multi-currency accounting following implementation of uniform chart of accounts	10 February 2005
Prakas on reporting date for commercial banks and specialised banks	13 September 2006
Accounting rules and reporting	
Prakas on reporting requirement for registered NGOs and licensed microfinance institutions	25 February 2002
Prakas on adoption and implementation of chart of accounts for microfinance institutions	25 December 2002
Prakas on reporting date for microfinance institutions	13 September 2006
Accounting rules and credit information	
Prakas on the accounting process for foreign currency transaction	17 February 2000
Prakas on using language, currency unit and exchange rate for accounting records and reports	13 December 2007
Prakas on credit reporting	24 March 2011

The Public Accounts Committee (PAC)

Public sector accounting plays a dominant role in government ministries, departments and SOEs in Cambodia. Under Cambodian laws and regulations, there appears to be no independent body, which is separate from the government, which carries out an independent review of all public expenditures incurred by the government ministries, agencies and enterprises. It shows that the Finance and Banking Commission (FBC) performs the role of a Public Accounts Committee in an ad hoc fashion. However, the FBC has no official role or procedural documents and its constitution has yet to be drafted. The PAC, made up of members of the National Assembly, instils public confidence in government financial operations.

The general functions of most public accounts committees are to examine the accounts of government and SOEs to ensure that the accounts of the public sector are appropriate and in accordance with budget, and are applicable to the service for which they were charged or allocated (MEF, 2005).

The law on financial management in the public sector

Public sector accounting is highly influential when it comes to economic performance in Cambodia. Public sector accounting has been under the administration of the law on financial management since 2000. The law contains the general provisions on revenues and expenditures of the state budget. The revenues are divided into current revenues, duties and taxes, non-fiscal revenues, capital revenues, internal capital revenues and foreign capital revenue. Revenues are further shown as current year, previous year and the difference between them. Expenditures are divided into general expenses, central administration, provinces, capital expenditure, committed credits, payment credits, domestic financing, foreign financing and repayment of loans (MEF, 2005).

Economic and political influence on the accounting profession

Following independence, all Cambodian enterprises were required to prepare their financial statements based on the influence of the French accounting model. As a result, the French companies involved in major economic activities such as trade and mercantile activities in Cambodia operated from France, and French accountants carried out the accounting record-keeping function in Cambodia (NBC, 2006; Chan *et al.*, 2007; Yapa *et al.*, 2016). The Cambodian legal system was based on the French civil code and the approach to accounting practice was essentially legal in accordance with the Vichy law (emerging from France) of 4 April 1942 and a subsequent decree of 12 August 1969 (Chan *et al.*, 2007).

A few decades after independence and the introduction of new economic development programmes, accounting developments were accelerated with the establishment of the Department of Accounting within the MEF, which developed three new uniform codes of account for (1) commercial enterprises, (2) industrial enterprises and (3) construction enterprises, which were unified in 1987.[5]

As the economy of Cambodia expanded to the private sector from 1993, the role of the MEF changed from only regulating the state to also producing a legal and financial framework for the private sector and, with the support and influence of the French government, through the French National Accounting Council (Conseil National de la Comptabilité), started preparing a new public and private sector accounting system. In November 1993 the MEF prescribed a chart of accounts (Prakas No. 012 PK-RKSHV, 7 November 1993) for the public and private sectors and a plan for accounting rules and guidelines for all financial statements (Narayan and Godden, 2000), which clearly reflected the French economic influence in its structure, classifications and accounting approaches (Chan, 2007). The accounting system was followed by a number of other pieces of economic reform legislation, changes to public sector financial management and the establishment of an Auditor General and the NAA of Cambodia in January 2000. In 2002 the French economic recommendations were incorporated into further refinement of the accounting rules and the creation of a French-style professional accounting entity – the National Accounting Council (clearly modelled after the French Conseil National de la Comptabilité), a consultative body to review and give its opinion on all accounting regulations and laws and to develop the conceptual framework and accounting standards (Chan, 2007).

The Kampuchea Institute of Certified Public Accountants and Auditors (KICPAA)

The Western accounting system was introduced to Cambodia in the nineteenth century by the French to support colonial rule, and the country's legal and accounting systems developed along the lines of those in France. The Khmer Rouge regime, led by Pol Pot, destroyed most of the professionals in all disciplines in Cambodia, including accountants, as well as the social and physical infrastructure in the country. The influence of globalisation and resultant economic reforms coupled with markets and capital have also resulted in reforms to the accounting profession. In March 2003 the KICPAA was established by the MEF. Although the KICPAA was technically independent it was regulated and governed by the MEF and KICPAA's day-to-day functions were still directly influenced by the state (Narayan and Godden, 2000; Chan *et al.*, 2007; Yapa *et al.*, 2016). KICPAA offers memberships to individuals and firms and recognises both local and international qualifications. KICPAA appears to have been influenced by and modelled on French professional bodies such as the Ordre des Experts Comptables and the legacies of the Soviet-style central-planning era, as the structure and role of KICPAA reflects the model of the accounting profession as a state-controlled regulator rather than an independent professional body (Narayan and Godden, 2000). The World Bank's (2007: 9) analysis of accounting and auditing in Cambodia was critical of the competency of accountants and auditors and the capability of the KICPAA, claiming that it was unable to 'move the profession forward or project its image as an effective regulator of the public accountancy profession in Cambodia'. The World Bank (2007: 9) indicated that the majority of KICPAA members hold foreign accountancy qualifications, most with the British-based Association of Chartered Certified Accountants (ACCA) and some other professional associations from Australia, the UK and New Zealand and were granted membership in KICPAA without further examination or requirements. However, despite listing over 100 qualified members, only 58 members of KICPAA were active (and only 10 of the 15 locally registered firms were active). Yet while most of the members were foreigners (with British-based ACCA qualifications) only Cambodian citizens would be allowed to provide audit services from 2010. The ADB (2010) analysis of the accounting profession in Cambodia was equally scathing, noting that in 2005 there were only 10 locally certified accountants working in Cambodia. Although there were attempts to boost accounting qualifications and training, the World Bank (2007) concluded that Cambodia's accounting profession is dominated (in terms of membership numbers) by members of the UK-based ACCA; many of the entities in the corporate sector do not have access to professionally qualified accountants and the accountants who did work in Cambodia were not well trained or supported. The influence of major accounting firms in Cambodia has become more evident in recent times. By 2002 there were seven accounting firms including three of the 'Big Four' largest international accounting firms in the world that have offices in Phnom Penh: Ernst & Young International, KPMG and PricewaterhouseCoopers (*Cambodia Daily*, 2002). While there has been some attempt to regulate international firms by restricting the power to offer statutory audit or accounting work under the Cambodian accounting law,[6] it is questionable under global trade agreements as to how long these restrictions can be sustained.

At present, KICPAA members comprise accountants and auditors who are members of foreign professional accountancy organisations, such as the ACCA, the Chartered Professional Accountants of Canada, the Certified Practising Accountants of Australia, and the Institute of Chartered Accountants in England and Wales (ICAEW). Membership of KICPAA is mandatory for all individuals who wish to perform accountancy services in Cambodia. Finally, in addition to being an Associate of IFAC, KICPAA is also a member of the ASEAN Federation of Accountants.

Despite the fact that KICPAA has no direct responsibility in adopting national accounting standards, which are full International Financial Reporting Standards (IFRS) and also IFRS for Small and Medium-sized Entities, it reports that it does contribute to the development of standards by providing technical assistance and support to the National Accountancy Council, which is the accounting standard setter.

At present, KICPAA assists its members with implementation of the standards by offering workshops and continuing professional development courses on the standards and developments in the area. Additionally, the institute has stated that it is working with the government to establish a company registrar for companies to file statutory audited financial statements. However, these plans have been ongoing since 2009 with no clear indication of progress.

While KICPAA has no direct responsibility for the adoption of public sector accounting standards, it has been promoting the adoption of International Public Sector Accounting

Standards (IPSAS) to the government entities responsible for the adoption of such standards: the NAA and the MEF. In 2012, having granted assistance from the World Bank, the government agreed to meet the disclosure requirements under cash-basis (IPSAS) and gradually transition over time to accrual-basis standards. Subsequently, in 2014, the KICPAA co-organised a workshop on IPSAS with the ICAEW for officials of the MEF. The institute reports that it continues to use its best endeavours to promote the benefits of IPSAS and circulate guidance issued by IPSAS Board.

KICPAA is encouraged to report when there is an official timeline or roadmap in place to transition from cash-basis IPSAS to accrual-basis plans and to consider if the institute should have a participatory role in the process. KICPAA is also encouraged to consider sharing exposure drafts issued by the IPSAS Board with the NAA and MEF as the relevant public sector stakeholders.

The accounting profession in Cambodia can be characterised by competition between international institutions (such as the ACCA) seeking to exert influence within a former French colony and a local accounting body (KICPAA) concerned with maintaining local regulation and protection. While French influence drove institutional structures, the current forces are associated with the global accounting firms (Big four) and professional associations (such as ACCA).

Accounting education

During the period of French influence, and until about 1975, the Cambodian education system was predominantly based on the French system, divided into primary, secondary, higher and specialised technical and vocational levels.[7] To date, only one study (Seng, 2009) has focused on accounting education in Cambodia. Seng's (2009) study discusses Cambodia's historical and political development and the structure of the Cambodian educational system. However, he ignores the British involvement in accounting in Cambodia. Cambodia has nearly 15 public sector universities and about 35 private universities. The Cambodian government has made arrangements with some public and private sector universities with a view to improving accounting education throughout the country as one of its developmental objectives (Chan *et al.*, 2007). Two universities, Royal University of Law and Economics[8] (RULE) and Build Bright University, are working closely with the KICPAA to coordinate the accounting qualifications required by the local market. Both universities provide an Associate of Business Administration degree programme (two-year duration). Successful completion of the KICPAA subject modules enables graduates to become qualified accountants and Certified Public Accountants. The lack of qualified staff to provide a standard accounting education in universities and the lack of rapport with industry and business has hindered the development of university accounting educational programmes (Yapa *et al.*, 2016).

Not surprisingly for such a young market economy, there is virtually no properly coordinated local professional accounting education, at least in the sense that a Western observer might expect. The British-based ACCA accounting qualification[9] is well accepted by Cambodian accounting and audit firms and the ACCA has sought to recruit large numbers of potential accounting students, including university graduates, for the Cambodian market.

Influence of the 'Big Four' accounting firms on accounting education in Cambodia

Currently, there are seven major accounting firms in Cambodia, including three of the 'Big Four' firms.[10] The majority of the accounting staff in the international firms are from overseas and conduct the audit work of subsidiaries of foreign firms located in Cambodia, as well as joint ventures and SOEs at the request of the government (Seng, 2009). The KPMG work is mainly for government projects, non-governmental organisations (NGOs), private businesses and projects funded by international agencies (run by either government or NGOs).

As the Cambodian university system has generally been unable to offer quality accounting degree programmes, major accounting firms in Cambodia depend on the ACCA accounting and auditing training qualifications. The Big Four reported that the inflow of UK-based ACCA educational facilities in the recent past has influenced Cambodia's accountancy towards a British model, supporting their own training schemes and in-house professional development programmes. This suggests that in Cambodia accounting education and training are now driven by both the consultancy demands and in-house needs of the transnationals and NGOs, with a clear preference for British-based accountancy training over the historic colonial French system. Accounting education in Cambodia can be characterised as being exposed to international influences from British professional accounting institutions that have supported the move to a market economy since 1993, supplanting any remnant of French influence.

Future directions

While economic and political reforms are taking place in Cambodia, during the last decade, the stock market (CSX) has been undergoing a significant change. It is attractive to investors, especially foreign investors. Considering the fact that over the last few years more than 50 per cent of market turnover came from the trading transactions performed by foreign investors this will be a significant factor for the future growth of the Cambodian economy and market.

In the area of accounting and financial reporting in Cambodia, major changes have taken place, particularly in regard to the economy, political framework, regulatory structure and standard setting in public and private sectors. With the enactment of various laws on accounting and auditing, Cambodian accounting regulation entered a new phase of co-regulation where accounting standards of the KICPAA have been given legal backing. Accordingly, any business enterprise that acted in contravention of the provisions of this Act would be committing an offence. This may be seen as an attempt to respond to the fact that the environment in which accounting operates in Cambodia has undergone rapid development in the past decade. One of the objectives of developing the legal framework in accounting and auditing is to increase public confidence and safeguard the interests of investors and consumers. This was the main focus of the newly appointed government in Cambodia.

Accounting in Cambodia is also subject to international influences such as the International Accounting Standards Board (IASB). As a member of IASB, the KICPAA is obliged to support the work of IASB by informing its members of IFRS, working towards implementation of IFRS as far as possible, and specifically incorporating IFRS into local standards. To date, the authorities in Cambodia have adopted only a very few accounting standards that cover some of the local accounting requirements. Given the current trend towards globalisation of capital markets, and the importance of foreign investments to developing countries in general, Cambodia can expect to be under increasing pressure in the future to fully adopt internationally acceptable accounting and auditing standards, and to ensure that the regulatory mechanisms in place are adequate and effective for enforcing such standards.

Under progressive moves towards an open market economy and globalisation, more 'private sector' accounting practices were legislated and a state-controlled Cambodian professional body (KICPAA) was instituted. This creation of post-soviet accounting rules was influenced by the French approach towards accounting regulation based on a common state-regulated chart of accounts. When there was the desire to develop a more fully formed accounting system and establish an accounting association it was to the French government and the French accounting regulators that the Cambodian authorities turned. While this illustrated the dominant influence of the state (at this point in time) and a residual influence of the French colonial powers, it was just a passing phase as international standards have been implemented and international accounting bodies such as the ACCA have grown in influence. There is evidence for the growing dominance of the ACCA and other external professional bodies in this setting and the relative absence of local investment in the accounting profession despite clear regulatory efforts to prefer Cambodian accountants in the area of auditing. In a sense the growth of a globalised accounting profession is not particularly surprising, but that it occurs despite the radical and fundamental disjunction and transformations that had been experienced by Cambodia illustrates the strength and broad applicability of global firms and professional accountancy associations.

While the accounting and auditing profession is progressing with the help of international financial agencies and professional accounting bodies, the accounting professionalisation process has to go further to develop the accounting profession in Cambodia. Future researchers may be able to focus their research on the following issues. The first is evaluation and assessment of the accounting system in Cambodia. As the public sector (e.g. IPSAS) and the corporate sector (e.g. IFRS) have been working together in the recent past, it is worthwhile to evaluate the effectiveness of the private–public relationship in accounting in Cambodia. The second is the involvement of gender in the accounting profession. The role of women in the accounting profession has not been addressed in the literature on Cambodia. Most importantly, sustainability in accounting in Cambodia has not been explored. Finally, it is important to focus further research on evaluation of the effectiveness of assistance provided by international donors and how improvements in Cambodian accounting can be made through such assistance to develop the profession alongside international and institutional development.

Notes

1 French-educated Saloth Sar (later known as Pol Pot) (middle-class leftist) with others (Son Sen, Ieng Sary) organised an uprising against the government of King Sihanouk in Cambodia. See *How Pol Pot Came to Power* (Kiernan, 2004).
2 The term 'Khmer' generally refers to the dominant ethnic group in Cambodia. 'Cambodia' and 'Cambodge' are Europeanised spellings of 'Kampuchea', which is a country with several ethnic groups, including Chinese, Chams (Muslims), Khmers, Malays and Vietnamese. 'Kampuchea', in turn, is a modernised version of 'Kambuja', the Khmer name first used in the tenth century (Haas, 1991).
3 Further information about the CSX is available in English at the exchange's website: http://csx.com. kh/laws/prakas/listPosts.do (accessed 25 January 2019).
4 More information about investment and investment incentives in Cambodia may be found on the Council for the Development of Cambodia websites: www.cdc-crdb.gov.kh, www.cambodia investment.gov.kh (accessed 25 January 2019) and also www.cambodiainvestment.gov.kh/why-invest-in-cambodia/investment-enviroment/economic-trend.html (accessed 26 January 2019).
5 Council of Ministers' decision No 49 SSR (11 April 1987).
6 They need to set up joint ventures within local firms or incorporate local firms as member firms in order to apply for provisional operation licences to provide audit/accounting services in Cambodia. Cambodian accountants may form an accounting partnership with limited liability, although any new firms require approval from the MEF before they can provide statutory services.
7 Although higher education has increased in recent years, it has not yet reached the level of the period prior to the rule of the Khmer Rouge. Higher education is available at the Royal University of Phnom Penh, the Royal Agricultural University, the Royal University of Fine Arts, the Faculty of Medicine, the Faculty of Law and Economics, the Faculty of Business (National Institute of Management), the Institute of Technology of Cambodia (formerly the Higher Technical Institute of Khmer–Soviet

Friendship) and the Maharishi Vedic University (an Australian-funded institution in rural Prey Veng Province). Private education exists at all levels of the education system (Chan, 2007).

8 RULE was established in 1948 as the National Institute of Law, Politics and Economics. In 2003 the institute officially became a university. In 2003 the university had almost 5,000 students.

9 www.accaglobal.com/uk/en.html (accessed 25 January 2019).

10 Ernst &Young International, KPMG Cambodia and PricewaterhouseCoopers.

References

ADB (2005). *Economic Trends and Prospects in Developing Cambodia*. Phnom Penh: Asian Development Bank.

ADB (2010). ADB support to strengthen the accounting profession in Cambodia – Putu Kamayana. Asian Development Bank. www.adb.org/news/speeches/adb-support-strengthen-accounting-profession-cambodia (accessed 21 January 2019).

ADB (2016). *Member Fact Sheet*. Phnom Penh: Asian Development Bank.

Cambodia Daily (2002). Audit authority seeks hard proof of corruption. *Weekend, Saturday*, 5–6 September.

Chan, C. B. (2007). *The Re-emergence of the Accounting Profession in Cambodia*. Unpublished PhD Thesis, La Trobe University, Melbourne, Australia.

Chan, C. B., Yapa, P. W. S. and Jacobs, K. (2007). The re-emergence of accounting profession in Cambodia. Fifth Asia-Pacific Interdisciplinary Research in Accounting Conference (APIRA), Auckland, New Zealand, 8–10 July.

Haas, M. (1991), *Cambodia, Pol Pot, and the United States: The Faustian Pact*. New York: Praeger Publishers.

Kiernan, B. (1985). *How Pol Pot Came to Power: A History of Communism in Kampuchea, 1930–1975*. London: Verso.

Kiernan, B. (2004). *How Pol Pot came to Power: A History of Communism in Cambodia, 1930–1975*, 2nd edn. New Haven CT: Yale University Press.

MEF (2005). *Reports on Economic Performance*. Phnom Penh: Ministry of Economy and Finance, MEF press. Information in English on the MEF is available at http://fmis.mef.gov.kh/en/ (accessed 25 January 2019).

Narayan, F. B. and Godden, T. (2000). *Financial Management and Governance Issues in Cambodia*. Manila: Asian Development Bank.

NBC (2006). Economic and monetary reports. National Bank of Cambodia. www.nbc.org.kh/quarter_bulletins/bulletin%2%2021.pdf (accessed 25 July 2006).

Seng, D. (2009). Accounting education in Cambodia. *International Journal of Education Research*, 4(2), 43–54.

US Department of State (2018). 2018 Investment climate statements: Cambodia. www.state.gov/e/eb/rls/othr/ics/2013/204614.htm (accessed 25 January 2019).

World Bank (2007). *Report on the Observance of Standards and Codes (ROSC): Cambodia, Accounting and Auditing*. May 15.

World Bank (2018a). *Cambodia Economic Update, April 2018*. http://documents.worldbank.org/curated/en/740941525786311189/pdf/126030-WP-PUBLIC-may-10-9-am-cambodia-time-Cambodia-Economic-Update-V04.pdf (accessed 22 January 2019).

World Bank (2018b). The World Bank in Cambodia: Overview. September 2018. www.worldbank.org/en/country/cambodia/overview (accessed 22 January 2019).

Yapa, P. W. S, Jacobs, K. and Bopta, C. H. (2016). The field of accounting: Exploring the presence and absence of accounting in Cambodia. *Accounting, Auditing & Accountability Journal*, 29(3), 401–427.

PART III

Audit, governance and accountability

14

INTERNATIONAL STANDARDS ON AUDITING (ISAs)

Conflicting influences on implementation

Pran K. Boolaky, Peter Ghattas, Teerooven Soobaroyen and Oliver Marnet

Introduction

In contrast to the very significant body of research into the adoption of International Financial Reporting Standards (IFRS), there has been less interest in auditing practices and standards, conceptualised primarily in terms of (1) processes, routines and procedures by which an external auditor forms an opinion of the financial statements as a fair representation, and (2) settings and conditions within which an external auditor or external audit firm is 'licensed' to operate and, where relevant, how the auditor or audit firm is evaluated in compliance with applicable laws, regulations and/or professional ethics/standards. Auditing standards typically seek to codify aspects from these two perspectives and purport to offer some 'legitimacy' of the external auditing process and a degree of reassurance to outside parties as to the basis by which an audit opinion has been expressed (Simunic *et al.*, 2016; Boolaky and Soobaroyen, 2017). In the light of high-profile corporate failures and the finding that audit firms have not always applied the expected diligence and oversight, the issue of audit quality has been the subject of extensive work, primarily in the context of developed countries (Gendron and Bédard, 2001; DeFond and Zhang, 2014) but with a heavy reliance on quantitative approaches and potentially limitative proxies of audit quality (e.g. Ahmed and Goyal, 2005). Such approaches have been criticised for being less concerned about audit practices and processes in the field (Humphrey, 2008; Hazgui and Gendron, 2015; Power and Gendron, 2015). Financial statements could thus be prepared in accordance with international accounting standards but concerns may remain as to the reliability of an auditor's assurances if there are questions about the basis (and potentially varying standards) adopted by external auditors in providing such an assurance. It is in this regard that research into the implementation of International Standards on Auditing (ISAs), and the contribution (if any) played in the local arena, has begun to take some prominence in developed as well as developing countries, albeit that empirical evidence is substantially lacking in both contexts (Needles *et al.*, 2002; Fraser, 2010; Simunic *et al.*, 2016). The International Auditing and Assurance Standards Board (IAASB) reports that, as of December 2017, 128 jurisdictions[1] were using the clarified ISAs or were committed to using them in the near future, albeit on different bases of adoption (clarified ISAs are explained later in this chapter). Of this total, over 80 jurisdictions are classified as emerging economies by the IMF.[2]

This chapter sets the scene for further research and empirical forays on the adoption and use of auditing standards generally, and ISAs specifically, by providing (1) a review of the (limited) academic literature on ISAs, (2) a broad picture of ISA 'implementation' (or the apparent variations or lack of implementation) in developing and emerging economies and (3) a specific illustration of how ISAs have permeated a developing economy (Egypt). We first contribute to the extant knowledge on the consequences of policies and strategies instigated by transnational institutions (e.g. IFAC, World Bank; global audit firms) as outlined in Humphrey *et al.* (2009) and Humphrey and Loft (2013), in developing and emerging economies. Second, we extend an understanding of ISA implementation at the national level by outlining the relevant contextual factors and dominant actors in the case of developing and emerging economies.

ISA implementation: a review of prior studies

Work by the International Auditing Practices Committee (IAPC) – reconstituted in 2002 as the IAASB – on object and scope of audits of financial statements, engagement letters and general auditing guidelines led to the 2001 recodification of IAPC's *Guidelines* as ISAs. In 2004, the IAASB introduced the Clarity Project[3] with the aim of enhancing the clarity of ISAs either as part of a substantive revision or through a limited redrafting of the original standards, particularly in response to pressures (Humphrey and Loft, 2013) from powerful stakeholders such as the International Organizations of Securities Commissions (IOSCO). Supporters of ISAs cite greater confidence through enforceability, higher levels of assurance on financial statements, encouragement for international investment, particularly for emerging and developing countries, a base for elaborating domestic auditing standards, and a reinforcement of the agency-based monitoring mechanism. In addition, the use of ISAs by large accounting firms globally would ensure a consistent message to their clients on audit outcomes and enable efficiencies in the audit process internationally (Needles *et al.*, 2002).

Needles *et al.* (2002) set out a number of factors that might account for the delay by countries to engage with ISAs, namely (1) how accounting is itself subject to economic, political and social influence and unless accounting/reporting issues are resolved, it is difficult to move to the process of reviewing accounting/reporting; (2) external auditing typically draws its authority from law (e.g. company law) and is thus more dependent on legislative influences in each country; (3) large global accounting firms tend to see themselves as purveyors of best practice and are often ideally positioned to resist or influence the development and implementation of standards; (4) local market regulators could traditionally rely on domestic auditing standards to influence the audit process but the use of ISAs would remove this influence; and (5) inadequate professional education and training in accountancy, which in turn leads to weak auditing practices. To a limited extent, these factors emerge in a few empirical studies of auditing standards and ISAs, which can be broadly categorised in terms of (1) quantitative cross-country analyses and (2) qualitative single country assessments.

Boolaky and Soobaroyen (2017) sought to examine the level of adoption/commitment to ISAs on a cross-national basis (89 developed and developing/emerging countries) and the country-level factors that might explain the extent of commitment by a given jurisdiction. Informed by the neo-institutional perspective, the authors found evidence that a broad set of coercive, mimetic and normative variables (lenders'/borrowers' rights, foreign aid, regulatory enforcement, protection of minority interests, prevalence of foreign ownership, educational attainment and more democratic forms of political systems) were positively associated with higher levels of commitment to ISAs. The empirical analysis effectively supports Needles *et al.*'s (2002) expectations and highlights how economic and 'non-economic' factors are associated with ISA adoption. However, which factors would be more prevalent in the case of emerging and developing countries has not been clearly established and is far more complex than an issue of 'narrow nationalism' (Fraser, 2010). The likely consequences (cost and benefits) of adoption have also been alluded to, although there are methodological challenges in teasing out the effects for auditors and audit firms. Kohler (2009) did attempt to measure the costs and benefits of ISA adoption at the EU level and concluded that the benefits could outstrip the costs by a ratio of 9 to 1, subject to it being imposed wholesale and enforced consistently by national audit regulators (with no opt-outs). Following the implementation of local auditing standards in Egypt, Khlif and Samaha (2014) found that internal control quality improved post adoption and this was positively associated with a reduction in audit report lag. Although seen as supportive of local auditing standards, the authors acknowledged the weak legal enforcement and high level of secrecy of the Egyptian context.

From a qualitative/case study perspective, ISA studies reveal a complex set of interactions between the different actors in the field (national jurisdiction) involving principally the audit firms (large international and/or local ones), local professional accountancy bodies, state-backed regulatory agencies (audit oversight bodies, stock market regulators, sectoral regulators such as the central banks), the government itself (in terms of a broader political agenda) and 'outside' influencers (e.g. World Bank, IFAC). Mennicken's (2008) study of ISA implementation by a Russian audit firm in 2002 provides an early account of changing micro-practices in an emerging economy and the actors' motivations and experiences in doing so. While the key motivation was related to an organisational interest to join the 'elite' group of international Western-based firms, the practical implementation of ISAs was less obvious given the ISA's inherent limitations in actually guiding and standardising audit practice as such. There was little involvement of the state in this case. In contrast, Al-Awaqleh (2010) evaluates Jordan's decision to adopt ISAs by interviewing local users, preparers, auditors and regulators. Stakeholders generally supported ISAs due to cost implications, limited local expertise/oversight and undue influence, which could be exerted on (or by) professionals if local standards were implemented instead. Hence, the reliance on ISAs was seen as both a relatively less costly alternative and one which in the main would preclude interference at the local level and be seen as legitimate from an international perspective. At the same time, an emphasis on international pronouncements has led to an enforcement gap in that there is a lack of familiarity with ISAs among local regulators. Lastly, Brody *et al.* (2005) analysed the audit landscape in Poland and in spite of the European Union's directives and international developments, the local profession and audit regulator were found to have retained the locally developed auditing standards; which provide only general guidelines on audit objectives and procedures. However, even if the local audit regulator was minded to address the gap, the authors argued that there remains an absence of detailed guidelines which could preclude auditors from adequately implementing these standards; and in parallel for the regulator to have the necessary tools for an effective oversight. Yet, there appeared to be a stronger preference for maintaining the local audit standards and their regulatory infrastructure.

Overall, our review provides a limited but multifaceted picture of ISAs in developing and emerging economies; both as a technical-legal artefact (a guide and regulation to undertake a particular process) and as a social practice (a set of routines and ways of working in an audit firm within a particular context). From the policy-maker's perspective, there seems to be some consensus on the benefits of ISAs for developing countries, primarily as a confidence building exercise and in tandem with the adoption of IFRS. However, issues of relevance, local enforcement and fit to the local (professional) circumstances emerge. Theoretically, therefore, it seems apt for implications of ISAs to be analysed from a broader social, economic and political per-spective, and from the status of accounting and audit practices/profession in a given national context.

ISAs in developing and emerging economies

Our snapshot of the extent of ISA implementation in developing and emerging economies is based on a documentary analysis of the *World Bank Reports on the Observance of Standards and Codes* (ROSC, 2002–2010) on accounting and auditing. ROSC reports are the outcome of a field visit and review of documentation by a team of World Bank (WB) and International Monetary Fund (IMF) consultants.[4] The review team is tasked with interviewing corporate stakeholders, professional bodies, regulators and government agencies. We found recurring issues of: not providing ISAs that were appropriately translated, thereby leading to the possibility of practitioners misinterpreting the ISA requirements; non-compliance with a large number of ISAs; and, lastly, for a majority of these countries, a lack of education and training appearing to significantly hamper the development of auditing standards and the adoption of ISAs.

The second stage of this desk research draws on the approach of Boolaky and Soobaroyen (2017) to investigating the ISA adoption status of developing and emerging countries. IFAC's *Basis of ISA Adoption by Jurisdiction* (IFAC, 2012) reports on a survey of member countries at that time. Boolaky and Soobaroyen (2017) sought further clarification of the ISA status post-2012 by reviewing the Statement of Membership Obligations (SMO) reports filed by member coun-tries and other publicly available sources.[5] As a result, we report in Tables 14.1 and 14.2 the status of the 60 developing and emerging countries, respectively, in alphabetical order and arranged geographically.

What is first noticeable is that just over half of the surveyed developing and emerging eco-nomies have opted for a wholesale adoption of ISAs either as a part of a legal change or as a regulation by the standard setters. In the African context, it is also noted that many of the ex-British colonies whose accounting and auditing practices have been (and remain to a large extent) influenced by UK practices and professional bodies appear to have taken a more deter-mined route towards ISA adoption, albeit that there are exceptions (Nigeria and Egypt). Whole-sale adoption by law is more prevalent in the European context and may reflect a general aspiration in response to the European Union's interest in the codification of auditing standards for the wider benefit of all countries within the economic block, and in line with Kohler's (2009) recommendations.

In the Central and South American context, the picture is more mixed with many countries progressing rather slowly. A review of the SMO reports suggests the influence of Spain, and principally in relation to the use of translated versions of ISA. Furthermore, some the South American economies (e.g. Bolivia) are keen to maintain local auditing standards. Finally, in the Asian/Middle Eastern context, there is again some variation but with the largest economies either adopting ISAs with modifications or retaining control over local auditing standards. An analysis of the breakdown of the 'other' category shows that many of the countries seek to retain a local version of auditing standards while seeking to progress (how quickly is not always clear) towards a convergence with ISAs. A case in point we review in detail in the next section is Egypt, which has had local standards on the basis of the 2005 ISA edition but which that have yet to be fully updated or adapted to the new or revised standards. Given that the earlier versions of ISAs were deemed to be not sufficiently clear (and hence the need for Clarified ISAs), a reli-ance on prior versions in various countries (including Egypt) may suggest challenges in applying the standards adequately.

Table 14.1 ISA adoption by region

	By law	By standard setters	Modified adoption	Others
Africa	Mauritius	Botswana Ghana Kenya Lesotho Malawi South Africa Uganda Zambia Zimbabwe	Nigeria Senegal	Cameroon Ivory Coast Egypt Ethiopia Madagascar Morocco
Central/South Americas	Costa Rica	Brazil Colombia El Salvador Guatemala Jamaica	Mexico	Bolivia Dominican Republic Ecuador Nicaragua Peru Uruguay Venezuela
Asia/Middle East	Mongolia	Cambodia Jordan Kazakhstan Turkey	Bangladesh India Malaysia Pakistan Philippines Thailand	China Indonesia Nepal Sri Lanka United Arab Emirates Vietnam Kyrgyz Republic
Europe	Bulgaria Romania Georgia Macedonia, FYR Russian Federation	Bosnia and Herzegovina Serbia Ukraine	Albania Poland	

Source: This table is compiled for this chapter, from data based on IFAC sources and from the evidence collected in preparation for Boolaky and Soobaroyen (2017).

Table 14.2 also displays the regulatory enforcement score (1 is highest, 0 is the lowest) for each surveyed country (World Justice Project, 2012; average from 2009–2012) and the Democracy Index published by the Economic Intelligence Unit (*The Economist*, 2012), on a scale of 0 to 10. Full democracy ranged from 8 to 10, flawed democracy 6 to 7.9, hybrid 4 to 5.9 and autocracy 0 to 3.9. It is not always the case that the commitment to ISAs is associated to a higher democracy index. However, most countries with the higher scores tended to have adopted ISA on a wholesale basis either by law or by the standard-setting body. Most of the countries in our sample had a regulatory enforcement score of less than 0.5 and this suggests that the adherence to ISA standards (whether adopted by law or otherwise) will be subject to (relatively) weak monitoring and enforcement.

Just under half of the surveyed developing and emerging countries have gone for a stronger commitment to ISAs (principally with the local standard setter embedding ISAs) but there is

Table 14.2 Regulatory enforcement, political systems and ISA adoption

Countries	Regulatory enforcement	Political regime/system	Basis of ISA adoption			
			By law	By standard setters	Modified adoption	Others
Albania	0.4	5.8			x	
Bangladesh	0.2	5.8			x	
Bolivia	0.4	6				x
Bosnia and Herzegovina	0.1	5.5		x		
Botswana	0.2	9.7		x		
Brazil	0.3	7.3		x		
Bulgaria	0.5	6.9	x			
Cambodia	0.1	4.9		x		
Cameroon	0.2	3.4				x
China	0.2	3				x
Colombia	0.5	6.5		x		
Costa Rica	0*	8.05	x			
Côte D'Ivoire (Ivory Coast)	0.1	3				x
Dominican Republic	0.5	6.3				x
Egypt	0.1	3.9				x
El Salvador	0.5	6.4		x		
Ecuador	0.46	5.7				x
Ethiopia	0.2	4.2				x
Georgia	0.2	4.9	x			
Ghana	0.5	5.7		x		
Guatemala	0.2	6		x		
India	0.4	7.6			x	
Indonesia	0.5	6.5				x
Jamaica	0.2	7.3		x		
Jordan	0.5	3.8		x		
Kazakhstan	0.2	3.3		x		
Kenya	0.4	4.8		x		
Kyrgyz Republic	0.2	4.3				x
Lesotho	0*	6.36		x		
Macedonia, FYR	0.1	6.2	x			
Madagascar	0.1	4.8				x
Malawi	0.1	5.5		x		
Malaysia	0.3	6.2			x	
Mauritius	0*	8.07	x			
Mexico	0.3	6.8			x	
Mongolia	0.1	6.5	x			
Morocco	0.5	3.9				x
Nepal	0.1	4				x
Nicaragua	0.1	5.8				x
Nigeria	0.5	3.6			x	
Pakistan	0.4	4.4			x	
Peru	0.5	6.3				x
Philippines	0.5	6.3			x	
Poland	0.6	7.2			x	
Romania	0.3	6.8	x			

Countries	Regulatory enforcement	Political regime/system	Basis of ISA adoption			
			By law	*By standard setters*	*Modified adoption*	*Others*
Russian federation	0.2	4.4	x			
Senegal	0.58	6.09			x	
Serbia	0.1	6.4		x		
South Africa	0.6	7.9		x		
Sri Lanka	0.1	6.4				x
Thailand	0.5	6.4			x	
Turkey	0.55	5.76		x		
United Arab Emirates	0.3	2.5				x
Uganda	0.2	5.1		x		
Ukraine	0.2	6.5		x		
Uruguay	0.2	8.1				x
Venezuela	0.2	5.3				x
Vietnam	0.2	2.8				x
Zambia	0.1	5.6		x		
Zimbabwe	0.1	2.6		x		
Total			8	21	11	20

Source: This table is compiled for this chapter, from data based on IFAC sources and from the evidence collected in preparation for Boolaky and Soobaroyen (2017).

Note: Zero scores with an asterisk ($\star$) – data was not available.

little in the way of assessment of whether this has been effective so far. The remaining countries have, in the main, been slower and more circumspect in their approach to ISAs particularly in the presence of existing auditing regulators on the local scene. While reviewing the SMO reports (particularly in relation to the categories of 'modified adoption' and 'others', i.e. partial or limited adoption), it became apparent that the historical context figured extensively in the explanations as to the current status. The Egyptian case below provides us with an opportunity to delve further on this point.

The micro-level picture: an Egyptian case

The following case of Egypt[6] helps to contextualise the professional and regulatory elements that underlie the challenging path towards ISA adoption in developing and emerging countries. The evidence relates to a broader study of audit practices and regulation, and was gathered from 32 face to face interviews conducted between December 2014 and June 2016 with senior members of the Egyptian Society of Accountants and Auditors (ESAA), Egyptian Financial Supervisory Authority (EFSA), auditors of local small, mid-size and Big Four firms, as well as academics. Participants were contacted on the basis of their involvement in the local profession and, subsequently, by referral. The interviews, conducted in Arabic, ranged from 30 minutes to about three hours. It presents a story of long-standing external pressure to adopt international standards such as ISAs in a country where local institutions have remained weak, inadequately resourced and dominated by the state. This context has led to an undue favouring of dominant players in the country, while there has not been adequate monitoring of audit practice and, in particular, ISA implementation.

Since 1979, the IMF, the WB and the United States Agency for International Development (USAID) have repeatedly provided Egypt with financial and technical loans to fund the application of comprehensive economic (including accounting and auditing) reforms but there have been few noticeable improvements (Lofgren 1993; Momani 2003). During the 1990s, the Egyptian government entered into an agreement with the IMF and the WB with the aim of privatising the public sector and restructuring the Egyptian capital markets (Zohny, 2000). Consequently, a new capital market law was issued which initially mandated the use of international reporting standards. This requirement led to the necessity of issuing local Egyptian Standards on Auditing (ESA) (World Bank 2002; Abd-Elsalam and Weetman, 2003). In 1997, this task was assigned by the state, represented by the minister of economy and foreign trade, to a new Permanent Committee for Standards of Accounting and Auditing, which the minister chaired along with one representative from the following governmental institutions; the Central Auditing Organization (CAO),[7] the Capital Market Authority (CMA), the Departments of Companies, two professional associations, the Egyptian Institute for Accountants and Auditors (EIAA)[8] and the ESAA, and one accounting academic[9] (Ministerial Decree 478, 1997).

The Capital Markets Law was amended to dictate the use of the newly issued Egyptian standards (Ministerial Decree 503, 1997). In 2000, six ESAs were issued, mainly addressing the content and process for an auditor's report (Ministerial Decree 55, 2000). Additionally, it was mandated that ISAs could be applied for issues that the ESAs did not specifically address (Ministerial Decree 625, 2000). In 2008, the current version of ESAs was issued, comprising 38 ESAs and a general audit framework (Ministerial Decree 166, 2008). The still valid 2008 ESAs were based on the 2005 version of ISAs.

The most prominent player in the auditing standards-setting process is the ESAA, which functions as an 'elite body of accounting professionals', as described by the WB and the IMF in their ROSC (World Bank, 2002). ESAA's 2,100 membership represents about 14 per cent of the number of registered auditors in Egypt (ESAA, 2016). The majority of ESAA members are auditors in the local offices of Big Four firms, its board is dominated by Big Four partners, and its president has been the same Big Four lead partner since 1977. The ESAA takes pride that their members are the only Egyptian certified auditors by examination and practical experience – unlike other certification routes available for Egyptian auditors. Deficiencies of the Egyptian audit market at both the auditor and the firm level stem from a few factors. First, ESAs are fairly new from the perspective of practitioners and at the same time rather outdated. Second, Egyptian auditors were never subject to any form of oversight. Third, the accounting education system in Egypt is weak and auditors lack adequate knowledge in many technical areas and professional aspects such as auditor independence and conflict of interest (Raslan *et al.*, 2016).

According to the WB (2002), the standards-setting committee within ESAA is the de facto ISA standards setter in Egypt. This committee handles the translation of ISAs from English to Arabic and its adaptation to the local Egyptian laws. Based on the interviews with local stakeholders, there is no evidence that the ESAA standards-setting committee involves ESAA members or the other stakeholders in the standards-setting due process (i.e. exposure drafts). The 10 years' time lag between IFAC's current ISAs and the ESA 2008 version is another criticism of the ESA standards-setting process (ESAA, 2016). In light of the limited financial technical resources, the ESA standards-setting process is completely dependent on the 'voluntary' contributions of ESAA and of its member firms. Indeed, the WB (2002) highlighted ESAA's domination of the Egyptian standards-setting process whereby the selecting, drafting and translating of relevant ISAs into ESAs were left to the ESAA, in spite of this being the responsibility of the State bodies.

Once the above tasks are done, the drafts are submitted to the State's permanent standards-setting committee for ratification. Despite the substantial presence of government and state players within the permanent committee, their role is limited to suggesting modifications on the applicability of the standards to the Egyptian legal framework. While the role of these state actors could, on paper, be considered to be influential in setting accounting and auditing standards, their limited technical knowledge created a void for local affiliates of Big Four firms to exploit. Due to their international networks and resources, technical expertise and financial resources, the local affiliates were thus able to carve out a dominant position on ISA adoption in Egypt.

The research highlights how the market dominance by Big Four firms of accountancy and audit services in developing and emerging economies (Hopper *et al.*, 2017) is significant. While similar arguments could be made in the context of developed countries, it is the knock-on effect on the development of a local profession and a competent local oversight function that are seen to be more problematic. In relation to the latter, the first form of oversight ever to be levied on Egyptian auditors came from the Auditor Oversight Unit (AOU) of EFSA. EFSA, a member of the International Forum of Independent Audit Regulators (IFIAR), was established in 2009 as a part of the Egyptian government's efforts to restructure its capital markets and in accordance with loan agreements with the IMF (EFSA 2008; IFIAR, 2012; Raslan *et al.*, 2016). Inspired by the US-style Public Company Accounting Oversight Board and in order to meet IFIAR requirements, the EFSA established the AOU as its compliance and oversight arm. According to Egyptian law, the 375 auditors listed with EFSA are registered in their personal capacity and not in their firm's name, and are the subject of the AOU's regular oversight. The AOU's main responsibilities include setting the entry criteria for registering auditors and a mechanism for audit compliance reviews. Yet, the AOU's achievements have so far been limited to managing the auditors' registration, since the AOU consists only of a handful of employees handling registration, compliance reviews and continuous professional development. Compliance reviews remain somewhat minimal and primarily involve a checklist of the auditor's independence profile and duties, and information about their firm e.g. human resources policies and quality control QC manual. According to AOU staff, this questionnaire was developed after reviewing the Egyptian and International Standards on Auditing, and based on what is done by regulators in developed countries.

The introduction of EFSA as a new regulator had a varying impact on the three types of audit firms operating in the Egyptian market. The first type of firm is the small local firm with one partner, who is the only registered auditor of the firm, but most of these firms will not have clients listed on the main equity market. The second type is mid-size or large local firms with a nominal international affiliation.[10] The third type includes the Big Four firms and other 'top tier' international firms, which are in close contact with their network in terms of staff training and technical resources including the application of the network's audit software and quality control manual.

The local firm's application of ISAs in their audit engagements varied between the three types of Egyptians firms. Small-size firms are limited to the use of the 'current' version of ESA, issued in 2008 and based on the 2005 version of ISA. Although most of the auditors we interviewed are aware that the current ESA version is poorly written, outdated and does not reflect the new Clarified ISAs (issued 2009), it is still the legally required set of standards and it is in Arabic. The consequence is that local auditors, particularly small-size firms, are applying an outdated, pre-Clarified version of ISA. This is a situation that not only affects the growth potential for such firms, but also limits their knowledge base.

As, for the second tier of Egyptian auditors (i.e. mid-size or large local firms with nominal international affiliation), the extent of ISA implementation varied between firms and was dependent on the nature of the firm and the type of their audit engagements. Some interviewees highlighted that they do use ISAs when dealing with audit engagements that have a foreign client (i.e. either Egyptian companies with foreign subsidiaries or an Egyptian company as subsidiary of a foreign company). They also rely on some of the staff's English proficiency to be able to translate the requirements to other staff members. Other mid-size firms depend on the updated Arabic versions of ISAs from Jordan or Saudi Arabia. In effect ISAs are being 'implemented' but not necessarily in terms of the most timely version and on a comprehensive basis. Therefore, questions arise as to whether particular standards are ignored or not considered due to the delay.

The Egyptian case provides a more detailed local understanding of ISA adoption and implementation in the context of a developing country. ISA adoption is often conceptualised by international institutions as being the end goal and the reflection of a successful outcome. When faced with such pressure, governments frequently seek to accelerate and portray compliance, but the standards-setting institutions are evidently not ready, leading only to adoption in name. In such cases, local Big Four firms typically take precedence to provide the technical know-how to adapt ISAs to the local environment but, at the same time, seek to benefit from the competitive position they hold in the market. This not only hinders the ISA standards-setting process (which normally should consist of a wide variety of local constituents for consultation) but may also negatively affect the subsequent oversight by regulators. For instance, one could question how a local regulator, who has just relied on the expertise of local Big Four in the adoption of ISA, could subsequently carry out a meaningful and objective oversight function on its own advisers?

Future directions

Limited research attention to the development and practice of auditing standards can be associated with the lack of access to primary data on the working practices of audit firms. Humphrey (2008) suggests that audit research 'at a distance' has thrived with the use of closed-ended questionnaires, experimental designs and the reliance on financial or arguably simplistic proxies. For instance, audit quality has often been associated with the type of firm (Big Four or non-Big Four) regardless of the circumstances in which these firms operate. Yet, it is not always apparent that Big Four's global networks of offices and staff operate on the basis of different ownership and control arrangements (e.g. branch offices, local representative firm or affiliates) and the looseness or tightness of this relationship may well affect the quality of the audit outcomes.

Increasingly, audit firms, particularly large ones, operate at the crossroads of a potentially conflicting set of social, economic, cultural and political influences. In the context of developing and emerging economies, large firms are often the primary intermediary organisation involved in advisory, audit and other certification activities for the benefit of public, private and international (e.g. financing or development agencies) institutions. The firm's reputation and standing are on one hand related to their credentials and experience, and on the other hand, to the processes and practices pertaining to audit tasks that have been over time codified in the auditing standards. With regards to the latter, there is a lack of understanding as to how these standards become operationalised and how auditors form an opinion and judgements (e.g. about sufficiency of evidence, reliability of particular controls) in relation to the standards. The Egyptian case reflects the difficulties for practitioners to embed these standards within their existing practices and the varying level of motivation among practitioners to adopt ISAs.

At the same time, the reputational advantage of being ISA compliant (however this comes to be defined in the local context and/or by IFAC) takes precedence because there is a clear material interest (e.g. more 'international' clients) from the audit firms' perspectives and that of policy makers (i.e. more international investment; better country governance scores). In this way, institutional level factors in terms of how and why particular jurisdictions seek to convey adoption (in part or fully or even a commitment to it) takes precedence in the analysis rather than concerns about substantive and functional improvements in auditing practice.

There are two key strands to be considered for future research and in particular (1) do auditing standards improve audit quality or other audit outcomes (using a longitudinal research and cost/benefits analysis) and (2) how and why would certain stakeholders (government, audit firms or accountancy bodies) seek to encourage the adoption of ISAs. We would therefore encourage a more in-depth and theoretically informed investigation of this phenomenon.

A further dimension to the study of ISA adoption is the role of audit regulators. As a result of the various ROSC reports (Hopper *et al.*, 2017; Boolaky and Soobaroyen, 2017), there has been a proliferation of accounting and audit regulators in developing and emerging countries, whose remit has been inspired by institutions established in developed countries (e.g. UK Financial Reporting Council, United States Public Company Accounting Oversight Board). There is an urgent need to develop an evidence base on the effectiveness of audit regulators worldwide, and how these regulators have engaged with the oversight of auditing standards (including ISAs) and the outcomes thereof. The dynamics of regulatory space (e.g. Malsch and Gendron, 2011; Hazgui and Gendron, 2015) could be an appropriate theoretical frame for teasing out more explicitly the issues relating to the adoption and embedding of ISAs in some of the developing and emerging economies, and in particular to investigate the complex set of interactions between the different actors in the field, their roles, agendas and influence.

Thus, it seems apt for ISA adoption and implementation in the context of emerging and developing countries to be analysed from a broader social, economic and political perspective, and from the positioning of accounting and audit services in the national context. Theoretical implications call for further investigation into auditing practices and standards, with particular focus on diligence, oversight and audit quality in the field. This might serve to address concerns about the reliability of an auditor's assurances and the basis (and potentially varying standards) adopted by auditors in providing such an assurance. In conclusion, we suggest that the adoption and implementation of ISAs and their contribution (if any) as a consequence of policies and strategies instigated by transnational institutions deserve much greater attention than they have received to date.

Notes

1 For the IAASB's list of countries, see www.iaasb.org/clarity-center/support-and-guidance (accessed 8 February 2019).
2 Editors' note. We define emerging economies in Chapter 1 by reference to the IMF's *World Economic Outlook 2018* and the Statistical Appendix to that report. www.imf.org/en/Publications/WEO/Issues/2018/09/24/world-economic-outlook-october-2018 (accessed 8 February 2019).
3 www.iaasb.org/clarity-center.
4 World Bank *Report on Observance of Standards and Codes* (ROSC), www.worldbank.org/en/programs/rosc (accessed 15 August 2018).
5 A summary profile per country is available on the IFAC website: www.ifac.org/about-ifac/membership/member-organizations-and-country-profiles?
6 This section is drawn from a broader study of Egyptian audit practices (Ghattas, 2017).
7 In 1964, Egypt created the Central Accounting Organization as the main entity for setting future budgets, overseeing public funds and conducting audits for all public entities and governmental entities (Farag, 2009).
8 The Egyptian Institute for Accountants and Auditors (EIAA) was established with the initial help of the USAID through a two million US dollar grant. One of the EIAA's aims was to establish an

Independent Board for Accounting and Auditing Standards and to provide training programmes for Egyptian auditors. However, the EIAA activities were paused due to a lack of funding (Farag, 2009). Recently, the EIAA resurfaced and continued its operations, yet the ESAA continues to have the leading position as the primary accounting and auditing professional association in Egypt.

9 In 2013, the Prime Minister changed the makeup of the Permanent Standards-Setting Committee. The committee maintained the same bureaucratic composition as the previous standards-setting body with two notable changes. First, the committee is now headed by the president of EFSA instead of the minister and, second, the academic member is replaced by an auditing expert (practitioner), a Big Four partner (Egyptian Cabinet, 2011; EFSA, 2014).

10 Typically, there is an agreement with an international audit firm to carry its brand, but they do not receive any technical assistance. They are often not subject to the international network's audit quality review.

References

Abd-Elsalam, O. H. and Weetman, P. (2003). Introducing international accounting standards to an emerging capital market: Relative familiarity and language effect in Egypt. *Journal of International Accounting, Auditing and Taxation*, 12(1), 63–84.

Ahmed, K. and Goyal, M. K. (2005). A comparative study of pricing of audit services in emerging economies. *International Journal of Auditing*, 9(2), 103–116.

Al-Awaqleh, Q. A. (2010). Factors that influence the adoption of international standards on auditing in Jordan. *International Management Review*, 6(2), 28–34.

Boolaky, P. K. and Soobaroyen, T. (2017). Adoption of International Standards on Auditing (ISA): Do institutional factors matter? *International Journal of Auditing*, 21(1), 59–81.

Brody, R. G., Moscove, S. and Wnek, R. (2005). Auditing standards in Poland: Past, present and future. *Managerial Auditing Journal*, 20(1), 36–46.

DeFond, M. and Zhang, J. (2014). A review of archival auditing research. *Journal of Accounting and Economics*, 58(2–3), 275–326.

EFSA (2008). Law no. 84/2008: The establishment of the EFSA's Auditors Oversight Board. Egyptian Financial Supervisory Authority, The Egyptian Cabinet, Cairo.

EFSA (2014). Decree 220/2014: The formation of the Accounting and Auditing Standards-Setting Committee, 2014. Cairo, Egypt.

Egyptian Cabinet (2011). The formation of the Accounting and Auditing Standards-Setting Committee. Cairo, Egypt.

ESAA (2016). *Action Plan Developed by The Egyptian Society of Accountants & Auditors (ESAA)*. International Federation of Accountants (IFAC).

Farag, S. M. (2009). The accounting profession in Egypt: Its origin and development. *The International Journal of Accounting*, 44(4), 403–414.

Fraser, P. N. (2010). A single set of worldwide auditing standards: The road is long. *International Journal of Disclosure and Governance*, 7, 298–309.

Gendron, Y. and Bédard, J. (2001). Academic auditing research: An exploratory investigation into its usefulness. *Critical Perspectives on Accounting*, 12(3), 339–368.

Ghattas, P. (2017). *A Study of Professionalization, Standards and Oversight in Egypt: Closure, Capture and Spectacle*. Unpublished PhD thesis, University of Southampton.

Hazgui, M. and Gendron, Y. (2015). Blurred roles and elusive boundaries: On contemporary forms of oversight surrounding professional work. *Accounting, Auditing and Accountability Journal*, 28(8), 1234–1262.

Hopper, T. H., Lassou, P. and Soobaroyen, T. (2017). Globalisation, accounting and developing countries. *Critical Perspectives on Accounting*, 43, 125–148.

Humphrey, C. (2008). Auditing research: A review across the disciplinary divide. *Accounting, Auditing and Accountability Journal*, 21(2), 170–203.

Humphrey, C. and Loft, A. (2013). Contemporary audit regulation – going global! in Caprio Jr., G. (Ed.), *Handbook of Key Global Financial Markets, Institutions, and Infrastructure*. Elsevier, 31, 333–343.

Humphrey, C., Loft, A. and Woods, M. (2009). The global audit profession and the international financial architecture: Understanding regulatory relationships at a time of financial crisis. *Accounting, Organizations and Society*, 34, 810–825.

IFAC (2012). Basis of ISA adoption by jurisdiction. New York, International Federation of Accountants, www.ifac.org/about-ifac/membership/compliance-program.

IFIAR (2012). Core principles for independent audit regulators. International Forum of Independent Audit Regulators, www.ifiar.org/download/core-principles/ (accessed 15 August 2018).

Khlif, H. and Samaha, K. (2014). Internal control quality, Egyptian standards on auditing and external audit delays: Evidence from the Egyptian stock exchange. *International Journal of Auditing*, 18(2), 139–154.

Kohler, A. G. (2009). *Evaluation of the Possible Adoption of International Standards on Auditing (ISAs) in the EU.* University of Duisburg-Essen.

Lofgren, H. (1993). Economic policy in Egypt: A breakdown in reform resistance? *International Journal of Middle East Studies*, 25 (3), 407–421.

Malsch, B. and Gendron, Y. (2011). Reining in auditors: On the dynamics of power surrounding an 'innovation' in the regulatory space. *Accounting, Organizations and Society*, 36(7), 456–476.

Mennicken, A. (2008). 'Connecting worlds': The translation of International Auditing Standards into post-soviet audit practice. *Accounting, Organizations and Society*, 33, 384–414.

Ministerial Decree (478, 1997). *Decree no. 478/1997: The Establishment of the Permanent Committee for Standards of Accounting and Auditing*, 1997. Ministry of Economy and Foreign Trade, Cairo, Egypt.

Ministerial Decree (503, 1997). *Decree no. 503/1997: Issuing the Egyptian Accounting Standards*, 1997. Ministry of Economy and Foreign Trade, Cairo, Egypt.

Ministerial Decree (55, 2000). *Decree no. 55/2000: The formation of the Permanent Accounting and Auditing Standards-Setting Committee*, 2000. Ministry of Economy and Foreign Trade, Cairo, Egypt.

Ministerial Decree (625, 2000). *Decree no. 625/2000: Issuance of the Egyptian Standards on Auditing (ESA)*, 2000. Ministry of Economy and Foreign Trade, Cairo, Egypt

Ministerial Decree (166, 2008). *Decree no. 166/2008: The issuance of the Egyptian Standards on Auditing*, 2008. Ministry of Investment, Cairo, Egypt.

Momani, B. (2003). Promoting economic liberalization in Egypt: From US foreign aid to trade and investment. *Middle East*, 7(3), 89.

Needles, B. E., Ramamoorti, S. and Shelton, S. W. (2002). The role of international auditing in the improvement of international financial reporting. *Advances in International Accounting*, 15, 181–201.

Power, M. K. and Gendron, Y. (2015). Qualitative research in auditing: A methodological roadmap. *Auditing: A Journal of Practice and Theory*, 34(2), 147–165.

Raslan, I., Hegazy, M. and Eldawla, N. K. (2016). Quality control elements and auditor fraud risk assessment: An experimental study. *Journal of Accounting and Finance*, 16(2), 151–176.

Simunic, D. A., Ye, M. and Zhang, P. (2016). Audit quality, auditing standards, and legal regimes: Implications for International Auditing Standards. *Journal of International Accounting Research*, 14(2), 221–234.

The Economist (2012), *Democracy Index*, The Economist Intelligence Unit. www.eiu.com/Handlers/WhitepaperHandler.ashx?fi=Democracy-Index-2012.pdf&mode=wp&campaignid=DemocracyIndex12.

World Bank (2002). *Egypt, Arab Republic – Report on the Observance of Standards and Codes (ROSC) – Accounting and Auditing*, http://documents.worldbank.org/curated/en/589181468023039456/Egypt-Arab-Republic-Report-on-the-Observance-of-Standards-and-Codes-ROSC-accounting-and-auditing (accessed 15 August 2018).

World Justice Project (2012). World Justice Project Rule of Law Index 2012–13. https://worldjustice project.org/sites/default/files/documents/WJP_Index_Report_2012.pdf.

Zohny, A. Y. (2000). The suitability of US security laws and regulations to serve as a model law for Egyptian financial markets. *Arab Law Quarterly*, 5, 5–47.

15

DEVELOPMENT AND IMPACT OF CORPORATE GOVERNANCE IN EGYPT

Tarek Abdelfattah and Khaled Hussainey

Introduction

In this chapter, we review the major developments of corporate governance (CG) in Egypt, empirical evidence on CG in Egypt and its impact on firm performance, financial distress, corporate disclosure practice, compliance with International Financial Reporting Standards (IFRS), earnings management, auditing-related issues and internal control quality. We identify gaps in the literature and suggest ideas for future research.

Egypt is one of the countries of the Middle East and North Africa (MENA) region. As the most populous country in the Arab world and the third most populous in Africa (CIA, 2018), Egypt plays an influential role, politically and economically, in the Middle East and Arab world. It was the first country in the region to introduce commercial, civil and other laws in the late nineteenth century and the first to organise its own national accounting profession and form its own institute of auditors (Abd-Elsalam, 1999). The Charter of Accounting and Auditing Professions was issued in 1958 (Larsen *et al.*, 2014: 491). The Egyptian legal system is based on codified laws with the written constitution being the highest governing norm. A new constitution was adopted in 2014. Egypt has been influenced by both French and Anglo-American laws, British and American. The French influence was on company law, which was based mainly on French civil law. Other laws and rules were established based on the concepts of Anglo-American common law, such as the Charter of Accounting and Auditing professions of 1958, Capital Market Law (95/1992) and CG rules. Egypt has a diversified economy where revenues from tourism and the Suez Canal are the main sources of foreign exchange. Over the last two decades, Egypt has been undergoing a transformation into an increasingly market-oriented economy. The Egyptian Exchange (EGX)[1] is one of the oldest stock exchanges in the world and, the first to be established in the MENA region, it dates back to the nineteenth century. EGX has a strong relationship with international organisations such as the World Federation of Exchanges (WFE) and the World Bank. It supports and promotes Western initiatives, standards and concepts that ensure transparency, sustainability and governance in the Egyptian market. EGX has been included in the global Emerging Market Investible Index since 1996 and in the Morgan Stanley Index since 2001.

In January 2011, Egypt experienced significant political turmoil after the Egyptian revolution. Falls in tourism and foreign investment since 2011 have severely affected the Egyptian economy, leading to lower growth rates compared to the pre-revolution average (EGX, 2011). Due to the transformational reform programme implemented by the Egyptian government in 2014 and support from some Arabic countries, higher levels of foreign investment have contributed to a slight rebound in gross domestic product (GDP) growth after a particularly depressed post-revolution period. Foreign direct investment flows to Egypt grew in 2015 by 14 per cent to $4.8 billion, driven by investments in oil and construction projects (UNCTAD, 2015). The annual rates of GDP growth increased from an average of 2 per cent between 2011 and 2014 to 4.2 per cent in 2017. Egypt floated its currency, reduced the fuel and electricity subsidy and passed a value-added tax in 2016. The implementation of the reform programme, along with the gradual restoration of confidence and stability, are starting to yield positive results. As a result, the International Monetary Fund (IMF) approved a three-year loan package worth $12 billion, to help restore macroeconomic stability and promote inclusive growth in Egypt. By the end of 2017, foreign direct investment flows to Egypt had increased to $8.1 billion (UNCTAD, 2017; World Bank, 2017).[2]

Using the cultural classification of Hofstede, Egypt shows high secrecy, high uncertainty avoidance and high power distance (Abd-Elsalam and Weetman, 2007; Dahawy *et al.*, 2010). According to Gray's model of cultural influences on accounting systems, accounting practices in Egypt tend to be more conservative and less transparent, combined with strong central government control and a mix of public/private ownership of many companies listed on the Egyptian stock exchange. It is uncommon for Egyptian companies to cross-list in foreign stock exchanges and file with foreign regulatory agencies in accordance with internationally recognised standards (Ebrahim and Abdelfattah, 2015). Similar to other developing countries, there is a tendency to resist changes and check all events in order to avoid uncertainty.

Corporate governance

In line with many other countries around the world, Egypt paid attention to CG early in 2000. To support the Egyptian economic reform programme and to attract direct foreign investments, the Egyptian government recognised the need for a number of regulatory changes to promote transparency through implementing international standards and the best practices of CG. Therefore, Egypt has been involved over the past two decades in a number of initiatives and CG reform activities aiming to increase the awareness of CG and to encourage the application of its best practices. Three versions of the Egyptian CG code have been issued, the most recent in 2016. The development of CG in the MENA region and particularly in Egypt can be classified under two waves. The focus of the first wave was mainly on increasing the awareness of CG and developing codes with guidelines and rules of good CG, while the second wave focuses on implementation issues.

The first wave of corporate governance in Egypt

CG refers to the system of internal and external checks and balances which ensure companies are both accountable to their stakeholders and conducting their business in a socially responsible way (Solomon, 2013: 14). Some of these internal and external governance mechanisms are included in several laws that govern the incorporation of companies and listed companies in the Egyptian Exchange. The first assessment of CG practices in Egypt was conducted in 2001 by the World Bank and the IMF against the CG principles of the Organisation for Economic Cooperation and Development (OECD, 2010). They reported that more than 60 per cent of the principles were applied in Egypt. The assessment identified some areas to be strengthened, including disclosure of ownership and control structures; disclosure of financial and non-financial information; training and capacity building for regulators and the private sector; role and effectiveness of shareholders' meetings; practices of boards of directors; professional conduct of auditors (World Bank, 2001).

As a response to the report, in August 2002 Egypt issued new listing rules that prohibit insider trading, encourage good CG practices by issuers, require an audit committee, and impose for the first time penalties on issuers in case of failure to disclose on time. In 2004 and 2005, the EGX was the world's best-performing emerging markets exchange. The penalties encouraged many illiquid companies, especially small and closely held companies, to delist. By the end of 2007, the number of listed companies had dropped from 1,151 at the end of 2002 to 435 listed companies. However, the market capitalisation during the same period increased from LE122 billion to LE768 billion (Abdel-Shahid, 2003; Mustafa, 2006).

Some governance-related concepts such as non-executive directors and audit committees were first introduced in Egypt's new listing rules of 2002. Consequently, the development of the audit committee as a governance tool in Egypt, as in other emerging markets, is still at a relatively early stage. Moreover, there were no rules governing the balance between executives and non-executive directors. The concept of independent board member was not clearly applied in most Egyptian companies (Bremer and Elias, 2007). Most of the Egyptian efforts to promote transparency and CG have been aimed at the 50 most active companies that account for 80 per cent of trading volume (Abdelsalam *et al.*, 2008).

As a sign of improvement, the World Bank updated its evaluation of the application of CG principles in Egypt to 85 per cent of the OECD principles (World Bank, 2004). Board responsibilities, and disclosure and transparency, were identified as two areas of weakness in CG in Egypt. The report of the World Bank (2004) highlighted the slow adoption of an audit committee, lack of rules governing members' independence, relatively limited accessibility of information to non-executive directors, and the dominance of role duality. The report recommended drafting a code of CG, adopting the rule of 'comply or explain', and considering the concept of 'independent director'.

In 2003, Egypt established the Egyptian Institute of Directors (EIoD), the first institute dealing with CG in the region, aiming to spread awareness and to improve good CG practices not only in Egypt but also in the MENA region (Koldertsova, 2010). The institute is responsible for educating and promoting CG principles. It collaborates with many leading international organisations such as the World Bank, the International Finance Corporation (IFC) and the Centre for International Private Enterprise. The EIoD organises conferences, seminars and training sessions on CG, targeting interested stakeholders. Examples of training programmes include a certified director programme, fundamentals of CG, CG in family-led companies and CG for state-owned enterprises (Bremer and Elias, 2007).

As a response to the World Bank's recommendations, the EIoD issued the Egyptian Corporate Governance Code (ECGC, 2005) for listed companies in October 2005. The code was written in Arabic and English and consisted of nine chapters that provided guidelines and governance rules for listed companies related to the scope of implementation, general assembly, board of directors, internal audit department, external auditor, audit committee, disclosure of social policies, avoiding conflict of interest, and CG rules for other corporations. However, this first version of the code was criticised for the lack of enforcement that may affect its implementation. The code did not follow the rule of 'comply or explain' and it indicated that the rules were neither mandatory nor legally binding; rather, they promoted and regulated responsible and transparent behaviour in managing corporations according to international best practices and means that strike equilibrium between various party interests (ECGC, 2005: 4).

The EIoD was the first in the region to issue CG Code for state-owned companies in July 2006 (ECGC, 2006). This code introduced the principles of governing state-owned companies by presenting an organisational and legal framework within which such companies should operate. In addition, the code focused on the actions of the State as a regulator versus its role as an owner. It presented the principles for equitable treatment of all shareholders, including the State as a shareholder, conflict of interest issues, disclosure and transparency, and responsibilities of the board of directors. Furthermore, the EIoD issued a manual for audit committees in May 2007 and launched a campaign to update the first version of CG Code.

The Egyptian efforts to promote CG have been recognised by international organisations such as the World Bank in its third ROSC report for Egypt (World Bank, 2009) and the IFC report (IFC, 2010) indicating significant progress in CG awareness in the MENA region in general and Egypt in particular (IFC, 2010).

Egypt started moving towards the approach of 'comply or explain' in March 2011 when the EIoD issued an amended version of the Egyptian Corporate Governance Code (ECGC, 2011) for private companies. According to this version, companies are recommended to comply with its recommendations and to clearly explain, in case of non-compliance, why certain recommendations have not been complied with. In addition, ECGC (2011) has introduced a definition of an independent board member as follows:

> A member of the board of directors whose relationship with the company is limited to being a member of its board. This member does not represent any shareholder, does not have material transactions with the company, and does not receive any salary, commission, or fees except the compensation for meeting attendance, transportation allowance, and board compensation as decided in the general assembly. Moreover, the member does not have any special interest in the company or any relatives or relationships with any of the board members or senior executives. In addition, the member is not a previous senior executive, company's consultant, or external auditor, during the three years that precede his appointment.
>
> *(ECGC, 2011: 8)*

Similarly, in July 2011, the Central Bank of Egypt issued a decision on the CG guidelines and instructions for banks in Egypt. Instructions had been distributed to all banks registered with the Central Bank of Egypt in August 2011 to begin creating or developing systems of governance. Banks had been committed to the application by 1 March 2012 at the latest. In case any bank could not abide by any of the required instructions, it should display it to the Central Bank accompanied by strong justifications for its consideration, which underlines the importance of adhering to the key rule of governance, namely, 'comply or explain' (Shehata and Dahawy, 2014).

A new support for CG practices in Egypt was provided by the European Bank for Reconstruction and Development (EBRD), which started its activities in Egypt in 2012. The EBRD's board of directors approved in 2017 its strategy for Egypt, highlighting that, while there is a voluntary code of CG in place, its implementation in practice needs to be further encouraged and strengthened. Therefore, the bank is aiming to supplement its investment in both the state and private sectors with appropriate CG programmes (Cigna *et al.*, 2017).

The second wave of Egyptian corporate governance

The second wave of CG in Egypt started by shifting the main focus from governance rules and principles towards the issues of commitment and implementation (Koldertsova, 2010). Generally, two main changes have been introduced in Egypt after issuing the ECGC in 2011: the first is enforcing some CG rules through the listing rules, and the second is issuing the third version of the CG Code in 2016, considering the comments and recommendations of the international organisations and the worldwide best practices (Abdelfattah, 2018).

Developing the legislative infrastructure was the first objective of the EGX strategy 2013–2017. To achieve this objective, EGX updated the listing rules to enhance CG application and to match international best practices. A new set of listing rules was introduced in 2014 to improve market transparency and minority protection rights.[3] Some rules were updated in 2015 and 2016 to ensure a wider application of CG and more investors' protection.[4] These rules include the disclosure requirements of some aspects such as financial reporting, corporate actions, material events, shareholding structure, board and general assembly meetings (EGX, 2015).

An example of the mandatory CG requirements introduced in the listing rules is the requirement that audit committees in listed companies should consist of at least three non-executive board directors, two of whom are independent. The listing rules assign authority to the audit committee concerning nomination, remuneration, dismissal, resignation and all matters related to the external auditors. Listed companies are also required to disclose immediately the minutes of their board meetings and general shareholders' meetings.

Having at least two independent directors on the board of a listed company is another example of the mandatory CG requirements introduced in the listing rules. According to the ECGC (2011), companies were recommended to have a majority of independent non-executive board members. Although the 2011 code introduced a definition of independent director, an adjusted detailed definition was presented in a more recent version of the Egyptian Corporate Governance Code (ECGC, 2016) in August 2016. New additional requirements for approval of related party transactions have been introduced in the listing rules.

The general assembly of a company is required to approve related party transactions in advance and also to approve each contract separately, allowing the shareholders commercial scrutiny before giving their approval. The listing rules require listed companies to promptly disclose information about any shareholder agreements before the company's shares are traded. These developments in the listing rules reflects the EGX's enforcement power and should improve the quality of governance practices of Egyptian listed companies. As the focus of the second wave of CG is implementation, there is a need for more monitoring and enforcement.

The second step was to publish the third version of the Egyptian Corporate Governance Code (ECGC, 2016) in August 2016. It provides a comprehensive set of guidelines to ensure a better implementation of CG best practices. In the new version, the EIoD has considered the latest international and regional practices and standards in good governance and addressed the full spectrum of companies in Egypt. The Code was introduced as indicative guidelines for all legislative and regulatory bodies when enacting and updating regulations and legislation related to CG in Egypt.

ECGC (2016) also follows the approach of 'comply or explain' and considers it as a fundamental pillar that upholds enforcement of the implementation of the principles. To enhance users' understanding of concepts and terminologies employed in the Code, detailed definitions have been presented. One of them is the adjusted definition of an independent director that is defined as:

> a non-executive Board member that is not a shareholder in the company, who has been appointed as an expert within the Board, and has no other relation with the company except his/her membership in that Board. This member is not a representative of the company's owners, and has no material transactions with the company, and

is not paid any salary, commissions, or fees, except compensation as a Board member. The independent director should neither have personal interest in the company, nor be a relative by blood or marriage or otherwise up to second degree relationship to any of its shareholders, Board directors, or executives. This member also should not be a senior officer, adviser or external auditor of the company for the three years prior to his/her appointment. Importantly, his/her tenure of membership as an independent director should not exceed a maximum six consecutive years, otherwise he/she will become a non-independent director.

(ECGC, 2016: 17)

In addition to highlighting the role of the State and its institutions in supporting the concept and applications of governance, the code presents the four main pillars of CG: the general assembly, board of directors, board committees and control environment. It emphasises the role of the board of directors and its responsibility for the effective implementation of governance. In addition to the composition and diversity of the board, the code presents the different types of committees such as audit committee, nomination committee, remuneration committee, risk management committee and governance committee. It clarifies their responsibilities and how they can assist the board in performing its functions.

As well as emphasising the role of external auditors, more focus is given to: the control environment and its components; internal control, internal audit, risk management, compliance department; and CG department. The code also presents the disclosure channels and highlights the importance of non-financial disclosure with clarification of the material information that should be disclosed. Finally, the code presents a number of policies and manuals that companies need to develop and apply to organise their internal approaches to CG.

Prior corporate governance research

In this section, we review prior empirical studies that investigate CG practices in Egypt.[5] We group selected studies in three themes. The first is related to CG quality; the second is the impact of CG on corporate performance and behaviour; and the third is CG and corporate disclosure.

CG quality

With regard to CG quality, a limited number of empirical studies has examined the determinants of CG quality in Egypt. For example, Elsayed (2010) found that board leadership structure is driven by firm size, age and ownership structure. However, the impact of CG on various accounting and auditing issues has been extensively examined in the Egyptian context.

The role of the audit committee was examined by Abdel-Meguid *et al.* (2014). They focused on audit committee functionality in Egypt and highlighted a substitutive association in which a weakness in a CG mechanism is compensated by the existence of a functioning audit committee, and a complementary association in which strength in a CG mechanism is reinforced by the existence of a functioning audit committee. The study examined the effects of six CG characteristics – board size, role duality, board independence, auditor type, blockholder ownership and managerial ownership – on the likelihood of audit committee functionality. Their study found a positive association of board independence and board size with audit committee functionality. The results showed a negative relation between auditor type and audit committee functionality, which indicates a substitutive governance effect.

Using a questionnaire survey, Kamel and Elkhatib (2013) investigated the perceptions of accounting academics, external auditors and financial managers/senior accountants on the role of audit committees in Egypt and their potential impact on the quality of financial reporting. The independence of audit committee members and their experience in accounting or other related subjects were ranked by respondents as the most important qualities to consider when appointing the members of audit committees. The study reported that the majority of respondents believe that a well-functioning and well-structured audit committee will constrain financial reporting fraud and will lead to a higher quality of financial reporting in Egypt.

Khlif and Samaha (2016) examined the moderating effect of auditor size on the audit committee as an internal control relationship. The study focused on the activity of the audit committee as it may represent a good proxy for the real functioning of the audit committee in the Egyptian context where companies may focus on the form of the committee rather than the substance. They reported a positive association between audit committee activity and the quality of internal control. The study highlighted the governance role of Big Four auditors in having a positive moderating effect on the relationship between audit committee activity and the quality of internal control in Egyptian listed companies.

Corporate performance and behaviour

Abdelsalam *et al.* (2008) examined the effect of board composition and ownership structure on corporate dividend policies in Egypt using a sample from the top 50 listed companies. The study covered the period between 2003 and 2005, before the Egyptian CG code was issued, and measured board composition using three variables: board size, independence and role duality. The results indicated no association between board composition and dividend decision or pay-out ratio. The authors reported a significant positive association between institutional ownership and both dividend decision and pay-out ratio. They concluded that despite the high institutional ownership and the closely held nature of the firms, which imply lower agency costs, the payment of a higher dividend was considered necessary to attract capital during the transitional period.

Elsayed (2007) examined the impact of CG on firm performance. He found that CEO duality does not affect performance. He did find, however, that the impact of CEO duality on performance varies across industries, and that CEO duality positively affects firms with low performance. In addition, Shahwan (2015) and Hassouna *et al.* (2017) found that CG practices have no impact on financial performance.

Elsayed and Wahba (2013) examined the relationship between institutional ownership and inventory management. They highlighted that the effectiveness of one CG mechanism is more likely to be contingent on some contextual variables and that the effect of one mechanism can depend upon others. The study examined the link between inventory management and some internal CG mechanisms. They found that institutional ownership is positively associated with inventory management when managerial ownership is high, CEO duality is in place or board size is large, while a significant negative association is observed when the conditions are reversed.

Ebrahim and Abdelfattah (2015) examined the effect of CG characteristics and independent audit quality on the compliance with IFRS requirements in Egypt. They found that compliance with recognition and disclosure requirements of income tax accounting during initial IFRS adoption in Egypt is significantly affected by the sophistication level of a company's management and its owners. Companies with foreign members on the board and higher levels of institutional ownership were more likely to recognise deferred taxes in their financial statements and comply with related disclosure requirements. Their conclusion was that companies with more-sophisticated management and owners are more likely to engage a high-quality auditing firm with an international affiliation. Ultimately, this integration leads to better compliance with IFRS requirements.

The association between CG and earnings management was examined by Khalil and Ozkan (2016). They found that non-executive board directors and audit committee per se are not sufficient to adequately constrain opportunistic earnings management in Egypt. They highlighted the interaction between board independence and the ownership levels. The effect of non-executive directors on earnings management practices was contingent on the levels of ownership held by executive directors and large shareholders, in addition to the composition of the audit committee. At higher levels of ownership, large shareholders and managers follow good practices of CG, such as increasing the number of outsiders on the board, to signal their commitment to high-quality financial reporting and not manipulating earnings opportunistically. While high-quality auditors were associated with a lower magnitude of earnings management, the study reported that CG mechanisms are unlikely to act in isolation. In a recent study, Nasr and Ntim (2018) used a sample from the top 100 listed companies in EGX over the period from 2011 to 2013 to investigate the effect of CG characteristics on accounting conservatism. The results indicated that only board independence was positively associated while board size was negatively associated with accounting conservatism. Role duality was found to be insignificant in this study.

In a study of the impact of CG practices on the auditor's client acceptance decision in Egypt, Ebaid (2011) used a 2×2 experimental design, comprising strong versus weak board of directors and strong versus weak audit committee, finding that auditors significantly assess higher (lower) favourable client acceptance judgements for the strong (weak) board of directors or/and the strong (weak) audit committee. The study concluded that the voluntary adoption of CG practices by Egyptian companies enhances the quality of the financial reporting process, and therefore affects auditors' decisions, especially the client acceptance decision.

CG and disclosure practices

With regard to the third theme of CG and disclosure practices, the extent of CG voluntary disclosure in the annual reports and websites of a sample of listed companies on the Egyptian Stock Exchange is assessed in Samaha *et al.* (2012). They found that the level of CG disclosure is low. Companies with duality in place and higher ownership concentration measured by blockholder ownership provide less CG disclosure while companies with a high percentage of independent directors on the board disclose more CG information. Samaha *et al.* (2012) reported that Egyptian listed companies provide higher disclosure for mandatory items under the EAS. They highlighted that non-compliance can be interpreted by some socio-economic factors in Egypt.

The association between CG and the extent of corporate voluntary disclosure of Egyptian listed companies is examined by Samaha and Dahawy (2011). They found that audit committee presence is the most significant mechanism affecting voluntary disclosure practices in Egypt. Companies with a higher ratio of independent non-executive directors disclose more information voluntarily. Their study reported a negative association between the levels of voluntary disclosure and blockholder ownership.

Using a sample from listed companies for the year 2007, Afify (2009) investigated the impact of CG implementation in the Egyptian context on audit report lag. The study indicated that more independent boards and the presence of audit committees reduced audit report lag while CEO duality was positively associated with audit report lag.

Desoky and Mousa (2012) investigated the CG practices and focused on the extent of transparency and disclosure as main pillars of CG. Using a sample of the top 100 listed companies in EGX for the year 2010, authors reported a case of weak practice of CG and attributed this to the voluntary nature of the Egyptian CG code. They highlighted that CG in Egypt was in its first stage of application. The results of the study indicated that the extent of disclosure and transparency is positively associated with firm size and foreign listing.

Future directions

Challenges from corporate governance practices

Egypt has made significant progress in enhancing CG. In particular, the second wave of CG in Egypt focuses on the implementation issues. This offers opportunities to gain benefits of market confidence as well as business integrity by attracting more direct foreign investments to the stock market. However, challenges remain. One is the issue of board independence. The method of appointment of non-executives and independent members and the tenure of non-executive directors are potential factors that may threaten board independence in Egypt. The threat has been highlighted in the OECD 2010 report. The 2016 version of the Egyptian governance code, therefore, adjusts the definition of board independence and tenure (e.g. an independent director should not exceed a maximum of six consecutive years on a board).

Culture impact is the second challenge that faces Egyptian state-owned enterprises (SOEs). Power distance might create unlimited power for authority that might negatively affect the implementation of a CG code. Legislative changes are needed to mitigate the possible negative consequences of high power distance and uncertainty avoidance.

CG practices of family firms provide a third challenge in Egypt. Generally speaking, these firms have independent boards according to the definition of the 2016 governance code. These companies, however, may choose friends or relatives to be the chair or the CEO. These companies also might have different committees according to the 2016 governance code, but the final decision is always taken by the chair of the board. Therefore, special care should be taken when evaluating the CG implementation of family firms in Egypt.

Another challenge is CG implementation and communication costs. The cost of designing a good governance system, implementing it and then communicating governance practice to stakeholders through financial communication channels (e.g. annual reports, corporate websites) might discourage Egyptian companies from seeking an effective application of a good governance system.

To mitigate these challenges, efforts are needed to improve the accounting profession in Egypt and we offer some suggestions. Professional bodies could consider the importance of CG to the Egyptian business environment and they should include CG as a core module for candidates who wish to obtain their certificates. Egyptian universities and colleges should increase the awareness of CG by introducing new courses or new programmes on CG. Universities and research institutions should also encourage research on CG to provide a cost–benefit analysis of the implementation of a CG system in Egypt. Collaborations between universities, stock exchanges and large Egyptian companies should also support the effective implementation of the CG system in Egypt.

Research potential

Prior studies have focused mostly on the top 100 listed companies. They have justified their choice by the high possibility of these companies following the best practices of CG. However, following the second wave of CG, there is a need to examine CG practices in listed companies outside the top 100 and in financial institutions. There is a need to investigate the CG practices in family-owned companies and governmental companies. Moreover, there is a need for longitudinal studies that span across different regulatory periods that witnessed gradual changes in the Egyptian CG code.

Researchers should focus on demonstrating the validity and robustness of their research method in order to support a strong contribution to knowledge. There is particular need to demonstrate the validity and robustness of any CG index, whether it relates to compliance or disclosure. Researchers have to balance the need to reflect the unique characteristics of the Egyptian context with a desire to show comparability with studies on other countries. Robustness of the model specification and consideration of endogeneity are also essential features.

As the EGX was a pioneer in introducing the sustainability index, the S&P/EGX and ESG index for the first time in the region, there is a need to clarify the links between CG, social responsibility and sustainability and to avoid any trade-off between the three aspects of the ESG index.

Agency theory is dominant in most prior CG studies. Researchers are encouraged to employ other relevant theories, such as neo-institutional theory, to provide more insights into the evolving of CG concepts and practices in emerging capital markets. In addition, future research in the Egyptian context may focus on some specific sectors that lead the capital market.

Most prior studies of CG and disclosure in the Egyptian context have focused on the quantity of disclosure without paying as much attention to the disclosure quality. Scholars in future research are encouraged to investigate the quality of disclosure. In addition, the unique features of Egyptian governance rules need to be considered in constructing a credible instrument for a governance index. Moreover, most prior studies have employed a quantitative methodology. There is a need to add more insights by employing a qualitative approach. Future research may give more attention to the relationship between CG and capital structure choices of Egyptian listed companies.

The concept of audit committees in Egypt is in its early stage compared with the US and other developed countries (Kamel and Elkhatib, 2013). There is a need to know how the role and performance of audit committees have evolved in the Egyptian context over time. Although a number of prior research studies have examined the effect of audit committee, there is a lack of research about the effect of other committees such as compensation committees and risk committees in the Egyptian context where a secretive culture and risk avoidance are prominent.

Finally, while the code of CG introduced and defined independent members, the issue of real independence is still a debatable issue in the Egyptian context. The Egyptian case may provide a unique opportunity to investigate how political and socio-economic variables may affect the effectiveness of CG practices in the MENA region, where some countries have witnessed relatively recent political volatility or instability.

Notes

1 The previous name was Cairo and Alexandria Stock Exchange (CASE). More information is available at the following source: www.egx.com.eg/en/history.aspx (accessed 28 January 2019).
2 More details are available at the following sources:

  a www.worldbank.org/en/country/egypt/overview
  b www.egx.com.eg/en/Reports.aspx (accessed 28 January 2019).

3 In February 2014, the Financial Regulatory Authority Board of Directors issued Decree No. 11 of 2014 on the listing rules.

4 The Financial Regulatory Authority Board of Directors issued the following decrees to amend some listing rules: Decree No. 114 of 2015 dated 20 September 2015 and Decree No. 35 of 2016 dated 23 March 2016.

5 There is often a time lag between carrying out a research project and the publication of the results. The sample period of the research reported in the literature review (but not necessarily the date of publication) reflects the CG guidelines of the research period.

References

Access date for all URL references is 29/09/2018.

Abdelfattah, T. (2018). The second wave of corporate governance in Egypt: Challenges ahead, in Jamali, D., Bodolica, V. and Y. Lapina (Eds.), *Corporate Governance in Arab Countries: Specifics and Outlooks*. Virtus Interpress, 70–88.

Abdel-Meguid, A., Samaha, K. and Dahawy, K. (2014). Preliminary evidence on the relationship between corporate governance attributes and audit committee functionality in Egypt: Beyond checking the box. *Corporate Governance: The International Journal of Business in Society*, 14(2), 197–210.

Abd-Elsalam, O. (1999). *The Introduction and Application of International Accounting Standards to Accounting Disclosure Regulation of a Capital Market in a Developing Country: The Case of Egypt*. Unpublished PhD Thesis, Heriot-Watt University, Edinburgh, UK.

Abd-Elsalam, O. and Weetman, P. (2007). Measuring accounting disclosure in a period of complex changes: The case of Egypt. *Advances in International Accounting*, 20, 75–104.

Abdelsalam, O., El-Masry, A. and Elsegini, S. (2008). Board composition, ownership structure and dividend policies in an emerging market: Further evidence from CASE 50. *Managerial Finance*, 34(12), 953–964.

Abdel-Shahid, S. (2003). Does ownership structure affect firm value? Evidence from the Egyptian Stock Market. https://ssrn.com/abstract=378580.

Afify, H. (2009). Determinants of audit report lag: Does implementing corporate governance have any impact? Empirical evidence from Egypt. *Journal of Applied Accounting Research*, 10(1), 56–86.

Bremer, J. and Elias, N. (2007). Corporate governance in developing economies: The case of Egypt. *International Journal of Business Governance and Ethics*, 3(4), 430–454.

CIA (2018). Egypt, in *The World Factbook*. Central Intelligence Agency. www.cia.gov/library/publications/the-world-factbook/geos/print_eg.html.

Cigna, G., Djuric, P. and Sigheartau, A. (2017). Corporate governance in transition economies: Egypt country report. www.ebrd.com/documents/ogc/eygpt.pdf.

Dahawy, K., Shehata, N. and Ransopher, T. (2010). The state of accounting in Egypt: A case. *Journal of Business Cases and Applications*, 3, 1–12.

Desoky, A. M. and Mousa, G. A. (2012). Corporate governance practices: Transparency and disclosure-evidence from the Egyptian exchange. *Journal of Accounting, Finance and Economics*, 2(1), 49–72.

Ebaid, I. (2011). Corporate governance practices and auditor's client acceptance decision: Empirical evidence from Egypt. *Corporate Governance: The International Journal of Business in Society*, 11(2), 171–183.

Ebrahim, A. and Abdelfattah, T. (2015). Corporate governance and initial compliance with IFRS in emerging markets: The case of income tax accounting in Egypt. *Journal of International Accounting, Auditing and Taxation*, 24, 46–60.

ECGC (2005). The Egyptian Corporate Governance Code. http://ir.egytrans.com/pdf/Egyptian%20Code%20of%20Corporate%20Governance.pdf.

ECGC (2006). The Egyptian Corporate Governance Code for state owned enterprises. www.eiod.org/uploads/Publications/Pdf/Publications/egyptsoecodeofcg/untitled1/index.html.

ECGC (2011). The Egyptian Corporate Governance Code. www.ecgi.org/codes/documents/code_egypt_2011_englishtranslation2016.pdf.

ECGC (2016). The Egyptian Corporate Governance Code. www.ecgi.org/codes/code.php?code_id=464.

EGX (2011). Annual report. The Egyptian Exchange. www.egx.com.eg/English/Services_Reports.aspx.

EGX (2015). Communication to stakeholders. The Egyptian Exchange. www.sseinitiative.org/wp-content/uploads/2015/04/Egypt_Comm_Stake_Eng.pdf.

Elsayed, K. (2007). Does CEO duality really affect corporate performance? *Corporate Governance: An International Review*, 15(6): 1203–1214.

Elsayed, K. (2010). A multi-theory perspective of board leadership structure: What does the Egyptian corporate governance context tell us? *British Journal of Management*, 21(1), 80–99.

Elsayed, K. and Wahba, H. (2013). Reinvestigating the relationship between ownership structure and inventory management: A corporate governance perspective. *International Journal of Production Economics*, 143(1), 207–218.

Hassouna, D., Ouda, H. and Hussainey, K. (2017). Transparency and disclosure as an internal corporate governance mechanism and corporate performance: Egypt's case. *Corporate Ownership and Control*, 14(4–1), 182–195.

IFC (2010). Corporate governance success stories. International Finance Corporation. http://gccbdi.org/Media/Articles/IFC%20Corporate_Governance_Success_ Stories_MENA.pdf.

Kamel, H. and Elkhatib, S. (2013). The perceptions of audit committees' role in an emerging market: The case of Egypt. *Journal of Economic and Administrative Sciences*, 29(2), 85–98.

Khalil, M. and Ozkan, A. (2016). Board independence, audit quality and earnings management: Evidence from Egypt. *Journal of Emerging Market Finance*, 15(1), 84–118.

Khlif, H. and Samaha, K. (2016). Audit committee activity and internal control quality in Egypt: Does external auditor's size matter? *Managerial Auditing Journal*, 31(3), 269–289.

Koldertsova, A. (2010). The second corporate governance wave in the Middle East and North Africa. *OECD Journal: Financial Market Trends*, 2, 219–226.

Larsen, J., ElDeeb, M. and AbdelFattah, T. (2014). *Modern Advanced Accounting*. McGraw-Hill International limited.

Mustafa, M. (2006). Corporate governance and firm performance: Evidence from Egypt. The 7th Annual UAE University Research Conference.

Nasr, M. A. and Ntim, C. G. (2018). Corporate governance mechanisms and accounting conservatism: Evidence from Egypt. *Corporate Governance: The International Journal of Business in Society*, 18(3), 386–407.

OECD (2010). Business climate development strategy – Egypt. www.oecd.org/global-relations/46341513.pdf.

Samaha, K. and Dahawy, K. (2011). An empirical analysis of corporate governance structures and voluntary corporate disclosure in volatile capital markets: The Egyptian experience. *International Journal of Accounting, Auditing and Performance Evaluation*, 7, 61–93.

Samaha, K., Dahawy, K., Hussainey, K. and Stapleton, P. (2012). The extent of corporate governance disclosure and its determinants in a developing market: The case of Egypt. *Advances in Accounting*, 28(1), 168–178.

Shahwan, T. M. (2015). The effects of corporate governance on financial performance and financial distress: evidence from Egypt. *Corporate Governance*, 15(5), 641–662.

Shehata, N. F. and Dahawy, K. M. (2014). 2013 review of the implementation status of corporate governance disclosures: Case of Egypt. *Corporate Ownership and Control*, 11(2–6), 591–601.

Solomon, J. (2013). *Corporate Governance and Accountability*, 4th edn. John Wiley and Sons.

UNCTAD (2015). *World Investment Report*. United Nations, New York. http://unctad.org/en/Publications Library/wir2015_en.pdf.

UNCTAD (2017). *World Investment Report*. United Nations, New York. http://unctad.org/en/Publications Library/wir2017_en.pdf.

World Bank (2001). The Arab Republic of Egypt. Report on The Observance of Standards and Codes (ROSC): Corporate governance country assessment. www-wds.worldbank.org.

World Bank (2004). Report on The Observance of Standards and Codes (ROSC), Corporate governance country assessment, EGYPT. www.worldbank.org/ifa/rosc_cg_egyp2.pdf.

World Bank (2009). Report on The Observance of Standards and Codes (ROSC), Corporate governance country assessment, EGYPT. www.worldbank.org/en/programs/rosc.

World Bank (2017). Doing business 2017 report. www.doingbusiness.org.

16

INSTITUTIONAL CHARACTERISTICS AND OUTCOMES OF CORPORATE GOVERNANCE IN BANGLADESH

Research challenges

Abdus Sobhan and Sudipta Bose

Introduction

Importing corporate governance (CG) codes based on the Anglo-American model (Paredes, 2003) acts as an impetus for the growth of CG research in emerging economies. A utilitarian tradition, investigating the association between CG and outcomes embodies the implicit assumption that a CG system based on the Anglo-American model is context-free regarding ensuring the well-being of corporations and protecting the interests of shareholders and stakeholders. Other researchers contend that studies based on a utilitarian tradition provide an under-socialised view and downplay the role of institutions on CG practices (Aguilera and Jackson, 2010). Researchers highlighting the role of distinctive institutions question both the suitability (Singh and Zammit, 2006; Young *et al.*, 2008) and effectiveness of a CG system based on an Anglo-American model in an emerging economy context (Sobhan, 2016).

We provide a systematic review of existing research on CG in Bangladesh, as a case study for emerging economies more broadly. We view CG as the whole set of legal, cultural and institutional arrangements that determine the relationships between corporations and all stakeholders and the influence of these stakeholders on strategic corporate decision making (Aguilera and Jackson, 2010). Bangladesh provides a particularly apt context to encapsulate research on CG based on the Anglo-American model in the context of emerging economies because the recent economic growth of Bangladesh is phenomenal (ADB, 2017). However, most of the formal institutions of Bangladesh (e.g. family concentrated ownership and control of companies, inefficient and ineffective judicial system, rampant corruption) co-exist with its informal institutions (e.g. high power distance and secretive culture) (Sobhan, 2014). These institutional settings of Bangladesh are distinct from those prevailing in Anglo-American countries and conflict with recently imported CG guidelines based on the Anglo-American model (Sobhan, 2016).

We build on the results of the systematic review to propose avenues for future research. We suggest successful empirical strategies that could be used in the emerging economy context, derived from the experience of Bangladesh in particular, including data sources, theoretical approach and statistical estimation techniques often overlooked in prior studies. This chapter, therefore, stimulates interest in CG research in the emerging economy context in general, and Bangladesh, in particular.

Bangladesh: an institutional overview

On achieving national independence in 1971, the ruling regime in Bangladesh initially adopted socialism to pursue economic growth, nationalising all large companies. By 1975, a lack of efficient management and resultant enormous operating losses in the newly nationalised large companies led international financial institutions (IFIs) and donor agencies to convince the ruling party to abandon socialism and embrace market-based capitalism (Ahmed and Uddin, 2018). Slow initial economic growth has subsequently accelerated to the point where Bangladesh is claimed as a new 'Asian Tiger' (Garber, 2017).

However, existing institutional characteristics of Bangladesh were not suited for market-based capitalism (Uddin and Choudhury, 2008). Many institutional features of Bangladesh conflict with those prevailing in Anglo-American countries (Sobhan, 2014). Bangladesh is categorised as a country with high levels of collectivism and power distance (Hofstede *et al.*, 2010). It has persistent high levels of corruption according to Transparency International Bangladesh (TIB, 2016), weak property rights and judicial ineffectiveness (The Heritage Foundation, 2018), weak implementation and enforcement of regulations as indicated by the World Justice Project (WJP, 2018), significant difficulties in enforcement of contracts (World Bank, 2018), a small and volatile stock market (World Bank, 2017), and a passive managerial labour market (Siddiqui, 2010). Uddin and Choudhury (2008) argued that such institutional characteristics hamper the efficient operation of the formal rational framework.

A tradition of family ownership and control of corporations existed before independence (Kochanek, 1996). Following the brief period of nationalisation under market-based capitalism, the large corporations were privatised to families having an affiliation with the contemporary ruling parties (Uddin and Choudhury, 2008). Subsequently, not only did these few families accumulate economic power (Nuruzzaman, 2004), but they also strengthened their political alliances leading to a geometric increase in the proportion of businesspeople and industrialists as Members of Parliament on the national assembly (56 per cent in the 2009–2014 parliament) (Jahan, 2015). Several academics considered Bangladesh as an ideal example of 'crony capitalism' (Uddin and Hopper, 2003; Haque *et al.*, 2011a).

The Asian financial crisis in 1996 led the IFIs to pressurise Bangladesh to adopt a CG code based on the Anglo-American model (Uddin and Choudhury, 2008; Sobhan, 2016). In consequence Bangladesh CG Guidelines (hereafter BCGG) were issued in 2006 by the Bangladesh Securities and Exchange Commission (BSEC). The BCGG-2006 are aligned with the OECD's Principles of CG and consistent with the Anglo-American model, subsequently becoming part of the listing rules of both Dhaka Stock Exchange and Chittagong Stock Exchange.

A more severe stock market fall in 2010 reduced market capitalisation by an amount equivalent to 22 per cent of gross domestic product (GDP) as of October 2012 (ADB, 2014). The IFIs responded with a $300 million Second Capital Market Development Programme. One objective was to ensure that the BSEC would adopt an amendment to the existing BCGG-2006 to require 'compulsory' adherence by listed companies. The BSEC amended the BCGG-2006 by including more provisions and changing its basis of compliance from 'comply or explain' to 'comply' guidelines only in 2012. A further update to BCGG, incorporating detailed provisions on the independent director, the role of chairperson and introducing nomination and remuneration committees, was adopted by the BSEC in June 2018.

Research themes – theories and methods

We searched journals ranked from 2 to 4★ by the UK's Chartered Association of Business Schools (ABS) and/or from B to A★ by the Australian Business Deans Council (ABDC) to find relevant papers on CG in Bangladesh, published between January 2001 and January 2018 using the search term 'Bangladesh' together with 'corporate governance' or 'board of directors', 'ownership', 'family control' and 'audit' in the title, abstract and/or keywords. Our time frame recognises that CG research in Bangladesh has received much attention since the stock market crash in 1996 but quality publication takes time to materialise. We also searched for forthcoming papers on the website of those journals where at least one article was found in a previous search as of 31 January 2018. We have also included two publications on CG in Bangladesh written by non-academic institutions. We excluded any multi-country study in which CG in Bangladesh was extensively explored. The outcome was 47 papers from 20 journals (Table 16.1). We made our best effort to capture all significant contributions to Bangladesh CG research but we apologise in advance for any unintentional omission.

Figure 16.1 presents publications by year and ABS journal ranking.[1] The quantity and quality of publications has increased, indicating a strengthening contribution to knowledge

Table 16.2 summarises theories and research methods. As indicated in Panel A we find a clear distinction between theories used by studies that investigate the effectiveness of or level of compliance with the CG guidelines and studies that examine the association between CG mechanisms and outcome variables. While institutional theory in some form dominates the earlier

Table 16.1 Publications on corporate governance in Bangladesh

Journal Name	Total	ABS rank	ABDC rank
Accounting, Organizations and Society	1	4★	A★
Accounting, Auditing and Accountability Journal	5	3	A
British Accounting Review	2	3	A
Corporate Governance: An International Review	2	3	A
Critical Perspectives on Accounting	2	3	A
Asia Pacific Journal of Management	1	3	A
Journal of Business Ethics	6	3	A
Applied Economics	2	2	A
Journal of Contemporary Accounting and Economics	2	2	A
Pacific-Basin Finance Journal	1	2	A
Accounting Research Journal	1	2	B
Advances in Accounting	4	2	B
Asia-Pacific Journal of Accounting and Economics	1	2	B
Australian Accounting Review	1	2	B
International Journal of Accounting & Information Management	3	2	B
Journal of Accounting in Emerging Economies	2	2	C
Managerial Auditing Journal	6	2	B
Research in International Business and Finance	2	2	B
Journal of Banking and Finance Law and Practice	1	–	A
Others (Not published in academic journals)	2	–	–
Total	47		

Note: These 47 publications are indicated by asterisks in the full list of references.

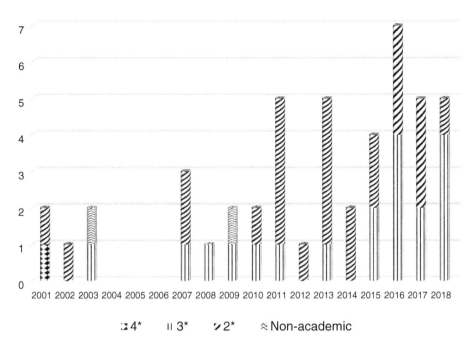

Figure 16.1 Publications by year and ABS journal ranking

Table 16.2 Theoretical frameworks and methods in papers reviewed

Panel A: Theoretical framework applied

Theory	Total
Agency or extended agency theory	17
Institutional theory in various versions	9
Legitimacy related	4
Stakeholder theory	2
Signalling theory	3
Resource dependence theory	3
Others	3
The theory is not explicit	14
Total★	**55**

Panel B: Research methods used

Method	Total
Publicly available data	34
Interviews and other qualitative methods	7
Survey supplemented by archival data	3
Multi-method	1
Analytical	2
Total	**47**

Note: ★ Eight papers used two theories each.

stream, agency theory and its extension dominate the later stream. Overall, agency theory is the most used theoretical framework, which is unsurprising as CG research is dominated by agency theory (Aguilera and Jackson, 2010). Reflecting a common acceptance of a multi-theoretical approach to examine CG (Aguilera and Jackson, 2010), eight studies used two theories each.

From Panel B, the majority of papers depends on publicly available data. The limited use of primary data suggests that primary data collection is challenging Bangladesh, which, like other emerging economies, suffers from a lack of research orientation.

Institutions and CG in Bangladesh

Management control of firms and its impact on shareholders as well as stakeholders has long been an interest of researchers (Uddin and Hopper, 2001, 2003; Uddin, 2009). Uddin and Hopper (2001) provide detailed case study evidence on how internal and external accountability changed when a state-owned enterprise became a family firm through privatisation. The owner-managers used the internal and external accounting systems not only to maximise family interests but also to inhibit accountability and transparency to both internal and external stakeholders (Uddin and Hopper, 2001). Uddin and Hopper (2003) and Uddin (2009) reported similar conclusions that family owners manipulate management control to serve their own interests instead of those of general shareholders.

The Bangladesh Enterprise Institute (BEI, 2003), a private sector think tank, first investigated the status quo of the Bangladesh CG framework in 2003 and reported that stakeholders lacked legal, institutional and economic motivations to maintain a robust CG framework. Haque *et al.* (2011a), based on a 2004–2005 questionnaire survey, evidenced a negative relationship of their self-constructed CG index with the political connection of the sponsor family, ownership concentration, family-aligned board and family-aligned management. Since the BCGG-2006 came into effect, Siddiqui (2010) has investigated its appropriateness in Bangladesh and few studies explore the level or substance of compliance with it (Uddin and Choudhury, 2008; World Bank, 2009; Sobhan, 2016; Ahmed and Uddin, 2018). Siddiqui (2010) contended that the domestic regulatory agencies and other actors adopted the shareholder-based model to prove their legitimacy to the IFIs, although the institutional characteristics of Bangladesh are more compatible with the stakeholder-based approach of CG. Using Weber's notion of traditionalism and rationality as a theoretical lens, Uddin and Choudhury (2008) find that substantive rationality resulting from traditional institutional characteristics of Bangladesh hampered formal rationality of CG. They show that sponsor families, having traditional attitudes, craft ceremonial boards of directors, grant limited authority to non–family affiliated managers, stage-manage annual general meetings and dominate external auditors who lack independence. This evidence indicates a widespread non-compliance with the BCGG-2006. In contrast, the World Bank (2009), based on compliance as reported in annual reports, documented that the average level of compliance with the BCGG-2006 is 82 per cent.

Sobhan (2016) reconciles the contradictory findings of Uddin and Choudhury (2008) and the World Bank (2009) by demonstrating overstatement of compliance in annual reports. Sobhan (2016) reports an average level of overstatement of compliance in annual reports, calculated as a gap between compliance as reported in annual reports and compliance as stated by company secretaries or chief financial officers in a confidential survey. The author also documents that overstatement of compliance is positively associated with family control but negatively associated with the presence of an institutional investor on the board of directors. Similarly, Ahmed and Uddin (2018) evidenced that structural and cultural conditions affect agential perception and consequent actions leading to symbolic compliance by family business groups and lax monitoring of compliance by regulatory agencies. In sum, studies that explore compliance and underlying determinants consistently documented that institutional characteristics and family control and ownership hamper substantive compliance with the BCGG-2006.

Besides compliance with CG guidelines, we find two studies that focus on Corporate Social Responsibility (CSR) governance. Kamal and Deegan (2013) investigated and found CSR governance disclosures, although increased rapidly over 1996–2009, to still fall significantly short of international standards. Similarly, the theoretical analysis of Rahim and Alam (2014) demonstrates that CG and CSR do not converge in Bangladesh due to the ineffectiveness of ancillary institutional characteristics.

CG and outcomes

As the primary objective of a paper is to test the association between hypothesised test variables and the dependent variable, our review focuses on the association between CG used as the hypothesised test variable and a dependent outcome variable.

Family firms and outcomes

Family ownership and control also attract significant empirical attention as a determinant of performance and accounting-related outcomes. We find six prior studies of this type. The impact of family ownership and control on Type I and Type II agency problems (Young *et al.*, 2008) informs the hypotheses of most of these studies.

Family firms have a positive association with firm performance (Muttakin *et al.*, 2014, 2015b) and real earnings management (Razzaque *et al.*, 2016), and a negative association with audit quality choice and pricing (Khan *et al.*, 2015). Muttakin *et al.* (2014) extend family firm research by demonstrating that family firms managed by first-generation entrepreneurs outperform other firms. Other evidence is mixed. Although family ownership is found to be positively associated with firm performance (Muttakin *et al.*, 2014, 2015b), and negatively associated with audit quality choice and pricing (Khan *et al.*, 2015) and CSR disclosures (Muttakin and Khan, 2014), it maintains a U-shaped relationship with real earnings management (Razzaque *et al.*, 2016) and intellectual capital (IC) disclosures (Muttakin *et al.*, 2015a).

Other ownership characteristics and outcomes

An important ownership characteristic that captures much empirical attention can be labelled as insider ownership although researchers describe it variously as managerial ownership, board ownership and sponsor ownership. In our view, all these ownership measures represent the same ownership construct as, in many Bangladeshi companies, the board of directors, and management is nothing but an extension of sponsors (Farooque *et al.*, 2007a; Sobhan, 2016). On the board of directors, independent and non-sponsor affiliated executive directors are few and they have either negligible or no ownership interest in the companies.

The studies on insider ownership are generally informed by incentive-alignment and entrenchment hypotheses (Morck *et al.*, 1988), an extension of agency theory. The empirical evidence is often conditional on the measurement of variables or statistical technique applied to estimate the association of interest. Khan *et al.* (2013) and Karim and Hasan (2012) evidence a negative relationship of managerial ownership with CSR disclosures and audit fees respectively while Rashid (2016) documents a mixed association between managerial ownership and agency costs; the association depends on how the agency costs are measured. Rashid (2016) also finds that managerial interest converses with that of shareholders at both very high and low levels of managerial ownership, which is inconsistent incentive-alignment and entrenchment hypotheses.

The association between board ownership and firm performance depends on the measurement of the performance variable and the statistical techniques applied. While Farooque *et al.* (2007a) find a non-linear association, Farooque *et al.* (2007b) report a negative association between board ownership and firm performance under ordinary least squares estimation. However, neither finds a significant association between board ownership and firm performance when two-stage least squares estimation is used. Karim *et al.* (2013) report a statistically insignificant relationship between board ownership and auditor choice. Additional evidence on insider ownership includes a significant negative relationship between sponsor ownership and auditor fees (Khan *et al.*, 2011) and no association between sponsor ownership and auditor choice (Karim and van Zijl, 2013).

Institutional ownership, although often viewed as an essential monitor of management under the Anglo-American corporate governance model, attracts limited attention by Bangladeshi researchers. We find six prior studies that test institutional ownership. While Karim and Van Zijl (2013), Bose *et al.* (2016) and Bose *et al.* (2018) find a positive association of institutional ownership with green banking disclosures, financial inclusion disclosures and auditor choice respectively, Farooque *et al.* (2007b) and Khan *et al.* (2011) report negative associations of institutional ownership with firm performance and audit fees respectively. Bose *et al.* (2017a) find that institutional investors are more attracted to banks with a higher level of philanthropic giving. Foreign ownership, despite its lower level in Bangladesh compared to other countries, is explored in four studies. These studies find consistent evidence that foreign ownership is positively associated with CSR disclosures (Khan *et al.*, 2013), IC disclosures (Muttakin *et al.*, 2015a), and auditor choice (Karim and Van Zijl, 2013; Karim *et al.*, 2013).

Bangladesh privatised a number of its state-owned enterprises after it moved to market-based capitalism (Uddin and Hopper, 2001). However, the government still has a significant percentage of ownership in several companies. Several studies investigate government ownership. Robin *et al.* (2018) report a positive association between government ownership and cost efficiency for the banking sector. In contrast, Zheng *et al.* (2017) document a positive (negative) association between government ownership and risk-taking behaviour (capital adequacy ratio) for the banking firms. Karim and Van Zijl (2013) document a negative association of government ownership with auditor quality choice for non-financial companies but there is no significant finding across the full sample comprising both financial and non-financial companies. Bose *et al.* (2017b) find that government ownership of banks positively moderates the positive association between financial inclusion disclosures and market-based performance of banks.

Turning to the types of ownership traits, Khan *et al.* (2013) document a positive association between public ownership and CSR disclosures while Khan *et al.* (2011) do not find any association between public ownership and audit fees. Farooque *et al.* (2010) report a co-deterministic relationship between ownership concentration and firm performance and Haque *et al.* (2011b) report that ownership concentration is positively associated with the proportion of debt in the capital structure.

CG mechanisms and outcomes

CEO duality, regarded as inconsistent with CG best practice under an Anglo-American corporate governance model, has received research attention but with mixed findings (Table 16.3, Panel A). Board independence is another critical CG mechanism in the Anglo-American model,

Table 16.3 Corporate governance mechanisms and outcomes

Panel A: CEO Duality

Outcome	Significance of association	Reference
Audit quality	Negative	Karim *et al.* (2013)
CSR disclosures	None	Khan *et al.* (2013)
IC disclosures	None	Muttakin *et al.* (2015a)
IC disclosures where there is CEO duality in the sponsor family	Negative	Muttakin *et al.* (2015a)
Agency costs, various	Inconclusive	Rashid (2015)

Panel B: Board independence

Outcome	Significance of association	Reference
CSR	Positive	Khan *et al.* (2013)
IC disclosures	Positive	Muttakin *et al.* (2015a)
Green banking disclosures	None	Bose *et al.* (2018)
Financial inclusion disclosures	None	Bose *et al.* (2016)
Efficiency of banks	None	Robin *et al.* (2018)
Agency costs	Inconclusive	Rashid (2015)
CSR disclosures when a firm is politically connected	Positive	Muttakin *et al.* (2018b)

Panel C: Political connections

Outcome	Significance of association	Reference
Corporate governance index	Negative	Haque *et al.* (2011a)
Performance in non-family firms	Negative	Muttakin *et al.* (2015b)
Agency costs	Positive	Khan *et al.* (2016)
Cost efficiency	Negative	Robin *et al.* (2018)
CSR disclosures	Negative	Muttakin *et al.* (2018b)
Perpetuation of human rights violations	Positive	Siddiqui and Uddin (2016)

again with mixed results in our sample of papers (Table 16.3, Panel B). Bangladesh is portrayed as a prominent example of crony capitalism (Uddin and Hopper, 2001). It is not surprising that political connection or state-business nexus is featured as a determining factor for several firm-level outcomes (Table 16.3, Panel C).

Other board-level variables receive scant attention from researchers, possibly because of mixed findings or difficulty in accessing data (Table 16.4).

External audit as CG and outcomes

The empirical evidence is mixed but probably weighted against the general conjecture that Big Four or their affiliated local audit firms are more effective in a CG role than non-affiliated local audit firms. Belal *et al.* (2017) provide interview evidence that Big-Four-affiliated local audit firms in Bangladesh do not follow the rigorous standard of the Big Four because of low audit

Table 16.4 Other corporate governance measures

CG measure	Outcome	Significance of association	Reference
CEO power	CSR disclosures	Negative	Muttakin *et al.* (2018a)
	Relation between board capital and CSR disclosures	Negative	Muttakin *et al.* (2018a)
Board size	Green banking disclosures	Positive	Bose *et al.* (2017b)
	Financial inclusion disclosures	None	Bose *et al.* (2016)
Board meeting frequency	Agency costs	Inconclusive	Rashid (2015)
Board capital	CSR disclosures	Positive	Muttakin *et al.* (2018a)
Board gender diversity	Financial inclusion disclosures	Negative	Bose *et al.* (2016)
Audit committees	CSR disclosures	Positive	Khan *et al.* (2013)
Audit committees	IC disclosures	Positive	Muttakin *et al.* (2015a)
Audit committee size	Financial inclusion	Positive	Bose *et al.* (2016)
Audit committee independence	Financial inclusion	None	Bose *et al.* (2016)
Risk committee and risk management unit	Accounting and market-based performance of banks	Positive	Nahar *et al.* (2016)
CG index (as defined by researchers)	Leverage in capital structure	Positive	Haque *et al.* (2011b)

fees and poor client-base. Previous evidence finds no difference between Big-Four-affiliated and local audit firms in Bangladesh, be it audit fees (Siddiqui *et al.*, 2013), accrual quality (Habib and Islam, 2007) or issue of unqualified audit reports when banks failed to maintain adequate provision for classified loans (Siddiqui and Podder, 2002). Inferior performance is seen where accrual quality is lower (Kabir *et al.*, 2011) and audit delay is higher (Imam *et al.*, 2001) for Big-Four-affiliated audit firms. Favourable effects are seen where Big-Four-affiliated audit firms negatively moderate the positive association between business group and earnings management (Muttakin *et al.*, 2017) and the positive association between politically connected firms and agency costs (Khan *et al.*, 2016).

Future directions

Challenges associated with data collection

The imbalance in research methods applied by prior researchers (Table 16.2, Panel B) suggests that collection of primary data in Bangladesh as an emerging economy is daunting, but a detailed reading of the method sections of published papers that relied on primary data suggests practical solutions. First, access to prospective interviewees, both company managers and professional accountants, becomes more plausible when researchers themselves have professional association memberships (e.g. Uddin, 2009; Belal *et al.*, 2017). Second, a research collaboration between an academic and a professional accountant working in a company seems a practical solution to develop practical insights into CG practices (e.g. Uddin and Choudhury, 2008). Finally, personal contacts and strong alumni connections could be used to collect survey data (e.g. Sobhan, 2016).

The primary source of secondary data is annual reports of companies although some studies collect data from company prospectuses, government reports, initial public offering documents, right share issue documents, the status of shareholdings of directors of listed companies published by the Dhaka Stock Exchange (DSE), and monthly review reports by DSE and newspapers (e.g. Muttakin *et al.*, 2015b, 2018b; Rashid, 2015; Razzaque *et al.*, 2016; Bose *et al.*, 2018). There are no dedicated databases available for Bangladeshi firms' financial data, CG and share prices. Some international databases provide data for relatively large Bangladeshi companies. For some Bangladeshi companies, Datastream provides share price data, while Compustat provides financial and share price data. Bankscope database provides financial data for banking companies whereas Bureau van Dijk provides financial and corporate governance data for banks and some non-financial companies, but only the current year's CG data. A growing number of studies have used the Compustat database (e.g. Bose *et al.*, 2016, 2017a, 2017b, 2018), and Datastream (e.g. Farooque *et al.*, 2007a; Khan *et al.*, 2015; Muttakin *et al.*, 2015b; Rashid, 2015, 2016). However, all studies need to rely on annual reports for firms' CG data, as will future researchers.

Further research on institutions and CG in Bangladesh

The prior research on institutions and CG in Bangladesh, using a context-bound approach, made a significant contribution to CG research in emerging economies. However, the potential of context-bound research has not still been fulfilled. First, the existing research has yet to identify an appropriate model of CG for emerging economies like Bangladesh. Siddiqui (2010) argued that a stakeholder model is more suited in emerging economies like Bangladesh. A future theory-building research is warranted to find out an appropriate model of CG for emerging economies like Bangladesh.

Second, although researchers focus on the role of overall institutions on CG practices, a limited number of in-depth studies exists on how an institutional element (e.g. culture, religion, corruption) affects CG practices. For instance, Bangladesh is populated mostly by people who follow Islam as their religion and it is simultaneously a highly corrupt country. Islam does not permit corruption and, therefore, a contradiction exists between two major institutional elements. A future study could explore the influence of this conflict between specific institutional elements on CG practices.

Finally, emerging economies are continually changing. For instance, ownership and control of companies are shifting to the second or third generation of a sponsor family (Muttakin *et al.*, 2014; Ahmed and Uddin, 2018). These later generations differ on at least two grounds. They are relatively more educated, some having attended Anglo-American educational institutions. Prior research has demonstrated that education, in particular Western education, changes cognitive abilities and infuses benefits of the Anglo-American model. The second or third generation may, therefore, face a different level of dilemma regarding effective compliance with the CG guidelines. We suggest future studies could explore the difference in compliance with the BCGG managed by different generations of families and by CEOs educated in local and Western institutions. Similarly, the BCGG is also changing rapidly. The 2012 and 2018 codes are progressively more stringent and extensive. A future study could investigate the changes in the level of compliance due to the change in the BCGG. An innovative study design is required to find real improvement as there is a possibility of over-reporting of compliance in annual reports (Sobhan, 2016).

Further research on CG and outcomes

First, analysis of existing studies on CG and outcomes indicates a strong imbalance towards CSR disclosures and firm performance. Although characteristics of emerging countries like

Bangladesh are well suited for CSR research, future research should explore the influence of CG on a broader set of firm outcomes. For instance, future research can examine the impact of family firms or CG elements on firms' cost of equity and cost of debt. Although, analysts' forecast data is not available in Bangladesh, realised return could be used as an alternative proxy for the cost of equity.

Second, we need future research to resolve some of the mixed and conflicting findings. For instance, family firms are performing better but substantively comply less with an Anglo-American based CG code. Does it imply that better compliance with an Anglo-American based CG code is harmful to the performance of family firms in emerging economies? Similarly, board independence positively influences CSR (Khan *et al.*, 2013) and IC (Muttakin *et al.*, 2015a) disclosures but does not affect green banking (Bose *et al.*, 2018) and financial inclusion (Bose *et al.*, 2016) disclosures. Are independent directors less effective in the banking sector than in non-financial sector? If yes, why?

Third, the research on the association between CG and outcome variables is dominated by agency theory and, therefore, downplays context. With few exceptions, most of the papers on the association between CG and outcomes do not acknowledge the role of contextual peculiarities of Bangladesh on the association between CG and outcomes. For instance, how do the institutional characteristics of Bangladesh affect the cognitive and related abilities of independent directors and therefore the association between the independence of board directors and outcome variables? A prevailing view is that independent directors are not independent of the controlling family (Ahmed and Uddin, 2018). However, some of the independent directors are highly educated, experienced and socially reputable and therefore are possessors of substantial social and human capital. They can be weaker in monitoring the family managers due to the relationship but may play important strategy and networking roles. This argument suggests that researchers should go beyond agency or institutional theory to acknowledge the role of institutional dynamics and individuals' social and human capitals simultaneously while conceptualising the causal relationships between CG and firm outcomes.

Finally, our literature review finds that many studies do not follow a proper methodology in examining the association between CG and outcome variables. For example, many studies do not attempt to deal with the endogeneity issue. It is now commonly accepted that CG is an endogenous variable and, therefore, without adequately dealing with the endogeneity issue, it is not possible to claim a causal relationship between CG and outcome variables. We therefore suggest future researchers use more-sophisticated statistical estimation techniques for minimising the endogeneity issue and establishing the robustness of their findings.

We hope that this chapter will encourage other CG scholars to apply more innovative and rigorous research approaches while examining CG issues in Bangladesh and other emerging countries and contribute to our better understanding of CG in emerging economies.

Note

1 We used the 2015 *Academic Journal Guide* of the Association of Business Schools, subsequently renamed as the Chartered Association of Business Schools. We do not present a figure for ABDC ranking due to limitations of space.

References

(*) The asterisks indicate the 47 papers contributing to the analysis in Table 16.1.

Aguilera, R. V. and Jackson, G. (2010). Comparative and international corporate governance. *Academy of Management Annals*, 4(1), 485–556.

*Ahmed, S. and Uddin, S. (2018). Toward a political economy of corporate governance change and stability in family business groups: A morphogenetic approach. *Accounting, Auditing & Accountability Journal*, doi: 10.1108/AAAJ-01–2017–2833.

ADB (2014). Second capital market development program (tranche 2): Progress report on tranche release. Asian Development Bank. www.adb.org/sites/default/files/project-document/149775/43477-013-prtr.pdf (accessed 15 February 2018).

ADB (2017). Asian development outlook 2017 update: Sustaining development through public–private partnership. Asian Development Bank. www.adb.org/sites/default/files/publication/365701/ado2017-update.pdf (accessed 18 May 2018).

*BEI (2003). Comparative Analysis of Corporate Governance in South Asia: Charting a Roadmap for Bangladesh. Bangladesh Enterprise Institute. http://bei-bd.org/wp-content/uploads/2015/03/whc4f4bb192762221.pdf (accessed 18 July 2018).

*Belal, A., Spence, C., Carter, C. and Zhu, J. (2017). The Big 4 in Bangladesh: Caught between the global and the local. *Accounting, Auditing & Accountability Journal*, 30(1), 145–163.

*Bose, S., Bhattacharyya, A. and Islam, S. (2016). Dynamics of firm-level financial inclusion: Empirical evidence from an emerging economy. *Journal of Banking and Finance Law and Practice*, 27(1), 47–68.

*Bose, S., Khan, H. Z., Rashid, A. and Islam, S. (2018). What drives green banking disclosure? An institutional and corporate governance perspective. *Asia Pacific Journal of Management*, 35(2), 501–527.

*Bose, S., Podder, J. and Biswas, K. K. (2017a). Philanthropic giving, market-based performance and institutional ownership: Evidence from an emerging economy. *The British Accounting Review*, 49(4), 429–444.

*Bose, S., Saha, A., Khan, H. Z. and Islam, S. (2017b). Non-financial disclosure and market-based firm performance: The initiation of financial inclusion. *Journal of Contemporary Accounting & Economics*, 13(3), 263–281.

*Farooque, O. A., Van Zijl, T., Dunstan, K. and Karim, A. (2007a). Corporate governance in Bangladesh: Link between ownership and financial performance. *Corporate Governance: An International Review*, 15(6), 1453–1468.

*Farooque, O. A., Van Zijl, T., Dunstan, K. and Karim, A. W. (2007b). Ownership structure and corporate performance: Evidence from Bangladesh. *Asia-Pacific Journal of Accounting & Economics*, 14(2), 127–149.

*Farooque, O. A., Van Zijl, T., Dunstan, K. and Karim, A. W. (2010). Co-deterministic relationship between ownership concentration and corporate performance: Evidence from an emerging economy. *Accounting Research Journal*, 23(2), 172–189.

Garber, J. (2017). There's a new 'Asian Tiger'. *Business Insider Australia*. www.businessinsider.com.au/bangladesh-is-the-new-asian-tiger-2017-4?r=US&IR=T (accessed 18 June 2018).

*Habib, A. and Islam, A. (2007). Determinants and consequences of non-audit service fees: Preliminary evidence from Bangladesh. *Managerial Auditing Journal*, 22(5), 446–469.

*Haque, F., Arun, T. and Kirkpatrick, C. (2011a). The political economy of corporate governance in developing economies: The case of Bangladesh. *Research in International Business and Finance*, 25(2), 169–182.

*Haque, F., Arun, T. G. and Kirkpatrick, C. (2011b). Corporate governance and capital structure in developing countries: A case study of Bangladesh. *Applied Economics*, 43(6), 673–681.

Hofstede, G., Hofstede, G. J. and Minkov, M. (2010). *Cultures and Organizations: Software of the Mind*. New York: McGraw-Hill.

*Imam, S., Ahmed, Z. U. and Khan, S. H. (2001). Association of audit delay and audit firms' international links: Evidence from Bangladesh. *Managerial Auditing Journal*, 16(3), 129–134.

Jahan, R. (2015). The Parliament of Bangladesh: Representation and Accountability. *The Journal of Legislative Studies*, 21(2), 250–269.

*Kabir, H. M., Sharma, D., Islam, A. and Salat, A. (2011). Big 4 auditor affiliation and accruals quality in Bangladesh. *Managerial Auditing Journal*, 26(2), 161–181.

*Kamal, Y. and Deegan, C. (2013). Corporate social and environment-related governance disclosure practices in the textile and garment industry: Evidence from a developing country. *Australian Accounting Review*, 23(2), 117–134.

*Karim, A. W. and Hasan, T. (2012). The market for audit services in Bangladesh. *Journal of Accounting in Emerging Economies*, 2(1), 50–66.

*Karim, A. W. and Van Zijl, T. (2013). Efficiency and opportunism in auditor quality choice in emerging audit services markets: The case of Bangladesh. *International Journal of Accounting & Information Management*, 21(3), 241–256.

*Karim, A. W., Van Zijl, T. and Mollah, S. (2013). Impact of board ownership, CEO-chair duality and foreign equity participation on auditor quality choice of IPO Companies: Evidence from an emerging market. *International Journal of Accounting & Information Management*, 21(2), 148–169.

*Khan, A. R., Hossain, D. M. and Siddiqui, J. (2011). Corporate ownership concentration and audit fees: The case of an emerging economy. *Advances in Accounting*, 27(1), 125–131.

*Khan, A., Muttakin, M. B. and Siddiqui, J. (2013). Corporate governance and corporate social responsibility disclosures: Evidence from an emerging economy. *Journal of Business Ethics*, 114(2), 207–223.

*Khan, A. R., Muttakin, M. B. and Siddiqui, J. (2015). Audit fees, auditor choice and stakeholder influence: Evidence from a family-firm dominated economy. *The British Accounting Review*, 47(3), 304–320.

*Khan, A. R., Mihret, D. G. and Muttakin, M. B. (2016). Corporate political connections, agency costs and audit quality. *International Journal of Accounting & Information Management*, 24(4), 357–374.

Kochanek, S. A. (1996). The rise of interest politics in Bangladesh. *Asian Survey*, 36(7), 704–722.

Morck, R., Shleifer, A. and Vishny, R. W. (1988). Management ownership and market valuation: An empirical analysis. *Journal of Financial Economics*, 20, 293–315.

*Muttakin, M. B. and Khan, A. R. (2014). Determinants of corporate social disclosure: Empirical evidence from Bangladesh. *Advances in Accounting*, 30(1), 168–175.

*Muttakin, M. B., Khan, A. R. and Subramaniam, N. (2014). Family firms, family generation and performance: Evidence from an emerging economy. *Journal of Accounting in Emerging Economies*, 4(2), 197–219.

*Muttakin, M. B., Khan, A. R. and Belal, A. R. (2015a). Intellectual capital disclosures and corporate governance: An empirical examination. *Advances in Accounting*, 31(2), 219–227.

*Muttakin, M. B., Monem, R. M., Khan, A. R. and Subramaniam, N. (2015b). Family firms, firm performance and political connections: Evidence from Bangladesh. *Journal of Contemporary Accounting & Economics*, 11(3), 215–230.

*Muttakin, M. B., Khan, A. R. and Mihret, D. G. (2017). Business group affiliation, earnings management and audit quality: Evidence from Bangladesh. *Managerial Auditing Journal*, 32(4/5): 427–444.

*Muttakin, M. B., Khan, A. R. and Mihret, D. G. (2018a). The effect of board capital and CEO power on corporate social responsibility disclosures. *Journal of Business Ethics*, 150(1), 41–56.

*Muttakin, M. B., Mihret, D. G. and Khan, A. R. (2018b). Corporate political connection and corporate social responsibility disclosures: A neo-pluralist hypothesis and empirical evidence. *Accounting, Auditing & Accountability Journal*, 31(2), 725–744.

*Nahar, S., Jubb, C. and Azim, M. I. (2016). Risk governance and performance: A developing country perspective. *Managerial Auditing Journal*, 31(3), 250–268.

Nuruzzaman, M. (2004). Neoliberal economic reforms, the rich and the poor in Bangladesh. *Journal of Contemporary Asia*, 34(1), 33–54.

Paredes, T. A. (2003). A systems approach to corporate governance reform: Why importing US corporate law isn't the answer. *William & Mary Law Review*, 45, 1055.

*Rahim, M. M. and Alam, S. (2014). Convergence of corporate social responsibility and corporate governance in weak economies: The case of Bangladesh. *Journal of Business Ethics*, 121(4), 607–620.

*Rashid, A. (2015). Revisiting agency theory: Evidence of board independence and agency cost from Bangladesh. *Journal of Business Ethics*, 130(1), 181–198.

*Rashid, A. (2016). Managerial ownership and agency cost: Evidence from Bangladesh. *Journal of Business Ethics*, 137(3), 609–621.

*Razzaque, R. M. R., Ali, M. J. and Mather, P. R. (2016). Real earnings management in family firms: Evidence from an emerging economy. *Pacific-Basin Finance Journal*, 40, Part B, 237–250.

*Robin, I., Salim, R. and Bloch, H. (2018). Cost efficiency in Bangladesh banking: Does financial reform matter? *Applied Economics*, 50(8), 891–904.

*Siddiqui, J. (2010). Development of corporate governance regulations: The case of an emerging economy. *Journal of Business Ethics*, 91(2), 253–274.

*Siddiqui, J. and Podder, J. (2002). Effectiveness of bank audit in Bangladesh. *Managerial Auditing Journal*, 17(8), 502–510.

*Siddiqui, J. and Uddin, S. (2016). Human rights disasters, corporate accountability and the state: Lessons learned from Rana Plaza. *Accounting, Auditing & Accountability Journal*, 29(4), 679–704.

*Siddiqui, J., Zaman, M. and Khan, A. (2013). Do Big-Four Affiliates Earn Audit Fee Premiums in Emerging Markets? *Advances in Accounting*, 29(2), 332–342.

Singh, A. and Zammit, A. (2006). Corporate governance, crony capitalism and economic crises: Should the US business model replace the Asian way of 'doing business'? *Corporate Governance: An International Review*, 14(4), 220–233.

Sobhan, M. A. (2014). *Corporate Governance Reform in a Developing Country: The Case of Bangladesh*. Unpublished PhD thesis, University of Edinburgh Business School, UK.

★Sobhan, M. A. (2016). Where institutional logics of corporate governance collide: Overstatement of compliance in a developing country, Bangladesh. *Corporate Governance: An International Review*, 24(6), 599–618.

The Heritage Foundation. (2018). 2018 Index of economic freedom. www.heritage.org/index/pdf/2018/book/index_2018.pdf (accessed 20 June 2018).

TIB (2016). CPI 2016: Bangladesh slightly improves scores and ranking. Transparency International Bangladesh. www.ti-bangladesh.org/beta3/images/2017/S_FinalCPI-EnglishPressrelease2016.pdf (accessed 25 May 2018).

★Uddin, S. (2009). Rationalities, domination and accounting control: A case study from a traditional society. *Critical Perspectives on Accounting*, 20(6), 782–794.

★Uddin, S. and Choudhury, J. (2008). Rationality, traditionalism and the state of corporate governance mechanisms: Illustrations from a less-developed country. *Accounting, Auditing & Accountability Journal*, 21(7), 1026–1051.

★Uddin, S. and Hopper, T. (2001). A Bangladesh soap opera: Privatisation, Accounting, and regimes of control in a less developed country. *Accounting, Organizations and Society*, 26(7–8), 643–672.

★Uddin, S. and Hopper, T. (2003). Accounting for privatisation in Bangladesh: Testing World Bank claims. *Critical Perspectives on Accounting*, 14(7), 739–774.

★World Bank (2009). Report on the Observance of Standards and Codes (ROSC). www.worldbank.org/en/programs/rosc (accessed 15 June 2018).

World Bank (2017). Bangladesh Development Update: Towards More, Better and Inclusive Jobs. http://documents.worldbank.org/curated/en/710651506517681504/pdf/120089-WP-PUBLIC-BDU-September-27-2017.pdf (accessed 18 July 2018).

World Bank (2018). Doing business 2018: Reforming to create jobs. www.doingbusiness.org/~/media/WBG/DoingBusiness/Documents/Annual-Reports/English/DB2018-Full-Report.pdf (accessed 18 July 2018).

WJP (2018). Rule of Law Index 2017–2018. World Justice Project. https://worldjusticeproject.org/sites/default/files/documents/WJP_ROLI_2017-18_Online-Edition_0.pdf (accessed 19 June 2018).

Young, M. N., Peng, M. W., Ahlstrom, D., Bruton, G. D. and Jiang, Y. (2008). Corporate governance in emerging economies: A review of the principal–principal perspective. *Journal of Management Studies*, 45(1), 196–220.

★Zheng, C., Moudud-Ul-Huq, S., Rahman, M. M. and Ashraf, B. N. (2017). Does the ownership structure matter for banks' capital regulation and risk-taking behavior? Empirical evidence from a developing country. *Research in International Business and Finance*, 42, 404–421.

17

NGOs IN GHANA

Accountabilities, performance and motivations

Gloria Agyemang, Brendan O'Dwyer, Charles Antwi Owusu and Jeffrey Unerman

Introduction

Non-governmental organisations (NGOs) are nonprofit organisations that address development and/or advocacy missions. In many emerging economies they play significant roles contributing to economic development and to the promotion and advancement of human rights. Collectively they are responsible for the deployment of aid to hundreds of millions of the most impoverished and vulnerable people on the planet. The funds they deploy often derive from the global north for development projects in the global south. In 2017, Official Development Assistance reached a total of US$146.6 billion globally, an increase of 1.1 per cent in real terms from the previous year (OECD, 2018). Much of these funds are deployed through NGOs.

Accounting scholars have studied several issues related to the roles of accounting and accountability mechanisms in these organisations. Prominent among these issues have been the study of hierarchical, upward, downward and holistic accountability (Unerman and O'Dwyer, 2006a, 2006b; O'Dwyer and Unerman, 2007, 2008, 2010; O'Leary, 2017). Other studies have also addressed performance management processes within NGOs (Chenhall *et al.*, 2010, 2013, 2016; Hall and O'Dwyer, 2017).

This chapter reviews the key findings from several research studies of NGOs operating specifically in Ghana and draws on a key research project by Agyemang *et al.* (2009a) that studied the effectiveness of NGO accountability in Ghana. NGO activity in Ghana is widespread covering all aspects of the economy including poverty reduction, education, health and agriculture. The studies undertaken in Ghana provide examples of the issues that NGOs working in emerging economies have to manage, and the roles of accounting and accountability in enhancing the effectiveness and efficiency of this management. Within the NGO accounting literature, NGO activity in several other emerging economies has also been studied, including in South Africa (Marini *et al.*, 2017), Sri Lanka (Jayasinghe and Wickramasinghe, 2011), Tanzania (Goddard and Assad, 2006; Assad and Goddard, 2010) and Uganda (Dixon *et al.*, 2006; Awio *et al.*, 2011) to name a few.

This chapter commences by introducing the Ghanaian NGO landscape. It then progresses with an explanation of the key theoretical issues of hierarchical and holistic accountability associated with the study of NGOs in the accounting literature. In doing this it draws upon research projects from Ghana. Attention is then turned to research on NGO performance management in Ghana. The chapter concludes by providing directions for future research.

NGOs and overseas assistance in Ghana

Ghana is considered a lower middle income country by the World Bank (World Bank, 2016). It has a population of 28 million people with 39 per cent of the population living below the poverty line. It met the Millennium Development Goal of reducing poverty by half between 2000 and 2015 (DFID, 2014). Despite this, it still receives a significant amount of aid from Overseas Development Assistance, multilateral and bilateral donors and grants. The OECD development finance gives a sense of the amounts involved (see Table 17.1).

This aid covers all the main sectors of activity including the social, economic and production sectors with key areas being education, health and water. Several national development organisations have strategies to support development in Ghana. For example, DFID, the UK Department for International Development, has a strategy of supporting the government of Ghana with human capital development, economic development and with improving governance. In the health and education sectors its work is undertaken by many NGOs.

Currently, the Ghanaian government lacks an accurate database for all registered NGOs in Ghana. However, according to interview research with, and data provided by, the governmental Department of Social Welfare, there is a conservative figure of over 5,000 NGOs operating in Ghana (Awuah-Werekoh, 2015). This number is made up of local grassroots organisations, faith-based organisations, community-based organisations and international development and relief organisations, among others. These organisations operate in all the 10 administrative regions in Ghana.

Hierarchical and holistic accountability

O'Dwyer and Unerman (2008) introduced two concepts of accountability with respect to NGOs as a way of framing the reporting practices between NGOs' funders and their beneficiaries. These are 'hierarchical accountability' and 'holistic accountability'. Hierarchical accountability is accountability of a short term, functional nature that emphasises reporting by local NGO offices to key stakeholders such as donors or suppliers of resources. Over time, the accounting literature has started to use the term 'upward accountability' to refer to such reporting to donors and suppliers of finance about the use of those resources. Holistic accountability, on the other hand, refers the broader forms of accountability that look beyond just accountability to the donors or funders. Holistic accountability includes accountability to funders (hierarchical accountability) but also accountability to beneficiaries, other organisations and the environment. The term 'downward accountability' has been used to refer to the reporting to, and interactions with, beneficiaries. Research has been undertaken to provide an understanding of the practices of upward and downward accountability.

In a project funded by the Association of Chartered Certified Accountants (ACCA) that studied NGO accountability from the perspectives of local officers working in 30 NGOs at the grassroots level in Ghana, Agyemang *et al.* (2009a) analysed the different mechanisms of upward

Table 17.1 Development Assistance to Ghana USD million (2015 prices and exchange rates)

2014	2015	2016
1,013	1,769	1,324

Source: Based on *Development Aid at a Glance 2018 Edition* (www.oecd.org/dac/financing-sustainable-Development).

and downward accountability used in a number of NGOs in Ghana. The report identified five types of accountability mechanisms (see Agyemang *et al.*, 2009a: 13) including disclosure statements and reports, performance assessment and evaluation document, participatory meetings with beneficiaries, self-regulation and social auditing reports.

The mechanisms of accountability used by the sample NGOs in the study covered both hierarchical and holistic accountability. Disclosure statements and reports, and performance assessments and evaluation are documents that are required by donors and oversight agencies and form the backbone of hierarchical accountability. Generally they contain financial information about projects as well as operational data about the projects. Performance assessment and evaluation reports assess the impact of projects. Typically the performance evaluation is conducted at the end of a project, while assessments are conducted mid-way through a project.

Holistic accountability includes accountability to all stakeholders. For example, participation as an accountability mechanism reflects the process of involving beneficiaries in decisions about projects. Social auditing is a process whereby the NGO assesses and reports on its social performance and ethical behaviour (Ebrahim, 2003) and can be considered part of holistic accountability. Its use enables the views of a range of stakeholders (such as beneficiaries, donors and NGO officers) to influence the organisational goals and values of the NGO. Self-regulation may also be considered part of holistic accountability. Within self-regulation accountability mechanisms, the NGO sector develops for itself standards and codes of behaviour. In Ghana, for example, a key network of NGOs is the Resource Centre Network that works with many NGOs to promote knowledge management services within the water, sanitation and hygiene sector in Ghana.

Upward accountability

Upward accountability is the reporting relationship between NGOs and their funders where local NGO offices receiving funds are required to provide formal quantitative financial reports to the suppliers of funds about how these resources have been used. Typically these reports specify the amounts received and how much has been spent on development activities during the period. The purpose of these reports is to demonstrate to the funders that resources have been used appropriately for the purposes for which they had been given. Additionally, these upward reports to funders enable them to assess whether the aid interventions have achieved their targets and goals. They enable funders to have oversight and control (O'Dwyer and Unerman, 2008). Importantly, funders have also indicated their desire to learn about local conditions impacting development.

Achieving the benefits of upward accountability

From the perspective of local NGOs working on development projects, there are several benefits associated with upward accountability mechanisms. Agyemang *et al.* (2009a) identified key benefits as providing transparency about the work of the NGOs at the grassroots to donors, thereby contributing to the building of a relationship of trust between local NGOs and funders. This was considered important by local NGOs because it assured them of funding and thereby sustainability of operations. Quantitative performance information was considered useful because it enabled a demonstration of what had been achieved. Local NGOs in emerging economies often are highly dependent on external funding and often lived in fear of funding being curtailed. Regular upward accountability through the disclosures about use of funds ensured that there was continuous communication between funders and officers that helped the development of good working relationships and ensured ongoing financial resources.

Despite these benefits there are aspects of hierarchical accountability that were considered problematic. First, hierarchical accountability was seen as being too controlling. The focus was on the specific requirements of the funders. In Agyemang *et al.* (2009a), NGO officers explained that they often felt compelled to address only the issues that donors required in the reports and that they would often not address other issues that were equally or more important. One example given was the reporting bias on female gender issues, which officers complied with in order to be assured of funding, though they felt a more balanced account on both males and females was more appropriate.

Second, the focus of upward accountability reports was on the short term, with reports required on a quarterly basis in most instances. This meant there was not enough emphasis on longer-term developmental needs of NGO activities. As an example, officers often discussed the need for beneficiaries to be trained before the development interventions could take place. They argued, however, that the required quarterly reporting did not allow them to fully demonstrate how this training could yield longer-term benefits. Thus, in some instances the required accounting did not reveal the full extent of the contribution and benefits derived from the training provided.

Another key issue associated with hierarchical accountability was the perception that it did not enable contextual issues associated with local work to be shared with funders. Quantified performance indicators were useful, but more qualitative reporting was important for the interpretation of performance metrics. The officers were very much aware that donors and funders may need an understanding of the local contexts, but their perception was that the narrative section of the upward reports was ignored by funders. This is because there was no follow up from the funders about the challenges they faced. Hierarchical accountability did not include reciprocal reporting so they remained unsure of how the reports were used.

The impact of these three problems meant that there was a risk that funds channelled through NGOs may not be effectively used. Several researchers have studied these problems associated with upward accountability (Rahaman *et al.*, 2010; Awio *et al.*, 2011). In a more detailed follow-on study, Agyemang *et al.* (2017) explained how the NGO officers in Ghana managed or coped with what they thought of as problems associated with hierarchical accountability processes.

Seeking 'conversations for accountability'

The above issues demonstrate an imbalance of power between local NGO officers and external funders. This power imbalance means that local officers are required to comply with the requirements of external funders. Agyemang *et al.* (2017) suggest that much of this compliance is tactical. Fieldworkers felt frustrated because their perception was that the 'real issues' on the ground were ignored by funders. They complied with the requirements but often did not share their real views on issues with funders. The fieldworkers found the accountability to be constraining and they sought more conversations with the funders, and a sense of 'committed listening' (Fry, 1995). Some research work has suggested that in such situations NGO officers manipulate and strategise (Elbers and Arts, 2011). Agyemang *et al.* (2017) found, however, that fieldworkers found ways of working within the upward accountability processes to enable them to meet their understandings of the needs of the development projects in Ghana. There was a strong sense of 'felt responsibility', an intrinsic and deeply felt sense of responsibility towards their tasks and the needs of beneficiaries (Fry, 1995; O'Dwyer and Boomsma, 2015). This meant that the fieldworkers engaged in activities to support the development process, which they believed were necessary to support their work, though not required by the upward accountability process. The 'world of action' (Jordan and Messner, 2012) and doing things to support their beneficiaries was very important to them. Thus, for example, the officers provided extended training periods for beneficiaries to ensure they could achieve the benefits of the interventions financed by funders.

What the fieldworkers sought was a level of mutual accountability where the funders could reciprocate by providing them with information about their plans and how they used the upward accountability reports etc. This would then help develop a relationship where they could fully share contextual information with funders. Agyemang *et al.* (2017) argue that this was beginning to take place, albeit informally.

Downward accountability

Downward accountability covers interactions between an NGO and its beneficiaries. It often takes place through participatory meetings. The purpose of downward accountability is to provide ways of involving beneficiaries in shaping the activities of the NGO. It offers ways in which the NGO funders and officers, through engaging with beneficiaries, can understand and respond to the needs of their beneficiaries.

There are variations in the approaches taken to achieve downward accountability and additionally there are differences in the effectiveness with which these approaches are implemented.

Agyemang *et al.* (2009a) identified two approaches to downward accountability used the NGO case studies they examined. Local NGO officers held community consultations and dialogues with their beneficiaries. These meetings were often held at the start of projects so the beneficiaries could help with the design and planning of projects. This type of downward accountability was often required by donors and was undertaken to assess and identify the needs of beneficiaries. Within the upward accountability reports officers had to show that the consultations had taken place.

The second type of downward accountability process is the participatory review, which often takes place during the development process and at the end of the project. Some reviews included beneficiaries and any partner organisation that had contributed to the project. For example, a project aimed at children as direct beneficiaries would include teachers and parents in the participatory review meetings. During the review the beneficiaries are encouraged to reflect on the impact the development intervention has had. Evidence from Agyemang *et al.* (2009a) suggests that beneficiaries engage actively in the process, providing both positive and negative comments about the value of the development aid projects to them.

Achieving downward accountability

In undertaking the consultations and community dialogues NGO officers have to be sensitive to the cultural settings in which they operate. In some rural areas, for example, there might be a requirement for meetings to be held separately for men and women. Often the participatory review meetings are organised as focus group meetings. As part of the ACCA NGO Project (Agyemang *et al.*, 2009a) five focus group meetings were held to assess the effectiveness of this as a method for interacting with beneficiaries. Agyemang *et al.* (2009b) report on this experience, pointing out that the method seemed to be an effective method for drawing out the views of beneficiaries because they spoke out with confidence and shared their views of the NGO work freely. They were critical of some aspects of the work of NGOs. For example, beneficiaries of a micro-credit finance scheme criticised the length of repayment period of the scheme, arguing that this time period did not reflect the trading cycles they operated under.

From the experience of holding these focus group meetings, Agyemang *et al.* (2009b) argue that the method offers the opportunity for engaging effectively with stakeholders such as beneficiaries.

Problems of downward accountability processes

While there are clear benefits associated with downward accountability processes, there are also associated problems. Where the downward accountability processes are part of the upward accountability requirements of donors, it is possible that the real needs of beneficiaries are not identified or reported upon. Instead the needs as specified by donors are addressed. It is also possible that beneficiaries will not share their true views as they need the resources provided within the projects and they may perceive a risk of losing these resources/projects if they comment negatively. Agyemang *et al.* (2009a) explained that often financial and cost information is not shared with the beneficiaries. Many beneficiaries did not have a high level of financial literacy and also were powerless vis-à-vis the NGO officers as well as the donors. Agyemang *et al.* (2009a) provide examples of how the NGO officers suggested that they had to manage the 'capacities' (meaning the lack of education) among beneficiaries.

In a section labelled 'Accountability and the Powerless', Agyemang *et al.* (2009a) illustrate clearly key problems with downward accountability in Ghana. First, strategic benefits associated with downward accountability processes may not be achieved because beneficiaries have weak negotiating skills and limited bargaining power. Second, beneficiaries had a strong fear of losing resources and therefore often were acquiescent and compliant. Third, beneficiaries often did not have the time or scope of understanding to fully engage with the NGO processes. Agyemang *et al.* (2009a: 31) state:

> beneficiaries are often overwhelmed with challenges from day-to-day living, so do not have the ability to spend much time reflecting or providing feedback to the officers. This is often coupled with, and compounded by, a relatively low capacity by many beneficiaries to understand fully the issues and external pressures involved in a particular aid project.

Rights-based approaches to development and downward accountability

Downward accountability forms an integral part of a development approach known as the 'rights-based approach' (O'Dwyer and Unerman 2010; O'Leary, 2017). The UN HRBA Portal (2018) defines the human-rights-based approach as:

> a conceptual framework for the process of human development that is normatively based on international human rights standards and operationally directed to promoting and protecting human rights. It seeks to analyse inequalities which lie at the heart of development problems and redress discriminatory practices and unjust distributions of power that impede development progress.

Under this philosophy, the plans, policies and processes developed by development agencies and NGOs are therefore not to be offered as charity but are enshrined in international law, placing obligations and duties upon NGOs and donors. The approach involves first identifying the rights of people as laid down in international conventions. Once these are identified then attempts are made to empower people to claim these rights. NGOs and their officers are seen as duty bearers accountable to the beneficiaries. Elements of the rights-based approach include active and meaningful participation, with beneficiaries often seen as the directors of development. While this approach to development is widely used, research in Ghana has not overtly investigated its effectiveness. O'Leary (2017) provides a rich account of rights-based approaches in two case studies in India. Her findings suggest that when self-determination and empowerment associated with rights-based approaches are promised by NGOs to beneficiaries, different forms of monitoring and evaluation are introduced in addition to the traditional upward and downward accountability processes. Accountability therefore is seen as a process to achieve a specific promise, and the underlying motivations of actors need to be understood.

Performance management in faith-based NGOs in Ghana

The first section of this chapter has explained key aspects of NGO accountability that have been associated with accounting research into NGOs in Ghana. There are other examples of NGO research in Ghana which touch upon accountability issues but focus on specific types of NGOs and the work they perform in Ghana.

Owusu (2017) undertook a doctoral study of two faith-based NGOs in Ghana. This study combined research into the nature of faith-based NGOs and also considered performance management practices of the two NGOs, asking whether the faith mission and values of faith-based NGOs contribute towards achieving development. The study is interesting also for its consideration of whether accountability is influenced by NGO organisational missions and values.

Faith-based NGOs have historically, as well as more recently, played major roles in development (Boehle, 2010; Tomalin, 2012). They tend to have holistic or dual missions that aim to improve the material well-being and poverty alleviation of people as well as to enhance their spirituality (Woolnough, 2011, 2014). There is thus a development mission objective as well as a faith or spiritual mission objective.

Ghana was chosen as the context for examining the role of faith-based NGOs because Christianity is followed by almost 72 per cent of the population and faith holds a very important position in the social fabric of the country. Christianity dominates many national discourses and the way things are undertaken by people in their daily lives.

In his study, Owusu (2017) analyses two local NGOs that operate in development focusing on the needs of children in one case (the Omega case study[1]) and on agricultural development in the second case (the Alpha case study). Both organisations are Christian faith-based organisations but their funding arrangements differ. Alpha was the development arm of a well-known international church and obtained funding through donation contracts and grants. Omega, on the other hand, received funds from individuals who sponsored children.

Performance management practices depend on NGO mission as defined by donors

A key aspect of performance management is the identification of objectives. Being faith-based organisations the expectation was that the two missions, development and spiritual, would form the objectives of each NGO. Surprisingly this was not the case and differed between the two case studies.

Omega clearly had objectives that specified both development and spiritual missions. The NGO was mandated by its international donors and sponsors to ensure a holistic development of children. It was clearly stated that 'accepting Christ and becoming a practising Christian' was a key objective. There were also more social, economic and material developmental objectives. NGO officers actively interacted with churches to achieve both development and spiritual objectives. They were actively prevented from working with the national and local government. Monitoring and evaluation revolved around these dual mission objectives. First, performance management practices included the use of a spiritual scorecard that showed the spiritual performance in metrics such as the number of registered children who have accepted Christ as the Lord and their personal saviour; the number of Bibles distributed to children and their caregivers; a child's ability to attend church regularly. Sponsored children had to write letters to their sponsors and the number of letters written and their contents formed part of the performance monitoring of the achievement of faith goals. But additionally, to reflect the performance and achievement of development mission, there were also measures of the achievement of more physical and tangible projects. Examples of metrics used to manage performance in this area included the number of projects completed; the number of children and caregivers provided with housing; the number of water bore-holes drilled in communities; the number of children offered funding to successfully complete primary or secondary education; the number of children receiving medical treatment abroad for complicated diseases; the number of shoes distributed to beneficiaries. To Omega's international NGO financial sponsors, developmental and spiritual missions were important and each had to be reported upon in the upward accountability reports. Performance management practices were multi-dimensional to reflect the multi-dimensional objectives associated with the holistic approach to development taken by this faith-based NGO.

In the case of Alpha, the activities of the NGO officers were bounded by a development-oriented mission of agricultural growth and the goal of achieving food security in local communities. Thus, the entire focus of performance management was on the achievement of agricultural objectives that formed the development mission for this organisation. The officers were encouraged to engage with national organisations working on the national agricultural development agenda. Direct reference was made by the NGO's officers to their desire to influence the government of Ghana's attempts at achieving the UN's Millennium Development Goals. Unlike Omega, the mission statement of Alpha emphasised development and poverty alleviation through empowerment without any reference to faith. Performance management practices focused on metrics that related to the development mission. For example, the 2016 annual report stated the number of poultry, maize and soy bean farmers that had been trained. The financing from the international NGO took the form of either contracted financing or the provision of grants. With contracted financing the projects were performed under contracts as specified by donors. In such projects, donors had absolute control to dictate what had to be undertaken in communities. They set the goals for projects and local NGO officers then monitored performance against the prescribed quantitative targets around development-oriented needs in the areas of food, water, shelter, clothing and health care. Where funding was provided as grants, the local NGO officers had more freedom to decide on strategy, operations and monitoring. Although faith and spirituality were not measured or reported upon, Owusu (2017) in his analysis explains how the shared Christian value system between the local and international NGO led to a more informal upward accountability relationship.

In his conclusions, Owusu (2017) argues that NGO accountability and performance management play out in different ways in faith-based NGOs in Ghana. Where the goal of faith is an overt mission objective (as in Omega), performance measures included metrics related to faith, and operations needed to be undertaken with local churches to facilitate the achievement of these goals. On the other hand, where development was the mission of the NGO, faith worked in the background and was not measured. As suggested by O'Leary (2017), the underlying motivations for NGO work need to be understood.

Ultimately, however, it was the type and source of funding that was responsible for differences in performance management practices. The mission depended on funding sources. In the situation where funding sources for operations emanated mainly from individual Christian sponsors, the 'faith' mission was driven by these sponsors, who may be considered the most 'powerful' stakeholder in holistic accountability relationships. The development mission of poverty alleviation is considered as background activity to the 'faith' mission of the organisation. On the other hand, where funding for activities comes from contractual and multiple donor sources, NGO officers concentrate mainly on the development mission of poverty alleviation. The relationship with government becomes important and it is considered to be a powerful stakeholder in relation to holistic accountability because of its role in development.

Future directions

NGOs play a significant role in the deployment of substantial amounts of aid in the alleviation of impacts of poverty worldwide. In so doing, they help hundreds of millions of the most impoverished people on Earth realise their basic human rights. Well-designed accounting and accountability mechanisms are crucial in improving the effectiveness and efficiency with which this finite aid is deployed by and through NGOs, thus improving the life experiences of those living in extreme poverty. NGO accountability issues therefore remain important for the development of emerging countries such as Ghana.

By reviewing key literature in this area, this chapter has provided insights into the roles that NGO accounting and accountability mechanisms can and do play in enhancing the effectiveness and efficiency of aid delivery in Ghana. While, at a broad level, the insights apply across NGO accounting and accountability globally, at a more fine-grained level several insights are context-specific. To derive maximum impact from academic research into NGO accounting and accountability, it is therefore important for future studies to provide insights that are context-specific while also helping develop more generic improvements in the shape of NGO accounting and accountability mechanisms regionally and globally.

Achieving this impact will require future studies to do more than simply replicate existing studies in new contexts, such as going much further than commenting on whether the individual NGOs studied are using upward, downward, hierarchical and/or holistic mechanisms. As this field of research matures, such studies only have the potential to make diminishing incremental contributions to advancing the academic literature. There therefore needs to be a focus in future on more nuanced studies of NGO accounting and accountability that are designed to provide major new insights – often in new contexts.

Theories of upward, downward, hierarchical and holistic NGO accountability, developed over a decade ago, have been very helpful in structuring interpretive analyses that highlight key elements from complex data about NGO accounting and accountability practices. However, as this field matures there is a need for more-refined theories to be developed that both help derive more context-specific insights and are adapted to evolving (and improving) NGO accountability practices. Development and refining of theories in the area of NGO accounting and accountability is thus an additional direction and important element of future NGO accounting and accountability studies that can make an impact both on the academic literature and on policy and practice around NGO accounting and accountability.

This impact is particularly important because donor agencies remain accountable to their taxpayers, and their missions and motivations drive NGO activities in the global south. While it may be understandable that the values, missions and motivations of funders sometimes drive the activities and behaviours of local NGOs, they need to do so in ways that maximise the chances of the world's most impoverished and vulnerable people realising their basic human rights. As the insights covered in this chapter have shown, NGO accounting and accountability mechanisms have a significant role to play in this effectiveness and efficiency of translating donations into poverty alleviation on the ground.

Note

1 Omega and Alpha are pseudonyms for the real organisations.

References

Agyemang, G., Awumbila, M., Unerman, J. and O'Dwyer, B. (2009a). *NGO accountability and aid delivery.* ACCA Research Report. London, Certified Accountants Educational Trust (ACCA).

Agyemang, G., Awumbila, M. and O'Dwyer, B. (2009b). A critical reflection on the use of focus groups as a research method: Lessons from trying to hear the voices of NGO beneficiaries in Ghana. *Social and Environmental Accountability Journal*, 29(1), 4–1.

Agyemang, G., O'Dwyer, B., Unerman, J. and Awumbila, M. (2017). Seeking 'conversations for accountability': Mediating the impact of non-governmental organization (NGO) upward accountability processes. *Accounting, Auditing & Accountability Journal*, 30(5), 982–1007.

Assad, M. J. and Goddard, A. R. (2010). Stakeholder salience and accounting practices in Tanzanian NGOs. *International Journal of Public Sector Management*, 23(3), 276–299.

Awio, G., Northcott, D. and Lawrence, S. (2011). Social capital and accountability in grass-roots NGOs: The case of the Ugandan community-led HIV/AIDS initiative. *Accounting, Auditing & Accountability Journal*, 24(1), 63–92.

Awuah-Werekoh, K. (2015). *Accountability systems of Non Governmental Organisations (NGOs): Case study from Ghana.* Unpublished doctoral thesis, University of Birmingham.

Boehle, J. (2010). Religious NGOs at the UN and the millennium development goals: An introduction. *Global Change, Peace & Security*, 22(3), 275–296.

Chenhall, R. H., Hall, M. and Smith, D. (2010). Social capital and management control systems: A study of a non-government organization. *Accounting, Organizations and Society*, 35(8), 737–756.

Chenhall, R. H., Hall, M. and Smith, D. (2013). Performance measurement, modes of evaluation and the development of compromising accounts. *Accounting, Organizations and Society*, 38(4), 268–287.

Chenhall, R. H., Hall, M. and Smith, D. (2016). Managing identity conflicts in organizations: A case study of one welfare non-profit organization. *Nonprofit and Voluntary Sector Quarterly*, 45(4), 669–687.

DFID (2014). Operational plan 2011–2015 DFID GHANA. United Kingdom Government.

Dixon, R., Ritchie, J. and Siwale, J. (2006). Microfinance: Accountability from the grassroots. *Accounting, Auditing and Accountability Journal*, 19(3), 415–427.

Ebrahim, A. (2003). Accountability in practice: Mechanisms for NGOs. *World Development*, 31(5) 813–829.

Elbers, W. and Arts, B. (2011). Keeping body and soul together: Southern NGOs' strategic responses to donor constraints. *International Review of Administrative Sciences*, 77, 713–732.

Fry, R. E. (1995). Accountability in organizational life: Problem or opportunity for nonprofits? *Nonprofit Management and Leadership*, 6, 181–195.

Goddard, A. and Assad, M. J. (2006). Accounting and navigating legitimacy in Tanzanian NGOs. *Accounting, Auditing and Accountability Journal*, 19(3), 377–404.

Hall, M. and O'Dwyer, B. 2017. Not because they are nonprofit: The importance of nonprofit organisations to understanding accounting, organizations and society. *Accounting, Organizations and Society*, 63, 1–5.

Jayasinghe, K. and Wickramasinghe, D. (2011). Power over empowerment: Encountering development accounting in a Sri Lankan fishing village. *Critical Perspectives on Accounting*, 22, 396–214.

Jordan, S. and Messner, M. (2012). Enabling control and the problem of incomplete performance indicators. *Accounting, Organizations and Society*, 37, 544–564.

Marini, L., Andrew, J. and van der Laan, S. (2017). Tools of accountability: Protecting microfinance clients in South Africa? *Accounting, Auditing and Accountability Journal*, 30(6), 1344–1369.

O'Dwyer, B. and Boomsma, R. (2015). The co-construction of NGO accountability: Aligning imposed and felt accountability in NGO-funder accountability relationships. *Accounting, Auditing & Accountability Journal*, 28, 36–68.

O'Dwyer, B. and Unerman, J. (2007). From functional to social accountability: Transforming the accountability relationship between funders and non-governmental development organisations. *Accounting, Auditing & Accountability Journal*, 20, 446–471.

O'Dwyer, B. and Unerman, J. (2008). The paradox of greater NGO accountability: A case study of Amnesty Ireland. *Accounting, Organizations and Society*, 33(7–8), 801–824.

O'Dwyer, B. and Unerman, J. (2010). Enhancing the role of accountability in promoting the rights of beneficiaries of development NGOs. *Accounting and Business Research*, 40(5), 451–471.

O'Leary, S. (2017). Grassroots accountability promises in rights-based approaches to development: The role of transformative monitoring and evaluation in NGOs. *Accounting Organizations and Society*, 63, 21–41.

OECD (2018). Official Development Assistance Data. www.oecd.org/dac/stats/officialdevelopment assistancedefinitionandcoverage.htm.

Owusu, C. (2017). *Accountability in NGOs: Evidence of Two Christian Faith-Based Organizations in Ghana.* Unpublished PhD thesis, Royal Holloway University of London.

Rahaman, A., Neu, D. and Everett, J. (2010). Accounting for social purpose alliances: Confronting the HIV/AIDS pandemic in Africa. *Contemporary Accounting Research*, 27(4), 1093–1129.

Tomalin, E. (2012). Thinking about faith-based organizations in development: Where have we got to and what next? *Development in Practice*, 22(5–6), 689–703.

UN HRBA Portal (2018). https://hrbaportal.org/faq/what-is-a-human-rights-based-approach (accessed 5 November 2018).

Unerman, J. and O'Dwyer, B. (2006a). On James Bond and the importance of NGO accountability. *Accounting, Auditing and Accountability Journal*, 19(3), 305–318.

Unerman, J. and O'Dwyer, B. (2006b). Theorising accountability for NGO advocacy. *Accounting, Auditing and Accountability Journal*, 19(3), 349–376.

Woolnough, B. E. (2011). Christian NGOs in relief and development: One of the Church's arms for holistic mission. *Transformation: An International Journal of Holistic Mission Studies*, 28(3), 195–205.

Woolnough, B. E. (2014). Good news from Africa: Community transformation through the Church. *Transformation: An International Journal of Holistic Mission Studies*, 31(1), 1–10.

World Bank (2016). *Data for lower middle income, Ghana.* Washington, DC: World Bank Group. https:// data.worldbank.org/income-level/lower-middle-income, click on Ghana link at foot of page (accessed 9 November 2018).

18

ACCOUNTABILITY AND LABOUR GOVERNANCE IN A 'STATE OF DENIAL'

Javed Siddiqui, Melita Mehjabeen and Sharmin Shabnam Rahman

Introduction

This chapter stems from a concern for accountability and labour governance in the ready-made garments sector (RMG) in Bangladesh. The objective of this chapter is to examine the role of the state in the context of human rights violations in the Bangladeshi RMG industry against the backdrop of the Rana Plaza collapse of 2013. On 24 April 2013, Rana Plaza, an eight-storey commercial building in Bangladesh that hosted eight RMG factories, collapsed killing more than 1,100 workers. The Rana Plaza collapse, the worst industrial accident since the Bhopal disaster in 1984 (*The Economist*, 2013), raised serious concerns regarding labour governance and accountability in global supply chains. Bangladesh is the second largest global exporter of RMG products in the world, mainly due to its ability to produce RMG products at the cheapest possible price. Consequently, all major global retailers use Bangladesh as their supply chain (*Daily Star*, 2018). The quest for profitability pursued by multinational companies (MNCs), coupled with the availability of cheap labour, has resulted in developing countries being increasingly used as supply chains for global brands.

Due to the failure of nation states to address the supranational challenges in global supply chains, a growing range of voluntary private labour governance has emerged (O'Rourke, 2006; Bernstein and Cashore, 2007; Vogel, 2008). Such standards, led by the private sector, are implemented by strict inspection regimes monitored directly by the MNCs. Thus, in global supply chains, activities relating to corporate social responsibility (CSR) typically take the form of voluntary, private-sector-led assurance initiatives aimed at ensuring adherence to various codes of conduct and industry specific self-regulation (Fransen and Burgoon, 2014). However, several recent papers have questioned the efficacy of such private inspection arrangements (Reinecke and Donaghey, 2015; Sinkovics *et al.*, 2016). Also, accounting researchers have largely been critical of the potential of such certification arrangements to create a myth. Boiral (2013) observes that the certification arrangement may present a reassuring façade that hides organisational uncertainties in inherent organisational practices and capabilities. Boiral and Gendron (2011) point out that the dissemination of certification creates a global phenomenon that exploits the ritualistic nature of audits, and its capacity to create a disconnect between the audit and actual organisational performance.

Reinecke and Ansari (2016) demonstrate how the assumption of a political role, where the brands take complete responsibility by co-authoring and implementing regulations, can significantly allay concerns regarding labour governance in supply chains in developing countries, but point out that to allow the MNCs to take a political role, the state must be prepared to play the role of an enabler. Alamgir and Banerjee (2018) observe that globalisation and the subsequent emergence of transnational governance does not necessarily imply that postcolonial states have all been weakened. Rather, in certain areas of the economy the state has a very strong presence, whereas in others market actors and foreign capital dominate. Siddiqui and Uddin (2016) demonstrate that the presence of a strong state–business nexus may result in gross violation of human rights in global supply chains, resulting in large-scale industrial accidents. The economic interests pursued by the politician-businesspeople in charge of the state may significantly handicap the private governance regime's ability to effectively improve accountability and labour governance in supply chains. This presents the context for this chapter.

Like many other developing countries, Bangladesh has a corrupt political climate that has led to the creation of a culture that only permits wealthy people to be elected to public offices (Siddiqui and Uddin, 2016). While many politicians think the easiest way to earn money is through business, many businesspeople believe their engagement in politics would help them expand their business (Zaman, 2011). According to a declaration of candidates, 57 per cent of the current members of the parliament are businesspeople (*Daily Star*, 2011). Mahmud *et al.* (2008) point out that a parliament dominated by businesspeople will tend to make laws to protect their own income, legal or illegal. The state–business nexus, coupled with dysfunctional democracy has allowed the government to apply a common discourse of denial in response to a wide range of issues, from allegations of rampant corruption to human rights violations.

The theoretical perspective in this chapter draws from the work of Stanley Cohen. An important part of Cohen's (1993, 2001) work involves looking at the discourse of official denial. Such a framework has been useful in analysing the discourse of the government of Bangladesh (GoB) and the Bangladesh Garments Manufacturers and Exporters Association (BGMEA), the apex body of the RMG manufacturers in Bangladesh, in response to allegations of human rights violations. Using Cohen's framework, this chapter demonstrates how the state–business nexus has helped the formation of a wider culture of denial in a society where significant violations of human rights are either overlooked or ignored. In such a 'state of denial', effective implementation of the private governance regime on human rights in the RMG sector would be challenging.

The next section presents the theoretical framework used in this chapter. This is followed by a section that discusses the institutional context of the RMG industry in Bangladesh. Using Cohen's notion of denial, the subsequent sections then analyse the events leading to the Rana Plaza collapse, the response of the state in light of the crisis of legitimacy created by the collapse, and the state's subsequent reverting to the denial mode. The conclusion section then summarises the main issues addressed in this chapter and the potential ways forward.

Theorising denial

Although the term 'denial' is relatively uncommon in accounting and management literature, it is frequently used in the field of psychiatry, psychology and personality. Freud included 'denial' as a major defence mechanism (Freud, 1936: 36). Following Freud, researchers in psychiatry and criminology attempted to provide several theories of denial. Cohen (1993) used Freud's typology of defensive mechanisms to investigate the government's response to allegations of human rights violations. Cohen (2001: 3) points out that denial can be private, official and cultural and observes (Cohen, 1993) that whereas private denials are individualistic, official denials are actively supported and sustained by the state using a significant number of resources. In totalitarian societies, the extreme form of such collective denial may involve a complete rewriting of history. In such a case, denial is not an individual or personal matter – rather, it is embedded into the ideological disguise of the state. Cultural denials are not individualistic, and not necessarily complemented by the mechanisms of the state. Rather, the entire society moves into a collective mode of denial. This is where societies are based on different types of atrocities and human rights violations that are known, but never openly acknowledged. Although such denials may sometimes be initiated by the state, they are sustained by the cultural norms of the society.

Having identified the different forms of denial, Cohen borrowed heavily from Sykes and Matza (1957) to offer different techniques of denial, and points out (Cohen, 2001: 38) that three of the five techniques of neutralisation, as offered by Sykes and Matza, use the term 'denial' (Cohen 2001: 1). The first of the five techniques is the 'denial of responsibility'. Such denials may range from a primitive, childish 'I didn't do it' to a more articulate 'I didn't know what I was doing', depending on the gravity of the offences committed. The second technique is the 'denial of injury'. This is where the offender attempts to neutralise the wrongfulness of the offence by downplaying the actual impact of the injury. This is subtler compared to the third technique, the 'denial of the victim', where the victim is accused of being the wrongdoer and the action of the perpetrator is portrayed as a mere retaliation. 'Condemnation of the condemners' technique is sometimes applied to deflect attention from one's own wrongdoings to the motives and character of the critics. Here, critics are generally presented as hypocrites. In the final technique, delinquents 'appeal to higher loyalties' to deviate attention. In a political world, such higher loyalties are generally expressed in a discourse that justifies the actions by highlighting the political ideology of the actors.

An important part of Cohen's work involves looking at the discourse of official denial. According to Cohen (2001: 14), only the governments of a handful countries in the world pay no attention to outside criticism, primarily regarding atrocities committed on its citizens and other human rights issues. Such situations do not warrant an official denial, as the state does not respond to outside pressures. The socio-economic factors dictating the world economy, however, force most governments into having to appease the superpowers and important international agencies such as the United Nations, the World Bank and the International Monetary Fund. Such active reactions take three forms: the classic official denial, the conversion of a defensive position into an attack on the critic, and the partial acknowledgement of the actions.

Classic official denials have three variants: literal (nothing happened), interpretive (what happened is really something else) and implicatory (what happens is justifiable). According to Cohen (2001: 68), most governments would use official discourse directed towards establishing their interpretation of the events. Interpretive denial may involve governments in legally challenging whether a particular course of action is in violation of, for example, internationally accepted norms on human rights. An important version of interpretive denial is the denial of responsibility. Here, the state might acknowledge that something wrong had happened but apply discourse to establish that the responsibility for that action actually lay with other groups, the usual suspects being militant groups and vague 'third forces' (Cohen 2001: 109). As part of implicatory denial strategy, the government sometimes also may claim that events of human rights violation are isolated, and do not reflect the overall condition of the country. 'Appeals to higher moral authority' is another variant of implicatory denial, which may also involve 'condemnation of the condemners' by questioning the moral authority of the critics.

The second form of active reaction is adopting a 'counter-offensive strategy'. Here, all allegations are refuted as lies, propaganda and ideological prejudice. Counter-offensive techniques against international bodies (for example, human right activist groups) range from identifying errors in various reports prepared by condemners, questioning their source of financing and their political bias. Internal critics may be branded as treacherous, unpatriotic or irresponsible. The third form of active reaction is partial acknowledgement. According to Cohen (2001: 69), this strategy is adopted either due to a change in political regime, or when the evidence is too embarrassing to be able to deny. Partial acknowledgement involves use of discourse claiming that the events were either isolated or happened during the previous political regime. In both cases, an assurance is provided that such incidents will not happen in the future.

Human rights and accountability in Bangladesh: the 'State of denial'

In recent times, the Bangladesh economy has been able to maintain sustainable economic growth. However, a continued dysfunctional political system, lawlessness and corruption have remained the biggest threats to Bangladesh's development (*Daily Star*, 2015). Transparency International has consistently ranked Bangladesh as one of the most corrupt countries in the world (TI, 2017). A survey conducted by Transparency International Bangladesh (TIB) in 2013 revealed that politicians, police and the judiciary were perceived to be the most corrupt sectors in the country (*Daily Star*, 2013). Unsurprisingly, the country has a poor record when it comes to corruption and accountability in the public sector and on human rights issues (Siddiqui, 2001). As reported in Siddiqui and Uddin (2016), the government of Bangladesh has persistently used a discourse of denial in response to allegations of corruption and human rights violations. For instance, in 2005, an article published in *The Economist* branded Bangladesh as the 'State of denial', referring to the government's indifference to rising threats of militancy and Islamic fundamentalism (*The Economist*, 2005). In 2006, when the country was branded as the most corrupt in the world by the TI, a senior minister in charge of a ministry that was ranked to be the most corrupt within the GoB applied a counter-offensive technique in denying the allegations:

> We outright reject the report as it is false, baseless, confusing and politically motivated to malign the government as well as the country abroad … we hope that the TIB will withdraw its report immediately.
> *(LGRD minister, GoB, BDnews24.com, 9 July 2006)*

Adopting a typical 'condemning the condemner' technique described by Cohen (1993), the minister also questioned the moral standing of the chairperson of TIB:

> He himself a corrupt person … how he find out the corruption of others. Such a person like has no moral right to brand the country as a corrupt one … he simply wanted to tarnish the image of the government and the country as well.
> *(LGRD minister, Government of Bangladesh, Bdnews24.com, 9 July, 2006)*

In 2012, the World Bank cancelled a US$1.2 billion credit to Bangladesh to build a bridge on the river Padma because of allegations of corruption involving several senior ministers of the GoB (BBC, 2012). The Prime Minister (PM) of Bangladesh, in her reaction, adopted a counter-offensive strategy, questioning the political motive of the World Bank:

> They want us to beg. They want us to continue as guinea pigs.
> *(PM of Bangladesh, Guardian, 2012a)*

The finance minister of Bangladesh also termed the integrity department of the World Bank, which initiated the corruption charges, as a 'highly inefficient body that should not exist'

(Risingbd, 2013). Such discourse of denial is consistent with Cohen's depiction of a counter-offensive strategy, where 'accusations of treachery and lack of patriotism cannot be applied to international critics' (Cohen, 2001: 113).

The discourse of denial has also been applied in response to allegations regarding the state's failure to ensure human rights. The organisation *Human Rights Watch*, in its country report of events in Bangladesh for 2017, mentioned that the human rights situation in Bangladesh had worsened further, mainly due to the government's failure to hold the security forces responsible for serious human rights violations including secret detentions, enforced disappearances, torture and extrajudicial killings (HRW, 2017a). However, the government continued to deny allegations of human rights in its part, describing the report as a 'smear campaign' (HRW, 2017b). The government's tendency to apply a discourse of denial on human rights issues was highlighted in the country report of the Asian Human Rights Commission:

> Denial of human dignity has become part of the fabric of daily life in Bangladesh, and outright denial of this reality is the default setting of the GoB.
>
> *(AHRC, 2013)*

HRW (2017c) also accused the government of restricting press freedom through censorship.

Denial of human rights in the RMG sector pre-Rana Plaza

Bangladesh has emerged as the second largest global exporter of garment products (*Daily Star*, 2016). This is mainly because Bangladeshi textile employees are among the lowest paid in the world (Apparel Resources, 2018). Consequently, the country is used as a supply chain by many large, global manufacturers of RMG. The industry is regulated by its apex body, the BGMEA, established in 1987. Since its inception, the BGMEA has enjoyed tremendous power as the major actor regulating the RMG industry. It draws its legitimacy from the state–business nexus that exists in Bangladesh. A report prepared by the US senate observes that nearly every member of parliament in Bangladesh is either a direct owner of an RMG factory or has close ties with them (US Senate, 2013). Leaders of the BGMEA, an apex body dominated by factory owners, have openly opposed workers' rights to bargain collectively and form unions (Siddiqui and Uddin, 2016). In recent years, several high-profile incidents of building collapses and factory fires have raised serious questions regarding BGMEA and the government's ability to ensure human rights of the workers in this sector.

On 24 April 2013, an eight-storey building collapsed completely in Savar, a sub-district of Dhaka, the capital of Bangladesh. The building, named Rana Plaza, hosted several garment factories where around 5,000 worked daily, producing garments for renowned global manufacturers. The collapse killed more than 1,100 workers. Further probes into the incident revealed how workers were forced to enter a building that had been declared as unsafe by engineers, mainly to meet order deadlines set by the foreign buyers (*The Economist*, 2013). While the Rana Plaza incident may have been the most-publicised industrial accident in the RMG sector in Bangladesh, it was certainly not the first. On 24 November 2012, a deadly fire broke out in Tazreen Fashions, an RMG factory producing apparel for leading global manufacturers, leaving 117 workers dead (*Guardian*, 2012b). In addition, the RMG sector has witnessed frequent labour unrest in recent years, primarily due to the poor wage structure being offered to the workers (BBC, 2010).

Despite the gravity and frequency of such incidents, however, the global brands, in their pursuit of profit, continued to use Bangladesh as their supply chain. The government's awareness of this competitive advantage has perhaps allowed the use of a denial discourse that it is familiar with. For example, the PM referred to the Tazreen fire incident as 'an act of sabotage'

(Reuters, 2012). Also, after the Rana Plaza incident, a senior minister in the cabinet attempted to blame the opposition party for the building's collapse:

> The fundamentalist BNP [the party in opposition] had called the shutdown. I was told some hired supporters went there and shook the gates ... and the pillars. This might be the reason behind the collapse.... When part of a building caves in, it affects the whole. This might have happened.
>
> *(Huffington Post, 2013a)*

Such discourse is consistent with the denial of responsibility technique:

> Yes, something bad happened, but don't blame us. Responsibility lies with shadowy army groups, vigilantes, rogue psychopaths, proxy armies, vague third forces ... or 'unknown elements'.
>
> *(Cohen, 2001: 108)*

The government's persistent strategy to use a discourse of denial has allowed the BGMEA to adopt a similar strategy. After the Tazreen fire, the BGMEA followed the lead of the government by blaming unknown 'conspirators' (BGMEA President, 1 January 2013, as reported in the *Independent*, 2012).

Historically, the RMG owners have been opposed to allowing the workers to have a voice in the industry. The Bangladesh Independent Garments Workers Union, formed in 1995, was refused registration as a national union, mainly due to the objections raised by owners of RMG industries (ILO, 1995). Attempts to form trade unions are often thwarted by severe repression, dismissal, arrest, assault by hooligans hired by employers, and other practices which are in violation of the International Labour Standards and Codes of Conduct (ILO, 2003). In August 2010, HRW wrote a letter to the PM of Bangladesh asking the government to stop harassment of the organisers of trade unions in the RMG sector:

> We call on you to publicly guarantee the safety and security of labour rights activists from BCWS and other trade union organizations who lawfully protested against their conditions of employment. The government has engaged in a harsh rhetorical campaign against the protesters, branding them as 'provocateurs,' 'saboteurs,' and even 'terrorists' and claiming they incite violence and unrest in the RMG sector, appearing to allege, without providing any evidence that the protestors are responsible for the violence.
>
> *(HRW, 2010)*

In its letter, HRW mentioned the name of one union leader who was detained by the national security intelligence as he was trying to negotiate a national minimum wage for the workers in the garment sector. He was later found dead. In a letter dated 11 April 2012, HRW urged the government to 'immediately launch a comprehensive and impartial investigation of the disappearance, torture, and murder of (the union leader), and publicly report the findings' (HRW, 2012). Again, the GoB denied any involvement in the abduction of the trade union leader. The PM, in an interview with CNN, denied even recognising the trade union leader:

> Which union he belongs to? What is the name of the union, do you know that? Nobody knew that he was a labour leader. He was killed somehow ... it was our police that recovered his dead body.
>
> *(Bangladesh PM, Interview with CNN, 2 May 2013)*

Thus, the pre-Rana Plaza environment in the RMG sector in Bangladesh was characterised by frequent accidents, followed by street demonstrations by the RMG workers who wanted a voice. However, the presence of an explicit collusion between the government and the RMG owners resulted in the consistent denial of workers' demands for safer working conditions.

The Rana Plaza collapse: a crisis of legitimacy and eventual acceptance of private sector governance

The Rana Plaza collapse mounted further pressure on the government, already held culpable by the media for its failure to monitor the structural safety of the RMG factories (*The Economist*, 2013). After the Rana Plaza collapse, the US government postponed the generalised system of preference facility (a facility that allows duty-free access of some products from specific countries to the US market) due to the failure of the GoB to ensure workers' rights, especially in the RMG sector. In response, the BGMEA blamed local civil society groups and labour unions for tarnishing the image of the country and threatened legal actions against them in charges of sedition (Siddiqui and Uddin, 2016). This is consistent with a counter-offensive strategy of denial, where critics are termed as 'treacherous, unpatriotic, or irresponsible' (Cohen, 2001: 21). The disturbing images of the Rana Plaza rubble quickly circulated across the international media. There were threats of boycotting products, putting further pressure on MNCs who used Bangladesh as a cheap outsourcing location (Huffington Post, 2013b). Thus, the Rana Plaza incident created a severe crisis of legitimacy for the government as well as the international buyers of RMG products from Bangladesh.

In response to public outrage (*New York Times*, 2014), the MNCs were forced to make quick interventions to the regulatory arena guiding the RMG. Two separate initiatives were introduced: the Bangladesh Accord for Fire and Building Safety (hereafter, Accord), led by European brands; and the Alliance for Bangladesh Worker Safety (hereafter, Alliance), led by US-based companies. Both initiatives relied heavily on inspections by independent safety inspectors who provided reports on fire and building safety. The GoB, under pressure from foreign governments and international agencies such as the ILO, not only allowed private actors to assume the role of a regulator in this sector, but also signed a tripartite agreement with the trade unions and activists to ensure better working conditions in the RMG sector (GoB, 2013). Thus, events following the Rana Plaza collapse resulted in a shift in the government's strategy from denial to partial acceptance of responsibility (Siddiqui *et al.*, 2018).

Five years since Rana Plaza: return of the denial regime?

Five years on from Rana Plaza, the private governance regime appears to be effective in promoting better working conditions. In 2017, a statement issued by Alliance claimed that the working conditions in RMG factories in Bangladesh are demonstrably safer compared to 2013 due to their compliance programmes (Sourcing Journal, 2017). This is confirmed by a report published in the *Financial Times* in April 2018, reporting that 84 per cent of the initial problems that existed at the time of the Rana Plaza collapse had been fixed. Also, 96 companies that had failed to carry out renovations in line with the recommendations made by the compliance auditors have been barred from acting as suppliers for the signatory brands for Accord and Alliance (*Financial Times*, 2018). Due to the success of the private inspection regimes, the brands wanted to enter into a new agreement that would extend their mandate to govern the RMG sector in Bangladesh by a further three years (UNI Global Union, 2017). However, the RMG owners and the government were irked by the private actors' willingness to look into politically sensitive issues such as worker's voice and wage structures (Siddiqui *et al.*, 2018). Also, market trend following Rana Plaza indicated that the Western buyers were actually 'buying more from Bangladeshi factories than ever before', due to their failure to find alternative locations offering such cheap products (*Financial Times*, 2017). This perhaps resulted in a reversal to the denial mode for the GoB. In July 2018, the commerce minister announced that private sector inspection regimes initiated by Accord and Alliance were no longer required for the RMG sector in Bangladesh and gave the private sector regulators six months to leave Bangladesh (Commerce Minister, GoB, as reported by New Age, 2018b). Another senior cabinet minister claimed that the post-Rana Plaza reforms carried out by the GoB were sufficient in ensuring safer working conditions in the RMG sector in Bangladesh, and the presence of Alliance and Accord was no longer necessary (New Age, 2018b).

In another event, the Commerce Minister cited Bangladesh's sovereignty as a reason for asking Alliance and Accord to leave:

> Bangladesh is a sovereign country. There is no such monitoring body like Accord and Alliance in any other countries in the world. We are a self-respecting nation, there's no more need for the Accord-Alliance.
>
> *(Commerce Minister, GoB, as reported by New Age, 2018a)*

This is consistent with the strategy of an appeal to higher loyalty, expressed in a discourse that justifies actions by highlighting the political ideology of the actors (Cohen, 1993). However, private sector actors, and various international bodies, including foreign governments, asked the GoB to re-assess their position on the new Accord. In a statement issued on 27 July 2018, Accord observed that, although it had achieved substantial progress in the safety of workers in the Bangladesh RMG sector, any premature shutdown of Accord would still leave workers in unsafe circumstances.

> The premature shut down of the Accord; leaving workers in unsafe circumstances, would jeopardize the brands' ability to source from a safe industry and may make them reconsider sourcing decisions and review the reputational risk of Bangladesh as a sourcing country. In the last 5 years, the Accord has delivered a robust, high quality, transparent, inclusive system, and it has made substantial progress to achieve the safety of workers in Bangladesh's most important export industry. But the work is not yet completed and the national structure, notwithstanding assertions to the contrary, is not yet prepared to credibly take over the work of the Accord.
>
> *(Accord, 2018)*

However, so far, the GoB has showed no sign of changing its attitude towards the new Accord, potentially implying a return to its usual mode of denial.

Future directions

This chapter provides a foundation for further research in several areas in human rights accounting and social audit. So far, the human rights accounting literature (McPhail and Ferguson, 2016) has been predominantly based on the premise that although the state is primarily responsible for human rights issues, businesses also have an important role to play. Especially in the context of supply chains, the literature informs us of the state's inability to face super-national challenges involving violations of human rights (Bernstein and Cashore, 2007). This is based on the implicit assumption that the state is always willing to address issues relating to violation of human rights. In a recent paper, Reinecke and Ansari (2016) proposed a responsibilisation framework to demonstrate how the assumption of a political role, where the brands take complete responsibility by co-authoring and implementing regulations, can significantly allay concerns regarding labour governance in supply chains in developing countries. Using the case of Democratic Republic of Congo, the paper demonstrates that complex governance issues in supply chains can effectively be tackled if the private actors are willing to take a political role. However, a crucial element of Reinecke and Ansari's (2016) framework is the catalytic role of the state in the process of tackling a supply chain crisis. Here, the state does not dictate or enforce behaviour. Rather, as a catalytic actor, it can play a major role in enabling and legitimising private governance. Alamgir and Banerjee (2018) point out that globalisation and the subsequent emergence of transnational governance does not necessarily imply that postcolonial states have all been weakened. Rather, in certain areas of the economy the state has a very strong presence. State repression against dissenting workers and forcible relocation of populations to make way for development projects reconfigure the relationship between the state and its citizens. The discussion presented in this chapter indicates that economic interests pursued by the politician-businesspeople in charge of the state can significantly handicap its ability to play a catalytic role in transnational governance. Thus, this chapter forms a basis for further empirical exploration of the responsibilisation framework proposed by Reinecke and Ansari (2016) in a research context where the state is unable to play the role of a catalyst due to the presence of a strong state–business nexus.

This chapter also identifies the need for further examination of important human rights issues in business, such as child labour and gender discrimination, which are often attributed to the supply chain companies of large multinationals. The study of such issues in an emerging economy can contribute novel and interesting insights to both theory and practice in the accounting literature. This chapter, in line with law and criminology, contributes to the accounting literature by drawing on Cohen's work of denial. We report that the state itself is allegedly involved in human rights abuses. This nature of the state, consequently, creates the necessary conditions for businesses to disregard human rights, including in the RMG sector. The fundamental position of this network is 'denial of responsibility' for human rights violations in the RMG sector. This rhetoric of denial has consistently been applied by the highest level of the state, including the prime minister, and ministers have often adopted a counter-offensive strategy to vilify internal and external critics of human rights issues. The issue of social compliance audits, employed by multinational companies to check on subcontracting factories (NYU, 2015), also warrants intensive study. The efficacy of the auditing and assurance practices are often questioned especially in emerging economies, where the state lacks resources and political will to safeguard the working conditions and the rights of workers, which are often breached by businesses (Gallhofer *et al.*, 2011). By identifying the state's unwillingness to tackle labour governance issues, we encourage other researchers to add to our contribution to the advancement of this research agenda.

References

All URLs were checked for access on 18 January 2019.

Accord (2018). Accord statement on 4th high level meeting of the Bangladesh sustainability compact. 27 July. http://bangladeshaccord.org/2018/07/accord-statement-4th-high-level-meeting-bangladesh-sustainability-compact/

AHRC (2013). The state of human rights in Bangladesh, 2013. Asian Human Rights Commission, Hong Kong. www.humanrights.asia/wp-content/uploads/2018/09/AHRC-SPR-008-2013-HRRpt-Bangladesh.pdf.

Alamgir, F. and Banerjee, S. B. (2018). Contested compliance regimes in global production networks: Insights from the Bangladesh garment industry. *Human Relations*, https://doi.org/10.1177/00187267 18760150.

Apparel Resources (2018). Bangladesh's RMG wage lowest in the world: Oxfam. 22 January. https://apparelresources.com/management-news/human-resource/bangladeshs-rmg-wage-lowest-world-oxfam/

BBC (2010). Bangladesh garment factories shut after wage protests. 22 June. www.bbc.co.uk/news/10375797

BBC (2012). World Bank cancels Bangladesh bridge loan over corruption. 30 June. www.bbc.co.uk/news/world-south-asia-18655846.

BDNews24.com (2006), Bhuiyan rejects TIB report on corruption, demands immediate withdrawal. *BDNews24*, 9 July. http://bdnews24.com/politics/2006/07/09/bhuiyan-rejects-tib-report-on-corruption-demands-immediate-withdrawal.

Bernstein, S. and Cashore, B. (2007). Can non-state global governance be legitimate? An analytical framework. *Regulation & Governance*, 1(4), 347–371.

Boiral, O. (2013). Sustainability reports as simulacra? A counter-account of A and A+ GRI reports. *Accounting, Auditing & Accountability Journal*, 26(7), 1036–1071.

Boiral, O. and Gendron, Y. (2011). Sustainable development and certification practices: Lessons learned and prospects. *Business Strategy and the Environment*, 20(5), 331–347.

Cohen, S. (1993). Human rights and the crimes of the state: The culture of denial. *Australian and New Zealand Journal of Criminology*, 26(2), 97–115.

Cohen, S. (2001). *States of Denial: Knowing About Atrocities and Suffering*. US: Blackwell Publishers.

Daily Star (2011). Of political leadership, politics, and politicians. 24 February. www.thedailystar.net/newDesign/newsdetails.php?nid¼175230c (accessed 1 January 2016).

Daily Star (2013). Political parties, cops most corrupt. 10 July. http://archive.thedailystar.net/beta2/news/political-parties-cops-most-corrupt/.

Daily Star (2015). Corruption still a serious impediment for investment. 3 September. www.thedailystar.net/business/corruption-still-serious-impediment-investment-137005.

Daily Star (2016). Bangladesh remains second largest garments exporter against all odds. 17 July. www.thedailystar.net/country/bangladesh-remains-second-largest-garments-exporter-against-all-odds-1255084.

Daily Star (2018). Bangladesh remains the second biggest apparel exporter. 2 August. www.thedailystar.net/business/export/bangladesh-remains-the-second-biggest-apparel-exporter-1614856.

Financial Times (2017). Bangladesh garment-making success prompts fear for wider economy. 6 January. www.ft.com/content/5cd0d9ea-d316-11e6-9341-7393bb2e1b51.

Financial Times (2018). Rana Plaza five years on: Safety is greater but not guaranteed. 24 April. www.ft.com/content/7ec413ec-46e6-11e8-8ee8-cae73aab7ccb.

Fransen, L. and Burgoon, B. (2014). Privatizing or socializing corporate responsibility: Business participation in voluntary programs. *Business & Society*, 53(4), 583–619.

Freud, S. (1936). *The Problem of Anxiety*. New York, NY: W. W. Norton & Company.

Gallhofer, S., Haslam, J. and Van der Walt, S. (2011). Accountability and transparency in relation to human rights: A critical perspective reflecting upon accounting, corporate responsibility and ways forward in the context of globalization. *Critical Perspectives on Accounting*, 22(8), 765–780.

GoB (2013). National tripartite plan of action on fire safety for the ready-made garment sector in Bangladesh. Government of the People's Republic of Bangladesh. www.ilo.org/wcmsp5/groups/public/--asia/--ro-bangkok/--ilo-dhaka/documents/genericdocument/wcms_209285.pdf

Guardian (2012a). Bangladesh weighs options after World Bank pulls out of Padma Bridge project. 17 July. www.theguardian.com/global-development/poverty-matters/2012/jul/17/bangladesh-options-padma-bridge-world-bank.

Guardian (2012b). Bangladesh textile factory fire leaves more than 100 dead. 25 November. www.theguardian.com/world/2012/nov/25/bangladesh-textile-factory-fire.

HRW (2010). Letter to Prime Minister Sheikh Hasina regarding the harassment of apparel industry demonstrators and union leaders. 10 August. www.hrw.org/news/2010/08/10/letter-prime-minister-sheikh-hasina-regarding-harassment-apparel-industry.

HRW (2012). Letter to Prime Minister Sheikh Hasina Re. Wazed Killing of Aminul Islam. Bangladesh Center for Worker Solidarity. http://bdnews24.com/politics/2006/07/09/bhuiyan-rejects-tib-report-on-corruption-demands-immediate-withdrawal.

HRW (2017a). We don't have him: Secret detentions and enforced disappearances in Bangladesh. 6 July. www.hrw.org/report/2017/07/06/we-dont-have-him/secret-detentions-and-enforced-disappearances-bangladesh#.

HRW (2017b). No, Bangladesh, the truth is not a 'smear campaign'. 7 July. www.hrw.org/news/2017/07/07/no-bangladesh-truth-not-smear-campaign.

HRW (2017c). Bangladesh expands efforts to stifle free speech. 29 March. www.hrw.org/news/2017/03/29/bangladesh-expands-efforts-stifle-free-speech.

Huffington Post (2013a). After Bangladesh building collapse, police club workers protesting against the owner. 25 April. www.huffingtonpost.co.uk/entry/bangaldesh-building-collapse_n_3156765?ec_carp=1881910415849232693.

Huffington Post (2013b). Bangladesh factory collapse: Should you boycott Primark over workers' rights? 2 May. www.huffingtonpost.co.uk/2013/05/02/primark-boycott-bangladesh_n_3201576.html.

ILO (1995). Case no. 1862: Bangladesh. International Labour Organisation, Geneva. www.ilo.org/dyn/normlex/en/f?p=1000:50001:0::NO::P50001_COMPLAINT_FIE_ID:2896790:NO.

ILO (2003). International Labour Standards, International Labour Organization. www.ilo.org/global/standards/subjects-covered-by-international-labour-standards/occupational-safety-and-health/lang-en/index.htm.

Independent (2012). Wal-Mart distances itself from Bangladesh fire. 27 November. www.independent.co.uk/news/world/asia/wal-mart-distances-itself-from-bangladesh-fire-8360022.html.

Mahmud, W., Ahmed, S. and Mahajan, S. (2008). Economic reforms, growth and governance: The political economy aspects of Bangladesh's development surprise, in Brady, D. and Spence, M. (Eds.), *Leadership and Growth*. Washington, DC: World Bank on behalf of the Commission on Growth and Development, 227–254.

McPhail, K. and Ferguson, J. (2016). The past, the present and the future of accounting for human rights. *Accounting, Auditing & Accountability Journal*, 29(4), 526–541.

New Age (2018a). Accord, Alliance beyond Dec 31 not required, says Tofail. 31 May. www.newagebd.net/article/42556/accord-alliance-beyond-dec-31-not-required-says-tofail.

New Age (2018b). Accord, Alliance to leave Bangladesh after Dec 7: Tofail. 18 July. www.newagebd.net/article/46266/accord-alliance-to-leave-bangladesh-after-dec-7-tofail.

New York Times (2014). Battling for a safer Bangladesh. 22 April. www.nytimes.com/2014/04/22/business/international/battling-for-a-safer-bangladesh.html?_r=1.

NYU (2015). Beyond the tip of the iceberg: Bangladesh's forgotten apparel workers. Centre for Business and Human Rights, New York University, New York. http://people.stern.nyu.edu/twadhwa/bangladesh/downloads/beyond_the_tip_of_the_iceberg_report.pdf.

O'Rourke, D. (2006). Multi-stakeholder regulation: Privatizing or socializing global labor standards? *World Development*, 34, 899–918.

Reinecke, J. and Ansari, S. (2016). Taming wicked problems: The role of framing in the construction of corporate social responsibility. *Journal of Management Studies*, 53(3), 299–329.

Reinecke, J. and Donaghey, J. (2015). After Rana Plaza: Building coalitional power for labour rights between unions and (consumption-based) social movement organisations. *Organization*, 22(5), 720–740.

Reuters (2012). Bangladesh mourns, calls factory fire 'an act of sabotage'. 27 November. www.reuters.com/article/us-bangladesh-fire-idUSBRE8AQ0WE20121127.

Risingbd (2013). WB's integrity department should be punished, Muhith. 8 September. www.risingbd.com/english/WB-s_integrity_dept_should_be_punished_Muhith/6429.

Siddiqui, J. (2001). Environmental non-accountability in Bangladesh? The striking case of the Magurchara gas field disaster. *Social and Environmental Accounting Journal*, 21(2), 12–13.

Siddiqui, J. and Uddin, S. (2016). Human rights disasters, corporate accountability and the state: Lessons learned from Rana Plaza. *Accounting, Auditing & Accountability Journal*, 29(4), 679–704.

Siddiqui, J., Rahman, S. and McPhail, K. (2018). Tackling modern slavery through certification audits: An exploration of the effectiveness of the framing approach. Presented at the AAEE annual conference, University of Essex.

Sinkovics, N., Hoque, S. F. and Sinkovics, R. R. (2016). Rana plaza collapse aftermath: Are CSR compliance and auditing pressures effective? *Accounting, Auditing & Accountability Journal*, 29(4), 617–649.

Sourcing Journal (2017). Alliance says Bangladesh factories 'demonstrably safer' than pre-Rana Plaza. 16 November. https://sourcingjournal.com/topics/compliance/bangladesh-alliance-garment-factory-safety-74962/.

Sykes, G. M. and Matza, D. (1957) Techniques of neutralization: A theory of delinquency. *American Sociological Review*, 22(6), 664–670.

The Economist (2005). Bangladesh – State of denial. 16 June. www.economist.com/asia/2005/06/16/state-of-denial.

The Economist (2013). Disaster at Rana Plaza. 4 May. www.economist.com/news/leaders/21577067-gruesome-accident-should-make-all-bosses-think-harder-about-what-behaving-responsibly.

TI (2017). Corruption perceptions index 2017. www.transparency.org/news/feature/corruption_perceptions_index_2017.

UNI Global Union (2017). 2 Leading fashion brands join with unions to sign new Bangladesh Accord on Fire and Building Safety. 9 June. http://uniglobalunion.org/news/leading-fashion-brands-join-unions-sign-new-bangladesh-accord-fire-and-building-safety.

US Senate (2013). Worker safety and labour rights in Bangladesh's garment sector. Committee of Foreign Relations. www.govinfo.gov/content/pkg/CPRT-113SPRT85633/html/CPRT-113SPRT85633.html.

Vogel, D. (2008). Private global business regulation. *Annual Review of Political Science*, 11, 261–282.

Zaman, I. (2011). Corruption and anti-corruption in Bangladesh. Transparency International Bangladesh, Dhaka.

PART IV

Researchers' experiences and reflections

19

ETHNOGRAPHIC SIGNIFICANCE IN RESEARCHING MANAGEMENT ACCOUNTING

Bangladesh and Sri Lanka

Saiful Alam, Seuwandhi B. Ranasinghe and Danture Wickramasinghe

Introduction

Exploring how measurements, evaluations and controls function (and malfunction) in organisations and society, management accounting research has now extended its search into spatial variations. In the past three decades, this development has accompanied studies in developing countries illustrating how emerging discourses functioned or malfunctioned in relation to the local context, and the ramifications of this (Hopper *et al.*, 2009). Such ramifications were richly articulated when researchers took a variety of theoretical frameworks ranging from classical Marxist approaches through neo-Marxist variants to post-modern analysis. They illuminated variations, contradictions and ambiguities in management accounting practices in non-Western settings.

The findings of such research suggest that prevailing cultures and institutions in these countries make these differences and, as researchers contend, it is the people carrying these cultures and institutions who maintain these differences. Although the intimate relationship between accounting and people has long been studied (Argyris, 1964), the unique behaviour of people (both individuals and groups) in developing countries tends to produce atypical forms of management accounting practices in response to Western discourses that have been diffused around the globe. While several methodological approaches can be useful in capturing and illuminating such differences, the majority of researchers have preferred adopting ethnographic traditions which embrace and analyse people's everyday life to show how it is manifested in management accounting and control practices (Uddin and Hopper, 2001, 2003; Wickramasinghe and Hopper, 2005; Alawattage and Wickramasinghe, 2009a, 2009b; Alawattage *et al.*, 2018).

This chapter aims to unpack some recent experiences of two researchers who adopted an ethnographic tradition to study such accounting practices. One researcher studied Bangladesh's microfinance practices (Alam, 2017) where illiterate women produce 'oral accounts' as part of alleviating rural poverty, and the other took a similar approach to studying Sri Lankan tea plantation's management control practices (Ranasinghe, 2017) where tea-plucking women exploited the opportunities of neoliberalism to reconstruct the prevailing system of management controls.

We unpack these experiences: (1) to show how such research has to be executed under circumstances where the researchers manage; and (2) to highlight how ethnographic studies in accounting (and finance) can find something that other methodological approaches cannot see.

We provide an account of the matters of ethnography which outlines the foundation of the presentation of two pieces of ethnographic experiences. We then showcase an example of accounting research in less developed countries (LDCs), which has evolved since the early 1990s. This account is then extended to report on the voice of two researchers who had something to say about how ethnographic research in accounting can happen in developing country settings. Finally, its implications are discussed showing how novice researchers can benefit from such accounts of data, procedures of data collection as well as situational encounters the researchers face.

The art of ethnography

Ethnography involves:

> the researcher participating, overtly or covertly, in people's daily lives for an extended period of time, watching what happens, listening to what is said, and/or asking questions through informal and formal interviews, collecting documents and artefacts – in fact, gathering whatever data are available to throw light on the issues that are the emerging focus of inquiry.
>
> *(Hammersley and Atkinson, 2007: 3)*

Accounting researchers in LDCs (e.g. Uddin and Hopper, 2001; Jacobs and Kemp, 2002; Wickramasinghe and Hopper, 2005; Alawattage and Wickramasinghe, 2008, 2009a, 2009b; Jayasinghe and Thomas, 2009; Alawattage, 2011; Jayasinghe and Wickramasinghe, 2011) employed this approach as it is a 'valuable way to understand the way accounting works in actual organisational settings' (Jönsson and Macintosh, 1997: 367). This tradition enabled researchers to analyse the transformations taking place in emerging economies. They linked their ethnographies to British colonialism, its continued impact, and subsequent changes occurring through postcolonial ramifications. For this, they examined mundane relations, traditions and practices to understand their implications for unconventional management accounting and controls.

Such an approach is rooted in cultural anthropology, which inspired them to undertake fieldwork as the central activity of such studies (Wickramasinghe and Hopper, 2005; Alawattage *et al.*, 2007). These researchers plan how to immerse themselves in the field and learn as far as possible by thinking, feeling, seeing, smelling and sometimes working with those being researched. As far back as the 1960s, Powdermaker (1966) articulated that these forms of investigation can generate deep and rich analyses about the social world in relation to a specific phenomenon. Following this tradition, accounting researchers have analysed, for example, how reform programmes in developing countries where accounting plays a central role are embraced differently depending on location, and how unique practices are produced and reproduced. Alawattage and Wickramasinghe (2009b) illustrated the nature of such accounting. Given the nature of colonial power in management accounting controls prevailing in Sri Lankan tea plantations, their analysis showed that resistance to such controls has not been agitative like in orthodox organisations. Instead, workers at the grassroots presented themselves with silent forms of resistance which they called 'weapons of the weak'.

As has already been mentioned, such ethnographic studies are rooted in cultural anthropology, which promotes case study research allowing the researchers to undertake in-depth investigations of the culture of a people, of a group or of a community (Robben and Sluka, 2007). This involves micro-analysis of mundane practices which focuses on particularising the people therein. For example, when we observe a worker to know about her relations with the management, we may focus not only on the official statements about control arrangements, such as performance measurements, but also on her understanding of these arrangements, her reactions to them, and the voices and the ways in which her everyday work is organised for producing a particular life under such management. The researchers then understand the language she speaks, the way she dresses, her relationships with others, and, of course, they listen to her recent stories, which specify her everyday life embedded in such controls. Hence, the researcher is not satisfied with how things happen – rather she wants to know much about it in details, in pictures, in voices and in incidents.

Such research encompasses two paradoxical but interrelated research actions. One is about 'involvement', which aims to understand the psychological realities of a practice. This reality is understood through the eyes of indigenous members – as they understand it, as they speak to us about it and as show it to us, and as we see them. Even when the researcher sees something, she sees it through the eyes of the local member. The research borrows their eyes for this purpose. To complement this, she thinks, smells, feels, and, sometimes, acts as a participant. When this involvement is materialised, the researcher becomes immersed in the local setting and learns it as far as possible. For example, Wickramasinghe and Hopper (2005) became immersed themselves to see local village culture through the eyes of local members, making the researchers realise that their factory life was secondary to their village life. Though the villagers were officially attached to the factory as operational staff, their 'psychological reality' was that they really were detached from the factory in terms of their understanding of their assigned commitments. Instead, the village was manifested in the factory reproducing a cultural political economy of management accounting.

In contrast, the researcher must construct 'an abstract reality' by exercising a form of 'detachment'. This is because the local story told through the eyes of the locals cannot be a research outcome that can be delivered to the international research community. The local story is only an illustration for saying something – about a network of social relations, including the underlying rules about how such relations function – which is not necessarily real to the people studied (Robben and Sluka, 2007). How can this be done? First, you may contextualise a story-line through the eyes of the people therein illustrating what happened, through what, and how. Then, you may textualise the context by using the story to illustrate a social theory or using a social theory to illuminate that story. Hence, detachment is about the business of contextualising and textualising, which occurs iteratively. For example, the cultural political economy thesis mentioned above (Wickramasinghe and Hopper, 2005) was developed with a general understanding of the political economy of accounting (Tinker, 1980; Cooper and Sherer, 1984) but it was extended as a cultural political economy through a process of iteration which was operationalised in the interface between contextualisation and textualisation. Only the eventual text of research, which can be 'theoretically generalisable', can be delivered to the international community.

An account of ethnographic studies in LDC accounting

Ethnographic studies in accounting emerged with the use of the terms 'development' and 'accounting' in a compatible way. This began in the early 1990s when Professor Trevor Hopper at the University of Manchester set this agenda with his early PhD students including one of the authors of this chapter. The agenda has now produced a significant stream of research (Hoque and Hopper, 1994; Uddin and Hopper, 2001; Wickramasinghe *et al.*, 2004; Wickramasinghe and Hopper, 2005; Alawattage *et al.*, 2007; Hopper *et al.*, 2009, 2012, 2017), and has encompassed a new accounting journal, a research conference and research centres in European and American universities.

Such researchers are intensively engaged in their research sites over many months and sometimes years to produce rich and deep field narratives exploring interesting research issues. Some articulate the perspectives of marginal groups in developing countries that are not typically captured in mainstream accounting research. For instance, the ethnographic study of Jacobs and Kemp (2002) on three Bangladeshi small traders explained how the literacy level influenced the (presence) absence of (in)formal accounting. For them, less-literate shop keepers started to keep records once they learned to read and write. Moreover, social capital, alias norms of reciprocity and trust, could also play an active role in understanding the absence of written accounting in traditional society. Talking about informal accounting in a Sri Lankan fishing village, Jayasinghe and Wickramasinghe (2011) suggested that families and communities with less-literate cultures use customary thoughts and pre-literate oral accounting calculations. In this type of community setting, accounting is manifested in daily activities of inhabitants and comprises a set of conceptions rather than an act of writing or examination.

Accounting's role in subaltern lives was further explored through ethnographic studies. Alawattage and Wickramasinghe (2009b) in a tea plantation in Sri Lanka revealed how subaltern workers reconstruct governance and accountability structures. The subaltern resistance which they theorised as subaltern emancipatory accounting, evident through 'hidden transcripts' in their study for instance, came to light through prolonged engagement and participative observations. Drawing from a subaltern community in Sri Lanka, Jayasinghe and Thomas (2009) also employed ethnography to produce texts about social accounting practices which were the common language of the inhabitants' everyday lives. The case suggested that existing patronage-based political systems within subaltern social structure tend to preserve indigenous accounting systems. Through an ethnographic study on the politics of accounting, race and ethnicity relating to the pine industry of Fiji, Davie (2005) was able to narrate how accounting becomes a part of a discourse that is deeply rooted in notions of racial identity and discrimination, and how accounting becomes involved in perpetuating the existing institutionalised inequalities in a society.

Ethnographic designs are also employed in studying reconstructions of social structures in LDC contexts. For instance, through the ethnographic study of the 'field' of gem mining in Sri Lanka, Alawattage (2011) was able to illustrate the connection between calculative practices and the social structure of capital. He did this by employing an ethnographic design with broad access to the 'field', its structural properties, and to the particular forms of embodiment through which structural properties of the field are internalised by its agents.

Some others have explored issues related to culture and management accounting controls. For instance, Wickramasinghe and Hopper (2005) taking a cultural political economy perspective, demonstrated how management accounting controls change with changes to ownership regimes (state capitalism to market capitalism). As mentioned in the previous section, the authors build on rich ethnographic accounts of a textile mill located in a traditional cultural village in Sri Lanka. They emphasise that although culture is independent of the MOP (mode of production), they are related and play a powerful role in shaping social relations and controls. Another study by Wickramasinghe *et al.* (2004) taking a political dimension of postcolonial MOP in theorising management control in LDCs employed an ethnographic research design to study the privatisation of the national telecommunication service provider – Sri Lanka Telecom. The authors demonstrate how patronage politics interact with and transform bureaucratic management controls. These studies highlight the interesting issues that can be captured, especially culture research in accounting by being deeply immersed in their field where research is 'more painstaking in its execution and modest in its claims but bolder in its methods and theorisation' (Wickramasinghe and Hopper, 2005: 501). A cultural form of management control is further illuminated through the extensive fieldwork of Efferin and Hopper (2007). Drawing from Merchant's (1998) management control model, their ethnographic materials explored how ethnic identity and cultural ramifications play roles in the management control systems of a Chinese Indonesian manufacturing company. In a multicultural and ethnic environment, as the study reveals, management controls are multi-dimensional, incorporating the ethnic traditions, values and beliefs of employees with those of owners while maintaining conventional control mechanisms (e.g. result controls or bureaucratic action controls).

The importance of ethnographic studies has been emphasised to understand the management accounting and control of LDCs in particular (Hopper *et al.*, 2009). One of the key issues is the enactment of Western neoliberal policies by LDC governments despite socio-cultural differences. In an earlier ethnographic study, Uddin and Hopper (2001) examined how neoliberal structural changes brought transformation in control regimes in a Bangladeshi soap manufacturing company. For them, controls were the outcome of production and state politics. The rich ethnographic materials explored how a new despotic regime of control under private ownership emerged despite idealistic attempts to secure accountability, rational planning and control. Without such complete engagement in the field, the researcher could not discern how ensuing coercive controls might work in relation to the context studied. For example, a recollection of a researcher's night shift experience (Uddin and Hopper, 2001: 665) provided the first-hand knowledge about how managers were selective in tolerating work deviations and their effects on achieving budget goals.

Therefore, ethnography has been increasingly used to produce rich empirical materials in support of indigenous accounting, subaltern relations, and structural and control regime changes in LDCs. Nevertheless, these efforts are still at a nascent stage. Gender issues, poverty alleviation programmes and many other areas need to be explored through ethnographic approaches. In the next section, we present two contextual experiences from Bangladesh and Sri Lanka respectively to understand, first, management and control issues in a poverty alleviation programme and, second, gender implications of management control in a tea plantation.

Experiences in contextualising and textualising

From the context of Bangladesh

The researcher (Alam, 2017) here started with a perspective on post-Foucauldian features of organisations and society. He was inspired by how disciplinary society is now being transformed into a society of control where people are managed by networks of relations governed by statistical norms. He then undertook a six-month period of ethnographic fieldwork to understand the management accounting and control practices in the context of a microfinance institution (MFI) in Bangladesh. The underlying objective of this ethnographic work was to examine how people's (borrowers of microfinance in this case) social relations, ordinary language and everyday practices are implicated in the microfinance activities in the village and in the production of their life. This intense work informed us about the functioning of organisations beyond their boundaries and the creation of a form of control of society through social networks.

For ethnographic work, the author selected Sharifpur village from his home district, Lakshmipur in Bangladesh. He had been living in the area for 16 years before he moved to the capital city for higher studies. But he frequently visited his parents, who were living in the area. People usually seek financial advice from his father, as an executive officer in the local branch of a public sector commercial bank. His grandfather was a renowned religious authority in the area and people from all walks of life, irrespective of their religion, caste, class or gender, used to visit him to seek religious teaching and advice. His mother has been living in their ancestral home throughout her 38 years of married life. Being a housewife, she has a strong bond with neighbours and village women. The author's uncles, aunts, cousins and other relatives also live in the same village and some of them are MFI borrowers. Because of this multifaceted and deep-rooted connection with the local people, the author selected Sharifpur village as his ethnographic site. The selection had eased his access to the participants' private and public spaces, and secured a rich understanding of the context.

To understand the socially embedded nature of management accounting in the microfinance context, the author had to immerse himself in the fabrication of village life. He used the first few days to visit every house, meet his old friends and local elders. He spent many hours with the village men at local tea-stalls discussing national politics, village happenings and his days in Great Britain. His familiarity with the local people, language, culture and ways of life helped him to reach the borrowers and to observe their daily lives, their relations with the firm, their activities with their microfinance support, etc. During this fieldwork in the village, many conversations took place in the natural home environment of women borrowers. They were reached through personal connections in the village and conversations were arranged at participants' convenience. During some conversations borrowers were joined by their spouses and other members to share their experiences with the MFI. Apart from unstructured open-ended conversations with borrowers in the village, the author also conducted semi-structured face to face interviews with officers of the MFI at different levels in their office environment throughout the fieldwork period. These interviews were mostly designed to allow understanding of a wide range of issues including (but not limited to) managerial practices, adopted strategies, operational policies, banking procedures, the existing mission and future vision. The author also observed the activities of a local branch, borrowers' group activities in the village and their daily lives, while they recognised him as a researcher. In effect, he had gained a clear understanding of borrowers' personal monetary management, credit history and relation with the MFI. Throughout the fieldwork period, a personal diary was maintained to mark personal reflections on data collection.

Drawing from rich field materials, the study examined how diverse poverty management technologies are put in place and traditional oral accounts and social control mechanisms are appropriated for microfinance operation in the village. It ultimately provided an illustration of alternative forms of management accounting and control that were made operable in a rural setting. The research explored the creation of a variant of a society of control (Deleuze, 1992, 1995) through social ties, mutual relations and everyday interaction. With the growing spread of MFIs in rural settings, illiterate villagers were becoming familiar with financial conversations and used them in convivial settings. It also revealed how MFIs like the firm in this case relied on the community-specific sense of shame/guilt, identity, responsibility, etc. to make members aware of their personal responsibility and their duty towards others. In this context, a sensible relationship between community actors and MFIs seemed necessary to accommodate, sustain and reproduce social controls in the formal control mechanisms.

This study is believed to address some of the concerns raised by accounting researchers relating to the management accounting and control mechanisms of neoliberal poverty-alleviation programmes, like microfinance, undertaken by LDC governments (Hopper *et al.*, 2009). It also showed how accounting and control are integrated into mundane language

(Jayasinghe and Thomas, 2009; Jayasinghe and Wickramasinghe, 2011) and social norms (Efferin and Hopper, 2007), when neoliberal poverty-alleviation programmes travelled unchartered territories (e.g. private space of community inhabitants) of LDCs. More importantly, this research offered an alternative explanation to the society of control that Deleuze (1992, 1995) originally suggested for technocentric modern organisations with multinational operations. Considering microfinance as a terrain of the society of control, it argued that continuous control over borrowers was maintained through social networks and traditional modes of communication.

From the context of Sri Lanka

Our second research study (Ranasinghe, 2017), taking a postcolonial feminist perspective, employed an ethnographic research design to explore management control practices in a tea plantation in Sri Lanka. Here the intention was to explore the operation of mundane labour controls in the tea plantation, especially the controls over female workers (tea pluckers). The aim of the study was to theorise management controls from a postcolonial feminist perspective – a critical perspective of management controls from the position of marginalised postcolonial women.

The aim of the study was achieved through an intensive involvement in fieldwork spanning six months. Being a native of Sri Lanka, the researcher obtained access to the field through personal contacts with the CEO of the plantation company. With his clearance, fieldwork took place at two sites – the head office of the tea plantation and in one of its estates. The first two weeks of fieldwork were spent at the head office in Colombo where the researcher conducted interviews and conversations with the corporate management and other senior administrative staff. Some observations and photographs taken supplemented these. Daily ethnographic accounts were maintained digitally, taking note of the observations, interviews and the way in which the researcher made sense of what she saw, heard and felt. Through the interviews and documentary analyses, we gained an understanding of the management control systems in place and the important role of budgets in monitoring all aspects of estate performance. All this was evidenced, illustrated and detailed through the eyes of the researched.

The second part of this fieldwork occurred in a tea estate in a remote place – the Rathnapura region. This relocation of fieldwork needed a change of accommodation for the researcher. She found accommodation in close proximity to the tea estate through family contacts, and fieldwork was initiated with the support of the estate manager and the staff of the welfare department. Ethnographic accounts consisted of participant observations on the operation of mundane controls at the tea fields, divisional offices, estate office and other locations of the estate. The researcher travelled daily to the estate where she was given a space to work at the welfare office and was part of the daily activities of the estate. An intense engagement with the field and participants during the six months materialised with daily conversations with welfare staff and estate staff, and walks to the tea fields to engage with the tea-plucking women – conversing about and observing their work and life. Further, interviews and conversations were conducted with the estate management, supervisory staff and others (workers, trade unions, NGOs). In addition to these, company documents were analysed and archival records of tea plantations in Sri Lanka were gathered for analysis. This deep involvement in the research setting and the researched provided the researcher with detailed accounts of the agency of the women even though they were patriarchally controlled. The tension between the domination of patriarchal controls and subjects' subalternity was evidenced when the researcher was immersed with rich accounts and a deeper understanding of what was going on.

The methods used for data collection and the material so collected elaborated this tension: the control regime was operated over female workers (tea-plucking women) for them to be marginalised by the patriarchal element of the control configuration, constructing that sub-alternity. Via an analysis through a 'detachment' from the field, the researcher also found that this marginalisation was embedded in the colonial and postcolonial systems of plantation controls. The researcher then saw that these structural consequences had informed a form of agency in the lives of women. Findings highlighted the agency of women – even those who are marginalised – in a distinct control context, giving them the ability to influence the way in which they are being controlled. It was possible to make these observations when the women in question were presenting their life trajectories and underlying control regimes as they saw it, and as they interpreted them to the researcher. The researcher listened, saw and borrowed the phenomenon with a view to thinking about and contrasting it with the universal truth of the time. These paradoxical actions of 'engagement' and 'detachment' produced a management control story that was subjected to contextualisation and textualisation.

Consequently, it was argued from the position of postcolonial feminism that management control practices dominated and controlled subaltern female workers, perpetuating their subalternity. Despite this, the women's agency (subaltern agency) arising in a context of postcolonial transformations was able to influence these controls to some extent, subsequently displacing the controller's power and creating a form of postcolonial management control that offered opportunities to realise emancipatory elements. What is salient here is that researching management controls beyond the perspective of the controller (managerial centricity) can bring us more theoretical insights when it is approached from a perspective of the 'controlled'. In other words, our understanding of management controls is mostly as a top-down unidirectional form (Lowe and Machin, 1983; Anthony *et al.*, 1984; Lowe and Puxty, 1989; Luft and Shields, 2003; Hesford *et al.*, 2007) rather than one that could also be bottom-up and an outcome of the interactions between the controller and the controlled. This is what intense engagement through an ethnographic design enabled the researchers to unpack – a group of marginalised women at the bottom of the hierarchy from a developing country context, having added complexities of ethnicity, patriarchy, colonialism and postcolonialism. A noteworthy contribution from this research is perhaps the use of a postcolonial feminist perspective and researching from the position of the 'controlled' (female tea plantation workers) in a context where there is a dearth of research on gender issues in accounting and management control domains (e.g. Otley *et al.*, 1995; Berry *et al.*, 2009).

Discussion

These accounts signify some epistemological and methodological values of doing ethnographic research in management accounting and controls. Unlike positivistic and functional research, which deploy quantitative approaches, these ethnographic studies can uniquely and differently unpack the unknown details hidden behind the trajectories of hypotheses testing. These details provide not only particularising but also aspects that are important but neglected in mainstream research. However, mainstream researchers may ask the question of its validity. Mostly, they raise this question pointing out that the findings lack generalisation. As we outlined earlier in the chapter, the validity issue is addressed through the process of iteration between the contextualisation of a text and textualisation of a context. We attend to this more closely now. For this, we use Table 19.1, which depicts this iteration process in relation to two interrelated actions – contextualisation of a text and textualisation of a context.

Table 19.1 Managing the tension between involvement and detachment

	Forms of involvement	*Forms of detachment*
Bangladesh microfinance	Interviews with microfinance managers. Conversations with poor women. Observations of mundane practices. Secondary material reviews – about MF tools.	Seeing its relation to a society of control (Deleuze, 1992, 1995). Seeing microfinance as a form of self-accountability. Seeing the story as an illustration of present-day neoliberalism – new networks allow markets to penetrate new territories.
Sri Lankan patriarchal controls	Interviews with plantation managers. Conversations with tea plucking women. Observations of mundane practices. Secondary material reviews – about budgetary controls.	Seeing its relation to postcolonial and patriarchal controls (postcolonial feminism). Seeing an emerging pattern of subaltern agency. Seeing the story as an illustration of present-day neoliberalism – markets produce new population categories.

Contextualisation of a text

As we have seen, the forms of involvement which enact interviews, conversations, observations and documentary reviews portray a storyline within a context. The story being developed shows how the subjects (i.e. Bangladesh microfinance women and Sri Lankan tea-plucking women) are linked to the context (i.e. Bangladesh microfinance and Sri Lankan tea plantations), and how the context constructs those subjects. Because of this invariable and intimate relationship between the subject and the context, the phenomenon (i.e. self-accountability in microfinance and patriarchal management controls) being studied becomes a unique incident, operating in a particular social and political landscape. It is then a unique text but is linked to such a relationship between the subject and the context. When ethnography approaches a people in a research setting, the researcher sees a kind of people being contextualised. It is thus a story which provides details, incidents, plots and characters. The ethnographic researcher's prime duty is to develop this story. In so doing, one important principle must be noteworthy – the story is useless unless it is told in relation to the context within which this type of people live and die. If this principle is followed, different stories can be produced from different contexts – texts vary from one context to another. If there are significant theoretical reasons, these differences could be used for comparative analyses as well.

In the case of Bangladesh, the context was characterised by the historical tragedy of country's persistent poverty and primitive characters of its traditional society. When the researcher had conversations and made observations, these characteristics manifested in people's language, behaviour and related practices of microfinance, i.e. the psychological realities of a practice. In the case of Sri Lanka, the same happens but in relation to colonial and postcolonial legacies of social and organisational characters, which produce postcolonial and patriarchal forms of control. Its psychological realities are manifested when conversations happen and observations are made. The researchers eventually developed storylines echoing this connection within their respective contexts. The outcomes were decent texts, i.e. contextualised texts. In these texts, the macro-physics of these traditional societies are portrayed in micro-terms, and with unexplored details, plots and characters. But these elements must encompass only in a single storyline because there can be other stories based on the same elements. When such a text with a single story is ready, then the research is said to be mature enough for textualising the context.

Textualising a context

The task of constructing a text in an ethnographic study is the primary one, although it always iterates with a theory. This iteration cannot happen without an informing theory which shows the wider picture in which the text is constructed, and its relations with the established order of society or the discourses being developed and circulated. Hence, a choice of a suitable theoretical perspective can allow the researcher to identify a set of initial questions, to frame a mode of investigation, and to preview the relationship between the story and the context. However, this choice is often not final or perfect: sometimes, the researcher makes decisions to modify the same theory or triangulate it with other theories; perhaps, she would completely change it because the story would be much more interesting, but the theory would not explain it perfectly. Whatever the course of action, a theory must shadow the task of fieldwork informing the researcher on the direction she should take. If the researcher embarked on the fieldwork with virtually no theory, she would be enmeshed with a complication of multiple focuses and multiple unrelated questions. Hence, being unprepared with a suitable theory choice is unwise when embarking on fieldwork.

The Bangladesh study we mentioned above was planned, prepared and executed with the help of a suitable theory borrowed from Deleuze's idea of a society of control (see Table 19.1). At the literature review stage, this choice was made as the microfinance is a manifestation of the circulation of capital through networks of relations which form a society of control. Capital then circulates to the bottom of populations, where people try to consume the ideas of microfinance and to deploy the related tools for reproduction of this society of control. When this perspective was chosen, the researcher was disciplined to focus on the articulation of this social reality so that he explored the psychological reality of poor women in Bangladesh about their connections with the network relations of microfinance. The ethnographic accounts were then used to complement the theoretical perspective with illustrative details. Similarly, the Sri Lankan study was prepared with a dedicated theoretical choice – the postcolonial feminist theory (see Table 19.1). It points to the tyrannies of management controls shaped by the legacy of colonial domination and the overlapping patriarchal conventions of postcolonial society. The researcher wanted to illustrate this thesis with a focus on how agency can be materialised in the era of present-day neoliberalism. Again, as the researcher did not want to derail from this perspective from the early stage of the study, she faced little complication about any modification or triangulation. Consequently, she comfortably illustrated this theory of management control and its emancipatory possibility of women's agency.

Future directions

The discussion above is built on the two paradoxical actions in this type of research – involvement and detachment. The paradox can only be handled by using the theory consciously. Hence, the chapter concludes with an important message about the use of theory in ethnographic studies in management accounting where we explore how measurements, evaluations and controls function (and malfunction) in organisations and societies with their spatial variations.

As a response to the validity question normally raised by positivistic researchers, ethnographic researchers use a theory. However, this can happen in two alternative ways. One is about using a theory to illustrate the theory itself by a story where the latter acts as an illustrative device. In both cases (Bangladesh and Sri Lanka) this almost happened despite some iterations taking place. The theory rather than the story was visible, clear and primary in both cases. The other is about using a theory to illuminate or echo a story with illustrative highlights of theoretical dimensions. Here, the primacy is the story, but it is not merely a journalistic and investigative story – rather it is a story informed by a theory. Most anthropological researchers (e.g. Scott, 1985, 2009) take this approach, where the theory is seen only between the lines. However, when this happens it is important to note, again, the iteration occurring between the theory and story, but with an inclination towards the story rather than the theory. The choice is down to the researcher, but this choice does not need to be revealed – it is better to leave the nature of the orientation to the reader to enjoy.

References

Alam, M. S. (2017). *Management Accounting, Control and Microfinance Operation: Three Papers*. PhD thesis, University of Glasgow.

Alawattage, C. (2011). The calculative reproduction of social structures: The field of gem mining in Sri Lanka. *Critical Perspectives on Accounting*, 22(1), 1–19.

Alawattage, C. and Wickramasinghe, D. (2008). Appearance of accounting in a political hegemony. *Critical Perspectives on Accounting*, 19(3), 293–339.

Alawattage, C. and Wickramasinghe, D. (2009a). Institutionalisation of control and accounting for bonded labour in colonial plantations: A historical analysis. *Critical Perspectives on Accounting*, 20(6), 701–715.

Alawattage, C. and Wickramasinghe, D. (2009b). Weapons of the weak: Subalterns' emancipatory accounting in Ceylon tea. *Accounting, Auditing & Accountability Journal*, 22(3), 379–404.

Alawattage, C., Hopper, T. and Wickramasinghe, D. (2007). Introduction to management accounting in less developed countries. *Journal of Accounting & Organizational Change*, 3(3), 183–191.

Alawattage, C., Graham, C. and Wickramasinghe, D. (2018). Microaccountability and biopolitics: Microfinance in a Sri Lankan village. *Accounting, Organizations and Society*. https://doi.org/10.1016/j.aos.2018.05.008.

Anthony, R. N., Dearden, J. and Bedford, N. M. (1984). *Management Control Systems*. Illinois: Richard D. Irwin Inc.

Argyris, C. (1964). *Integrating the Individual and the Organization*. New York: Wiley.

Berry, A. J., Coad, A. F., Harris, E. P., Otley, D. T. and Stringer, C. (2009). Emerging themes in management control: A review of recent literature. *The British Accounting Review*, 41(1), 2–20.

Cooper, D. J. and Sherer, M. J. (1984). The value of corporate accounting reports: Arguments for a political economy of accounting. *Accounting Organisations and Society*, 9(3/4), 207–232.

Davie, S. S. K. (2005). The politics of accounting, race and ethnicity: A story of a chiefly-based preferencing. *Critical Perspectives on Accounting*, 16(5), 551–577.

Deleuze, G. (1992). Postscript on the societies of control. *October*, 59, 3–7.

Deleuze, G. (1995). *Negotiations, 1972–1990*. New York: Columbia University Press.

Efferin, S. and Hopper, T. (2007). Management control, culture and ethnicity in a Chinese Indonesian company. *Accounting, Organizations and Society*, 32(3), 223–262.

Hammersley, M. and Atkinson, P. (2007). *Ethnography: Principles in Practice*. London: Routledge.

Hesford, J. W., Lee, S.-H. S., Van Der Stede, W. A. and Young, S. M. (2007). Management accounting: A bibliographic study, in Chapman, C. S., Hopwood, A. G. and Shields, M. D. (Eds.), *Handbook of Management Accounting Research*. Oxford: Elsevier Ltd, 3–26.

Hopper, T., Tsamenyi, M., Uddin, S. and Wickramasinghe, D. (2009). Management accounting in less developed countries: What is known and needs knowing. *Accounting, Auditing & Accountability Journal*, 22(3), 469–514.

Hopper, T., Tsamenyi, M., Uddin, S. and Wickramasinghe, D. (2012). *Handbook of Accounting and Development*. London: Edward Elgar Publishing.

Hopper, T., Lassou, P. and Soobaroyen, T. (2017). Globalisation, accounting and developing countries. *Critical Perspectives on Accounting*, 43(March): 125–148. https://doi.org/10.1016/j.cpa.2016.06.003.

Hoque, Z. and Hopper, T. (1994). Rationality, accounting and politics: A case study of management control in a Bangladeshi jute mill. *Management Accounting Research*, 5(1), 5–30.

Jacobs, K. and Kemp, J. (2002). Exploring accounting presence and absence: Case studies from Bangladesh. *Accounting, Auditing & Accountability Journal*, 15(2), 143–161.

Jayasinghe, K. and Thomas, D. (2009). The preservation of indigenous accounting systems in a subaltern community. *Accounting, Auditing & Accountability Journal*, 22(3), 351–378.

Jayasinghe, K. and Wickramasinghe, D. (2011). Power over empowerment: Encountering development accounting in a Sri Lankan fishing village. *Critical Perspectives on Accounting*, 22(4), 396–414.

Jönsson, S. and Macintosh, N. B. (1997). CATS, RATS, and EARS: Making the case for ethnographic accounting research. *Accounting, Organizations and Society*, 22(3–4), 367–386.

Lowe, T. and Machin, J. L. J. (1983). *New Perspectives in Management Control*. London: The MacMillan Press.

Lowe, T. and Puxty, T. (1989). The problems of a paradigm: A critique of the prevailing orthodoxy in management control, in Chua, W. F., Lowe., T. and Puxty, A. G. (Eds.), *Critical Perspectives in Management Control*. New York: Palgrave, 9–26.

Luft, J. and Shields, M. D. (2003). Mapping management accounting: Graphics and guidelines for theory-consistent empirical research. *Accounting, Organizations and Society*, 28(2–3), 169–249.

Merchant, K. A. (1998). *Modern Management Control Systems*. Upper Saddle River, NJ: Prentice Hall.

Otley, D. T., Broadbent, J. and Berry, A. J. (1995). Research in management control: An overview of its development. *British Journal of Management*, 6(s1), S31–S44. https://doi.org/10.1111/j.1467-8551.1995.tb00136.x.

Powdermaker, H. (1966). *Stranger and Friend: The Way of an Anthropologist*. London: Norton.

Ranasinghe, S. B. (2017). *Management control, gender and postcolonialism: The case of Sri Lankan tea plantations*. Unpublished PhD thesis, University of Glasgow.

Robben, A. C. G. M. and Sluka, J. A. (2007). *Ethnographic fieldwork: An Anthropological Reader*. London: Blackwell Publishing.

Scott, J. C. (1985). *Weapons of the Weak: Everyday Forms of Peasant Resistance*. New Haven, CT: Yale University Press.

Scott, J. C. (2009). *The Art of Not Being Governed: An Anarchist History of Upland Southeast Asia*. New Haven, CT: Yale University Press.

Tinker, A. M. (1980). Towards a political economy of accounting: An empirical illustration of the Cambridge controversies. *Accounting, Organizations and Society*, 5(1), 147–160.

Uddin, S. and Hopper, T. (2001). A Bangladesh soap opera: Privatisation, accounting, and regimes of control in a less developed country. *Accounting, Organizations and Society*, 26(7–8), 643–672.

Uddin, S. and Hopper, T. (2003). Accounting for privatisation in Bangladesh: Testing World Bank claims. *Critical Perspectives on Accounting*, 14(7), 739–774.

Wickramasinghe, D. and Hopper, T. (2005). A cultural political economy of management accounting controls: A case study of a textile Mill in a traditional Sinhalese village. *Critical Perspectives on Accounting*, 16(4), 473–503.

Wickramasinghe, D., Hopper, T. and Rathnasiri, C. (2004). Japanese cost management meets Sri Lankan politics. *Accounting, Auditing & Accountability Journal*, 17(1), 85–120.

20

APPROACHES TO RESEARCHING MANAGEMENT ACCOUNTING IN THAILAND

Sirinuch Nimtrakoon and Mike Tayles

Introduction

We offer an overview and discussion of management accounting (MA) in Thailand based on published research. We take a broad view of MA including the use of management accounting practices (MAPs), management accounting and control systems (MCS), the users of MA information, the drivers of change in MA and the role of the management accountant. We have sections on the private and public sectors, and environmental MA as convenient subdivisions.

Following a background to Thailand and the business and economic environment of this developing country we consider a range of research papers, offering insight into their findings/ contribution, theoretical framework and research methodology. In our summary comments and discussion, we refer to gaps in our knowledge and the potential for future research.

Background to Thailand

Thailand is regarded as a developing country having an emerging economy. It has a population of approximately 69 million with a significant proportion living in and around the capital, Bangkok. In 1967 Thailand was one of the founder members of the Association of South East Asian Nations[1] (ASEAN). The country has experienced fluctuations in its fortunes and hence in the stability of its business, investment and international relations. It was significantly affected by the Southeast Asian financial crisis in 1997, although the World Bank reported that the Thai economy quickly recovered by implementing substantial reorganisation in its financial sector, reinforcing corporate governance, restructuring lending practices and enhancing incentives for increasing competition. It was also affected, but less severely, by the world financial crisis in 2008.

The economy, the business environment and image of Thailand have also been affected by political disturbances in 2005 and a coup in 2006, a subsequent return to democracy and more recently the army assuming control over the government in 2014. All this uncertainty has, to an extent, had an impact on business and investor confidence in the region; however, none of this has been dramatic, and business, commerce and investment has proceeded with a degree of stability.

Business in Thailand can be classified into four main sectors: the agricultural sector, which accounts for a majority of the population (and the poverty in the country); the manufacturing sector; the services sector (tourism and hotel industry, trade and telecommunications); and real estate (Bank of Thailand, 2016). The Stock Exchange of Thailand (SET) currently lists (600) public companies in a range of sectors and subdivisions. Predictably, some MA researchers target and report findings related to particular sectors or subdivisions. The SET also has a Market for Alternative Investments (MAI), around 150 companies, and suited to smaller and growing companies having fewer regulatory requirements (SET, 2018).

Some state-owned enterprises (SOEs) (also called government linked companies) are quoted on the SET but a majority of those listed are private sector companies. SOEs include the airport, petroleum, Thai Airways, Krungthai Bank and MCOT (media). As in many Asian countries, the government owns a substantial proportion of these companies and hence has an influence on policies and practices. Companies which are entirely in the public sector are concerned with utilities, the post, the agricultural bank, cigarettes and railways. Some overseas institutions are investors in the SET (for example, Bank of New York, HSBC); the remainder are Thai institutions and private investors.

In terms of foreign investment, Thailand has for a number of years been attractive for low-cost manufacturing, but as with other emerging economies there are moves to address this with a greater emphasis on strategy related to quality, technology and the encouragement of innovation and entrepreneurship in an effort to modernise the economy. There has been some success with this, resulting in some relief of poverty and a movement in its categorisation from a lower-middle to upper-middle economy within the last decade (World Bank, 2018). As a result, it has been identified as the fourth most attractive foreign direct investment (FDI) host within Asia.

Companies making decisions over FDI into Thailand face considerable uncertainty and risk and a choice of entry mode, such as through a wholly owned subsidiary (WOS) or a joint venture (JV). These carry implications of resource commitment and control. Kyaw and Theingi (2009) studied these two entry modes (WOS) and (JV) in relation to firm performance in the electrical and electronic industries in Thailand. They used the Du Pont style of ratio analysis to compare a range of performance measures of companies and conclude that JVs exercise better control over costs whereas WOS undertake better asset utilisation and management.

The Federation of Thai Industries has encouraged research into the competitive strategies of all companies in Thailand. Phusavat and Kanchana (2007) identify the competitive priorities of Thai manufacturing firms and from this discuss their manufacturing strategies and action plans. They focus on six criteria in their research, namely, quality, customer focus, delivery, flexibility, know-how and costs, seeking to rank them through focus on various dimensions of each priority. Their method was to survey 10 manufacturing firms by questionnaire, selecting successful manufacturers, close to the end of the value chain of their respective industries. They found that quality was the most important competitive priority, followed by customer and delivery, then flexibility. The same authors (Phusavat and Kanchana, 2008) used a similar survey approach to reveal competitive priorities in service companies. This disclosed quality, service provision, customer focus and know-how as highly important while cost and flexibility were perceived as generally important.

Management accounting in the private sector

Management accounting practices – overview

We develop a more focused discussion of MA with some output from our own research on MAPs in Thailand. This will create an overview in which to place the research of others as it reveals a spread of practices involving management control, performance evaluation and costing, which we use to structure the remainder of this section. We based our research on a survey instrument developed by Chenhall and Langfield-Smith (1998) in Australia, widely and internationally replicated and cited. Our research deals with a broad range of practices and reveals and ranks the adoption of and perceived benefit derived from a range of MAPs, both traditional and contemporary, as shown in Table 20.1. For convenience of interpretation the items listed are divided into three groups classified as relatively high, moderate and low adoption. Note, however, that even low adoption implies usage by over 60 per cent of respondents.

The descriptive research findings confirm the popularity of the use of traditional management accounting practices (TMAPs) whereas the adoption rates of many contemporary management accounting practices and their perceived benefits (CMAPs)[2] has lagged behind the prominence accorded to these techniques by some commentators.[3] Thailand is not unusual in this regard and we comment further on this at the end of the chapter.

In Nimtrakoon and Tayles (2010) we applied a contingency approach to explore the influence of environmental uncertainty, strategy, industry type and company size on these practices. Applying factor analysis to the results of the survey, we found that firms facing greater environmental uncertainty obtained greater benefit from MAPs, both contemporary (as expected) and traditional. Firms pursuing a prospector strategy perceived greater benefit from contemporary MAPs compared to defenders, but no difference was observed in the benefit from traditional MAPs between different users. Larger firms also perceived greater benefit from both contemporary and traditional MAPs compared to smaller SET quoted firms.

To explore further the strategy of Thai businesses and its link to MA, we used cluster analysis to analyse four different but related strategic typologies of firms and relate these to groupings of both contemporary and traditional MAPs (Nimtrakoon and Tayles, 2015). The strategic typologies researched were differentiation/cost leadership, prospector/defender, entrepreneurial/ conservative and build/harvest. Some statistically significant results emerged. As predicted, differentiator/prospector/entrepreneurial firms with a build strategy reported higher benefit from contemporary MAPs. On the other hand, cost leaders found higher benefit from traditional MAPs. Unusually, entrepreneurial firms also reported more benefit from traditional MAPs than conservative firms. Overall, and in line with findings in other parts of the world, it is observed that there is still considerable reliance on traditional MA with only modest development of the more modern or contemporary MA techniques taking place.

Various studies have shown there is a perceived benefit from use of contemporary techniques, which some would categorise as strategic management accounting (SMA). Corporate governance (CG), by contrast, is generally seen as a basis for the protection of stakeholders and it has already been pointed out that, following the Asian financial crisis, efforts were made to improve CG in the region. Arunruangsirilert (2016) undertook grounded theory research in order to explore possible inter-relationships between CG and the usage of SMA techniques. This draws on an International Federation of Accountants (IFAC) enterprise governance framework, which seeks to link CG and performance. Based on management interviews in companies in the information and communications technologies sector, a model emerges relating levels of governance with 'management activity' resulting in 'active behaviours' and hence a demand for more SMA information.

Arunruangsirilert and Chonglerttham (2017) subsequently used a quantitative approach to explore the association between CG and SMA in Thai companies. They used multiple regression techniques and following Arunruangsirilert (2016) above they tested the association between CG (such as independence of the chair and directors, more active boards of directors and audit committees) and the involvement of the accountant in strategic management processes and usage of strategic management techniques.

Table 20.1 The adoption and perceived benefit of management accounting practices in Thailand

Management accounting practices	Adoption	Benefit
High adoption		
Budgeting systems for controlling costs	1	1
Performance evaluation based on budget variance analysis	2	5
Capital budgeting techniques (e.g. NPV, IRR, Payback)	2	12
Performance evaluation based on return (profit) on investment	3	13
Product profitability analysis	4	2
Budgeting systems for planning cash flows	5	4
Cost-volume-profit analysis	6	3
Performance evaluation based on customer satisfaction surveys	7	7
Standard costing	8	6
Absorption costing	9	15
Budgeting systems for coordinating activities across business units	9	30
Performance evaluation based on divisional profit	10	23
Moderate adoption		
Benchmarking of product/service characteristics	11	14
Performance evaluation based on team performance	11	26
Customer profitability analysis	12	11
Formal strategic planning	12	9
Benchmarking of management processes	13	19
Benchmarking of operational processes	14	15
Long-range forecasting	14	25
Budgeting systems for planning day to day operations	15	38
Budgeting systems for compensating managers	16	24
Performance evaluation based on cash flow return on investment	16	17
Performance evaluation based on controllable profit	17	24
Cost modelling	18	16
Benchmarking of strategic priorities	19	22
Performance evaluation based on supplier evaluations	20	34
Variable costing	20	8
Low adoption		
Performance evaluation based on balanced scorecard	21	28
Economic (shareholder) value added (EVA/SVA)	22	31
Performance evaluation based on residual income	22	36
Backflush costing	23	29
Product life cycle analysis	24	33
Target costing	24	21
Throughput accounting	24	23
Cost of quality	25	27
Activity-based costing (ABC)	26	10
Operations research techniques	27	37
Activity-based budgeting (ABB)	28	18
Activity-based management (ABM)	29	20
Zero-based budgeting	29	32
Performance evaluation based on employee attitudes	30	39
Kaizen costing	31	33
Value chain analysis	32	35

Source: Based on Nimtrakoon and Tayles (2015).

Control and performance evaluation

Teeratansirikool *et al.* (2013) make a link between competitive strategies and firm performance through studying the mediating role of performance measurement. Their data is from a survey of CEOs and uses differentiation/cost leadership strategy. They find that both competitive strategies positively and significantly enhance performance through performance measurement and, further, that firms' differentiation strategy has a direct and significant impact on performance and an indirect impact on performance through financial measures. Their work reveals that there is a much greater perceived role for financial measures, rather than for non-financial measures, in the Thai companies surveyed.

Performance measurement is the subject of a paper by Phornlaphatrachakorn (2017) in which a complex model is proposed involving benchmarking, integrated performance measurement and the balanced scorecard. The research examines the relationship of the above variables, describing them as 'strategic performance measurement', and their effect on organisational creativity, effectiveness and productivity; then ultimately the effect of all of these on 'firm success'. It is a contingency style study using multiple regression analysis. All of the items are based on respondents' perceptions of their firm's use of the techniques and from questionnaire responses the author finds support for some, but not all, of the relationships proposed.

Financial performance measures feature heavily in accounting and, within management accounting, non-financial measures also have received a high profile in recent years. This is particularly following the development and promotion of the Balanced Scorecard (BSC) as one possible performance measurement framework. It is increasingly recognised that managers should not just manage by the financial numbers (which lag) but also by the non-financial numbers, often leading measures of organisational performance. Tourism, which accounts for approximately 10 per cent of Thai GDP, is the focus of Bangchokdee and Mia (2016) relating to the use by senior managers of performance measures in decentralised organisations, specifically hotels in Thailand. In a survey of hotels which operate a decentralised organisation structure, the researchers found a positive and significant relationship between an increasing level of decentralisation and an increasing use of performance measures. A positive and significant relationship was also found between hotel performance and managers' use of the performance measures. A greater role is perceived in this research for non-financial performance measures (which decompose into a BSC structure), which contrasts with the findings of Teeratansirikool *et al.* (2013) (above).

In a paper which places a focus on management accounting system (MAS) effectiveness, Lata and Ussahawanitchakit (2015) examine the effectiveness of MAS in relation to goal achievement, a broader measure than performance. They use a survey methodology within the automotive sector, a significant sector within Thai manufacturing. The IFAC (1998) (cited in Abdel-Kader and Luther, 2006) 'Evolution of Management Accounting' framework is used to identify 'management accounting system effectiveness' and they test the impact of this on goal achievement through the mediating functions of cost information accuracy, corporate practice efficiency and performance evaluation effectiveness. Their conceptual model is quite complex and the paper would benefit from greater theoretical explanation, justification and detail of the variables as some of the material can be difficult to interpret in such a short paper.

Thailand encourages small business development and entrepreneurship. One example of small business and performance-oriented research is by Mandhachitara and Allapach (2017), where they explore some key success factors, or drivers of small business performance. They point out that in small businesses there will be a more informal management style and less focus on hierarchical structures (and perhaps less formal MA as a result). The factors they explore are leadership style of the owner-manager, market orientation, marketing intelligence and their relationship to business performance, including financial and non-financial (marketing and customer) performance. They collected data from small businesses in the Bangkok region by a self-administered questionnaire. They find no direct relationship of leadership style to performance, but it does influence implementation of market orientation and through this performance and market intelligence.

Performance is also a topic in a supply chain management paper by Banomyong and Supatn (2011). This does not use performance as a dependent variable but aims to develop a tool or set of performance metrics for Thai SMEs in relation to supply chain performance. The tool was developed from the literature, tested on 44 SMEs and then benchmarked within the group and externally with a recognised high-performing company. Thai accountants should be interested in this increasingly important area and one relevant accounting finding was that logistics cost data were the most difficult to calculate as traditional MA practices were usually unable to identify specific supply chain activity costs and many SMEs did not have any knowledge of their own supply chain activity costs.

Costing

Activity-based costing (ABC) and its derivatives activity-based management (ABM) and activity-based budgeting (ABB) received significant exposure in the West during the 1990s. An early paper based on a Thai setting was Chongrutsuk and Brooks (2005). It addressed the adoption and implementation of ABC based on a survey of Thai companies from the SET and produced results similar to that reported in developed economies. It addressed organisational and technological factors which influenced the adoption of ABC and also considered problems of implementation and revealed, surprisingly, that the lack of any top management support or resistance by employees to change were not seen as particularly major problems or barriers to implementation, which they attributed to the Thai culture.

The issue of culture (individualism/collectivism and power distance) and ABC was addressed by Morakul and Wu (2001) who assert that Thailand's accounting techniques and practices are adopted from more developed countries, mainly the US. They conducted case studies of the implementation of costing systems (specifically ABC) in the utility industry (electricity generation) in three government-owned companies which were being prepared for privatisation. It is worth noting that government-owned enterprises retain a more traditional (Thai) culture than private companies, who are more open to Western influence and management style. The research used interviews and a questionnaire to explore the reaction of employees to the new system. They found support for the proposition that in large power distance cultures (such as Thailand) a higher employee resistance occurs if the system causes redistribution of power.

In more recent ABC implementation research, Intakhan (2014) explored ABC in Thai companies certified by ISO 9000, which is useful given the high-quality strategic profile. This discussed the concept of ABC implementation 'success' and examined the related contextual, organisational and behavioural variables influencing successful implementation. In research also addressing companies certified by ISO 9000, Vetchagool *et al.* (2019) demonstrated that those employing ABC achieved significantly stronger organisational performance than those registered with ISO 9000 who did not employ the costing technique. They attributed this to the correlation between ISO 9000 and ABC system processes.

While ABC has proved to be quite a popular technique and research topic, other forms of costing also warrant attention. One example is in the highly significant auto parts sector in Thailand and deals with value chain costing (VCC) and its impact on firm success (Ussahawanitchakit,

2017). It tested the hypothesised relationships between VCC (composed of value creation activity, interdependent network, supplier–customer relationship and continuous improvement) and customer response, customer satisfaction and customer acceptance, leading to competitive advantage and firm success. The model being tested involves complex relationships and on consulting the questionnaire it might be questionable whether it addresses value chain analysis rather than VCC; however, it is possible that one approach is, to an extent, implied by the other.

Management accounting in the public sector

In a paper informed by institutional theory, Sutheewasinnon *et al.* (2016) map the development of a performance management system (PMS) in the Thai public sector. Based on archival research and interviews with key actors in the process they demonstrate in detail how the system was developed. They observe that Thailand has a strong central government and highly institutionalised public sector, so their contribution is to show the different isomorphic pressures which were in evidence over time, the 'institutional entrepreneurs' who were actors and the strategies they used. The analysis is structured in stages starting with the recognition that a results- or output-based system would be more in line with New Public Management, than the current 'input-based' traditional budgeting system. The analysis follows the stages of development and explains the strategies that were adopted to forestall resistance, secure legitimacy and advance development.

In another significant piece of longitudinal qualitative research related to the Thai public sector, Chiwamit *et al.* (2017) studied diffusion of management accounting innovations in the context of government regulation. In particular, their emphasis was on how the regulator interacts, not only with the supplier, but also with the regulatee and how the latter can influence this process and hence imbue the standards employed with greater flexibility. The innovation concerned the implementation of Economic Value Added (EVA™) as part of a performance management system in a state-owned utility company (electricity generation) and a commercial bank. This was driven by a mindset focused on government reform and implementation of a performance management system, promoted by the Thai government and the then prime minister, Thaksin Shinawatra, as a step towards greater privatisation of public sector activity. They demonstrate how a global innovation (EVA™) was adapted to a regulatory environment, which encourages a rethinking of how management accounting innovations are 'involved in' and 'evolve in' the regulatory process.

Separate and different insights taken from this study were used to produce one of two case studies (the other on EVA™ in a Chinese SOE), which make a theoretical contribution to institutional theory around management accounting (Chiwamit *et al.*, 2014). This paper draws attention to the human agency involved in creating, maintaining and disrupting institutions. It focuses particularly on the respective and differing interests of actors surrounding the implementation of (in this case) the EVA™ initiative and highlights the 'societal relevance' of management accounting innovations. It is interesting how management accounting is influenced by the roles of various actors not usually identified with management accounting, for example, regulators, financial analysts, auditors, societal pressures groups, trades unions, etc.

Performance measurement in public hospitals is the subject of a paper by Buathong and Bangchokdee (2017). It addresses the familiar topic of participation by middle managers in performance measurement and control systems, the extent of subsequent use of these measures by the managers (following a BSC structure) and hence the impact of this on managerial performance. In a concise paper the authors use structural equation modelling to examine responses from middle managers in public hospitals, a larger-scale provider of health care than the private sector, and one under constant pressure concerning government funding.

In a different public sector setting, Upping and Oliver (2012) research the change to greater autonomy in Thai universities. They address changes to the accounting systems as a result of the modernisation of their management and governance, the catalysts for change having come from the Thai government, which has encouraged a New Public Management style, which in turn has required greater financial management information. The research deals with a survey of Chief Finance Officers and the paper is descriptive of the changes taking place. By analysing the questionnaire responses it is observed that universities which have become, or intend to become, autonomous place greater importance on changes to the financial accounting system, the budgeting system and cost accounting system than those not becoming autonomous, and related to this express concern over a lack of accounting staff competence to support this autonomy.

Environmental management accounting and CSR

The past decade has seen an increasing interest in research into corporate social responsibility (CSR) and social and environmental accounting (SEA) and some of this applies to management accounting. An environmental management accounting (EMA) paper which adopts a perspective of life cycle costing (LCC) is by Silalertruksa *et al.* (2012). This paper takes a life cycle approach to the evaluation of the use of diesel fuel compared to palm oil biodiesel, which has the potential to be developed in southern Thailand, thus contributing to the economy in addition to the environment. The authors point out that, based on current prices and acquisition costs, biodiesel would not be used unless a government subsidy was available. However, they demonstrate that when taking account of externalities (wider environmental/welfare costs etc.) some blends of biodiesel are competitive with petroleum diesel. Interestingly and perhaps significantly, the authors are not attached to accounting departments, but to energy and environment centres but this demonstrates where cross-functional research and collaboration can contribute.

The non-involvement of accountants in CSR/EMA is one of the factors addressed by Setthasakko (2010) in a discussion of the barriers to the development of environmental management accounting in Thailand. This research is based on interviews with CEOs, environmental officers and accounting directors carried out in three pulp and paper companies, an industry with a reputation for having a negative impact on natural resources and the environment. The barriers discussed are related to change management and organisational learning; too narrow a focus on economic performance and the pursuit of profit, and very little guidance or regulation on environmental management accounting. Demonstrating ongoing involvement in this topic and sector, Setthasakko (2015) uses interviews and a survey to address factors influencing adoption of EMA. She finds top management roles, knowledge sharing and building corporate image as the three primary factors influencing Thai firms to adopt EMA.

In a more general and critical paper applied to SEA, Kuasirikun (2005) explored the mindset of Thai accountants and the accounting profession, with findings mirroring those of Setthasakko (2010). For example, the perception that the objectives of the management or owners of companies relate to profit maximisation and that accounting is perceived to be for 'control and decision making' related to profit. Hence this was the focus of the accountant's training and the orientation that he/she should adopt. Respondents asserted that accounting reporting is for 'financially interested' parties so that is the 'audience' accountants should respond to. They saw SEA as having a greater marketing or public relations emphasis and therefore somewhat beyond the scope of accounting.

Future directions

We have provided a brief summary of MA in Thailand based on English language journals and our own insights. It is pleasing to see that over time this has grown in scale, scope and profile. We would seek to encourage it and any comment we make is intended to be constructive. Some promising and interesting research is emerging in the different sectors we cover. We have observed considerable research in the private sector, particularly in manufacturing, and slightly less in the service sector. A significant proportion of GDP is now generated by the service sector and there is potential for research to generate further insights here. Much of the research presented here is undertaken in larger businesses. More research would be welcome related to small or micro businesses, which are important contributors to the economy and an engine for growth. Furthermore, the private sector consists of both indigenous businesses and international companies; some comparison here might fruitful, not only in the use and usefulness of MA practices, but also in the different ways they come to be adopted and the management reaction to them. Given that agriculture plays a large part in the Thai economy, research may also contribute to increasing efficiency in this sector.

Papers addressing management accounting in the public sector are many, involving considerable case research. It would be useful if further research could address the efficiency and effectiveness of the use of some of the emerging MA practices, in addition to exploring the factors leading to their emergence or retirement. Research could also be focused on SOEs, companies with partial government ownership, to explore the effect of this on the operation and practices adopted, dealing with culture for instance and perhaps compared to the private sector.

Research addressing CSR and particularly environmental management accounting, most likely driven by the interests of the researchers and by local needs and opportunities, offers considerable future potential. What is interesting here is the extent to which it is outward looking and incorporates external data into MA, something which must be encouraged if more contemporary MA practices are to be adopted.

Corporate governance is a substantial topic of worldwide interest with implications much wider than MA. Fraud and corruption are of concern in many developing economies where the regulatory powers of government and enforcement are less strong; the present Thai government is giving this a high profile. While it is notoriously difficult for various reasons to research this topic, appropriate contributions of MA would be interesting.

Most papers give appropriate attention to prior literature but only some to the conceptual framework surrounding their enquiry, though most related to the private sector assume a neo-classical economics-based approach. Some make little reference to the theory involved, which results in an impression of testing what 'might be a good idea' without sufficient justification. Linked to this point, the models in some papers are almost too complex and do not give enough detail for the reader to judge the overall (face) validity of the work, though statistics are presented to support construct validity. In other words, there could be a slight concern that some publications might be driven by the 'pressure to publish', rather than any concern over what the contribution and implications might be.

In terms of theoretical frameworks, contingency theory seems to predominate, using either a selection or interaction approach (either without or with specific reference to performance); this is mostly applicable to quantitative work with a positivist philosophy. There are a small number of case studies presented through an interpretivist approach which also adopt contingency. In more recent papers, explaining development in the public sector, institutional theory is strongly in evidence.

A range of research methodologies, the use of grounded theory, longitudinal enquiry and critical analysis, in addition to traditional cases and surveys, are all welcome given an appropriately wide interpretation of management accounting. Further 'critical' work exploring the origins of and influences on management accounting development within a Thai environment would add to our understanding. This is especially so, given that Thailand, unlike some of its neighbours in ASEAN, has never been colonised. Some papers refer in their explanation to local culture. This is a large and complex topic and further research into Asian and Thai culture (a predominantly Buddhist influence) would be interesting.

The research we have featured involved a considerable amount of time and hard work in data collection and analysis. Much is positivistic, based on quantitative analysis; only more recently has some extensive qualitative and longitudinal research emerged. Cross-sectional surveys are the most popular method used, even where it would appear the researcher has visited a site and administered a questionnaire to which qualitative insight could be added. Hence the use of more interviews and qualitative research insight would be welcome to create more context and to explore with greater depth aspects which are not easily achievable in survey work. Most of the papers have been suitably explanatory, not simply being descriptive of the circumstances. While there are examples of very good and carefully argued and constructed papers, in some cases the arguments, constructs and interpretations tended to be a little unclear and this needs attention in developing higher quality papers.

Related to the current state of MA practice we have noted that there is considerable reliance on traditional MA. There are examples of the use of contemporary MA, but greater usage and more benefit is attributed by questionnaire respondents to traditional MA. Following on from this observation, there is also some evidence of a reliance upon financial performance measures rather than non-financial performance measures and hence a financial accounting mentality in some of the work we have seen. This is in spite of considerable exposure and promotion (especially in the West) of the dangers of an exclusive reliance on financial measures, a short-termist perspective, and the benefit from the use of non-financial performance measures, for example, the Balanced Scorecard.

Looking forward, researchers must raise awareness of, and practitioners must be open to, the potential of contemporary MA and, linked to this, the dangers of a financial accounting mentality. MA must not be seen as the internal face of financial accounting and some of the interviews supporting our own survey research in Thailand and our ongoing contacts on this topic, worryingly, gave this impression. However, it is satisfying that some of the papers we feature here point to examples of a wider and more contemporary orientation of MA and further examples of these should be encouraged. For example, for new practices to become embedded, accountants need to deal with and be comfortable with change. Researchers also need to focus on and publish about the change process and novel approaches in MA, for example diffusion of innovations.

Interestingly, research relating the role of the management accountant and manager perception of this role in Thai companies has not been apparent and this would be a welcome development. Results may point to the need for greater and wider training and education of accountants, particularly management accountants. This also applies to managers and their use of MA information, because with the development of distributed data systems, managers can increasingly become their own 'management accountants'. Management accountants must be promoted in the role of 'business partners' and develop a greater cross-functional perspective; this should be reinforced in the output of MA researchers. Management accountants and MA academics can be encouraged to form teams to address projects and/or local business problems where accounting can provide one perspective. Linked to this, there is scope for greater exchange between academia and practice to share insight into problems and solutions.

Thailand has considerable potential as a founding member of ASEAN and given the development in 2015 of the ASEAN Economic Community it can grow its profile still further within Southeast Asia and the world. In this context, management accounting can be a contributor, but it requires the continuous development of both management accountants and management accounting researchers.

Notes

1 The five founders of ASEAN were Indonesia, Malaysia, Philippines, Singapore and Thailand (in the Bangkok Agreement 1967). They were subsequently joined by Vietnam, Laos PDR, Cambodia, Myanmar and Brunei Darussalam.
2 We would categorise traditional MA being more narrow scope, formal, financial and historical information often derived from a financial accounting system, focusing on internal events, having a short-term perspective, with product or responsibility centre emphasis. The contemporary concept of MA refers to less formal, non-financial, and future-oriented information related to external actors such as customers, suppliers, competitors and society, a longer-term perspective, and a more strategic orientation with a more flexible time period.
3 Interestingly, activity-based costing (ABC) is perceived as high benefit (ranked 10) even though it is not commonly used by the organisations in SET (ranked 26). Follow-up phone calls revealed low adoption due to lack of expertise, its practical difficulty and the time and money involved in developing it. In a survey, similar to ours, undertaken a few years later, ABC was shown to be more highly adopted, while its benefit was not perceived any higher than our survey.

References

Abdel-Kader, M. and Luther, R. (2006). IFAC's conception of the evolution of management accounting. *Advances in Management Accounting*, 15, 229–247.
Arunruangsirilert, T. (2016). Corporate governance and strategic management accounting: A grounded theory. *Journal of Accounting Profession, Thailand*, 12(Sept), 34–47.
Arunruangsirilert, T and Chonglerttham, S. (2017). Effect of corporate governance characteristics on strategic management accounting in Thailand. *Asian Review of Accounting*, 25(1), 85–105.
Bangchokdee, S and Mia, L. (2016). The role of senior managers' use of performance measures in the relationship between decentralisation and performance: Evidence from hotels in Thailand. *Journal of Accounting and Organisational Change*, 12(2), 129–151.
Bank of Thailand (2016). Thailand's economic conditions in 2016. www.bot.or.th/English/Monetary-Policy/EconomicConditions/AnnualReport/AnnualReport/annual_2016_V2.pdf (accessed 11 July 2018).
Banomyong, R. and Supatn, N. (2011). Developing a supply chain performance tool for SMEs in Thailand. *Supply Chain Management: An International Journal*, 16(1), 20–31.
Buathong, S and Bangchokdee, S. (2017). The use of the performance measures in Thai public hospitals. *Asian Review of Accounting*, 25(4), 472–485.
Chenhall, R. H. and Langfield-Smith, K. (1998). Adoption and benefits of management accounting practices: An Australian study. *Management Accounting Research*, 9(1), 1–19.
Chiwamit, P., Modell, S., Yang, C. (2014). The societal relevance of management accounting innovations: Economic value added and institutional work in the fields of Chinese and Thai state-owned enterprises. *Accounting and Business Research*, 44(2), 144–180.
Chiwamit, P., Modell, S. and Scapens, R W. (2017). Regulation and adaptation of management accounting innovations: The case of economic value added in Thai state-owned enterprises. *Management Accounting Research*, 37, 30–48.
Chongrutsuk, W. and Brooks, A. (2005). The adoption and implementation of activity-based costing in Thailand. *Asian Review of Accounting*, 13(2), 1–17.
Intakhan, P. (2014). ABC success: Evidence from ISO 9000 certified companies in Thailand. *Asian Review of Accounting*, 22(3), 287–303.
Kuasirikun, N. (2005). Attitudes to the development and implementation of social and environmental accounting in Thailand. *Critical Perspectives on Accounting*, 16(8), 1035–1057.

Kyaw, N. A. and Theingi, H. (2009). A performance analysis of wholly owned subsidiaries and joint ventures: Electrical and electronic industry in Thailand. *International Journal of Business Studies*, 17(1), 107–125.

Lata, P. and Ussahawanitchakit, P. (2015). Management accounting system effectiveness and goal achievement: Evidence from automotive businesses in Thailand. *The Business and Management Review*, 7(1), 322–334.

Mandhachitara, R. and Allapach, S. (2017). Small business performance in Thailand: Key success factors. *Journal of Research in Marketing and Entrepreneurship*, 19(2), 161–181.

Morakul, S. and Wu, F. H. (2001). Cultural influences on the ABC implementation in Thailand's environment. *Journal of Managerial Psychology*, 16(2), 142–158.

Nimtrakoon, S. and Tayles, M. (2010). Contingency factors of management accounting practices in Thailand: A selection approach. *Asian Journal of Accounting and Governance*, 1, 51–78.

Nimtrakoon, S. and Tayles, M. (2015). Explaining management accounting practices and strategy in Thailand: A selection approach using cluster analysis. *Journal of Accounting in Emerging Economies*, 5(3), 269–298.

Phornlaphatrachakorn, K. (2017). Strategic performance measurement and firm success of Thai listed firms: A managerial accounting approach. *Chulalongkorn Business Review*, 39(Oct–Dec), 1–29.

Phusavat, K. and Kanchana, R. (2007). Competitive priorities of manufacturing firms in Thailand. *Industrial Management and Data Systems*, 107(7), 979–996.

Phusavat, K. and Kanchana, R. (2008). Competitive priorities for service providers: Perspectives from Thailand. *Industrial Management and Data System*, 108(1), 5–21.

SET (2018). List of SET listed companies and contact information. Stock Exchange of Thailand, www.set.or.th/en/company/companylist.html (accessed 29 June 2018).

Setthasakko, W. (2010). Barriers to the development of environmental management accounting: An exploratory study of pulp and paper companies in Thailand. *EuroMed Journal of Business*, 5(3), 315–331.

Setthasakko, W. (2015). The adoption of environmental management accounting in Thailand. *Journal of the Accounting Profession*, 11(Dec), 99–109.

Silalertruksa, T., Bonnet, S. and Gheewala, S. H. (2012). Life cycle costing and externalities of palm oil biodiesel in Thailand. *Journal of Cleaner Production*, 28, 225–232.

Sutheewasinnon, P., Hoque, Z. and Nyamori, R. O. (2016). Development of a performance management system in the Thailand public sector: Isomorphism and the role and strategies of institutional entrepreneurs. *Critical Perspectives on Accounting*, 40, 26–44.

Teeratansirikool, L., Siengthai, S., Badir, Y. and Charoenngam, C. (2013). Competitive strategies and firm performance: The mediating role of performance measurement. *International Journal of Productivity and Performance Management*, 6(2), 168–184.

Upping, P. and Oliver, J. (2012), Thai public universities: Modernisation of accounting practices. *Journal of Accounting and Organisational Change*, 8(3), 403–430.

Ussahawanitchakit, P. (2017). Value chain costing, competitive advantage and firm success: Evidence from Thai auto parts manufacturing businesses. *International Journal of Business*, 22(3), 230–250.

Vetchagool, W., Augustyn, M. M. and Tayles, M. (2019). ISO 9000, activity based costing and organisational performance. *Total Quality Management and Business Excellence* (forthcoming).

World Bank (2018). The World Bank in Thailand: Overview. www.worldbank.org/en/country/thailand/overview (accessed 29 June 2018).

21

RESEARCHING AND PUBLISHING ON ACCOUNTING IN EMERGING ECONOMIES

An experiential account

Junaid Ashraf, Trevor Hopper, Philippe Lassou, Olayinka Moses,
Kelum Jayasinghe, Teerooven Soobaroyen and Shahzad Uddin

Introduction

This chapter discusses substantive issues for academia generally, and for researchers actively or contemplating conducting research on accounting in emerging economies. The authors have all researched and published in this area, sometimes individually but more often collaboratively, all but one have supervised PhD students, and all have promoted networks of researchers in this area. Except for one author born in the UK, the others were born, received their education up to and including university, and initially worked in their home countries (Bangladesh, Benin, Mauritius, Nigeria, Pakistan and Sri Lanka) before completing their PhDs in the UK or, in one instance, New Zealand. All retain links with their birthplaces, through their research and university and professional contacts. While we do not claim expertise on accounting in all emerging economies, our careers have exposed us to much of this research, especially in Asia and Africa. This chapter draws on these experiences.

Progress to date

Pre-1980s accounting research in emerging economies was sparse despite work by pioneers, especially Segun Wallace who founded the annual publication *Research in Third World Accounting*, later renamed *Research in Accounting in Emerging Economies* (Hopper et al., 2009). The reasons for this are unclear but we would venture that it was due to academics in emerging economies lacking the resources and training to pursue research in their home countries and to attain articles of the quality required to gain publication in international refereed journals; and the reluctance of accounting departments in Western countries to encourage PhD students from emerging economies to research accounting in their home countries. These problems persist today though many more departments in Western countries are now open to, and indeed encourage, PhD students from emerging economies studying accounting issues in their home country. Also, the increasing availability of databases covering emerging economies has made

259

quantitative studies more feasible, though this has also been accompanied by a growth in qualitative studies. Consequently, a growing body of work on accounting in emerging economies has emerged in books (Hopper and Hoque, 2004; Hopper *et al.*, 2012), reviews in book chapters and journal articles (Hopper *et al.*, 2009; van Helden and Uddin, 2016; Uddin *et al.*, 2017; Hopper and Tanima, 2018), special issues of journals, e.g. *Critical Perspectives on Accounting* (CPA, 2010); *Accounting, Auditing and Accountability Journal* (AAAJ, 2017); and a new specialist journal, *Journal of Accounting in Emerging Economies*, all attracting quality submissions worldwide.

Moreover, networks of scholars and forums to discuss such work are growing. For example, in 2018 the University of Essex hosted the first successful Accounting and Accountability in Emerging Economies Conference, which will become a biennial event. The African Accounting and Finance Association (AAFA), founded in 2009, held its eighth annual conference in 2018, and the Asian Academic Accounting Association held its eighteenth annual conference in 2017. The special interest group of the British Accounting and Finance Association, Accounting and Finance in Emerging Economies, meets regularly, is vibrant, has many active members, and has organised workshops for emerging scholars to develop their articles prior to submission to leading journals. Moreover, there are growing links and cross-fertilisation of ideas between accounting and development studies researchers; for example the Development Studies Association held panel sessions for accounting in emerging economies. The area can no longer be regarded as esoteric or marginal. Over the past two decades, some emerging economies have invested in doctoral studies and Western accounting departments have benefited from an influx of such students. While not all choose to research issues concerning their home country, increasing numbers are doing so, often with encouragement from their department. In some departments, emerging economy studies are 'mainstream', and have PhD supervisors expert and willing to supervise such research. Possibly, due to growing globalisation, more articles in key accounting journals examining accounting and development are appearing.

In discussions with colleagues we often find that there is a perception that it is difficult to publish on accounting in emerging economies in leading journals. This may be correct for some journals, as the preliminary analysis of the contents of these journals in an ongoing research project by two of the authors to this paper indicates. From 2009 to 2018, of the 12,666 articles published by journals ranked A$\star$, A and B in the Australian Business Deans Council's Master Journal List, 1,159 (9.5 per cent) were on an emerging economy (based the International Monetary Fund's 2018 World Economic Outlook[1] classification). There is a slight upward trend of such publications over the past 10 years. While most journals' publications remain disproportionally on rich economies, publication of work on poorer countries, where most of the world's population reside, is possible. However, the number of publications on emerging economies varies across the journals. The only A$\star$ journal in the top 20 publishers of such articles was *Accounting, Organizations and Society*, which occupied nineteenth position overall, and accounted for 25.58 per cent of the 86 articles on emerging economies in the nine A$\star$ journals. This constituted 7.42% of the 1,159 articles on emerging economies by all the journals (an average per A$\star$ journal of 0.82 per cent) and only 2.65 per cent of all articles published in A$\star$ journals. In contrast, the 20 A-ranked journals published 406 articles on emerging economies (35.03 per cent of all such articles by all journals) (an average per A journal of 1.75 per cent). This constituted 8.54 per cent of the articles they published. The 28 B journals published 667 articles on emerging economies (57.55 per cent of all such articles published by all journals) (an average per B journal of 2.06 per cent). This constituted 14.22 per cent of the total articles they published.

The above investigation has found that the 10 journals that published the most articles on accounting in emerging economies from 2009 to 2018 were:

- *Accounting Auditing and Accountability Journal*
- *Advances in Accounting*
- *Asian Review of Accounting*
- *Asia-Pacific Journal of Accounting and Economics*
- *Critical Perspectives on Accounting*
- *International Journal of Accounting and Information Management*
- *Journal of Intellectual Capital*
- *Managerial Auditing Journal*
- *Pacific Accounting Review*
- *The International Journal of Accounting*

In contrast the following journals published two or fewer articles:

- *Accounting and the Public Interest*
- *Advances in Accounting*
- *Advances in Management Accounting*
- *Behavioral Research*
- *Current Issues in Auditing*
- *Journal of Accounting Education*
- *Journal of Accounting Literature*
- *Journal of Governmental and Nonprofit Accounting.*
- *Review of Accounting Studies*

The analysis of articles on accounting in emerging economies in leading journals from 2009 to 2018 suggests that claims that it is difficult to publish qualitative rather than quantitative research may be unfounded. Quantitative methods were used most (759 articles – 65.49 per cent of all articles published on emerging economies) but qualitative methods were used in 387 (33.39 per cent of all articles published on emerging economies). This may be because research articles submitted are predominantly quantitative. For instance, internal analyses of all submissions to the *Journal of Accounting in Emerging Economies*, edited by one author of this chapter, have found that approximately 90 per cent are essentially quantitative. Journals that regularly publish work on emerging economies often show a predilection for quantitative or qualitative studies. To gain publication one must choose carefully: which journal is appropriate for the methodology used and is open to work of this ilk. Of course, systematic bias among journals cannot be proved – they can only publish what is submitted to them. However, differences are striking – journals based in British Commonwealth countries appear more willing to accept articles on emerging economies than those in North America. Journal rankings change and newer, successful ones will rise, as in the past, e.g. the *Journal of Accounting in Emerging Economies* and *Qualitative Research on Accounting and Management*, both currently ranked as 2★ in the Association of Business Schools list regularly publish work on accounting in emerging economies. Also, regional accounting associations in Africa, Asia and the South Pacific have or are planning to launch their own journals. It is anticipated that their ranking will rise but this takes time for new journals.

Despite such progress, we urge journal editors and reviewers to be more sympathetic to and aware of accounting research in emerging economies, and to use referees sympathetic to and knowledgeable of the area. Be wary of editors' claims that their journal is open to all types of work – check whether this is matched by their contents. Moreover, although difficult to prove, and, like most authors suffering rejections we may be prone to blaming referees and editors rather than recognising the limitations of our work, we still experience suspicions of editor and referee bias. Examples include cases of editors of leading journals rejecting submissions because they believed the data was unreliably collected, and a desk rejection by the editor of a North American 'international' accounting journal of a paper on corruption based on extensive interviews with senior officials because the data could not be externally validated. Sometimes papers have been rejected outright by editors without any reasons given, or the main editor has rejected papers without giving a reason despite special edition editors selecting them for consideration after initial refereeing reports. In most instances the papers were eventually accepted by other leading journals. Like most researchers we have had our share of rejected papers, but these have been for valid reported reasons; and we have not encountered the problems recounted above when submitting empirical research on a developed country, though this could be attributable to good luck. These problems can be encountered for quantitative studies too. Often data sets on emerging economies cannot match the size and reliability of those for developed countries but if this automatically disqualifies publication then findings on emerging economies, and perhaps their unique issues, can go unreported.

This reiterates the importance of choosing a journal sympathetic to, and with a record of publishing, articles on emerging economies. Finally, we note the bias of citation counts – their neglect of articles on emerging economies is alarming. Sadly, and too often, researchers writing on emerging economies only cite research on developed economies in North American journals; or publications on important international accounting issues cite illustrations from papers on emerging economies because of their context but ignore the topics and insights they provide.

Issues facing researchers in emerging economies

Unfortunately, governments and related stakeholders in many emerging economies lack a clear vision or appreciation of the need for social science research (including business, accounting and finance). Public universities usually rank low in public spending priorities, and political or government influence may prioritise 'national interest' initiatives over those of the institution and its staff. Thus, universities are perceived as a cog in the machinery of economic development, to create a professional workforce for businesses and government organisations. Technical skills and being up to date with the latest professional developments dominate curricula of undergraduate and postgraduate business school programmes. Consequently, funding for accounting research is shunned, or 'applied' research deemed 'useful' to specific stakeholders is privileged over fundamental research. This provides academics with credibility to act as paid consultants and advisers, rather than conducting research. In this context, research, PhD training and supervision – often centred on outdated or inappropriate econometric and statistical models, and dated and narrow beliefs about journal rankings and what constitutes cutting-edge research – become technically oriented, with little regard for different ontological and epistemological positions or studying alternative theoretical perspectives on accounting (Alawattage *et al.*, 2017a, 2017b).

PhD training in emerging economies relies on the pool of skills and expertise available. This is a major constraint on the methodological and theoretical approaches PhD students are exposed to, and sometimes breeds research that is descriptive or exercises naïve empiricism, i.e. statistical (often technically good) testing of relationships between variables without sufficient articulation of the underlying theory, or merely descriptive case studies. This is reflected in articles submitted to accounting journals and proposals submitted to UK universities for admission to, and scholarships for, PhD study, from emerging economies. From our experience, insufficient regard to the theory underpinning the choice of variables acting as proxies for the theory is attributable to narrow and technical research training modules (if any) in PhD and Masters pro-grammes, and sometimes poor supervision. This is not unique to emerging economies but is more pronounced there. For example, one author, when a PhD director in accounting, found only six of 28 applicants from emerging economies (during 2017/18) had adequate training to undertake a PhD project on their own.

Many leading scholars on accounting in emerging economies are from developing countries but undertook their PhDs in developed countries. Scholarships were crucial. However, many UK universities, in the current Brexit and austerity climate, have reduced or cut PhD scholar-ships, particularly for non-European students, and due to the global economic crisis, govern-ments in emerging economies have cut, reduced or tightened conditions for scholarships to pursue PhDs abroad. For example, the Indonesian government has imposed extra conditions and restrictions: applicants must have published in an international journal before they can apply for competitive government sponsored scholarships; and the Saudi government recently pub-lished a restricted list of UK universities eligible for funding accounting or finance doctoral studies, which has the unintended consequence of restricting research to a narrower set of topics, methods and theoretical standpoints. Nevertheless, potential PhD students from emerg-ing economies must not despair, for several universities in other developed countries (e.g. Canada) are expanding their reach to applicants from emerging economies, often combining baseline scholarships with income from teaching and research assistance, which consolidates research training with teaching experience.

Greater use of domestic PhD programmes in universities in emerging economies has merit financially and academically but, to be successful, they must improve. More regional collabora-tion across universities to concentrate the most talented PhD trainers and supervisors, within better programmes, reinforced by visiting and prominent researchers from developed countries, would help. However, there is little sign of this happening, possibly due to the lack of funds, not least from major international financial institutions such as the World Bank, and the African and Asian Development Banks; and the lack of will from governments and universities. Nor is it cheap. One author investigated offering his UK university's PhD programme in an emerging economy but the cost of flights and accommodation for periodic visits by supervisors proved prohibitive.

The World Bank's emphasis on strengthening primary and secondary education (possibly justifiably) has limited support for university-level studies, especially at the doctoral level, in poorer emerging economies.[2] Exceptions tend to be oil rich countries within the World Bank definition used here, and richer emerging economies such as Indonesia and Malaysia. For example, in the early 1990s, the World Bank funded an Academic Staff Development scheme for University of Mauritius academics to pursue 'split-site' doctoral programmes in overseas institutions. Unfortunately, this funding proved short-lived and despite a local scheme being provided thereafter, inadequate local funding led to reduced PhD enrolments and completion rates. The appetite for university education in emerging economies is often filled by private universities; home and overseas campuses of universities based in a developed country; and, for those seeking accounting education, qualifications from Western accounting professional associ-ations pursuing global growth. However, the institutions involved often concentrate on teach-ing not research, and show little willingness to finance and supervise indigenous PhD students.

Recently the World Bank has shown more sympathy for developing higher education capa-city (including research) in emerging economies and infrastructures conducive to this end. Nevertheless, with exceptions, it has placed little emphasis on increasing accounting research capacity. Extractive industries, science, agriculture and to some degree health have been the Bank's priorities. For example, World Bank financing of Vietnamese higher education[3] in 2017 emphasised agriculture, science and technology; and a scheme (2013) for 19 African universities[4] created excellence centres for agriculture (6), health (6), science and technology (5) and oil (1). Given the World Bank's influence in many emerging economies, their policy statements and financial support often frame governments' priorities and expectations for higher education and research. In our discussions with officers in United Nations agencies and international financial institutions responsible for accounting policies in emerging economies, they complain that many World Bank officials are macroeconomists, with little appreciation of accounting's importance for development, hence it receives a low priority.

Resources are a major problem for accounting researchers in emerging economies. They can have no or limited access to necessary books and journals. Frequently, we have found that worthy potential presenters from emerging economies wishing to attend relevant workshops and conferences require financial support from conference organisers. Although funding for such activities varies across emerging economies, it is predominately meagre, and university managers facing limited financial resources may privilege key departments or disciplines (rarely accounting). Conferences are important avenues for developing research papers to a level suitable for submission to well-ranked journals. Most major conferences occur in Europe and North America but insufficient funding, visa restrictions and geographical distance make it extremely difficult for academics to attend conferences not only in developed countries but also within their region. For example, the cost of attending one conference (including air fare and visa fees) in Pakistan is equivalent to attending three to four academic conferences in the UK. Paradoxically, the cost and complexity of flights within Africa can make it cheaper for African academics to travel to conferences outside the continent. This is a major impediment to building communities of scholars nationally, regionally and internationally.

Timely access to publications and even access to the internet can be problematic. We know colleagues in emerging economies who have spent days downloading entire back issues of accounting and business journals when a free trial opportunity arose, in anticipation that they might eventually use them. Academics in developed economies can help alleviate journal access problems, for example, by publishing in journals with free or cheap access or making their articles available on websites and free access platforms such as ResearchGate.

Low academic salaries, promotions not linked to research achievements, and heavy teaching loads discourage academics in emerging economies from pursuing research. Low salaries often mean they have more than one teaching job. Workload allocation systems often do not account for 'research time'. For example, in major business schools in West Africa, many accounting academics must teach 450 contact hours a year, nearly four times that of counterparts in leading research departments in developed countries. In Indonesian universities, academics devote considerable time to managing large groups of students (often class sizes around 500–750) but are expected to publish in SCOPUS ranked journals. This encourages replicating econometric/statistical-oriented research questions/methods on topics more relevant to developed countries. In other emerging economies perverse journal ranking lists encourage academics to publish in local, often non-refereed journals, to meet publication requirements for promotion.[5] On the one hand, we frequently come across unrealistic performance appraisal systems in emerging economies that limit acceptable output to a narrow range of A⋆ and A journals, to increase their universities' ranking internationally.[6] On the other hand, they can be overly generous by accepting outputs in journals ranked equally, many of which are of dubious or low quality, and not refereed. Predatory publishing is also a concern but sometimes it is even encouraged to improve institutional research rankings (de Jager *et al.*, 2017). Thus, publication becomes a means to an end, with research output of little academic, policy or practice relevance and, worse still, sometimes findings that are nonsensical but the reason is of little concern. Also, exerting undue pressure on faculty to produce research outputs may encourage research based on large databases immaterial to emerging economies. The 'relevance' of research thus becomes a casualty of the game of pursuing higher rankings or promotion. Publication in and promotion of indigenous journals are to be encouraged, especially given the reluctance of many highly ranked, allegedly 'international' journals to publish articles on accounting in developing countries, but their papers must be fairly and rigorously refereed, and performance appraisal and incentive systems must reciprocate this effectively and realistically.

Factors leading to publication (or not)

The increase in emerging economy studies means the novelty factor is declining. Justifying publication because there is no similar study in country Y becomes less tenable, particularly if the paper makes little incremental contribution empirically or theoretically. Journal editors and reviewers have become more demanding about the significance of national context. Our experience of journal editing and editorial board membership is that many articles fail to get published because they fail to appropriately articulate the uniqueness of the context their accounting operates in, which is frustrating. Also, many studies are merely descriptive and do not identify any contribution to extant debates. If a paper does not significantly contribute to prior work, it will struggle to get published in a well-ranked journal.

Authors often presume that their selected country has unique features, intriguing to others. However, these are often common to other emerging (or even developed) countries. Based on our experiences of working as accountants and researchers in developed and emerging economies, we notice that many problems and issues are common to both types of work. However, a weak institutional environment, unstable democratic traditions, low literacy rates and many other factors in emerging economies can create conditions where some issues, e.g. corruption and good governance, become more pronounced.

Be bold. Too often papers exhibit, implicitly or explicitly, 'cultural cringe' – they presume accounting systems and standards in developed countries are benchmarks of best practice, are appropriate in emerging economies, and should therefore be adopted. Sometimes this is valid, but often research on their application reveals unexpected results. If so, our advice is do not casually attribute this to 'culture' (often left unexplained) or the country being underdeveloped, but systematically investigate such factors. What is unique or common must be systematically teased out and the results tied to related work in both developed and emerging economies. In brief, the reader will only be intrigued if the study adds new theoretical and/or empirical contributions.

Western theories can be apt. For example, some development economists use neo-classical economic theory, with interesting results (e.g. North *et al.*, 2013) though, as in accounting, methodological debates on the worth of such theories abound (Gray, 2016). However, the application of Western theories to a developing country needs thought and justification; and the research aims, methods and results should relate to, and draw from, relevant accounting research but also work in other disciplines such as development studies, development economics or anthropology (Alawattage *et al.*, 2017a). They often contain empirical and theoretical material relevant to accounting (though this may be implicit rather than explicit) and given that researchers in such fields often neglect or are not well acquainted with accounting issues, there are opportunities to publish in fields beyond accounting.

However, many researchers from emerging economies replicate quantitative work found in A★ journals, without regard to whether the issues, concepts and methods are apt for an emerging economy. The belief that only research using statistical methods (not necessarily invalid for some studies) constitutes good research can privilege an (uncritical) transposing of methodological and/or theoretical underpinnings from mainstream 'developed' country capital markets research on, for example, corporate governance and performance, earnings management and IFRS adoption, adoption of management accounting techniques, executive compensation, board composition and investor activism (Hopper *et al.*, 2017). Also, archival statistical and econometric studies in emerging economies may encounter small or no databases, sometimes with unreliable data, and small and weakly regulated capital markets, which limit possible publication in leading journals demanding statistically significant results from a large database. These topics are relevant to emerging economies but researchers in emerging economies may concentrate too much on them and this carries dangers. It can propagate a singular 'reality', which presumes that formal accounting and accountability systems – epitomised by practices such as IFRS, corporate governance codes, balanced scorecards and activity-based costing – will gradually pervade corporate and newly privatised organisations worldwide; it may unwittingly diffuse research ideologies unsuitable for sustainable development (Alawattage *et al.*, 2017a, 2017b; Soobaroyen *et al.*, 2017); and they may deflect attention from other important accounting issues in emerging economies, such as political accountability, the role of civil society organisations, the working of family dominated boards and executive committees, and state and political party interventions. Our experience as editors is that such topics receive insufficient attention (Carlos and Uddin, 2016; Uddin *et al.*, 2017; Ahmed and Uddin, 2018).

In addition, this encourages undue focus on the formal sector, whereas in many emerging economies the informal sector is a sizeable and growing driver of their economies. It accounts for 48 per cent of non-agricultural employment in North Africa, 51 per cent in Latin America, 65 per cent in Asia and 72 per cent in Sub-Saharan Africa operations (Benjamin and Mbaye, 2015). In Africa, it contributes 55 per cent of GDP and provides jobs for the most vulnerable people. The informal sector is characterised by micro businesses, but some are large with complex activities, operations, procurement sources and organisation, but little is known about their accounting. They may not keep conventional 'formal' accounting but does this mean they lack any accounting? Some record purchases and sales (quantities, days/dates, prices, etc.) but to what ends, why, and how can it be conceptualised? How did it emerge and why? Since these entities are often not subject to income and employment tax, and their essence may transcend profit making, their accounting's function and characteristics may have distinctive social and economic features. Similarly, agricultural accounting in emerging economies rarely features in accounting research, despite the agricultural sector being preponderant in many emerging economies. Potentially, research on such topics may yield greater results than the current vogue of testing the application of developed countries' 'formal' accounting prescriptions in emerging economies (Hopper *et al.*, 2017).

Some Western-based theories contain 'unrealistic' assumptions about behaviour and institutions in emerging economies. Wallace (1997), for example, raises concerns about applying agency theory to African accounting history. Consequently, researchers inclined towards qualitative and critical accounting, including ourselves, use theories and research methods that develop bottom-up findings grounded in local realities, e.g. how the 'two publics' and 'neopatrimonialism' relate to weak government accounting and accountability (Goddard *et al.*, 2016; Lassou and Hopper, 2016; Hopper, 2017; Lassou, 2017). Cultural, political and social issues differ across countries, and emerging economies are no exception. However, their weak institutional environment and unstable traditions can lead to political leaders and government officials pursuing material and/or political interests in ways unlike in the West (Uddin, 2009; Tsamenyi *et al.*, 2017). Many emerging economies acquired independence from colonial rulers in the middle of the last century, and sometimes territorial disputes ensued, which rendered the military a powerful institution, with profound effects on accounting and judicial practices (Ashraf and Uddin, 2015; Ashraf *et al.*, forthcoming). Accounting researchers using postcolonial research theories have aided understanding of such issues (Hopper *et al.*, 2009; Tsamenyi *et al.*, 2017), but more attention needs paying to historical circumstances around independence, their effect on institutions, and how individuals' emotions and identities affect accounting practices. Too often it is presumed that accounting in emerging economies will follow a capitalist neoliberal business model. However, this is unlikely to be invariably so, especially when social production and business is family based. In many emerging economies, economic practices deviate from Western-based models of economic development promulgated by donors, especially the World Bank and International Monetary Fund, and consequently their accounting prescriptions often fail or have unanticipated consequences (Uddin and Choudhury, 2008; Ashraf and Uddin, 2016; Ghattas *et al.*, 2018). We need to know more about the actual indigenous economy, how it can be conceptualised, the influence of social, cultural, religious and political factors, and the nature and role of accounting therein. Accounting research emphasising sociological rather than economic theories helps inform these interesting accounting issues, which need further exploration. This requires creativity and innovation outside mainstream forms of inquiry but sadly, many researchers, especially from emerging economies, still neglect their interplay with accounting (Hopper *et al.*, 2014). Given our predilection for and experience of conducting bottom-up, qualitative research, we strongly commend this, even to quantitative researchers, say by using mixed methods, to address these needs.

Questionnaire surveys, large-scale archival data analysis, and cross-sectional econometric analysis in pursuit of 'objective' measurement can provide a truncated view of reality. Surveys can be unreliable, given many subjects in emerging economies are unused to doing them and suspicious of their eventual usage. The most successful in our experience are administered personally to help alleviate these problems but this is time consuming and expensive, especially as travel is difficult in many emerging economies. It is often argued that getting sustained access to conduct case studies, especially to intensively scrutinise an organisation over time, is particularly difficult in emerging economies. Approaching any organisation to conduct accounting research usually triggers alarm bells with managers or owners (Devereux and Hoddinott, 2002). 'Accounting', interpreted as a 'money' matter, is seen as private and confidential. Our PhD students are invariably and understandably worried about the dangers of not securing access and conducting negotiations (preferably at the highest organisational level) to gain the data required. Moreover, when they are sponsored, e.g. by their own universities or government funding agencies, these institutions may raise concerns about the feasibility of qualitative research approaches. We know this is challenging, but we are unconvinced that access is more difficult than in a developed country or impossible, as the quantity of good intensive case studies on developing countries bear testament (e.g. Tanzania studies by Goddard and Assad, 2006; Goddard and Issa Mzenzi, 2015; Goddard *et al.*, 2016). One may have to persistently negotiate, exploit supportive personal contacts with influential gatekeepers, and wait months to get access to meetings with senior managers, especially when subjects are suspicious or unused to research requests, but we and our PhD students usually gain access to meetings and important documents such as annual reports, minutes of meetings and company magazines, all essential for triangulation and validity purposes. Getting access and reliable responses are research method skills and often need direct personal interaction. Sometimes the social fabric (closely knit) and customs of emerging economies help mitigate problems of gaining access. For example, in a Pakistan public sector organisation, changes driven by a pro-change managerial block but resisted by many lower level staff and labour were sensitive, which made access difficult. But a former student of the researcher was in the pro-change block, and a labour union leader in the resistance block was a friend of a friend. These 'connections' enabled him to access data that otherwise would have been inaccessible. Similarly, in another research project on corruption, connections through family and clan were vital for accessing subjects accused of theft by their seniors. The alleged perpetrators talked freely about this as they 'trusted' the researcher because of familial and clan connections (Ashraf *et al.*, in press).

Connections though are often insufficient to gain access to research sites but need complementing by assurances of high confidentiality and anonymity, often beyond that experienced in developed countries. Research ethics must still prevail. Sometimes, despite introductions by connections and formal letters of support, research participants refuse to sign a consent form for fear of leaving evidence that may identify them. Hence key participants are lost. In one instance a senior government official denied access on the dubious grounds that staff were forbidden to talk to researchers. Nevertheless, enough data from other sources was gathered to support publications in well-ranked journals, possibly because the topic was important, difficult and under-researched. Ethical issues arising from confidentiality or anonymity often emerge, especially on sensitive topics where the identity of the participants and/or of the organisation might be ascertained. How to deal with this while retaining the richness of the data and analysis thereof, and rights to publication, can be a difficult balance. They need addressing and formal confirmation gained at the beginning, not the end, of empirical research. However, gaining and maintaining sound access, and protecting informants, is part of a normal qualitative study and protocols on doing this should be part of research training.

However, not all qualitative work entails fieldwork. Discourse analyses of accounting documents have grown. For example, Jayasinghe and Uddin (2010) analysed how the World Bank used accounting rhetoric in their world development reports, policy documents and strategy papers to shape economies and societies. They combined discourse analyses with grounded qualitative research to investigate how accounting and development discourses in development projects in two Sri Lankan villages changed, and how recipients responded to and/or resisted control regimes promulgated by the World Bank and donors. Ashraf *et al.* (forthcoming) used a similar mixed methods approach to study how different discourses on an accounting valuation in a privatisation in Pakistan created political unrest resulting eventually in the downfall of the military government.

It is often claimed that intensive qualitative research is high risk compared to quantitative research. We disagree. Much quantitative research uses similar data sets to study similar problems. Coming second with your results will debar publication in a well-ranked journal. They want articles that make a significant original contribution. Rightly or wrongly, it is difficult to get replication studies published. In contrast, qualitative research generates a unique data set and can identify and study new or sensitive topics, often inaccessible by quantitative methods, and produce the original results desired by many leading journals.

However, whatever the methodology, the normal tenets of what constitutes an acceptable paper in well-ranked journals apply, rightly, to work on and from emerging economies. There is now a broad theoretical and empirical range of research on accounting in emerging economies requiring just as careful a literature review as for other areas, often across other disciplines. However, empirical work and policies in many developing countries may be sparse, and what is available may come primarily from reports commissioned by international financial institutions, aid agencies and governments. These are useful despite being policy and practice oriented, though sometimes their reports of achievements fail to pass close empirical scrutiny. One's topic and research questions are vital. The underlying theory must be strong, explicit and connected to the research questions and the empirical analysis, especially in qualitative work. Large data samples are vital in quantitative studies to gain meaningful statistical analyses.

However, data volume with respect to depth and intensity, is more important in qualitative studies. It is usually better to conduct an in-depth single case study rather than several less-intensive ones, as neither will produce convincing generalisable results (in a statistical sense). Rather the aim is to gain a deep understanding of complex, dynamic events over time. Convincing data analysis whatever the research methodology is essential. Too often this is poor in qualitative studies, which have their own distinct but demanding methods.

Researchers from emerging economies often suffer from English being their second or third language, but it is the international medium of publication. The importance of advanced writing skills cannot be underestimated, and many PhD programmes neglect this, as students have met relevant entry requirements for the English language. Once admitted, many are reluctant to devote significant time to such training and prefer instead to develop technical knowledge (e.g. methods). This is a mistake, for in our experience of refereeing and editing research papers from and/or on emerging economies, many are badly written, prematurely submitted and insufficiently aired to colleagues and appropriate workshops/conferences to gain critical feedback. This is sad, for many have unfulfilled potential. If poor writing skills, especially when English is a second language, is a problem, there must be a strategy to overcome this, e.g. co-writing with an experienced and fluent English speaker or attending workshops and courses on academic writing for publication.

The transition from the 'big book' PhD thesis to publishable papers, particularly for qualitative research, is difficult and often underestimated. Journal reviewers demand a more focused and condensed presentation. Some disciplines favour turning the PhD into a book or monograph but, rightly or wrongly, in accounting, journal articles are the most valued means of research dissemination. Another option is to write a thesis on a three-paper basis should university regulations permit (a common occurrence in market-based accounting and finance research). This can ensure a swifter route from PhD to publication, though many accounting topics and designs do not lend themselves to 'neat salami-slicing'.

Accounting research on emerging economies has made little discernible impact on policies of indigenous and global professional associations, standard setters, aid agencies and especially international financial institutions. Impact is becoming an important priority for researchers, though identifying and documenting the impact of accounting research is difficult. In the UK, the 2021 Research Excellence Framework (REF) that evaluates departments' research and allocates funds accordingly now contains an impact factor, normally demonstrated by case studies. Given that accounting is a practice with important but neglected problems in many emerging economies, opportunities to make an impact abound, and publishing houses such as Emerald actively seek to publish policy-centric articles. For instance, the *Journal of Accounting in Emerging Economies* is planning to publish a special issue on accounting standards in emerging economies in collaboration with the accounting policy wing of the United Nations Conference on Trade and Development. Taking the cue from development scholars and REF demands, one author works with a United Nations' disaster risk reduction policy group. This not only covers disaster management procedures and protocols but also accountability and member countries' governance. His involvement with a steering group of the United Nations International Strategy for Disaster Reduction (UNISDR) helped formulate a policy guide on accountability (under the UNISDR's Sendai Framework for Disaster Risk Reduction). Qualitative research may offer more opportunities for networking and practitioner involvement, say by identifying possible impacts at inception, providing regular feedback to stakeholders on initial findings, establishing a small panel of practitioner advisers and organising round tables. All create opportunities for policy change, organisational responses and stakeholder engagement that has an impact.

But why are some researchers more successful in getting publications in well-ranked journals? We believe the process and supporting networks are vital. Partnerships with leading scholars and institutions in developed countries are often crucial for researchers in and/or from emerging economies getting published and subsequently doing so unassisted. Young academics and PhD students bring interesting empirics from emerging economies. Seasoned academics can help them theorise these; link them to current theoretical, empirical and policy conversations; write papers in the style and standard expected by leading journals; and understand and address reviewers' comments. All the authors of this chapter from emerging economies initially collaborated with experienced academics in developed countries, often their PhD supervisor, to produce articles subsequently published in international accounting journals. But this does not mean that researchers from emerging economies must relocate to a developed economy. For example, colleagues of Junaid Ashraf in a Pakistani university often work with PhD supervisors or mentors in the developed world. Sometimes this results in young academics finding jobs in Western universities, where they start working with next generation of scholars from emerging economies and the cycle continues. In summary, building active processes of partnership and collaboration locally and internationally is vital.

These are taking place, albeit not sufficiently, in emerging economies. For example, one author works with the Comparative Asia Africa Governmental Accounting group (a public sector accounting forum) in Indonesia, which provides a platform for academics to discuss their research and helps establish connections with academics from developed countries. A major 'partnership' opportunity with scholars from developed countries arose from the external examiner system, once prevalent in Commonwealth/ex-British colonies, that mostly involved UK academics. This has declined, which is unfortunate as it fostered the sharing of research networks, knowledge and insights. The University of Mauritius, aware of this benefit, continues to recruit external examiners, often with key profiles (e.g. journal editor or associate editor), from foreign research-intensive institutions. CESAG Business School – a Francophone regional school in Dakar (Senegal) – has started recruiting from the diaspora of Africans trained in leading research-oriented Western universities and has created visiting faculty positions for some to leverage their expertise and to address its shortage of well-trained university academics. It is too early to assess its impact, but it is likely to prove positive. Organising international conferences and workshops also develops research networks. Hosting the eighth AAFA conference made CESAG aware of the sizeable number of African academics in Western-based universities willing to partner with AAFA to help strengthen their research (including co-investigations and publications with colleagues at the institution).

The diaspora of accounting researchers trained and working in developed countries can provide crucial support for researchers 'back home'. Undoubtedly, we would know much less about accounting issues in emerging economies had these self-perpetuating partnerships not existed, but we would know more had international political and economic actors financed experienced researchers from developed countries to do fieldwork alongside novices in emerging economies. Research partnerships crucially need funding. Schemes funded by donors from developed countries, e.g. the Global Challenges Research Fund and the British Academy-Newton Funds, have helped, but the increasing commercialisation of universities in developed countries discourages developing new research partnerships further afield. Moreover, funders are inclined to fund projects with tangible and quick results, rather than those involving less-determinate processes. This needs to change.

Future directions

We have demonstrated that research and publications in emerging economies are growing, and this has become a significant field within accounting academia. There are undoubtedly scholars in emerging economies with significant potential to make further substantial contributions, but they face major hurdles, especially: teaching-focused higher education institutions; outdated or absent good PhD training; lack of resources and scholarships for higher studies; limited access to recent journals and books; and no or poor research-centric performance measurements for academics. These issues exist in developed countries but are more acute in emerging economies.

We have also argued that key factors accounting for the slow growth of publications on accounting in emerging economies in leading accounting journals are: lack of reflection on national contexts; descriptive and atheoretical papers; undue replications of Western studies and theories; ignoring topics relevant to the context; ignoring the informal sector and undue focus on the formal sector; inappropriate and/or a restricted range of research methods; possibly limited or restricted access to research sites; and writing in a second language. We illustrate that work on accounting in emerging economies can be published in leading journals, but this requires careful selection of where to submit and sometimes collaborations with senior academics working abroad. These factors are intertwined with improving PhD programmes and establishing conducive structural mechanisms and research processes for academics in emerging economies.

However, a growing number of researchers in emerging economies are publishing in leading journals but the numbers are small, and their regional associations and universities have or are planning well-refereed journals with aspirations to high academic standards, edited by leading academics from developing countries. These need support and recognition, especially given the limited outlets for publication in leading Western journals. However, ideally, the requirements for publishing articles in leading journals should match those on developed and emerging economies. The issue is helping scholars and institutions in emerging economies to do this.

Progress is slow but it is being made. Pursuing research on accounting in emerging economies is exciting; it can have positive policy impacts that, inter alia, may help reduce poverty and increase attainment of the United Nation's Millennium Development Goals. Given its relative neglect and youth it contains many issues, often virgin territory, for researchers to make theoretical, empirical and policy advances relevant to emerging economies but also richer ones, where pockets of poverty are increasingly emerging. While this poses challenges these can be overcome and doing so effectively is rewarding personally and for society.

Notes

1 See www.imf.org/external/pubs/ft/weo/2018/01/weodata/groups.htm.
2 See, for example, https://link.springer.com/chapter/10.1007/978-90-481-3694-0_6, and http://foundation-partnership.org/ulf/resources/tettey_staffretention.pdf.
3 See www.worldbank.org/en/news/press-release/2017/05/15/world-bank-funds-us155-million-to-support-autonomous-higher-education-in-vietnam (accessed 25 April 2018).
4 See www.worldbank.org/en/news/press-release/2014/04/15/world-bank-centers-excellence-science-technology-education-africa (accessed 25 April 2018).
5 An idiosyncratic system of academic performance appraisal and promotion operates in some Middle Eastern countries (notably Saudi Arabia) whereby the academic is not rewarded for journal publications (even in a top-ranked outlet) from his/her PhD thesis, on account of 'double-counting'. This is a disincentive for academics to target publications post-PhD. Instead, he/she must find a different research topic, which is somewhat counterproductive.
6 All these rankings allocate a significant chunk of 'points' for publications in 'top' international journals.

References

AAAJ (2017). Special issue: Accounting, auditing and accountability research in Africa. *Accounting, Auditing & Accountability Journal*, 30(6), 1206–1423.

Ahmed, S. and Uddin, S. N. (2018). Towards a political economy of corporate governance change and stability in family business groups: A morphogenetic approach. *Accounting, Auditing and Accountability Journal*, 31(8), 2192–2217.

Alawattage, C., Wickramasinghe, D., Tsamenyi, M. and Uddin, S. N. (2017a). Doing critical management accounting research in emerging economies. *Advances in Scientific and Applied Accounting*, 10(2), 177–188.

Alawattage, C., Wickramasinghe, D. and Uddin, S. N. (2017b). Theorising management accounting practices in Less Developed Countries, in Harris, E. (Ed.), *The Routledge Companion to Performance Management and Control*. New Yord: Routledge, 287–305.

Ashraf, J. and Uddin, S. N. (2015). Military, 'managers' and hegemonies of management controls: A critical realist interpretation. *Management Accounting Research*, 29(1), 13–26.

Ashraf, J. and Uddin, S. N. (2016). Regressive consequences of management accounting and control reforms: A case from a less developed country. *Critical Perspectives on Accounting*, 41(2), 18–33.

Ashraf, J., Hopper, T. M. and Muhammad, F. (in press). Accounting signifiers, political discourse, popular resistance and legal identity during Pakistan steel mills attempted privatization. *Critical Perspectives on Accounting*, https://doi.org/10.1016/j.cpa.2018.08.002.

Benjamin, N. and Mbaye, A. (2015). Informality, growth and development in Africa, in Monga, C. and Lin, J. Y. (Eds.), *The Oxford Handbook of Africa and Economics*. Oxford University Press.

Carlos, A. and Uddin, S. N. (2016). Social capital, networks and interlocked independent directors: A Mexican case. *Journal of Accounting in Emerging Economies*, 6(3), 291–312.

CPA (2010). Special issue on accounting in Africa. *Critical Perspectives on Accounting*, 21(5), 361–442.

de Jager, P., de Kock, F. and van der Spuy, P. (2017). Do not feed the predators. *South African Journal of Business Management*, 48(3), 35–45.

Devereux, S. and Hoddinott, J. (2002). Issues in data collection, in Devereux, S. and Hoddinott, J. (Eds.), *Fieldwork in Emerging Economies*. Boulder, CO: Lynne Rienner.

Ghattas, P. B. M., Soobaroyen T. and Marnet, O. (2018). Auditing the Egyptian auditors: An analysis of compliance reviews by the local public oversight body. Interdisciplinary Perspectives on Accounting Conference Proceedings, July, 2018, Edinburgh, Scotland.

Goddard, A. and Assad, M. J. (2006). Accounting and navigating legitimacy in Tanzanian NGOs. *Accounting, Auditing & Accountability Journal*, 19(3), 377–404.

Goddard, A. and Issa Mzenzi, S. (2015). Accounting practices in Tanzanian local government authorities: towards a grounded theory of manipulating legitimacy. In *Public Sector Accounting, Accountability and Auditing in Emerging Economies*, Hoque, Z., Parker, L. D., Covaleski, M. A. and Haynes, K. (eds)., 109–142. Emerald Group Publishing Limited: Bradford.

Goddard, A., Assad, M., Issa, S., Malagila, J. and Mkasiwa, T.A. (2016). The two publics and institutional theory: A study of public sector accounting in Tanzania. *Critical Perspectives on Accounting*, 40, 8–25.

Gray, H. (2016). Access orders and the 'new' new institutional economics of development. *Development and Change*, 47(1), 51–75.

Hopper, T. M. (2017). Neopatrimonialism, good governance, corruption and accounting in Africa: Idealism versus pragmatism. *Journal of Accounting in Emerging Economies*, 7(2), 225–248.

Hopper, T. M. and Hoque, Z. (2004). Changing forms of accounting and accountability within emerging economies. *Research on Accounting in Emerging Economies – Special Supplement 2*, 1–18.

Hopper, T. M. and Tanima, F. (2018). Accounting in less developed countries retrospectively and prospectively, in Roslender, R. (Ed.), *The Routledge Companion to Critical Accounting*. Routledge, 260–282.

Hopper, T. M., Tsamenyi, M, Uddin, S. N. and Wickramasinghe, D. (2009). Management accounting in less developed countries: What we know and need to know. *Accounting, Auditing and Accountability Journal*, 22(3), 469–514.

Hopper, T. M, Tsamenyi, M., Uddin, S. and Wickramasinghe D. (Eds.) (2012) *Handbook of Accounting and Development*. Cheltenham: Edward Elgar.

Hopper, T. M. Ashraf, J. Wickramsinghe, D. Uddin, S. N. (2014). Social theorisation of accounting: Challenges to positive research, Jones, S. (Ed.), *Routledge Companion to Financial Accounting Theory*. New York: Routledge, 452–471.

Hopper, T. M., Lassou, P. and Soobaroyen, T. (2017). Globalisation, accounting and development. *Critical Perspectives on Accounting*, 43, 125–148.

Jayasinghe, K. and Uddin, S. (2010). Continuity and change in World Bank development discourses and the rhetoric role of accounting. Asia and Pacific Interdisciplinary Research in Accounting Conference Proceedings, July, 2010, Sydney, Australia.

Lassou, P. J. C. (2017). State of government accounting in Ghana and Benin: A 'tentative' account. *Journal of Accounting in Emerging Economies*, 7(4), 486–506.

Lassou, P. J. C. and Hopper, T. M. (2016). Government accounting reform in an ex-French African colony: The political economy of neo-colonialism. *Critical Perspectives on Accounting*, 36, 39–57.

North, D. C., Wallis, J. J., Webb, S. B. and Weingast, B. R. (2013). Limited access orders: An introduction to the conceptual framework, in North, D. C., Wallis, J. J., Webb, S. B. and Weingast, B. R. (Eds.), *In the Shadow of Violence: The Problem of Development in Limited Access Societies*. New York: Cambridge University Press, 1–23.

Soobaroyen, T., Tsamenyi, M. and Sapra, H. (2017). Accounting and governance in Africa: Contributions and opportunities for further research. *Journal of Accounting in Emerging Economies*, 7(4), 422–427.

Tsamenyi, M. Hopper, T. M. and Uddin, S. N. (2017). Changing control and accounting in an African gold mine: An emergence of a new despotic control. *Journal of Accounting & Organizational Change*, 13(2), 282–308.

Uddin, S. N. (2009). Management accounting in a private manufacturing company: Rational vs familial/traditional control. *Critical Perspectives on Accounting*, 20(6), 782–794.

Uddin, S. N. and Choudhury, J. (2008). Rationality, traditionalism and the state of corporate governance mechanisms: Illustrations from a less developed country. *Accounting, Auditing and Accountability Journal*, 21(7), 1026–105.

Uddin, S. N., Jayasinghe, K. and Ahmed, S. (2017). Scandals from an island: Testing Anglo-American corporate governance frameworks. *Critical Perspectives on International Business*, 13(4), 349–370.

van Helden, J. G. and Uddin, S. N. (2016). Public sector management accounting in emerging economies: A literature review. *Critical Perspectives on Accounting*, 41, 34–62.

Wallace, R. S. O. (1997). African labour systems, maintenance accounting and agency theory: Some fundamental questions. *Critical Perspectives on Accounting*, 8(4), 393–407.

INDEX

Stock Exchange 18, 45; Americas **16**; Bangladesh, Dhaka, and Chittagong 95, 101, 197, 205; Bhutan 101; Cambodian 158, **160**; Chinese, Shanghai and Shenzhen 56, 58, 63, 106, 116; Colombo 101; Egyptian (EGX) 184–185, 191–192, 193n1; foreign 42, 185; Hong Kong 106; India, Bombay and National (NSE) 38, 98, 101; international 116; Korean 158; London 38, 106; Maldives 101–102; Nepal 101; non-existence in Afghanistan or Bhutan 95, 99; overseas 106; Pakistan 101; Russian 42, 48; Sri Lanka 101; Syrian 137–138; Thailand (SET) 248; Vietnamese 84
stock markets: Bangladesh 197–198; Brazil 16, 22; Cambodian 157–158, 165; Chinese 58, 62, 67n3, 105–107, 111, 116; Egyptian 192; regulators 173; in SAARC countries 101; Vietnamese 85
strategic management accounting (SMA) 249
Syria 140, 143n1, 144n7; audit firms, entry of 140; commerce dominated 141; interface with global context 143; Islamic influence 137; issues that impacted 142; new role of auditors in 138; political and economic developments 137; popular uprising 136; socialist and isolated 139; turbulence 143; unrest in 136, 142; violence in 4, 8, 135
Syria, accountancy developments in 144n6; of profession 135–136; state control over profession 139; state-supported body 137
Syria isolation 139; era 138; long period of 4–5, 135, 141; political and economic 137–139, 142
Syrian accounting standards 137; Association of Certified Accountants (ASCA) 137–140; CA 141; companies 138; culture 143; perception of history 141; revolution 140
Syrian accountants 5, 135–144, 143n4; context 135–136, 142; context, divided 140; economy, privatisation of 136; Golan Heights annexed 136; influence of Islam on 137; people 136–141; Unified Accounting System (UAS) 137

TACIS programme 48, 54n4
Thai accountants 252, 254; Airways 248; businesses, strategy of 249; companies 249, 251–252, 256; culture 252, 256; economy 247, 255; GDP 251; government 253–254; Industries, Federation of 248; institutions 248; manufacturing 251; manufacturing firms 248; public sector 253; SMEs 252
Thai accountants 254; environment, management accounting development within 256; firms 254; government 255; universities 254
Thailand **76**, 156, 255–256; accounting techniques and practices 252; Bank of 248; business environment 247; competitive strategies of companies 248; contemporary MAPS (CMAPs)

249; development of environmental management accounting 254; employee resistance to redistribution of power 252; encourages small business development 251; entry mode 248; foreign investment 248; founder member of ASEAN 247; founding member of ASEAN 257n1; ISA adoption **175**, **177**; management accounting in 7, 9, 247, 254; management accounting practices (MAPS) 248, **250**; performance measures in decentralised organisations 251; potential as founding member of ASEAN 257; Stock Exchange of (SET) 248–249, 252, 257n3; strong central government 253
Transparency International Bangladesh (TIB) 197, 224

Unified Accounting System (UAS) in Continental Europe 86
Unified Accounting System (UAS) in Vietnam 4, 83, 85; amended 86; co-existence of 86, 90; conflicts with/provides guidance on VAS 87; explanation of how accounts are applied to typical economic transactions 88; regulators primarily revise 89
US–Vietnam Bilateral Trade Agreement liberalisation commitments 85

value chain 248; analysis **250**, 253; costing (VCC) 252–253
Vietnam 156; Association of Accountants and Auditors 91n7; Association of Certified Public Accountants (VACPA) 89; challenges in adopting IASB standards 90; Communist Party of (CPV) 84; Constitution of the Socialist Republic of 84; Depository Insurance of 84; Development Forum 85; enterprises 87; equity market 84, 86–87; government 85; institutional changes 88; institutional reforms 87; ISA adoption **175**, **177**; lacks strong professional bodies 89; National Assembly of 84, 89; National Council for Accountancy (NCA) 89; signed with ASEAN Free Trade Area 90n3, 257n1; Social Security of 84; Socio-Economic Development Strategy (SEDS) 85; transition towards market economy 85; *see also* Uniform Accounting System in Vietnam
Vietnam accounting 3; Association (VAA) 89; and auditing arrangements 89; approaches to setting regulations 86; changes in legal and policy documents 4, 90; converged with IASB standards 83; decisions 87; environment 4, 90; information, demand for/supply of 85; objectives of 88; reforms and developments 86; regulation 89; regulators 83, 87, 89–90; standards 89; system 86; traditional rule-driven 88
Vietnam accounting, IAS/IFRS adoption 87; debateable choice for 88; few economic

For Product Safety Concerns and Information please contact our EU
representative GPSR@taylorandfrancis.com
Taylor & Francis Verlag GmbH, Kaufingerstraße 24, 80331 München, Germany

www.ingramcontent.com/pod-product-compliance
Ingram Content Group UK Ltd.
Pitfield, Milton Keynes, MK11 3LW, UK
UKHW011454240425
457818UK00021B/809